31

D1322727

A Social History of France in the Nineteenth Century

Christophe Charle

Social History of France in the Nineteenth Century

Christophe Charle

Translated by

Miriam Kochan

BERG
Oxford/Providence 37546 495

English edition
first published in 1994 by
Berg Publishers
Editorial offices:
150 Cowley Road, Oxford, OX4 1JJ, UK
221 Waterman Street, Providence, RI 02906, USA

© Editions du Seuil, 1991

The translation of this book was made possible with the help of the French
Ministry of Culture.

Library of Congress Cataloguing-in-Publication Data
A catalogue record for this book is available from the Library of Congress.

British Library Cataloging in Publication Data
A catalogue record for this book is available from the British Library.

ISBN 0 85496 906 3 (Cloth)
0 85496 913 6 (Paper)

Printed in the United Kingdom by WBC Bookbinders, Bridgend.

This book is dedicated to the memory of my forebears:

Claude Charle, carpenter; Florimond Charle, cutler; Jean Auchère, potter and farmer; Alexandre Charle, cutler and Communard; Christophe Charle, painting valuer; Philippe Potier, railway employee; Jean Potier, railway conductor; Marie Chapelotte, housewife; Alphonse Auchère, cafe-owner; Léonide Potier, milliner; Charles Philippe Heim, gardener; Marthe Heim, office worker; who, with millions of other Frenchmen or foreigners, known or unknown, have composed this social history of France in the nineteenth century.

Contents

Introduction		1
I	**The Age of the Notables or Unattainable Social Peace**	5
1	**French Society *circa* 1815**	7
	A A Weakened Society	8
	a Demographic Balance Sheet of the Revolution and Empire	8
	b Cultural Balance Sheet	13
	B A Divided Society	15
	a Property, the Central Issue	15
	b Contrasting Rural Societies	16
	C A Society of Exclusion and Violent Revolt	22
	a Towns and Social Pathology	22
	b Excluded Men and Women and the Seeds of Revolt	24
	c Conclusion	26
2	**Notables, Educated Classes (*Capacités*), Peasants and Proletariat**	28
	A The Ruling Notables: The Logic of a System of Domination	29
	a The Central State, Bone of Contention among Notables	29
	b An Enlightened Class?	31
	B The Notables: Divided and Challenged	32
	a The Challenge from the '*Capacités*'	32
	b The Challenge from the Craft Workers	35
	C The Proletarian Threat	39
	a The Process of Contagion	39
	b The Factory Proletariat and those excluded from Industrial Society	40
	c A New Social Perspective	41
	D The Mid-Century Crisis, 1847–1851	43
	a Economic Crisis and Social Tensions	43
	b The Social Issues in the Mid-Century Crisis	46
	c Reconciled Notables and Lacerated Masses	48
	d Peasants: Saviours or Rebels?	48
	e Conclusion	52

Contents

3 Imperial Stabilisation and Society in Motion   53
A The Bonapartist State, a Stabilising or Destabilising
   Force?   54
   a The Political Establishment   54
   b The High Administration and the Upper Ranks of the
    Army   56
   c The Emergence of a Body of Officials   59
   d The Clergy, Ally or Opponent?   61
B The End of the Agrarian Ancien Regime   64
   a The 'Extinction of Pauperism' in the Countryside   64
   b *Nouveaux Riches* Peasants?   68
   c The Return of the Notables?   73
C An Urban Society in Motion   74
   a The Employers   75
   b The Workers between Field and Town   81
D The Democratic Thrust   91
   a The Failure of Social Bonapartism   91
   b The Towns and Paris, Social Laboratories   92
   c The Demand for Education and Culture   96
   d The 'New Strata'   99
   e The Militant Movement   100
   f The Commune   103
   g Conclusion   105

II The Emergence of a Democratic Society, 1870–1914   107

4 A New Class: The Peasants   109
A Integration in the Nation   110
   a Peasant France: An Overall View   110
   b Insertion in Republican Space   114
B Crisis as a Social Indicator   121
   a Readjustment to the Crisis   122
   b Social Effects of the Crisis   124
   c The Response to the Crisis: Unionism and
    Agrarianism   125
   d The Agricultural Proletariat's Intermittent Class
    Struggles   128
   e Agrarian Unanimism: The 1907 Vineyard Workers
    Movement   130
C Rural France and Peasant Societies   131
   a Overall Improvement in Way of Life   132
   b Antiquated Egalitarianism: Brittany   135
   c The South of the Massif Central: Unegalitarian
    and Antiquated   136

d Unegalitarian Modernity: The Paris Basin and the
Pas-de-Calais 137
e Conclusion 139

5 The Rise of the Middle Classes 140
A The World of the Petty Bourgeoisie, or How to Escape
from the Proletariat 141
a The Retail Tradesmen 141
b The Struggle to Live 142
c The Financial Balance Sheet 143
d The Political Balance Sheet 144
B The Employees: A New Proletariat 146
a Attempts at Definition 146
b Paternalism and Bureaucracy 148
c Employee Unrest 149
C The Officials: Servants or Rebels? 151
a From the Old to the New State 151
b Administrative Unrest 152
c Officials in the Central Administration and the Crisis
of Confidence in the State 153
d Newcomers 157
e A Protected World: The Officers 163
f A World Apart: Secondary School-Teachers, between
Elitism and Utopia 165
D The Liberal Professions: The Dream of a Classless
Society? 168
a Overall View 169
b The Doctors: Paths to Success 172
c The Legal Professions 174
d Conclusion 178

6 Old and New Elites 179
A Nobility and Notables: Decline or Adaptation? 180
a The Causes of the Decline 180
b The Provincial Notables 183
c The Paris Aristocracy 185
B The Bourgeoisies 188
a Overall View 188
b Closure or Openness? 189
c The Bourgeois Dynasties 191
d Lifestyles 195
e The New Men: Self-Made Men and Engineers 197
f The Lobbies 199
C The Elites of the Republic 201

Contents

	a The Political Elite	202
	b The Higher Administration	205
D	A New Elite? The *Intellectuels*	211
	a The Intellectual Professions in a Liberal System	211
	b Intellectual Power	214
	c Conclusion	216
7	**The Working Classes: Dissent or Integration?**	**218**
A	The Crisis of the Old Industrial World and the Rise of the New	219
	a Worker Divisions	219
	b Worker Geography	221
	c Mobility	222
	d Working Classes or Popular Classes? The Action at the Fringe	225
B	Worker Lifestyles	227
	a Budgets	227
	b Life Cycle	228
	c Hours of Work and Wages	229
	d Anthropology: Worker Wear and Tear	233
	e Workers in the Service Sector	235
C	Employer-Worker Relations	236
	a The Means of Worker Action	238
	b The Policy of the Employers	242
	c Rival Worker Tactics	247
D	From Dependence to Exclusion	251
	a Domestic Servants	251
	b Excluded Men and Women, the Hell or Purgatory of the Working Classes?	256
	c Conclusion	261
8	**The Ideal of a Democratic Society?**	**262**
A	Measuring Inequalities	263
	a Wealth and Incomes	263
	b Status	265
B	Mobility and Immobility	266
	a Changes in Social Status	267
	b The Narrow Door	268
General Conclusion		**271**
Bibliography		**273**
Index		**305**

Introduction

We have certain misgivings in giving the title 'A Social History of France' to a book which, despite its relatively modest size compared with the vastness of the material, aims to provide history students or lovers of history who do not have time to read all the material themselves with an up-to-date summary of the findings of research. Several first-rate syntheses have been published during the last ten years, but most of them are collective, thematic and very large books which students and interested readers can only consult in libraries. These books often assume a good basic knowledge and are directed at an informed or specialist public. In addition, because they are necessarily prepared over several years, the research they reflect is often already out of date especially on certain questions which have recently been revived. Other more academic textbooks on the market, despite their being classics, have also aged and are limited to dated problematics of the understanding of society.

The most recent books to appear, those by Gérard Noiriel and Annie Moulin on the workers and the peasants respectively, opt for a long-term view and a sectoral division of society. This book takes the opposite view in order to complement the new perspectives that have been opened up by analysing the social groups, the nobility, bourgeoisie, elites, middle classes, petty bourgeoisie, etc., knowledge of which has increased in recent years. A particular effort has been made to understand the dynamics and the relationships of these various groups or classes.

Growing specialisation by historians makes it increasingly difficult to fit the mass of detailed material contained in monographs into a unified frame. Each author multiplies as he pleases the specific features of his subject at the risk of incarcerating himself in 'his' world. The great danger in this is that the new knowledge will only benefit researchers in each field of social history and we will continue to work at a general level off the old models and the old ideas of the days when professors were not afraid of generalisations based on well-oiled economic and social mechanisms.

It would be foolhardy to claim to have avoided the two pitfalls described above. Any synthesis is provisional, all the more so when it is confined to a limited number of pages. Every historian has had to specialise and is bound to show some preference for his chosen fields.

Even if he or she has tried to read the works of his or her specialist colleagues in other fields, a mass of unpublished work will always be missed. Lastly, there is no substitute for direct contact with the documents. Exhaustiveness is an inaccessible ideal in contemporary history, especially for nineteenth-century France, and all the more so as new methods have multiplied approaches and unpublished sources.

If any synthesis is premature, at least it has the virtue of trying to formulate questions or new ways of asking them. Until the 1970s, French historiography was dominated by a Labrousseian, that is to say largely Marxist, interpretation. Recent efforts by historians have been directed not so much at combatting this interpretation as at circumventing it, complementing it or working at its margins but without offering counter-models or alternatives. While respecting the enormous contribution by Ernest Labrousse and his personal students, this book will aim primarily to integrate into a coherent overall view the discoveries of social micro-history and the monographs on specific groups which do not fit into the Marxist and Labrousseian perspective of a society which can be reduced to class issues and simple confrontations.

However, this concern for complexity is not synonymous with a convenient withdrawal into the empiricism or impressionism extolled by certain Anglo-Saxon historians of France. Exposing social conflicts and discussions which are of a different type from economic class struggles does not imply an absence of hierarchisation of the issues. This book argues in favour of an interpolation between the wholly political interpretations of the nineteenth century, which reduce history to the control of the ideological conflicts deriving from the Revolution, and the wholly economic interpretation in which the class struggle underlies every confrontation. The goal here is an interpretation that restores relative autonomy to the intermediate groups, to the State as an issue and a social force, to rivalries of corporate bodies and status groups, to nostalgia for the old social relationships or for utopias which seek in the future to rejoin a mythical past, to the differences in geographical areas, to cultural contrasts and to the tensions which also cross the classes, the pivots of orthodox Marxist theory.

The contrast, noted many times, between a convulsive political nineteenth century and a real society, developing slowly and following an aberrant path when compared with other European countries like England and Germany, can not be explained solely by French or even 'Gallic' atavism, or by the vision of the Revolution espoused by François Furet and Denis Richet as a skid which took three-quarters of a century to control.

The outline suggested for this book argues for the existence of two successive models of social domination, domination by the notables and what will for the sake of simplicity be called the democratic model, though the adjective should really be 'meritocratic'. The turning-point (roughly the 1870s) is only relative and is mainly for academic convenience. The first system organised social and political relationships on a 'real' base, land and economic capacity, from which all other power and social assets derived. The enigma to be explained is its early failure, blatantly revealed by the revolutions, uprisings and civil wars and even the defeat by Germany in 1870, despite the multi-form social power of the ruling classes.

The second system, whose genesis actually stretched from the 1830s to the 1880s, was no more immune from conflict (the rise of an organised worker movement, widespread popular discontent) or defeat (August 1914 was not so different from August 1870). However, this mode of social domination managed better than the preceding system to solve major conflicts peaceably and to prevent the endless rebirth of the coalitions of its enemies. The first period is marked by the aspiration for stability and suffered every unforeseen upheaval; the second embodied chronic instability and showed a remarkable capacity to withstand every challenge. The first mode of domination had the defect of making the hierarchy rest on exclusion; the second made the hierarchy acceptable to the dominated by practising an apparent inclusion and by offering credible alternatives to costly social dissidence. The various chapters of this book will strive to comprehend this dual social dynamic and the way in which one world of domination gave way to the other.

I
The Age of the Notables or Unattainable Social Peace

French Society *circa* 1815

A preliminary balance sheet of French society in about 1815, on the morrow of twenty-six years of wars and revolutions, would show the negative aspects of that troubled period unquestionably outweighing positive gains. However, an account which took in only the human and social balance sheet would yield a truncated view, because the cultural consequences of the transition from the Ancien Regime to post-revolutionary society had long-term social and political effects which were at least as important as the change in the legal structure of the country produced by the revolutionary and imperial remodeling. Many social factors inherited from the Ancien Regime were still present in the first half of the nineteenth century, notably the principles of social hierarchisation in the form of exclusion and the impassable barriers erected before a whole series of legally defined categories of persons. Similarly, the continued existence of the old economy produced periodic crises (food crises, deadly epidemics) which had social consequences differing little from those recorded before the taking of the Bastille.

Paradoxically, these disasters had more lasting repercussions than those which occurred before 1789 primarily because of the new political and ideological order. The destruction of the old system in which the Church provided social protection had not been fully replaced by the establishment of new institutions by the new liberal and individualist order. Virtually the only means of protest open to the new and dangerous classes thrown up by the shortcomings of the old economic system or the new, emerging industrial society were the acts of rebellion used by their fathers before them to assert themselves on the revolutionary scene. There was a whole complex of methods of popular resistance in extreme situations the extent of which is only explicable by the memory of the revolutionary days or provincial civil wars. The balance sheet for 1789-1815 is therefore made up both of new structures and types of collective activity and of the periodic revival of myths stirring the people to revolt, without which the social dynamic of the first half of the nineteenth century is incomprehensible.

A A Weakened Society

a Demographic Balance Sheet of the Revolution and Empire

The first scar left by these revolutionary and imperial years was demographic. The nineteenth century is framed by two equally vast mass slaughters, since an estimated 1.5 million died as a result of the battles and civil wars of 1789-1815, the equivalent of the losses in the Great War. Even if the losses from war and revolution were spread over a longer period than those of the First World War, their effects were more long-lasting precisely because of this spread. The poorer classes shared the responsibility for the steady fall in the birth rate from 1821 to 1825. To this must be added the many men who were disabled or unfit for work as a result of ill-tended wounds or physiological hardship during certain campaigns, and self-mutilated cripples who refused conscription. The high death rate during the food crises at the end of the Empire also originated in the lack of able-bodied men to cultivate the land in certain regions affected by conscription; in addition, the growth of children or adolescents who suffered these famines was stunted. Lastly, the collective psychology of some regions bore the enduring scar of the civil wars (the Vendée and the West in general, the Midi of the White Terror) and the 'home-sickness' or depression of forced recruits from non-French-speaking regions.[1]

The military archives themselves record this long-term 'weakening of the race'. Out of 1,033,422 conscripts examined between 1818 and 1826, 380,422 (over a third) were rejected as unfit. Faced with the high rate of exemptions for insufficient height, the government itself decided at the beginning of the Restoration to lower the minimum required height from 1.57 to 1.54 metres. Recruitment statistics show the scars of the poverty still existing at the end of the Empire and the beginning of the Restoration: a fall in average height was recorded in 1836-1837, that is to say, among young adults born in the black years between 1813 and 1815.[2]

Apart from these direct effects of an emergency situation, the experience of the wars had long-term social and psychological repercussions in the society of the early nineteenth century. Peasant resistance to increasing military obligation explains why the authorities retreated after 1815 and organised a system of drawing lots and

---

1. Y.-M. Bercé, 'Nostalgie et mutilations: psychoses de la conscription', in F. Lebrun and R. Dupuy (149), pp. 171–9.
2. A. Armengaud (23), p. 19; J.-P. Aron, P. Dumont and E. Le Roy Ladurie (125), p. 197.

substitution which transferred the blood tax to the most deprived. A map showing the strength of good citizenship in this respect clearly defines two contrasting Frances, the France of the 'Occitane' and northern and eastern France. The one felt less French and less bound to the remote central State; the other had experienced foreign invasion and occupation and even favoured military professions because its population saw the army as a means to upward social mobility given its educational advancement. In addition, its experience of exactions by enemy troops on the national soil made the necessity of a national defence, dependent on everyone, more easily comprehensible.

This ambivalent reaction to conscription also introduced an element of domination into the relationship between poor regions which exported substitutes and rich regions which bought them. That such an inegalitarian – and militarily inefficient – system continued to exist until 1872 is inexplicable without this haunting souvenir of the war years which imposed a historical compromise between ruling classes and comfortably-off peasantry. This was more especially the case as the areas where Legitimism and Ultraism were strongest were precisely those regions which resisted incorporation into the modern revolutionary State. Legislation thus played its part in dividing social groups on the military question, and France would pay dearly for this division in 1870. Substitutes were in fact principally recruited from amongst craftsmen and landless peasants; they could use the money put by as capital to make a start in life after release.[3]

The foreign and civil wars had further social effects. First, they uprooted a whole section of peasant youth, turning some into veterans attached to the Napoleonic legend, and others into diehard opponents of the new revolutionary and imperial State. The events of these years were also a factor in increasing peasant mobility. The forced mobility involved in conscription enlarged the horizon of hitherto settled populations, and this uprooting was conducive to a break with certain traditions; respect for the established state of affairs and blind adherence to established authority were damaged by the military and administrative instability of 1814-1815. On the other hand, in regions traditionally loyal to the central authority or hostile to the Revolution and the new order, voluntary mobility was one means of escape from the constraint of army service despite the investigations, internal passports and workers' registration books the Napoleonic State instituted.[4]

---

3. J.-P. Aron et al.(125), p. 25; Y. Pourcher (108), pp. 20 ff.: the Lozère had 177 absentees per 1,000 (the national rate was only 14) (p. 35); B. Schnapper (110), particularly pp. 118–20.

4. A. Châtelain (58), vol. 1, p. 24.

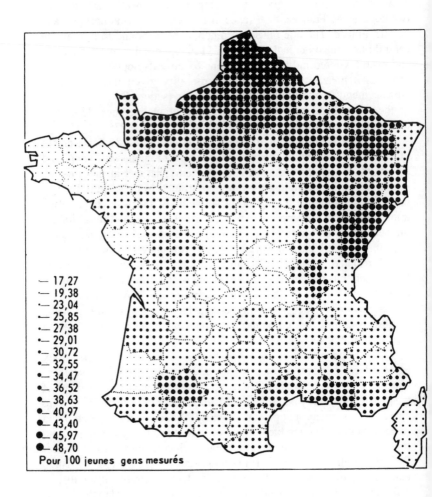

Source: Jean-Paul Aron, Paul Dumont and Emmanuel Le Roy Ladurie, *Anthropologie du conscrit français*, Paris, Mouton, 1972, p. 90.

MAP 1: The Proportion of tall men per 100 young men measured in 1819–1826.

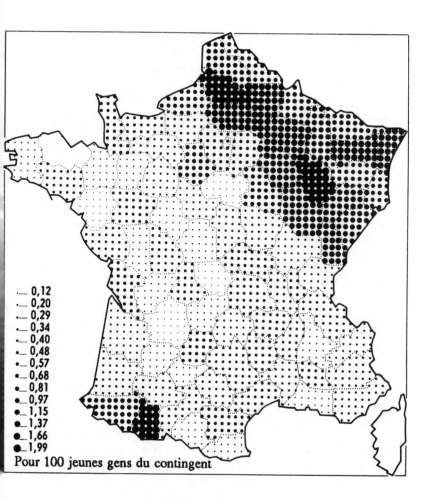

Source: Jean-Paul Aron, Paul Dumont and Emmanuel Le Roy Ladurie, *Anthropologie du conscrit français*, Paris, Mouton, 1972, p. 76.

MAP 2: The geographical origin of the 'elite' in 1819–1826 per 100 young men called up. (Departments with an above average rate of young men with further education: schoolmasters, pupils at seminaries, students.)

Demographers are also inclined to make these population movements responsible for the spread of the limitation of births in the peasantry. The chronological coincidence with the collapse of the framework of the Church for several years, the greater ascendancy of the towns resulting from the birth of revolutionary and imperial bureaucracy, and the social and cultural interchanges created by the wars all argue for a causal relationship.

During the first half of the century the spread of Malthusianism, which aimed to maintain a balance between resources and population without a notable decrease in the rural population, was still limited. The relatively rich agricultural regions and those where the Church's ascendancy was least, such as Normandy, the Garonne valley and the east of the Paris basin, were the earliest to practice limitation of births. Traditionalist regions, such as the West or mountainous areas, used the solutions of the preceding period to remedy overpopulation: temporary migration, higher age of marriage, or a high rate of celibacy, which sometimes took the form of large numbers of religious careers as in the south of the Massif Central.

In fact, although it was less dynamic demographically than in the eighteenth century, French society experienced the phenomenon of relative rural overpopulation before 1848. This overpopulation can be explained by the absence of large-scale movements from poor to rich regions, itself a consequence of slow agricultural modernisation and industrial development, and the relative decline in the rate of urbanisation compared with the eighteenth century. As during the Ancien Regime, less developed France was temporarily employed in the service of more developed France but, in the absence of adequate stable employment, did not settle there. The Revolution, by establishing if not the reality then at least the possibility of access by all to the land, was a strong deterrent to a rural exodus on the English model. The sharp rise in temporary migration during this period came both from this latent overpopulation and from the hope that the money earned would provide a way out of insecurity without the need to break with the native soil. It is estimated that 200,000 people (from a population of about 29 million) were affected by this migration at the beginning of the nineteenth century, and 500,000 in about 1850 (with peaks of over 800,000 at harvest-time).[5]

This temporary solution to lack of work in the dead season or to lack of cultivable land had positive effects only in the long term. The money thus saved was often used unproductively to pay taxes (shortage of cash being the scourge in poor and autarkic regions) or to buy land which was too cramped to provide a proper livelihood or to permit agronomic

5. Ibid., pp. 42–3.

improvements. Thus archaic rural France was caught in a vicious circle resembling today's underdevelopment.

The reason for this was the continued existence of the old demographic system, with its negative effects aggravated by the disorganisation of medical training and the welfare system during the revolutionary period. As prior to 1789, food crises were conducive to epidemics which were deadly for the ill-nourished populations. These periods of high death rate particularly affected the youngest members of society, while poverty drove parents to the extreme solution of abandoning their children, itself a factor in high infant mortality. Thus between 1824 and 1833, 198,505 of the 452,749 children admitted to welfare institutions, or 430 per 1,000, died in institutions or with the wet-nurses found for them. Death below the age of twenty remained very frequent, even for births in normal conditions: a third of the generation born in 1820 did not reach its twentieth year.

This close link between the economic situation, the demographic situation and social status, typical of old societies, appeared in full during epidemics or in the context of certain chronic diseases. Cholera for example, was a social index, particularly in 1832. The rich fled the towns, leaving the poor who remained a prey to death and to the poverty created by the halt in business resulting from the epidemic. The suddenness of the disease fed rumour; the working-class mentality was quick to attribute responsibility for the deaths to political adversaries or to assume the upper classes guilty of poisoning. Overcrowding in the central districts of Paris as well as the absence of hygiene accelerated contagion and increased the death rate.[6] The unemployed migrant workers returned home and spread the disease in north-eastern France with its concentrated habitations, tight communications network and mobile working population. The map of goitre, on the other hand, coincides with that of poor, mountainous France where the populations were strongly endogamous and suffered from certain food deficiencies.

b Cultural Balance Sheet

Literate and Illiterate — The biological contrasts also corresponded with cultural divisions. Illiteracy and a lack of schooling prevailed amongst the rural masses and townspeople, more particularly in western and southern regions, and amongst women more than men. In all, less than one million out of four million children attended school, and then irregularly. The ratio was of one to two between the north and the south

6. L. Chevalier (136), pp. 573–5; P. Bourdelais and J.-Y. Raulot (131), particularly pp. 110–20 and 222–4.

of the line running from Saint-Malo to Geneva (740,816 children north of the line against 375,931 to the south), whereas backward France had a higher population.[7]

All the indicators converge. Poverty prevented the communes from recruiting teachers. Even when schools did exist, the fact that children were employed in rural work or placed in domestic service, or even went as migrants to the towns, considerably reduced attendance. The use of a local language or dialect made all teaching of French more quickly forgotten. Finally, distances between farmsteads and lack of communication, together with the widespread feeling that elementary education served no useful social purpose for groups hereditarily destined to do the least skilled jobs, again reduced rates of progress in education and the elimination of illiteracy.

Women were at the bottom of the ladder in this respect. Their work locked them into the domestic duties of country life or unskilled craft work. Men, on the other hand, even in poor regions, could have the experience of temporary migration, a factor in acculturation to modernity. There were even extreme countervailing cases, for example in the Midi, from departments such as the Basses-Alpes or the Hautes-Pyrénées, where the export of schoolmasters to the lowlands became an industry in its own right, spreading education in its wake.

In actual fact, the profession of schoolmaster remained a part-time activity, often combined with a second profession during the slack season when the children were busy in the fields. Ill-esteemed, ill-paid, badly or little trained, the teachers were only able to convey the rudiments of education, following the old method of divided training for reading and writing which was unsuited to holding their pupils' attention. It was not until Guizot's law of 1833 that the State responded to a social demand for a rise, despite the factors just mentioned, in the acquisition of literacy. The July monarchy thus broke with the timidity of the Legitimist notables who were afraid that the spread of education would lose them their ascendancy over populations in peripheral regions.

Shortcomings in the Education of the Elites — The ruling class had the same ambiguous attitude to the education intended for the middle class (that is to say the bourgeoisie in the broadest sense) or even the elites. The aim of imperial reorganisation was to equip the new France with elites unified by a common education. The monopoly of the University, the militarisation of the high schools (*lycées*) replacing the central schools, the system of special schools and professional faculties, whose task was to supply the ruling cadres, were all orientated towards this end.

7. F. Furet and J. Ozouf (143), vol. 1, pp. 120–1.

The Restoration did not challenge this framework despite the charges of irreligion levelled by the Ultras at the imperial University. Church and regime were in favour of the parallel development of a competing network of religious institutions (religious boarding schools, small seminaries which actually accepted pupils with no religious vocation), while overall, the State network was increasingly elitist in its recruitment and its enrolment was slow to regain the levels of the colleges of the Ancien Regime (this did not happen before 1840). This long-lasting division as well as the notables' mistrust of opening up secondary education, which was blamed for the revolutionary troubles, continued to be a source of political conflict between factions of the ruling class from one generation to the next.

This social closure of elite education distorted the meritocratic ideal of the Revolution into an identical educational reproduction of the ruling circles, always educated according to the classical canons. This was tantamount to a regression compared with the pedagogic innovations of the Directory's central schools. In higher education, the narrow professionalisation of the special schools provided in the main an outlet for the technical cadres in State service, according to the ideas inherited from the monarchy. As for education for the liberal professions, it was concentrated to an excessive degree in Paris, and the educationally innovative faculties (arts and sciences) were limited to an ornamental social role; unless a few major stars turned their rostra into political tribunes, which in turn increased government suspicion of them.[8]

B A Divided Society

a Property, the Central Issue

The same modifications to the balance sheet appear when examining the innovations the Revolution and the Empire introduced into the social order. The principal factor which might have upset the structures of inherited property was the sale of the national assets. Despite the mass of books on the subject and the workshop re-opened at the time of the Bicentenary, it is still very hard to obtain a complete and balanced view; each regional or local case is specific.

The sale unquestionably involved a considerable transfer of property which interrupted the eighteenth-century movement towards the concentration of land, though without challenging the hierarchy of property. In fact, only a fraction of the property of the nation was really

8. M.-M. Compère (138), particularly pp. 160–7; T. Shinn (113); J.H. Weiss (120), V. Karady in J. Verger (347); N. and J. Dhombres (140).

sold to about a million Frenchmen, with large inequalities according to their initial social position. In Beauce, the nobility limited its losses by prior purchase of Church lands or by the re-purchase of alienated land with devalued money. Likewise in the Artois the nobility's share of the land fell by 3 per cent, while Church possessions were first purchased by townsfolk (who held 22 per cent of the land instead of 9 per cent before the Revolution) and by comfortably-off farmers (46 per cent of the land belonged to countryfolk instead of 38 per cent before 1789). In the vineyards on the Côte d'Or, 59 per cent of the purchasers were peasants but they only accounted for between a third and a quarter of the land sold while bourgeois carried off the finest domains.

The same pattern appears in the Beaujolais and Lyonnais where 4 per cent of the area of the department of the Rhône changed hands. However, peasant resentment was lessened by the fact that some bourgeois resold land in small lots for speculative purposes. In the West general stability came from the disturbances which hampered sales, but where they did take place, as in the Sarthe, competition between bourgeois and peasant turned in the bourgeois' favour. Lastly, in the area round Toulouse in the South, the prevalence of share-cropping barred poor peasants from a share in the feast. Only bourgeois from the towns and even some nobles appropriated the land freed by the Church, and these new landowners were sometimes more demanding than their more remote predecessors.[9]

The very fact that the Restoration had to ratify the new state of things in order to establish its power suggests that the return to the past, which the Ultras desired, would have destabilised the regime. From this point of view, the indemnity called 'the émigrés' billion' was a serious psychological blunder, despite the relative modesty of what it contributed to the beneficiaries of the state coffers.

b Contrasting Rural Societies

As before the Revolution, the preponderance of agriculture makes it particularly difficult to give an overall description of French society around 1815 because of the diversity of regional conditions, the co-existence of the old principles of hierarchisation based on status and the new principles based on wealth, and the unequal assimilation of social groups into the French nation. This was no longer legally a society of 'orders', but many features of the old order persisted, not least because the new, post-revolutionary society itself borrowed considerably from

9. J.-C. Farcy (65) and (66), pp. 227–34; D. Rosselle in G. Gayot and J.-P. Hirsch (144), pp. 314–18; R. Laurent (92), p. 86; G. Garrier (70), pp. 122–5; see also the local studies in (155); M. Denis (173), pp. 157–60; P. Bois (51), pp. 338–41; D. Higgs (146), pp. 8–9.

the former principles of social organisation in order to secure its bases. It is a well-known fact that the more antiquated a society, the more its social disparities are important (these disparities are often official and measurable by quantitative data). These are disparities not only among groups but among identical groups in different regions, and among lifestyles in homogeneous regions. The co-existence of these heterogeneous principles of social classification, combined with uneven progress in research and inadequate sources, makes any overall vision simplistic. It is preferable to measure the differences rather than attempt to arrange them on a single scale, which is what statisticians have tried to do for the past century.

Measuring Disparities — Wealth and the boundaries of status are prime measures of inequalities. The latter were inscribed in French law, since the political system gave a tiny minority who owned landed wealth the sole right to vote and gave the richest of them a share in government. This pyramid reached its peak in 1840 with a high point of 18,000 *censitaires* (men paying the *cens*, the direct tax qualification for voters) of more than 1,000 francs, and 56,000 people eligible for election appointed by 250,000 electors, themselves an elite from the 2.8 million municipal electors who only represented one adult Frenchman in five.

This system of notability, with gradients which were widened in 1830 by comparison with their 1815 levels, signified a compromise between the elites of a different historical age. It also marked an attempt to achieve political stability around large property under the Restoration, and medium-sized property under the July monarchy. It allowed the nobility, always at the top of the scale in landed wealth, to win back its influence without shutting the door on commoners, provided that they fitted into the mould partially inherited from the Ancien Regime. This system did not eliminate tensions but could, if conscientiously applied, engender a positive social dynamic. This is the same dynamic that Guizot, himself a new man, expressed in his famous formula 'Get rich by hard work and saving'.

Nevertheless, it contained two serious weaknesses. Although landed wealth was predominant in Restoration France, this principle of hierarchisation had the fault of not taking proper account of personal wealth resulting from trade or nascent industry. This created an element of tension with the new enriched bourgeoisie, which did not yet have the means to equip itself with landed investments yielding political rights. The second drawback of the system was that its narrowness created the opportunity for misuse of the dominant position. The political history of the Restoration is studded with examples of this; the 1820 law of the double vote, manipulation of electoral lists, manifold pressures, and a variety of measures to keep out the bourgeoisie with personal wealth. This delicate balance between the opening and closure of all the electoral systems, from the Consulate until February 1848, was maintained only by means of numerous savage interventions, even though this type of election was considered to be in harmony with the deep-seated social hierarchy of the country and had functioned in some sort of way and in a much more lasting fashion elsewhere in Europe. To those whom it excluded, it appeared a regression compared with the democratic phases of the Revolution; for those it privileged, it always concealed a danger of 'breaking away'.

For these people holding the traditional view, inequality was carved into the nature of things and to construct a political order without taking it into account was an aberration. The size of the inequalities of wealth between social classes had not actually been perceptibly reduced from pre-1789 levels, nor yet the hierarchy between ruling circles, even though new wealth had been able to emerge from the disturbances of the times or from new speculation. Thus, on the electoral lists of the First Empire, nearly two-thirds of the large bankers received more than 5,000 francs in income from land (or a fortune of 100,000 francs, without estimating their other income). Next on the scale of wealth came the personnel of the assemblies and the higher local administration, with trade occupying only a middle position. As the rise of trade had been more recent, it had not yet been able to make sufficient investment in landed property.[10] In fact, definition by ownership of land remained the main criterion of membership of the ruling class. Income from land was also indispensable to obtaining a high administrative position under the Empire and ensuing regimes, State service involving some payment from personal cash-boxes was a means of reserving the highest positions for the oligarchy and practising government on the cheap.[11]

In Paris and most of the large towns in the kingdom, the disparity between the average figures of declared wealth for the highest and lowest groups is in the order of 1 to 10,000. Even more telling is the fact that 68 per cent of Parisians died without assets. In Bordeaux, Rouen, Lille and Toulouse, this level of destitution was shared by 79, 75, 72 and 43 per cent respectively of the urban population under the Restoration. One per cent of informants in Paris held 30 per cent of total wealth. The corresponding figure in Toulouse was 1.5 per cent. The concentration was slightly less in the Beaujolais, where 50 per cent of total assets in 1820

10. L. Bergeron and G. Chaussinand-Nogaret (130), p. 62; on the persistent land-robe-trade hierarchy, particularly in the Midi, see M. Agulhon (121), pp. 262 ff.

11. A.-J. Tudesq (217); M. Rousselet (204); M.-J. Couailhac (139); N. Richardson (203); C. Charle (57); M. Agulhon (121), p. 78.

were held by 6.4 per cent of personal fortunes.[12] This wealth, originating primarily from the land, was very unevenly distributed both socially and spatially, defining contrasting rural structures.

Rural Structures — The line from Saint-Malo to Geneva, which d'Angeville developed on the basis of economic, anthropological and cultural criteria,[13] is also a line dividing types of rural societies, which themselves are not homogeneous. Even so, this schematic distinction between modern France and archaic France, also found in relation to urban structures, will be adopted for the sake of convenience.

Modern France: — A primary type of rural social structure is represented by the open-field regions, with capitalist agriculture, a heavy preponderance of middle-sized or large properties and tenant farming. In the Beauce, for example, the landowners, both bourgeois and noble, practised absentee landlordism and lived in the large towns on the periphery of the agricultural land. Only 5 per cent of the active local population lived off its private income from land. Against this, the majority of the active population was composed of wage-earners (divided equally between temporary day workers and permanent domestic servants). About 8 per cent formed a class of agricultural entrepreneurs, tenant farmers of large properties, owning relatively high mobile capital rather than land. Fifteen to 20 per cent of small and middle-rank peasants formed an intermediate class; some only worked their own land, others had help, still others had to rent out plots or even become part-time wage-earners.

Although it was predominantly agricultural, this modern rural society also contained other groups, whose existence was necessary given the high degree to which the products (particularly cereals and wool from merino sheep) were commercialised. These groups included merchants and traders (about 7 per cent) and artisans (millers, blacksmiths, carpenters, cartwrights, etc., who comprised about 5 per cent of the population).[14] This society corresponded to the model that the most enlightened notables wanted, since it was open to the agricultural improvements inspired by England. Social antagonism did exist, between lessor landowners and tenant farmers, between farmers who employed a workforce and day labourers and between buyers and sellers of grain; but the opportunity for rural progress, the relative shortage of manpower in relation to needs (at periods when agricultural work was heavy, some

---

12. A. Daumard in (24), vol. 3 no. 2, pp. 855, 870; G. Garrier (70), p. 293.
13. A. d'Angeville (123).
14. J.-C. Farcy (65) and (66), pp. 82–4.

of the day labourers were seasonal migrants from other areas), and the real possibility of making money and moving from one group to another prevented these tensions becoming the source of serious disturbance as was the case in poorer regions.

Unrest – as prior to 1789 and during the bad years of the Revolution – appeared at times of climatic vicissitudes which caused the six cyclical crises of the first half of the century (1805-1806, 1810-1812, 1816-1817, 1827-1828, 1836-1839, 1846-1847). According to the classic model developed by Ernest Labrousse, a bad harvest brutally forced up prices, and the situation was made worse by speculation on the rise by intermediaries or landowners with grain to sell. This plunged the whole wage-earning section of landless peasantry, who were particularly important in this type of agriculture, into poverty. Food riots were dealt with in the classic manner employed under the Ancien Regime: community charity workshops were created, the richest members of society were asked to contribute to subscriptions and, when assemblies turned riotous, armed repression was utilised. However, the position of day labourers and farm servants in this type of agricultural society was weakened by the return of peace in 1815 which ended the manpower shortage created by conscription. The result was a quasi-stagnation of the daily wage. Nevertheless, advances in agriculture and a general increase in wealth moderated crises (except in 1846-1847) and reduced total poverty. Under the July monarchy, the most deprived were able to find new jobs in the early railway yards or in Paris.

The greater the distance from this modern prototype, the greater the social disparities, and the harder it became to resolve tensions when the virtuous circle of agricultural innovation was not in operation. North-eastern France and Normandy are a prime intermediate example. The small property was much more important there, and the proportion of full-time wage-earners was smaller. Craft in a proto-industrial form (work at home with merchant manufacturers placing orders, or small workshops scattered in the villages) provided the complementary or principal means of livelihood to a considerable proportion of the rural population, for example about 15 per cent in the Calvados and Doubs under the July monarchy.[15] This lesser penetration of purely capitalist social relationships, as well as the greater shortage of resources, give agrarian affairs an aspect more closely resembling the Ancien Regime. For not only landless peasants but for rural craftsmen and a proportion of very

15. G. Désert (63), pp. 172; J.-L. Mayaud (151) and (194). Eighty per cent of the inhabitants of Doubs lived in the countryside and 65 per cent were solely farmers. In the upper Doubs there was a system of farm workshops engaged in producing edge-tools, clock- and watch-making or woodwork (p. 153).

small farmers too, the secondary source of support provided by common rights dating from before the Revolution was still a vital element in survival. Sullen resistance by the poor peasantry prevented revolutionary and imperial legislation from abolishing this heritage, which was inconsistent with the absolute conception of property imported from Roman law. In Côte-d'Or for example, 60 per cent of the area of the communes was still under common land in 1836-1838. Similarly, some communes in the East owned considerable property and their use was a bone of contention between the more affluent members of the rural community and those in less favourable circumstances. The richer elements urged that the land be sold; those at an intermediate social level wanted to lease new land to meet demographic pressure; while for the poorest, their sole source of support depended on customary rights.[16]

Archaic France: — These conflicts became bitter and turned into quasi-rebellion against the central power after the adoption of the Forest Code in 1827 and the attempt to apply it strictly under the July monarchy. The importance of woods and forests in poor and mountainous regions accounts for the dissidence by a section of the peasantry against this attempt to apply a new bourgeois order, nearly fifty years after a revolution which had not kept its agrarian promises. In the Var, Alpes, Dauphiné or Pyrénées, forest offences headed the list of criminal statistics.

Timber was in fact an indispensable component of the poor peasant's economy. In the Var, there were legal disputes not only between the communes and the landowners (often nobles) over common rights and ownership, but also at times between the inhabitants themselves, between supporters and opponents of rational or traditional use of woodland. Under the July monarchy the ravages of deforestation forced the State to take a stricter line, which revived hatred of the State's representatives and led to a recurrence of the earlier dissidence in these outlying regions.[17]

In agricultural southern and western France, the hierarchisation of rural society was even more traditional; the dependent relationship between poor peasants and day labourers on one hand and noble landowners and country bourgeois on the other took the form of methods of restrictive farming. Examples include share-cropping and a system of farm foremen in the South around Toulouse, and leases which landowners could reclaim at will in Brittany. The equivalent of the farming landowners or rich tenant farmers of the lands of the Nord were few in number. Placed in a

16. J.-L. Mayaud (151) and (194), p. 76; R. Laurent (92), p. 61.
17. M. Agulhon (160), pp. 49–92; J.-F. Soulet (156), vol. 2, pp. 155, 502 and 604 on the 'guerre des demoiselles' in the Ariège.

position of strength, the *rentier* landowners agreed only to short tenancies, which were hardly an incentive for peasants to introduce innovations when they would obtain scarcely any benefit from them. The existence of latent overpopulation also helped to strengthen the lessors' position.

The traditional ruling class was therefore not challenged, and even enjoyed a certain degree of popular support because the Revolution had left the poor rural classes with unhappy memories. Emigration of nobles had caused craftsmen to lose many customers and domestic servants to lose chances of employment; the rural classes had borne the main burden of conscription; and the blockade policy had partially destroyed trade and exports in outlying regions in the South and West. However, before 1830 the nobles, the Ultras in particular, united in the wish for revenge for their recent misfortunes, had to some extent abandoned their duties of social protection by giving priority to their public and political functions. They returned to their domains after the *Trois Glorieuses*, when it was perhaps too late; the rural problems no longer responded to the old-fashioned solutions which they advocated. The aristocratic model of the English gentry, which some people imitated in the western interior, proved unsuited to poverty-stricken zones where inhabitants looked to the towns to provide complementary means of livelihood.

C A Society of Exclusion and Violent Revolt

Agricultural progress took place mainly in advanced regions, whereas overpopulation was a feature in backward regions. The malady can be diagnosed from the bulge in temporary migrations already noted, the growth in emigration overseas – which rose from 2,500 people annually between 1821 and 1830 to 14,000 annually in 1831-1840 and then 26,000 annually in 1841-1850 – and a higher rate of permanent rural exodus as well as the accelerated growth of some towns, particularly Paris. The rate of urbanisation in France was again higher than in the Ancien Regime (21.5 per cent in 1836 against 19 per cent in 1806 and 20.5 per cent in 1790). Above all, the population of the county towns of *arrondissements*, the only population figures known precisely, rose by 31 per cent from 1821 to 1846, while total population only grew by 16.2 per cent in the same period. But the urban host societies were scarcely better placed to solve the problems of these poor, uprooted populations.

a Towns and Social Pathology

Most of the small towns which covered the country in a tight-knit web retained their traditional functions. They were market centres, the places where bourgeois and nobles lived; therefore they were where income from the land was spent and, for the most privileged sections of society, the home base of the new public function established by the Revolution and Empire. This old urban network had acquired new influence in the framework of the *censitaire* society. It was there that the bargaining and political struggles between cliques of notables took place, in which local political motives and personal rivalry very often took precedence over purely ideological discussions. The employment market for the migrants to these towns was thus in most cases limited to positions which were directly dependent on local notables for domestic and craft, commercial or redistribution jobs. In Toulouse under the Restoration, for example, the active population included more domestic servants than workers in transport or industry; a quarter were farmers and half were craftsmen.

Only nine towns in Restoration France had more than 50,000 inhabitants. Their size, except for Toulouse, could be explained by a specific economic function: four were ports (Marseilles, Rouen, Nantes and Bordeaux) and the rest were large administrative, commercial and craft or industrial centres (Lyons, Lille, Strasbourg and Paris). But these, like the mushroom villages into which new industries had been transplanted, were exceptions in the slowly changing urban picture.[18]

The expansion of these towns, dictated by their old structures and squeezed within limits which they were timidly beginning to break down, engendered a specific social pathology born of overcrowding in districts which had not been rebuilt and an inadequate municipal policy. The population growth in the largest towns at this period consisted essentially of input from without because their natural growth was negative, with death rates above the national average. Except for Paris, the migrants came mainly from adjacent departments. For example, in Marseilles in 1821-1822, 61 per cent of husbands and 69 per cent of wives were native-born, while 17 and 24 per cent respectively were born in the Bouches-du-Rhône, and the remainder originated from the Var, Basses-Alpes and south-eastern departments; only 21 per cent of newly married were of direct peasant origin.[19] In the 1820s therefore, urban migration was still a gradual process of moving into the hierarchy of the towns, a mechanism for rising in the social scale rather than an index of the disintegration of the society of origin. During the first half of the nineteenth century this pattern gradually changed. Immigration by skilled craftsmen became a secondary factor compared with migration born of poverty and rural overpopulation.

The change was fastest and most dramatic in Paris. Temporary migration by workmen from the Limousin building trade or scrap

18. B. Lepetit (150), particularly pp. 240–6; J. Merriman (99).
19. W. Sewell (208), pp. 155 and 163.

merchants and rag-pickers and water-carriers from the Auvergne had already taken place under the Ancien Regime. They were counter-balanced by migrations of workers belonging to fraternal societies of skilled artisans who made a 'tour de France', spending several years working in major cities, or the elite workforce from north-eastern France, attracted by the capital's luxury industries. The doubling of the population of Paris during the first half of the nineteenth century can be explained by a new phenomenon of permanent exodus by poor and deprived populations who could no longer find a livelihood in the overpopulated countryside. This influx of 'barbarians' into the town (in Marseilles they came partly from Piedmont) gave rise to social anxiety amongst the bourgeoisie who equated working classes with dangerous classes. The concentration of the poor in the large towns is an old truism, as the towns were the headquarters of welfare institutions, but in this period the concentration was aggravated because the countryside could not cope with the overpopulation. In Paris and in some towns a specific social pathology developed, aggravated by the inadequacy of the measures taken by the municipalities or the State authorities. Sanitary provisions did not keep pace, nor did social budgets, managed on the liberal principle of government on the cheap by authorities fearful of unleashing an endless spiral; any social measure, according to the notables and their municipal officials, risked increasing the number of poverty-stricken or professional beggars coming from outside. In actual fact, this restrictive policy increased the numbers of excluded people and deviants including children born out of wedlock (more than 60,000 in Paris), unmarried couples, prostitutes, beggars, vagabonds and temporary migrants composing the floating population of rented rooms. Crises caused by high prices and periods of unemployment extended this deep-seated poverty to almost half the urban population. On the basis of poorhouse admissions at the end of the Restoration, Louis Chevalier estimates the number of victims of chronic poverty in Paris at 350,000 out of 750,000 inhabitants.[20]

b Excluded Men and Women and the Seeds of Revolt

This society, which already combined the heritage of the Ancien Regime and the pathologies of emergent industrial society, also deliberately created other excluded categories; women, the young and prisoners. The exclusion of these groups was certainly aggravated by the conditions already mentioned, which often went hand in hand with urban or rural poverty.

If the labour question – which will be discussed in the next chapter –

20. L. Chevalier (136), p. 585.

succeeded in publicly piercing the screen of the ruling class's good faith, it did so precisely in connection with the groups which bore the handicaps introduced by the social order. First amongst these were the female workers, whose work (at home or in the factory) jeopardised the function of wife and mother, highly valued in the dominant Christian perspective. Given their generically low wages (half those of men), there was a risk that they would succumb to prostitution or to the crimes of abandoning their children, infanticide or theft. Secondly, the exploited child workers were hereditarily destined to the same downfall, so much so that contemporary demographers feared that they would never grow into real adults. The harshness of their employers and parents prematurely ruined their health and this, according to the reformers, could result in demographic and therefore military decadence. Bourgeois social observers and utopian reformers attributed these two pathological conditions solely to the effect of an industrial civilisation based on profit. In fact, they had more deep-seated foundations which were written into the Civil Code, and therefore existed prior to the expansion in manufacturing. The minority who had access to power had based it not only on the exclusion of the vast majority of men in the name of property, but also on exclusion by sex and age.

In fact, even when she belonged to the ruling class, the woman remained an eternal minor and dependant. Depending on bourgeois social strata, she was destined to facilitate first the accumulation of economic capital (by the system of unequal dowries between couples), and then of social capital. For their sons, parvenus for preference chose young girls of old social extraction, sometimes noble, who were capable of taking a worldly role or even a symbolic one, since it was women who organised the elite social activity of the salons.[21] In the urban working classes women were limited to unskilled jobs while amongst the peasantry, according to inheritance customs which had been more or less maintained despite the Civil Code, they served as an asset to be bartered for the reproduction of male lines – unless they were not the eldest and therefore excluded from their share in the family property. In certain southern regions, younger daughters, enforced spinsters, served as domestic servants to the eldest or as servants of the Church as nuns.

The young were in an intermediate position. If they were sons of good families they would change their status one day, but the late age fixed by the suffrage law and the correlation between this and the inheritance of capital put the date even further forward. But the age groups in question

21. Cf. M. Agulhon (122) and A. Martin-Fugier (193); A. Daumard (171). Y. Knibielher (148) relates this legal regression in the status of women compared with the eighteenth century with the theories spread by doctors on the 'natural' inequality between the sexes.

were still largely in the majority, not only in the total population but also in higher social circles. Here there was a seed of tension and revolt against this prolonged age of minority, imposed on a majority of young men knocking at the gates shut by the old who were perpetuating their power. At least this was how the young saw the situation, since the subject of gerontocracy was widespread at the time. The importance of student agitation under the Restoration and after, as well as the success of all the ideologies of revolt in these new *mal du siècle* generations can be explained by this artificial barrier set up after a Revolution when youth had, by contrast, enjoyed its full share of positions of power.[22]

To control all those who were challenging the still fragile order it had tried to establish, the Empire had invented the modern prison, populated by the people sentenced to the multiple penalties of imprisonment provided by the new Penal Code of 1810. The custodial system also confirmed social inequality, since the rich partly avoided it through the bail system, whereas the punishments incurred by the poor were increased if they could not pay the fines. At the end of the Empire there were 65,000 prisoners, a number which remained stable upto the 1830s. This high figure, which had increased rapidly since 1807-1808, necessitated the establishment of the system of county jails, where it was thought that manufacturing work by the inmates reduced the budgetary cost to the greatest advantage of unscrupulous general contractors. The correlation between the wheat price curve and the number of convictions for damage to property, the larger increase in crimes related to both vagabondage and begging, and the predominance of unmarried men, day labourers and young workers in the prison population underline the fact that in the new order of the notables, prison served to put to forced and under-paid labour any individual whom chronic unemployment and the unequal distribution of property excluded from a decent social life.[23]

c Conclusion

Every social level of every area of French society at the beginning of the nineteenth century was divided between nostalgia for a great aborted adventure and fear lest evil memories would return. The men of the movement were nostalgic for the egalitarian dream, former officers yearned for national greatness, the young bourgeois generations looked back to a time when youth held power. Corresponding to this was the fear of a return to feudal laws amongst the peasants, the fear of the Terror amongst the notables and the fear of abuse of liberties amongst the Ultras

22. A.B. Spitzer (214); J.-C. Caron (168) and L. Mazoyer (152).
23. J.-G. Petit (198), pp. 140-70.

which made the gulf between opposing groups all the wider. In addition, there was in the background the nostalgia for some forms of the paternalism of the Ancien Regime among the governed and the fear of what tomorrow might hold among the workers, whose position had deteriorated considerably in the Revolution. They had lost the possibility of defending themselves collectively and more humane welfare institutions, while they were the first victims of the organisation of custodial repression. This nostalgia interwoven with the fears explains the repeated constraints in the first half of the century, marked by the violence of the social conflicts and political antagonism, sometimes convergent, sometimes divergent, between notables, the *capacités* (the educated classes), peasants and the proletariat.

2

Notables, Educated Classes (*Capacités*), Peasants and Proletariat

The ruling class which unilaterally dominated the various spheres of social life in the first half of the nineteenth century presents a paradox. The notables appeared to hold all the levers of command: politics, administration, the traditional economy (land) or the new economy (industry and the emerging capitalist societies), and education. Yet unlike their British counterparts, they were not able to manage a smooth transition to a middle-class democratic society through a gradual historical compromise with the new emerging strata and the elite of the working class. What makes this paradox even harder to understand is that the English ruling classes had to confront a much more rapid process of urbanisation and industrialisation and an equally strong, if not stronger, popular protest movement than that which developed in France after 1830.

The explanation generally accepted is that memories of the Revolution and Terror petrified the various groups of notables, preventing them from evolving and combining. Some, dominant under the Restoration, remained attached to the most traditional system of rule based on the Church and the old nobility. Others, who had come to power after the 1830 revolution, were quite prepared to open the door to Legitimists of good will; this was the policy Guizot pursued after 1840. Conservative Orleanists, on the other hand, were against allowing the '*capacités*' and working classes to enter political society. For them, property and enlightenment had to go hand in hand in order to avoid any new 'demagogic' outbreak which would result in the ostracism of the ruling classes as happened in year II (1793-94). The object of this chapter is therefore to understand why the social dynamic of the years from 1830 to 1851 ended in violent confrontations between the various protagonists on the social scene (including labour uprisings under the July monarchy, the June days and the revolt, mainly by peasants and in the provinces against the coup d'état in December 1851). The notables had succeeded in re-establishing their domination by the end of the mid-century crisis, but at the price of a return to a dictatorial system which limited their own

freedom and only postponed the date of a new, equally radical, challenge
to their power.

A The Ruling Notables: The Logic of a System of Domination

a The Central State, Bone of Contention among Notables

The deep-seated foundations of the power to dominate which the notables,
and particularly the great notables, possessed have already been analysed
in the previous chapter. The notables owned not only the main means of
production, especially land, but also, from the 1830s, the new factories
and works based on industrial techniques imported from England. In fact,
the notables played an innovative role in both agriculture and
manufacturing by investing their capital in new national companies
(railway or mining companies, for example) and by going into partnership
with entrepreneurs or lending their capital to private companies. In any
case, the fact that political privilege derived solely from ownership of
land impelled the new bourgeoisie, even if it did not spring from the old
ruling class, to acquire the attributes of the ruling groups.

Nevertheless, what distinguished the notables from a bourgeoisie in
a later Marxist sense or from an old aristocracy was their grip on the State
and their specific use of its powers. They had established this monopoly
through representative institutions and administrations in which they kept
the highest positions for themselves. In a rural society, where
communications were slow and unreliable and where the economy was
fragmented, the main social links between the French regions – and their
very unequal development has already been seen – were the various
groups of notables, themselves organised hierarchically according to their
landed property, the basic measure of the extent of their social and
political power. The logic of such a system served in some ways to divide
authority into new small feudal systems which defended their individual
interests against the great national issues; hence the relative mediocrity
of political debate within the ruling class. But her absolutist tradition,
the memory of the civil wars, the peripheral attempts at revolt and the
imperial revolution had all rendered France incapable of establishing the
decentralising logic contained in a system of notables on the English
model.

As a result, varying distances from State power introduced
discrimination inside the ruling class itself, which changed over time;
the real notables were those in the highest positions and closest to State
power. The State was only a passive instrument in the hands of the ruling
class, used to respond to challenges from those excluded from the system.

It was also a means for political domination over ruling groups which did not enjoy an electoral majority at any one time. State patronage was more powerful than local patronage; on the other hand, official jobs, given out in a discretionary manner on the basis of political support, formed a trading currency between factions and a means of putting pressure on the electorate. Appropriation of the central State, from whence all other powers derived, was therefore the object of uncompromising conflicts since the power of the State could be used in a partisan manner. This shifty game between the various factions of notables can be seen in the criteria on which candidates were chosen at elections or again in co-options to the highest administrative posts during the purges which followed major changes in regime or majority. Patronage, recommendations and influence vis-à-vis non-political posts in this way perverted the principles of merit and ability stated in the Declaration of the Rights of Man.

The result of this loaded game was the very specific sociology of the political and administrative elites. André-Jean Tudesq has demonstrated this for the period around 1840, precisely the time when the liberals who came to power after 1830 were intending to break with the favouritism and unfair promotion which had marked the period of Ultra domination. Despite the lowering of the direct tax qualification (*cens*) required to vote and to be eligible for election after 1830, the deputies were still recruited from amongst the richest landowners (in 1840, 63.6 per cent of deputies paid more than 1,000 francs *cens*). Deputies also came increasingly from amongst officials, particularly higher officials (175 of the 459 deputies in 1840 were officials).[1] This unbalanced recruitment lay at the foundations of the confusion between the administration and politics and between politics and the politics of dubious practices or of social conservation. The public bodies, the magistracy, prefectoral corps and even the technical corps were filled with members of politicians' families or their protégés who traded services and bribes. This occasionally provoked scandals reminiscent of the venality of the Ancien Regime, including preferential deals, conditional resignations in order to make a job for a relative and exceptional promotion of those close to power.[2]

The pliancy of the system also explains why on two occasions (in 1830 and from 1846) the group in power was not able to defuse the rise of the opposition nor cope with the crises because of its growing and unperceived isolation from the real country. The illusion of parliamentary government counter-balanced by administrative pressure prevented any reform decided from above, since it would be political suicide for the

---

1. Tudesq, A.-J.(217), vol. 1, p. 369; Girard, L., Serman, W. and Gossez, R. (177), p. 15.
2. See the examples cited in Charle, C. (57), pp. 36 ff., and in Tudesq (217), vol. 1, passim.

party in power to abandon the very foundations of its domination and agree to the opposition's demands. However the Orleanists, and particularly supporters of Guizot, should have profited from their experience as opponents of the previous regime which had fallen into disgrace for the same reasons. This incomprehensible blindness by the actors in, or witnesses to, several political revolutions can be explained by ideological factors. Supporters of what can best be called the 'golden mean' (*juste milieu*) were convinced that they possessed the ultimate political truth.

b An Enlightened Class?

His Protestant origins ensured that Guizot, principal leader at the end of the July monarchy, was won over to the Enlightenment. He believed that it was possible to resolve social tensions by spreading education within the framework of the Christian religion. Such was the main object of his 1833 law on primary teaching. Similarly, in 1832, by re-establishing the Académie des Sciences Morales et Politiques suppressed by Napoleon, he thought that he was presenting the 'middle class' (that is to say, the bourgeoisie in the vocabulary of the day) with an organ for thought and social analysis which would avert the social dangers which had destroyed previous regimes. The Académie, like other contemporary academic or scholarly societies, initiated the publication of studies of social problems. The pamphlets and books by supporters of the established order, like those by their opponents who challenged the official viewpoint (for example, *L'Organisation du travail* by Louis Blanc, or *Qu'est-ce que la propriété?* by Proudhon published in 1840) helped to bring the labour question and pauperism to the fore, along with the equation of working classes with dangerous classes, which bourgeois opinion was finding it increasingly easy to accept in the 1840s.

These ethical and philosophical investigations may have nourished a latent social fear which would explain the panic which gripped the ruling class at the time of the 1848 revolution, but in reality they resulted in scarcely any practical reforms. That would have run counter to official liberalism, which rejected any State regulation of these matters as synonymous with a return to the Ancien Regime. The predominant viewpoint, which was ethical and Christian, placed responsibility for social problems not on society or the State but on the individuals who composed them. The poor and the workers themselves were therefore the first to be indicted. They were termed 'demoralised', that is to say leading a life which was not in accordance with the predominant ethic, through improvidence, drunkenness, weakness of character, laziness or through having grown accustomed to receiving aid. The employers were only criticised for their abuse of the weakest members of society[3] who were not able to defend themselves or for inadequate paternal action, except in the case of some Legitimists or social Catholics who were attached to the old order and therefore worried about excessive mechanisation and the disturbances created by the economic crises.

In the notables' social perspective, superior position involved duties towards inferiors, but even when freely fulfilled these duties did not confer rights on the lowly. To confer such rights would have gone outside the framework of the ethical hierarchy which shadowed the social hierarchy. Guizot summed up this concept in 1842: 'The superior classes are closely linked to the inferior classes; they represent them, protect them, do not oppress them'.[4] Mainly landowners, although some of them also engaged in more modern speculation, the notables transposed their domination of rural society onto the new, emerging industrial world. In this relationship the rich came to the aid of the poor at times of natural hardship and controlled every area of their lives as if they were children or servants, not men of the same status as themselves. The Mulhouse employers' paternalism was highly commended, because the factory became again an enlarged family such as the rural domain could become in certain regions where share-cropping, agricultural wage-labour or small-scale tenant-farming prevailed.

This social model, sometimes applied by the largest or most philanthropic manufacturers, was actually unsuited to the vast majority of employers who ran weak micro-enterprises and employed a temporary workforce. It was even less suited to sectors organised into the domestic system by merchant manufacturers who placed orders with craftsmen or semi-craftsmen, or even with peasant-workers. It was precisely in labour circles closest to craftwork that the predominant ideology was most challenged, as will be seen below. But it was also challenged within the ranks of the *'capacités'* (members of the liberal professions and minor officials), and even by some notables who were currently barred from power because of the monopolization of the State by groups who refused to give them a place in the sun.

B The Notables: Divided and Challenged

a The Challenge from the *'Capacités'*

As at the time of the French 'pre-revolution', the process of challenging

3. Like children, the only category affected by a law which was moreover made to measure in 1841, by and for industrialists. Cf. the famous investigation by Villermé (20).

4. Tudesq (217), vol. 2, pp. 566-605; quotation p. 604; on employers' conflicting conceptions of authority, see Stearns, P.N. (213).

the established order which culminated in the 1848 revolution was partially triggered off by characters belonging to the world of the notables. The basic reason for this has been demonstrated; the bias of the centralised electoral system moved it further and further away from the new trends in the economy and society by favouring inheritance, land, Parisian administrative power, stubborn conservatism and a politics of dubious practices, to the advantage of an increasingly small oligarchy. Rivalries among political factions were aimed at determining how to resolve the increasingly strong social tensions between the ruling groups, the middle classes and the petty bourgeoisie.

The masses were in any case excluded. The hope of enrichment held out to those classes situated at the immediate margins of the system, as an answer to their claim to participate in power, remained an enticement to the majority and was based on the laws of liberalism themselves. The 1840s experienced an economic upsurge which contributed to the enrichment of the petty and middle-rank bourgeoisie. However, the return of difficulties, in particular the serious crisis of 1846-1847, underlined the selective nature of the process; all the more so as industrialisation, along with the uneven modernisation of agriculture, highlighted regional disparities. Even in Paris, the most conducive setting for social ascent, every generation of the independent petty bourgeoisie risked sliding back to working-class or wage-earning status. A sample of small tradesmen in the IVth *arrondissement* shows that one out of every two shopkeepers' sons came down in the world, even if he started out from favourable circumstances.[5] However, the greatest critics of the established social order were people whose jobs or activities placed them outside this circle of economic earning. For the qualified petty bourgeoisie, minor officials or members of the liberal professions practising in the smallest towns or market towns – those who were called the '*capacités*' at the time – Guizot's advice 'Get rich by hard work and saving', was nothing more than an illusory perspective, perhaps even a contemptuous insult.

The 1840s were a time when the subjects of overcrowding in the liberal professions (particularly medicine), overproduction of qualified people and administrative malaise came out into the open.[6] It is by definition hard to assess the objective reality of these phenomena as these notions are actually an expression of the gap between the situation dreamed of, for which financial sacrifices had been made, and the final position which, even if it constituted promotion, did not match up to expectations in the majority of cases. Some statistical data records this structural blockage.

5. Le Yaouanq, J. (190), p. 93.
6. Léonard, J. (94), vol. 2, ch. 7; Pinkney, D.H. (199); Church, C. (137); Thuillier, G. (116).

In Grenoble in 1848-1850, for example, 38.9 per cent of deceased members of the liberal professions left no capital. These circles were also characterised by their Malthusian precocity: in Paris in 1847, 22.2 per cent remained unmarried (against 13.3 per cent of merchants and 16.1 per cent of officials) and the majority of those who started families had one child at the most.[7]

In addition to the increase in the educated workforce and the number of qualified personnel, one factor specific to those years increased malaise. Favouritism in public office was on the increase as the groups in power became entrenched, and this blocked the careers of most of the new men. Here too the way that French social space and the State apparatus were structured explain French specificity compared with foreign examples. The centralisation of the education system in Paris made it the place where young middle-class elements in quest of qualifications were socialised and politicised. Likewise, control of positions open to these qualified people by non-meritocratic methods made Paris a hotbed of challenge to this system of patronage and therefore of the notables in power. Outside Paris, the differences in rates of urban and economic growth meant that some towns or market towns could offer only inadequate outlets for the new members of the professions who settled there. In large towns, which attracted the most ambitious, success depended on the social selectivity of the clientele and involved integration into the ruling networks.

Increased legal charges were a symptom of the phenomenon of the growth of inequalities within those professions which were theoretically based on merit. Similarly, dubious procedures which some doctors employed to tout for patients (advertising, agreements with colleagues), the race for official medical posts and the beginning of the organisation of the medical profession in order to defend corporate interests all originated in the same unrest. Lastly, at a political level, periodical student agitation, particularly in Paris, in reaction to the authoritarian and Malthusian measures by a government desirous of increasing selectivity in access to higher education, and a strong presence of members of the *capacités* in opposition groups did not only indicate a trend in favour of the *Mouvement*, which wanted change. It also reflected a perception by the young bourgeois generations that the existing system was creating new privileges to the advantage of restricted groups, even if – perhaps above all if – they belonged to the *capacités*; and the system was doing this contrary to the initial programme of the 1830 revolution.[8]

---

7. Ibarrola, J. (185), p. 161; Daumard, A. (171), p. 173.

8. Léonard (94); Caron, J.-C. (168); on the quite specific place of lawyers as leaders of the opposition in the 1840s in the Limousin, see Corbin, A. (170), vol. 2, p. 792.

The antagonistic rejection by the parliamentary majority of the demand to extend the *cens* to the *capacités* finally demonstrated to the blindest observer the reality of this social barrier behind the political barrier, which was theoretically permeable by the accumulation of wealth. In the provinces, practising a liberal profession did not ensure an adequate standard of living because of the low purchasing power of the urban working classes, as well as the low economic development of the rural regions. Access to State power or to elective office was therefore the only possibility for those who did not inherit everything from their parents or who did not have the means to go to Paris to seek a wider setting for their talents.

This aspiration on the part of the *capacités* to play a political role was subsequently reflected in the social recruitment of the republican candidates and members elected in 1848 and the far Left in 1849; 37.3 per cent of the members of the Constituent Assembly in 1848 were lawyers, notaries, doctors and journalists, while 60.1 per cent of the Democratic Socialist members elected in 1849 were connected with the intellectual *capacités*.[9] These men were torn between two worlds in the electoral system; their cultural world, in which they formed a small elite in a country where ignorance was still predominant, and the world of the notables which was rejecting an increasing number of them because they were men without breeding. They therefore had every interest in obliterating the gulf, either by electoral reform purely to their own advantage, or, more generously, through the struggle for the introduction of universal suffrage in order to take their principles to their logical conclusion and to the general advantage. This would invest them with a new social function, replacing the old notables as leaders of the working classes.[10]

b The Challenge from the Craft Workers

However, this challenge would not have culminated in an enduring loosening of the notables' power without the growing, parallel and sometimes converging criticism and mobilisation by the skilled workers. The same dialogue with the deaf, or rather refusal of dialogue, as with the *capacités* can be observed between the new authorities born of the 1830 revolution and the mainly Parisian workers. As early as the summer

9. Best, H. (166), p. 58; Bouillon, J. (167), p. 81; Corbin (170), vol. 2, pp. 720-1: of 88 candidates and 23 elected members of the Limousin in 1848, 45 and 14 respectively, or over half, belonged to the '*capacités*'.

10. Lévêque, P. (188) and (189), p. iv. The precedent of the French Revolution, thanks to which these professions had gained administrative posts closed to them under the Ancien Regime, could only encourage these liberal or republican choices.

of 1830 the watchword of liberty, which had sealed the alliance between opponents of the Restoration and the masses, emerged as the principal issue in a conflict which became increasingly bitter as new groups of workers rejected the unalloyed liberal rules that the notables intended to maintain for regulating the labour market.

These two decades were marked by the rebirth of an autonomous popular movement with manifold origins and manifestations. The principal innovation was the assertion of social identity as a class by one section of the parties concerned. The earlier labour identity, as expressed in the tradeguilds, was narrowly limited to individual crafts, should internal competition (between the different '*devoirs*', i.e. fraternities of workers), not take precedence.[11] The other explosive element in labour identity lay in local and regional loyalties. For example, before being perceived as a mason, the migrant from the Limousin was regarded by Parisians, even Parisian workers, as a semi-peasant, a raw recruit, a sort of immigrant worker or foreigner, since he spoke in a provincial dialect and lived in temporary collective lodgings. A complete mental revolution had to take place before these workmen thought of themselves as workers and took part in the mid-century social and revolutionary movements in the capital on the same basis as workers in more elevated crafts.[12]

The conquest of the new identity by these divided workmen resulted from the events at the beginning of the 1830s and the systematic policy of exclusion of the working classes which the notables and bourgeoisie as a whole followed. The workers were not only rejected from the electorate, something which scarcely changed, but also gradually from the National Guard into which some of them had been incorporated after the July revolution. This exclusion also took the form of surveillance or criminalisation of all collective labour activities, including resistance groups, strikes and demonstrations in times of food shortages. In fact, this refractory, clamouring working class only represented a limited fraction of all those that could be encompassed by the description 'worker'.

The urban environment, particularly the large towns headed by Paris and Lyons, was at least as important for the emergence of this identity as the specific pursuit of manual labour. This setting provided the relative freedom of anonymity and social mixing, which enabled relationships with republican political militants and social theorists to be formed more easily. It helped to keep the political memory of revolt alive and ensure

11. Perdiguier, A. (15) and the introduction by Faure, A., p. 25: the young generation of guild members rejected the old organisations whose brawls harmed the corporative defence vis-à-vis the non-organised workforce.

12. Nadaud, M. (14), especially pp. 45 and 150 on the first strike by the Limousin masons in 1840; Corbin (170), vol. 1, pp. 217-9, and vol. 2, pp. 780-7.

Source: Edward Shorter and Charles Tilley, *Strikes in France, 1830–1968*, Cambridge, Cambridge University Press, 1974, p. 109.

MAP 3: The number of strikes per commune in 1833.

the existence of a minimal public for specifically working-class newspapers like *L'Artisan*, 'paper of the working class', published in the capital from September 1830, *L'Écho de la fabrique*, born in Lyons at the time of the silk-weavers' revolts at the end of October 1831, or *L'Atelier*, published in Paris from 1840.

In 1833 an unprecedented wave of strikes swept France; there were seventy-two strikes, or four times more than in any preceding year. This rise in activity was connected with the existence of workers' societies which co-ordinated activity among towns. The map of the 1833 strikes by commune, drawn up by Edward Shorter and Charles Tilly, illustrates this organisation. The old central France of crafts and artisanery shows up on it much more than the France of modern nascent industry. While there was one strike at Anzin and three at Lille, centres of the new proletariat of the new industry (and furthermore, there were still more craftsmen and home-workers than factory proletariat in Lille at that time), there were 13 strikes in Paris, 8 in Lyons, 3 in Saint-Étienne, 4 in Le Havre and 2 in Caen.[13] Tailors head the table for frequency of strikes in the period 1830-1847, followed by carpenters and masons; in other words, three guilds which had nothing to do with the industrial revolution and were, on the contrary, representative of the urban economy were the most active.[14]

There was therefore, a very perceptible timelag between the minority which developed this new image of itself, that is to say, challenged the individualist liberal order by claiming the right to resist it collectively, and the 'objective sociology' of the workers. Of the approximately 6.3 million workers in 1848, the majority worked in the crafts and artisanal trades sector and particularly in textiles, and were dispersed throughout the country. Despite considerable growth in the 1840s, the manufacturing sector took longer to accept the new social ideal which put the notion of working class in the foreground and claimed for it a new place in bourgeois society, to the extent that strikes and organisation were less frequent there; activity was more defensive than offensive, and was even waged on an individual scale.[15]

William Sewell has shown the continuity between the old corporatism and this assertion by the class of workers in trades. For them, it was a question of winning back a social power which the bourgeois revolutionary order had destroyed in the name of the parasitic landowners. By identifying the enfranchised bourgeoisie with a new nobility, these

13. Shorter, E. and Tilly, C. (114), map, p. 109.
14. Aguet, J.-P. (159), p. 366.
15. For example, the spinners and weavers in the Roubaix-Tourcoing region, still socially and locally linked to the manufacturers who supplied them with work, preferred to settle their differences through the intermediary of conciliation boards. Delsalle, P. (172), p. 227.

militants were reviving the battle plan of Sieyès against the old order in the name of the universality and utility of the new third estate, the workers.[16] This demand for social dignity therefore converged with the political demand of the *capacités* but was incompatible with the ethical and individualist viewpoint of the ruling classes. For them the worker, even if skilled, was closer to a domestic servant, bound to give service and not able to enjoy collective rights.

This antiquated image of social relationships and the harshness of the confrontations[14] can be explained by the dispersed nature of the productive process, the predominance of workshops or small shops, and the varied nature of workers' status. They were sometimes semi-employers, heads of workshops like the silk weavers in Lyons (the *'canuts'*), still identified in bourgeois opinion with the proletarian barbarians of the 1831 uprising. For the administrative authorities to recognise the 'working class' in the new sense as party to a dialogue would be to ruin the whole legal structure of the codes. For the employers, who were mainly small employers or weak middlemen, recognition would hasten their ruin to the advantage of the richest, or of heads of enterprises working with a labour force which was much more subdued because it was dispersed over the countryside or consisted largely of women, or to favour sub-contractors driven to accept anything during the dead season. The whole paradox was therefore that on several occasions this labour elite was able to create difficulties for supporters of the established order, despite its numerical weakness, hesitancy and ideological divisions, its dispersion in space, its atypical nature within the body of workers, its isolation from the peasantry and its ambiguous relationship with the intellectuals and the *capacités*.

C The Proletarian Threat

a The Process of Contagion

The two revolts in Lyons (1831 and 1834) provide a scientifically pure illustration of how revolutionary contagion took place, because, unlike the Paris uprisings, neither national politics nor student agitation come into the affair. The silk capital brought together 400 manufacturers, who did not in fact manufacture but formed a body of employers involved in providing the raw material, orders and the marketing of the finished product; 8,000 heads of workshops, owning their looms and employing labour, but entirely dependent on the commercial channels since theirs was a luxury product and subject to sharp fluctuations in demand; and

16. Sewell, W. (211), pp. 655-6, and (209).

20,000 workers, sometimes related to the head of the workshop, who could hope to set up on their own account.[17] The conflict of interests, although not corresponding to a Marxist proletarian/capitalist model, nonetheless came close to a modern class struggle because two links in the chain clashed in a pure market relationship; the 'rate' to be charged for the product determined workers' wages, the standard of living of the head of the workshop and his family and the necessary hours of work.

For the manufacturer to accept the rate, that is to say a uniform purchase price for the finished cloth, was to lose his main means of pressure, which was the use of competition to cut prices between silk-weavers and between workers in the town and in the country. Small, weak middlemen, the manufacturers controlled neither the raw material nor the outlets. In a very small minority amongst the population, ill-protected by the National Guard which was itself partly composed of workers, and far away from the capital which took time to send reinforcements, they also remembered the particularly hard times of the Terror in Lyons.

All these facts explain how, within a few weeks, an initially limited situation was converted into a symbol of the fracture which had emerged in bourgeois society. They also explain how, through the activity of a determined minority influenced by Saint-Simonian or republican missionaries, the silk-workers, renowned for their submissiveness, were able to conquer the second industrial city in the kingdom and for a few days set up a pre-figuration of the Commune in the face of the helpless authorities. Repression by the army and the courts and by measures restricting freedom themselves generated lasting class consciousness and wider solidarity. This was why every labour dispute, every disturbance born of urban poverty, was very rapidly able to sweep the mass of the working classes into open revolt and a new challenge of the class in power, which never negotiated or, if it did, never kept its promises.

b The Factory Proletariat and those excluded from Industrial Society

This makes it easier to understand the first aspect of the paradox mentioned earlier. The revolutionary contagion was the product of the intransigence of the class of notables who politicised the economic challenge from workers of the old type. They saw it as an attack on the order of individual property, while repressive violence drove the most conscious workers to seek wider alliances through associations on a national scale and links with political groups and socialist sects seeking

17. Rude, F. (205) and (206) and the evidence in Truquin, N. (19). On the revolutionary contagion in Paris, see Faure, A. (174).

an audience.

The second dimension of the paradox goes back to the development under the July monarchy of a second proletariat, much less conscious, much less organised and on which notwithstanding social observers concentrated all their attention. The majority were employed in the new collective factories and in the mines or in the large railway workyards. This proletariat was therefore primarily provincial, concentrated in textile industries in the Nord, in Normandy or Alsace, or in the mines of the Massif Central. It was weakened by its heterogeneity, since women, foreign workers and children could be more easily employed in the mechanised factories than in crafts. Unskilled and uneducated, it possessed only a small capacity to resist uprooting and demoralisation.

Consequently, it was a favourite subject of miserabilist descriptions by investigators of pauperism. In the eyes of these investigators, the danger these workers represented did not lie in their being so much a challenging force, like the previous group of workers, as a hotbed of social pathology which would destroy prevailing morals. According to social observers, whose opinions could mostly be confirmed by the facts, poverty, crowding, precarious accommodation, the conditions of factory work and periodic unemployment drove these '*miserables*' (the word acquired its new meaning at the time) to step outside the legal framework. Theft, abandonment of children, prostitution, individual revolt against the injunctions of the authorities, brawls and vagabondage were the crimes most frequently attributed to this sub-proletariat, notably in the large towns.[18] But what was only delinquency or urban pathology could, when aided by periods of economic crisis, political disturbances and conflicts stirred up by the class of craft-workers, swing towards a more general challenge even without political education or organisation. Hence the alternation of violent revolt and apathy, or even willing submission, to the employers.

The social conflicts between 1847 and 1851 did nothing more than recapitulate over a short period the various possible patterns of evolution of the working classes. But they assumed this amplitude not only because of the change in social perceptions within the predominant culture, but above all because of their spread in the ranks of the elite masses.

c A New Social Perspective

The importance of what can be conveniently encompassed under the heading of utopian socialism lies less in social projects or the later versions of these ideas in the socialist tradition than in the fact that another

18. Chevalier, L. (136); Sewell, W. (208); Petit, J.-G. (198), pp. 279 ff.

social viewpoint was thereby formulated and diffused. It represented another challenge to the monopoly of the hitherto dominant viewpoint. This viewpoint had been disputed only by an older doctrine, Catholic or Legitimist in inspiration, but the divergencies in that case did not bear on the same problems. By describing differently what should be central to the perception of social reality, these theories obliged official thinkers to redefine their own apologetics for the established order, thus putting them on the defensive.

Above all, the absence of real answers to the new questions posed (Why did industry give birth to a new form of poverty? Why did the rule of liberty engender the enslavement of the weakest, notably children?) created agitation within the middle classes, the bourgeois elements who were least well integrated into the prevailing system, and amongst leading contemporary writers. For the more organised working class to have been able to capture a certain public at the highest level of State for a few months between February and June 1848 (the creation of the Luxembourg commission and of the National Workshops, the first measures of social legislation), it had first been necessary that bourgeois and intellectual opinion, in the broadest sense, acknowledge as legitimate certain demands implied by socialist-inspired writings. If labour, not property alone, was the foundation of society then in order to cure the ills from which the workers suffered, this in fact implied 'the organisation of labour' (Louis Blanc), taking an interest 'in the largest and poorest class' (the theme of the Saint-Simonians) and permitting 'workers' associations' in order to right the balance vis-à-vis the property owners (Flora Tristan).

These writings, particularly those by worker-poets, proved that the workers, far from being the sub-men implied by the paternalist viewpoint of people like Villermé, possessed a dignity equal to the 'workers of thought', to use the terminology of 1848. Their poverty, far from being the punishment for their irresponsibility as the ruling class claimed, was on the contrary evidence of social injustice, since on some occasions workers managed to write poems or publish newspapers which proved their moral dignity. The idealisation of the masses by theorists or some romantic writers therefore combatted their identification with the dangerous classes.

Aside from the ideological debate, the 1840s saw the creation of a political weapon, which would again be of use after the revolution, and also of powers of social mobilisation, aided by certain romantic intellectuals who were patrons of the worker-poets or friends of the elite militants. This development stood in stark contrast to the denunciation in the press and in literature of the ruling class, which was shaken by the scandals at the end of the reign and whose image was thus damaged. This earlier psychological revolution partially explains the facility with which the faction in power capitulated before an uprising which was neither more nor less serious than any other; on one side there was demoralisation at the top, on the other there was a social project which, even if only espoused by a minority, had already acquired a certain legitimacy beyond those whom it was assumed to affect.[19]

D The Mid-Century Crisis, 1847–1851

a Economic Crisis and Social Tensions

These conceptual or social innovations offer an explanation for the new turn taken by political and social confrontations in the period from 1847 to 1851. But the direct cause of the national scale of the mid-century crisis, as well as of the need to invent new forms of domination, was the initial deep-seated destabilisation of the country by the agricultural crisis, and then the commercial and industrial crises, after 1846. As the previous chapter showed, the countryside was experiencing latent overpopulation and the scourge of indebtedness. The savage rise in prices caused by poor potato and cereal harvests plunged the rural population into poverty. The small farmer also suffered because his cash reserves were absorbed by taxes and by the interest he paid to money-lenders in order to pay for past purchases of land. The fall in demand for textile or craft products, caused by this peasant poverty or because of competition from better equipped factories, in its turn put rural weavers and craftsmen, so numerous at this period, out of work and further increased the proportion of the population living in penury.

Poverty, the source of disturbances, also nourished a rural class struggle. The crisis profited some; tenant farmers who sold their produce benefited from the sharp rise in prices, as did landowners who sold their surpluses or who received dues in kind from their farmers, and in particular the middlemen in whose interest it was to speculate on the rise by holding back sales, which in turn fed discontent, fear and rumour as it had in 1789.[20] In periods of penury, sources of supplementary income in poor regions (common rights and removal of forest resources, which infringed legislation) became all the more vital. This resulted in a covert war against the landowners and the authorities or their employees who refused what they regarded as a disguised form of theft, and what for the poor peasants was a normal method of redistribution, a right to survival analagous to what the workers called the right to work. Certain pointers and the common forms of agitation convey the fall in the standard of

---

19. Sewell, W.H. (209), ch. 9; Agulhon, M. (161), part 3; Rancière, J. (202).
20. Labrousse, E. (187).

living of the rural and urban working-class population in an economy dominated by primary consumer goods; these included a rise in the death-rate (23.9 per 1,000 in 1847 against 22 in 1844), an increase in the number of paupers in town and countryside, renewed growth of begging and delinquency, food riots to prevent cereals leaving for other regions or to force sales at 'normal' prices, pillage, attacks on the rich, at Buzançais (Indre), for example, where there was loss of life, and the development of xenophobia against foreign, particularly Belgian, workers in the Nord.

The intransigence of the ruling class and its inability to cope properly with the demands of the masses apart from the traditional charitable remedies, were two sources of peasant disaffection with the notables in some rural regions which later (after 1848) became 'red' bastions. The map of the 1846-1847 disturbances shows that they primarily occurred on the borders of departments, at points where convoys of corn passed through, and in zones where there was an old type of rural and urban proletariat, for example the whole mid-west (Mayenne, Ille-et-Vilaine, Indre-et-Loire, Indre and Vienne). This was a region with a dispersed rural textile industry intended for regional self-consumption, where agricultural yields below the national average meant that peasants without any land or very small plots felt the bad harvests all the more acutely.

On the other hand, departments with modern industry or large towns were relatively spared because the authorities, alive to the social danger, took quicker, more efficient measures to alleviate working-class poverty. The government also sent troops to those areas as a priority and demonstratively in order to forestall the threat. It used the troop train to move grain in the case of the Jura, the Vosge, in Lorraine and Alsace.[21] In most cases, however, the initiatives came from local, municipal or prefectoral sources. Inequalities between working classes of different status were therefore increased, while the limitations of official liberalism to tackle the problems were underlined. For example in Le Creusot, it was Schneider himself who arranged for corn to be brought from Marseilles to alleviate his workers' food problems. Similarly the managers of the Anzin company distributed bread rations to their miners and even bought American corn at Le Havre in order to bring down prices.[22] Paradoxically, the other regions spared the agitation were the poorest – the mountainous areas of subsistence agriculture – which is logical since there were fewer transactions and therefore less speculation in agricultural products there. Poverty could only show itself in migration, begging and vagabondage towards richer regions or various types of forest

21. Gossez, R., 'À propos de la carte des troubles de 1846-1847', in Labrousse (187), pp. 1-3.
22. Ibid., p. 118; Lévêque, P. (189), p. 34.

Key:
●● Interference with corn movements
   Interference and pillaging
   Interference and forced sale
   Forced sale on the market
Xx Riots
   Riots with pillaging or forced sales
   Disorder or unrest
▲▲ Other incidents

Source: From Rémi Gossez, 'A propos de la carte des troubles de 1846–1847', *Aspects de la crise et de la dépression, 1846–1851*, ed. E. Labrouse, Societé d'histoire de la révolution de 1848–1956.

MAP 4: Showing the unrest caused by the high price of corn in 1846–1847.

crime.[23]

The agricultural and, partly, the industrial crises were in fact overcome by the time of the political revolution. The first left psychological traces which explain why it was easy to rally the country to the decisions taken in Paris. Faced with economic problems, the great notables did not appear to best advantage. It even looked as if some were profiting from the poverty, since those who drew their income from land saw their revenues increase with the high prices. The temporary hearing given to moderate republicans in 1848 originated partly in these deficiencies of the old ruling class. On the other hand, their catastrophic policy vis-à-vis the peasantry (especially the tax of 45 centimes), in conjunction with measures taken too exclusively in favour of town workers and the depression in agricultural prices in 1848-1851, a consequence of overproduction, account for the revival of support for the notables' authority by the greater part of the peasantry.

b The Social Issues in the Mid-Century Crisis

The defeat of the new republican political personnel essentially resulted from the fact that they were caught in the pitiless confrontation between the main social forces revealed by the mid-century crisis. By a symbolic reversal, it was in fact the political revolution which restarted the economic crisis and drove the social groups to extreme solutions of collective violence or political radicalisation. The economic paralysis in the first months of 1848 was a sort of 'wall of money' *avant la lettre*. It showed the country that the old notables who were apparently dispossessed of political power still held the real economic power by their refusal to invest when faced with what they regarded as anarchy or a world turned upside down.[24] This slump in its turn engendered massive unemployment, particularly in the large urban centres, and this obliged the government to take emergency measures (national or municipal workshops) which the old ruling class identified with the premises of socialism.

In a parallel development, working-class poverty and the new climate of liberty developed a powerful working-class associative movement on the model of the militant elite first elaborated in the 1840s. However, this worker counter-power quickly became intolerable not only to the old ruling class but to the new middle classes, which owed their legal standing to universal suffrage. No more than the old ruling class could the

23. Armengaud, A. (124), pp. 184 ff.; Vigier, P. (219), vol. 1, pp. 49 ff.

24. Tudesq (217), vol. 2, pp. 1002 ff., and Gossez, R. (178), p. 56, on the conspiracy of the rich in worker opinion.

bourgeoisie of the *capacités* tolerate the birth of a new corporate body which by its concentration in the vital centres of power, notably Paris, influenced its decisions during the revolutionary days.

The June days of 1848 were the culminating point in a trend of rising working-class collective violence, not only in the Seine but in the whole country. This violence was preceded by intense social pressure. The other social groups had the impression that the working-class masses had a permanent hold on the streets with their marches and petitions. This increased fear and therefore economic stagnation which, in its turn, caused working-class radicalism to increase in a vicious spiral.[25] To re-establish confidence and break this spiral the new political elite, subjected to political and financial pressures by the old ruling class, then ended its earlier alliance with the organised Parisian workers. Relying on the minor bourgeoisie and the peasants, it aimed to defend the legitimacy of suffrage against the legitimacy of the street and destroy the counter-power of its former allies. The June revolt, orchestrated by the political leaders in order to rally the bourgeoisie as a whole, therefore seemed like a confrontation between two classes, but it was primarily a trial of strength between two brands of legitimacy: the legitimacy recently acquired by the educated bourgeoisie and the competing legitimacy of the working-class *capacités* which could rely neither on the other towns (where the employers were more powerful than in Paris) nor on the countryside plunged into poverty by the political crisis which began in February and worsened in June.

In order to win in Paris itself, the government made use of the young working-class generation which was less well integrated into urban life and therefore had the least corporative culture, and whose loyalty to the Republic was born of its poverty. Enrolment in the forces of law and order was actually the sole means of livelihood for this class. The ferocity of the mobile guards in battle against men who might have been their elder brothers or fathers probably expressed their resentment against a society which only offered them unemployment, whereas at the same time a section of the working class had won privileges at the expense of the most recent members of the same class.[26] The final result of the pitiless confrontation taken to extreme limits between the political elite and a section of the people thus harmed both protagonists, in a process which

25. Tilly, C. and Lees, L. (215), especially p. 1064; Gossez (178), pp. 39, 52, 61. There were 200 worker delegations to the public authorities in Paris up to 16 April 1848 and 339 professional petitions. Xenophobic pressure in the Nord, the destruction of machines and the sacking of convents at Lyons and Rouen were the most disturbing aspects of this collective violence. The large Paris demonstration on 17 March 1848 mustered up to 200,000 workers, or almost the whole working class of the capital.

26. Caspard, P. (169); Traugott, M. (216); Agulhon, M. (163), pp. 167 ff.

can be observed during other political crises. The Paris labour movement was lastingly weakened, while social fear drove the other social groups to transfer their confidence back to the old elites who held the keys to order and prosperity. The moderate republicans, despite their pledge to law and order, were in the event held responsible for having indirectly favoured 'anarchy' through the new liberties given to the 'trouble-makers'.

c Reconciled Notables and Lacerated Masses

The notables' return to the foreground at the end of 1848 was based on two social strengths; first, the traditional strength drawn from their earlier domination of the masses in regions with the most antiquated structures, and second, the new united strength coming from groups which had previously torn each other apart. This common front by the propertied classes enabled them to represent themselves to the peasant landowners, helpless and discontented in the face of agricultural slump and fiscal pressure, as genuine ramparts of law and order and guarantors of prosperity against socialism (that is to say, the rebellious and organised workers). In country areas most closely linked to the markets, and therefore best informed about the dangers from the towns, this reasoning was accepted, in the Paris Basin, for example, and in the Pas-de-Calais, northern Burgundy and Normandy. The restored notables' other stronghold was Brittany and the clerical West and the poor mountainous areas. Here, after the partial withdrawal of the notables during the period of the Constituent Assembly, universal suffrage once again found its natural 'guides', who in this case were the Legitimist nobles kept out of power under the July monarchy.[27]

However, rural unrest did not have unequivocal political and social effects. It could also serve the cause of the far Left, and this strengthened the social fear on the part of the party of Order which thought it controlled the whole countryside.

d Peasants: Saviours or Rebels?

In fact, the relative success of the democrat-socialists in the countryside in the legislative elections in May 1849 (winning about a third of the vote and 220 deputies) confirmed that the vote for Louis Napoleon Bonaparte on 10 December 1848, a vote challenging the old or current authorities, was not only a symbolic act or a symptom of the political immaturity of

27. Cf.the map in Tudesq (217), vol. 2, p. 1216; Vigier (219), vol. 2, pp. 171 ff.; Mayaud, J.-L. (194).

rural masses throwing themselves upon a saviour. The two votes in the space of six months revealed the emergence of a section of the peasantry as an autonomous social force which the great notables and, later, the republican middle classes had to take into account. This was a breach in the the notables' traditional power of domination, which was dependent on the consent and deference of the rural proletariat. Through the propaganda of the artisanal bodies and the liberal professions militating within the progressive republican party, the 'red' peasantry saw universal suffrage as the only means of unified struggle by a class divided in space and by different circumstances.

This red countryside partly resumed the peasant struggles of the French revolution, but also introduced new elements through their access to unprecedented methods of political organisation and expression (the *chambrées* in Provence, the collective reading of newspapers and booklets, secret societies) which peasants had never had in the past. These countrymen thus linked their claims with those of the Parisian workers in 1848, although their claims were basically very different; the Parisian workers were temporarily defeated, but they still voted for the progressive republic.

The emergence of this new political and social force thus gave birth to a new social fear within the ruling class. That land-owning peasants or artisans could support the 'reds', that is to say, in the eyes of conservative propaganda, the 'supporters of the equal distribution of wealth', upset the political strategy formulated to combat the most turbulent workers. The great notables still possessed the political and social majority through being able to count on the traditional rural classes, but their territorial hold had been broken and the democratic contagion of countryside by town, thought halted after the crushing of the workers' revolt in June, seemed to be spreading anew. The resumption of parliamentary power by the old ruling class was therefore not enough. It must now implement a systematic counter-revolution, since the 'enemy' seemed to grow stronger – to the very point where it no longer voted for the *capacitaire* bourgeoisie nor for Left-wing notables, but for leaders who were closer to it socially, or even drawn from its own ranks.

For two years (and no longer for a few days as in June), the party of law and order therefore brought a new class struggle into play in order to avert this threat. If fear is sometimes a poor adviser, the history of the Legislative Assembly does on the other hand, testify to the remarkable increase in class consciousness on the part of old notables, who used a whole arsenal of tools of domination to force the masses back into line. Not only was every manifestation of mass political autonomy repressed (by legal proceedings against the press and the persecution of all common action), but, most of all, the conservative majority wanted to shackle future generations with the help of the Church (Falloux law) and purge the electorate of undesirables, i.e. migrant workers and peasants, who did not give proof of three years of residence (the law of 31 May 1850). These were assumed to be vectors of revolutionary contagion.

The entry of a third individual actor, the *Prince-Président*, prevents a purely sociological interpretation of this confrontation. Without the coup d'état, it would probably have been resolved by the emergency elections with two clearly-defined camps, for which Frenchmen have had a fondness since the 1870s. However, the coup d'état cannot be summed up as the tactical action of one man and his supporters. Everyone who objected to those two camps yearned for an illegal solution of the imminent crisis, and their rapid rallying to the new power conveyed this; they included rural circles (this is a conveniently amorphous term for the collection of motley camp-followers), shocked by the ruling class's ostracism of the working classes and impervious to the far Left's millenarianism, the group of workers who did not identify with the republican far Left nor, *a fortiori*, with the old notables, and small, medium or large employers who longed for the rapid re-establishment of order, the guarantee of a business revival. In short, they constituted a negative majority for whom Bonapartism provided a programme which was simultaneously innovative and conservative, based on prosperity, a cure for sterile conflicts.

These composite social majorities and ecumenical policies, which reconciled the irreconcilable and were born of two political traditions, recur in French social history. Their periodic reappearance is proof that what was involved was a reaction to the phases of crisis and bitter conflicts through which the French regularly pass. The revolt against the coup d'état is a more complex matter to interpret.

The resistance to the coup d'état came in fact at the point where two movements converged: there was a social protest movement against the reactionary policy of the notables, and a purely political movement defending a republic which was beginning to take root amongst the people. This duality accounts for the lesser enthusiasm of town workers, who were more easily controlled and whose resentment, bred of the June events, diminished their enthusiasm for taking up arms again for a Republic which had partially betrayed them.

On the other hand, there was a new factor which, in retrospect, explains the *coup de force* and which at the time facilitated the rallying of the notables. This was the extent of the resistance in the provinces and particularly in the rural zones of the Midi (Lot-et-Garonne, Gers, Ariège, Hérault, Gard, Drôme, Basses-Alpes, Var) and the Centre (Nièvre, Allier, Yonne). For the first time, a movement with a strong rural and artisanal component (44 and 48 per cent respectively) was not solely based on an ordinary economic protest but was ingrained and had a general political meaning. It underlined the extent of unrest in country areas, particularly those linked to the market more than those in backward regions. It also highlighted the development of political awareness with the emergence of a genuine democratic policy, the militants of which were socially close to their followers and made local unanimity, hitherto limited to town workers, react to their advantage.[28]

There was probably a discrepancy between the extent of the democrat-socialists' regional success in 1849 and the number of departments which did in fact act on behalf of the democratic Republic and against the coup d'état. In order to spread, the 'red Vendée' of 1851, like the white Vendée of 1793, needed the advantage of distance from the capital (i.e. of a longer time before the authorities, initially caught unawares, could react). It also required the advantages of an adequate number of members of secret societies in its ranks, and easy interaction between towns, villages and the countryside. From this point of view, the structure of dispersed dwellings and the low quality of communications in the mountains of the Limousin, democrat-socialist but not insurgent, stood in contrast with the Provence countryside, sprinkled with village-towns and possessed of strong political sociability.[29]

Beyond these local differences, what was important was that in the collective memory the Republic was no longer a simple legal notion but a political and social programme for a new society freed from unilateral domination by a hereditary ruling class. These years of crisis, which seemed to end with a regression, were actually made up of a series of fundamental events with long-lasting effects for the future coalition of the social groups attached to this new social ideal.[30] However, an ordinary republican *a posteriori* interpretation would not be enough. The France which submitted to the coup d'état was not only the France of the West, afraid of the notables. It also partially coincided with the economically advanced France of the north-east and the Paris Basin, which petitioned massively in spring 1851 in favour of constitutional revision and therefore of the *Prince-Président*. In its way, it wanted a change from the decrepit order of notables incapable of stemming the rise of conflicts.[31]

28. Agulhon, M. (160); Margadant, T.W. (192), especially pp. 34, 87, 142, 183. As Agulhon notes, the statistics cited have only a relative value, as the repression was selective vis-à-vis the participants; hence the peasants are under-represented in respect of probable reality (M. Agulhon (162), pp. 194-5).

29. Corbin (170), vol. 2, pp. 838-9.

30. Huard, R. (184), p. 104; this was particularly true of the group of supervised interned persons who remained in France.

31. Ménager, B. (195), p. 108. Likewise, according to Corbin, the relatively rapid and lasting rallying to Bonapartism by the red Limousin is explained by the material benefits the new imperial order brought.

e Conclusion

Despite Marx's famous phrase in *Le 18 Brumaire de Louis Bonaparte*, the central crisis of the century cannot be reduced to a comic repetition of the events of the Great Revolution. Through the fears and the hopes that they left behind them (a sort of goalless draw in the class struggle), those four years of intense conflict created over the next thirty years lasting social and political reactions in both the dominated and dominating classes. In order to stay in power, every sector of the ruling class now knew that, in the new democratic system which could not be reversed, it had to possess a rural basis and control of the towns. Consequently it had to join with the other sectors with which it was in conflict, so as not to leave a gap through which popular demands might surge as they did in 1848. The fact that Bonapartism temporarily satisfied these three demands constituted its success. It did not therefore invent a new ruling class but renewed the initial Napoleonic compromise. It involved putting the Revolution into parentheses through a negative consensus of all those who feared the unleashing of the class struggle and wanted a strong State, a new social force which served as cement and apparent arbiter among contradictory interests.

3

Imperial Stabilisation and Society in Motion

After the serious social and political crisis of the mid-century, the Second Empire period presents the contradictory picture which the title of this chapter attempts to convey. The two political faces of Bonapartism, which witnesses emphasise, have long been well known. It is certainly necessary to avoid attributing too much influence over social evolution to the political cadre; but surely an authoritarian regime, more than any other, does claim to have an effect on the inner life of a country? Nevertheless, there is no escaping the conclusion that the social period lasting almost two decades (from December 1851 to May 1871, the Commune being the logical consequence of imperial policy) was a tapestry of contradictions. On the one hand there was the contradiction between a desire for modernisation and an opening up to the outside world imposed from above; on the other, there was the risk that by so doing the regime might undermine its own political bases, i.e., the committed notables and the peasants yearning for order and protection. There was also the contradiction between a policy which claimed to be social, and growing labour hostility which resulted in social agitation at the end of the reign and then the most serious French civil war. Lastly, there was the contradiction between a policy of State greatness and the inability to equip France with a functioning army, an appropriate administration, a re-modelled education system and adequate elites.

The case made for or against the Second Republic by its adversaries or its supporters could be revived in respect of the regime which was supposed to remedy the failings of its predecessor. To do so, however, would be to adopt the same illusion of a total domination of politics to which every government seeking legitimacy succumbs. The transition from authoritarian power to a presidential quasi-republic would probably have come to an end without the war of 1870. Furthermore, if the regression to authoritarianism in the unstable decade of the 1870s gave way to the permanent advent of the Republic and democracy, this was also paradoxically the result of social movements deliberately or involuntarily provoked by the Bonapartist State.

A The Bonapartist State, a Stabilising or Destabilising Force?

a The Political Establishment

The 1852 constitution broke with previous regimes by creating deep divisions within the political establishment. On one hand, ministers, senators and councillors of State (in so far as the latter fulfilled a political function) were the emperor's men. On the other, the deputies of the legislative body were, in theory, the product of universal suffrage.

Official candidature probably robbed popular selection of a large part of its meaning. Universal suffrage was ostensibly re-established on the morrow of the coup d'état in order to mark its difference from the policy of social segregation of the electors, resulting from the law of 31 May 1850 which was voted in by the party of law and order. In practice, the characteristics of the two groups were less divergent than might have been supposed, given the narrowness of the social groups from which this type of elite could be recruited. The process of democratising the political elites, begun in 1848, was interrupted and even reversed. The unequal financial position of the candidates (one set had the means of the State apparatus at its disposal, while the other only its own personal resources) discouraged all opposition from the start or forced opposition candidates to restrict themselves to electoral districts where local conditions limited the costs of propaganda; which meant in fact the large towns which had remained loyal to the Republic.

The first group participated in the exercise of power but had scarcely any autonomy by way of the constitution and in practice; there was no ministerial responsibility, no cabinet solidarity and no collective decisions. On the other hand, it enjoyed all the advantages of a classic monarchy, such as fat bribes, the practice of nepotism for close relations, length of office and absence of career hazards (senators were appointed for life, ministers held office for a long time and could depart with honour). Members of the ruling classes, through family heritage, were predominant amongst government personnel, but two groups were better represented than in the past. First and foremost there were the big businessmen, traditionally on the outside under the *monarchie censitaire*, and second there were a few new men, who broke with the conformism of the legal *capacités* of yore.

The first group included Achille Fould, a banker from a Jewish family converted to Protestantism, minister of State and later minister of Finance; Théodore Ducos, former Bordeaux deputy and minister of the Navy, born into a great ship-owning family and nephew of the consul Roger Ducos; and Armand Béhic, a businessman connected with the Rothschild-Talabot group, minister of economic affairs and then, from 1863-1867, holder of the joint portfolio of agriculture, trade and public works. Adolphe Vuitry, son of a notable under the July monarchy, councillor of State and then minister presiding over the Council of State, was also close to big business since his son-in-law was no other than the president of Crédit Lyonnais, Henri Germain; he himself would subsequently be president of PLM. Note too that the Pereires, close to Morny, the president of the *corps législatif*, and Eugène Schneider, manager of Le Creusot, had seats on the *corps législatif*; the latter was even its president at the end of the Empire. This close relationship between political power and the new economic power of big business explains how contemporaries had the impression that the two spheres were even more closely intermingled than before. The issues in the conflict had, as it were, moved from politics to civil society, or in other words, to arbitration between interest groups.[1]

The new men were no more numerous than under previous regimes, but they could allow themselves to emphasise their difference more than before because of the regime's democratic pretensions. For the emperor, they stood surety to his opening of the doors to the new strata and to emerging social questions. They therefore enjoyed a wider margin for manoeuvre than did other groups. The regime's two important ministers of public education are examples of this. Fortoul was an erstwhile Saint-Simonian, a member of the teaching profession, formerly belittled for his authoritarianism in the movement to regain control of the teaching personnel after the coup d'état. His innovative role has recently been revalued in the light of his concern to introduce science teaching at a secondary level. The prime example, however, is Victor Duruy, son of a Gobelins tapestry worker, teacher and inspector general, who had anti-clerical inclinations. He became a minister by special favour of the emperor for his help in writing Louis Napoleon's book on Julius Caesar. He launched the first important education reforms before the republicans, including the extension of free primary education, the opening of secondary education to girls, and the foundation of the *École pratique des hautes études*.

Until the last years of the reign, the parliamentary establishment was virtually remote from power. It received only a small allowance (which reinforced the system's oligarchical character), sat infrequently and had a secondary role as intermediary between the population and the centre, where it competed with the top administration. From a social and professional point of view however, the two groups had many common points which differentiated them from the political establishment of the Second Republic. The composition of the deputies showed many of the

1. On this point, see the very detailed book on the Foulds by F. Barbier (225).

characteristics of the personnel of the July monarchy: the same over-representation of officials (over a third of the legislative corps in 1852), a growing proportion of landowners living on their income from property (almost 20 per cent), the rich (23 per cent of deputies whose income is known were in receipt of more than 30,000 francs a year), and businessmen (a quarter, against 16.9 per cent under Louis-Philippe's regime). On the other hand, members of the liberal professions and intellectuals, as well as the lower ranks of the bourgeoisie who had made a break-through in 1848-1849, found their access to the political elite heavily curtailed.[2]

b The High Administration and the Upper Ranks of the Army

The administrative elites of the Second Empire were recruited from as narrow a social milieu as the political establishment. Bonapartist-inspired regimes placed great importance on this type of elite whose status was enhanced in relation to that of the political establishment. This enhancement can be seen from a variety of external indications, such as the increase in remuneration, particularly to the Council of State or to prefects, the building or improvement of the buildings where they worked, the gaudy costumes they wore and the decorations or titles granted them by the authorities. Prefects' salaries, for example, ranged from 20,000 to 40,000 francs whereas the earlier wage scale was from 10,000 to 30,000 francs. Councillors of State received 25,000 a year, while heads of ministries received from 20,000 to 30,000 but with lower entertainment allowances. The best-placed generals and marshals piled up income and bribes; for example, the holders of the six great commands created in 1859 received 260,000 francs. For high ranking officers, the colonial wars and their benefits, tacitly accepted to a greater or lesser degree, the decorations awarded and the gifts from the emperor on the occasion of specific conflicts all revived the practices of the First Empire.[3]

Here the nephew was following hard on the uncle's heels, but he did not succeed in creating an appropriate or entirely reliable administrative body. Like Napoleon I, Napoleon III in fact tried to reconcile the various elements of the ruling class by putting them into State service. The purge had already been largely carried out at the end of the Second Republic in order to exclude undesirables who had entered the high administration under cover of the February revolution. The purge which followed the coup d'état had been relatively limited: eight prefects were dismissed

---

2. From T. Zeldin (284), pp. 62–4, H. Best (166), pp. 58-9, and L. Girard, W. Serman and R. Gossez (177).

3. S.W. Serman (276), vol. 2, pp. 875–9.

and six were recalled, while 132 irremovable magistrates (out of several thousand) had been retired under a decree in March 1852. Consequently, men directly connected with the emperor or with those close to him were always in a minority within the high administration.[4]

Heir to the Napoleonic administration, the Second Empire increased the closed nature of the administrative elites still further. As a regime founded on commercial policies, it tended to reinforce the senior technical officials who were in charge of changes in the economy, finances and means of communication. This was a body recruited from its own ranks by competition or internal patronage, where veritable dynasties had lasted throughout regimes since 1830. The autonomy of the mining or the roads and bridges corps, the finance inspectors, receiver-generals and the audit office was strengthened. In these circumstances, the particularly high occurrence of administrative heredity in these bodies is not surprising: 55.5 per cent of finance inspectors, and 64 per cent of inspectors of roads and bridges in 1860 were sons of high officials. Likewise, 57 per cent of heads of ministries and 64 per cent of generals of divisions in 1870 were sons of officials, and in this case, of military men in particular.[5] Even the members of the most political bodies – prefects and councillors of State – experienced this administrative auto-recruitment, although to a lesser degree: 48.1 and 44.5 per cent of prefects and councillors of State respectively were born into an administrative milieu during the period 1852-1870. Of 220 prefects, 21 were sons of prefects, and 30 sons or sons-in-law of generals.

The nobility of the Empire was also linked to the administrative power. However, the majority of administrators belonged to the various groups of the bourgeoisie, either the genuine bourgeoisie of trade or property (between a fifth and a quarter of the total), or the bourgeoisie of the professional, particularly legal, classes. High officials of petty bourgeois origin, however, were the exception (five per cent or less of the total), although some individuals had glorious careers thanks to a variety of patronage or complicated curricula vitae. J.-J. Weiss is one example of this process. He was the son of a military musician, an orphan educated in a special military school and then a scholarship boy, a pupil at the *École normale supérieure*, a teacher and then an opposition journalist. He finally rallied to the Empire and was appointed director of Fine Arts in 1870.[6]

In fact, whereas the First Empire had partially profited from the

4. J.-P. Royer, R. Martinage and P. Lecoq (274); V. Wright, 'Les épurations administratives de 1848 à 1885', in P. Gerbod (247), p. 73.

5. From C. Charle (359), pp. 66-7, figures obtained from personal research or the books by V. Wright and S.W. Serman respectively; on the receiver-generals and finance inspectors, see also P.-F. Pinaud (104) and E. Chadeau (358).

6. V. Wright (247), p. 45.

revolutionary melting-pot to open its doors to some new men, the new requirement of a high educational level added another barrier to the patronage and recommendations indispensable to an administration dominated by notables' sons. This explains why another common characteristic of the Second Empire administrative elite was their Parisian origins, a factor favourable to admission to the great schools and attendance at the *École de droit* or the *École polytechnique*, the privileged means of access to the high administration, even to provincial professional bodies.[7] This common geographic origin facilitated the functioning of a centralised regime, wedded to national unity. Conversely – and the final collapse of the regime is partly explained by this – it resulted in a growing gulf between these elites and the real country, and in their own inability to step outside certain thought patterns, whereas provincial France and the nascent middle classes suffered State tutelage less gladly.

This homogenous recruitment did not exclude the existence of internal ideological cleavages among higher civil servants, with groups including sons of Orleanist personnel (even with Legitimist sympathies), pure Bonapartists and heirs of the great families of the regime, who were particularly numerous in the lower grades of public bodies as the years went by. Recent studies have challenged the received idea of the omnipotence of the high administration under a regime where the political figures played a minor role in its early phase. The power that most of these high officials possessed was probably linked to length of office: twenty-four prefects kept their positions for more than ten years, and these included the most coveted and most important prefectures. The same incumbent held the prefecture of Seine-Inférieure for the whole length of the reign, while Haussmann occupied the Paris city hall from 1853 to 1870. Vaisse was prefect of the Rhône from 1853 to 1863. Conversely, the heavy turn-over of occupants in small prefectures in poor departments scarcely made it possible to awaken these departments from their torpor.

For all that, prefects in the provinces had to take account of the notables, in spite of the extent of their administrative powers. Their origins and connections, as well as the need to possess rallying points in public opinion in order to support official candidatures, implied this mutual understanding. In addition, as has been seen, as the parliamentary establishment gained power under the liberal Empire the electorate

7. 22.2 per cent of prefects (1852-1870), 26.8 per cent of State councillors (same period), 33.6 per cent of heads of ministries (same period), 38 per cent of finance inspectors in 1860, 23.2 per cent of members of the supreme court of appeal (same date) and 16 per cent of inspectors of roads and bridges (same date) were born in Paris or in the Seine (from B. Le Clère et V. Wright (254), p. 176, V. Wright (282), p. 56, and (48), p. 72, and C. Charle (359), p. 59).

realised that the administration was no longer the only medium for obtaining government favours. The second element limiting the high officials' influence lay in internal rivalry, at both a departmental and a national level. The ministers and the emperor played on this because some regions of France were hard to control from Paris, despite the advance in rapid communications provided by the railway and the electric telegraph, and it would have been very hazardous to leave all power to an 'emperor with short legs', which was what the prefect should theoretically have been. The attorney-generals who had several departments under their authority, like generals of divisions, wrote reports about the prefects and the state of their areas, which supplied the ministers with contradictory pieces of evidence.[8]

c The Emergence of a Body of Officials

Possession of a prestigious higher administration was not a sufficient basis for a lasting dictatorship. The Second Empire also increased the State's strength considerably at every level. The army, indispensable to the maintenance of order and a crucial trump card at the time of the seizure of power, saw its manpower increased (to between 400,000 and 450,000 men), particularly the numbers of officers, non-commissioned officers, re-enlisted men and substitutes, who formed a quasi-professional army. To prevent a clash with the notables' privileges and to enable the comfortably-off peasantry, loyal supporters of the emperor, to avoid military service, the unfair and increasingly old-fashioned system of drawing lots and substitution was continued. Even more, through the 1855 law on exemption, the authorities themselves organised long service, reserved for the poorest elements in the masses, who were thereby elevated paradoxically to the rank of permanent ramparts of a bourgeois order which excluded them from normal life.[9]

On the other hand, the officer class was expanded and rejuvenated because the successive conflicts necessitated the creation of new posts for officers and non-commissioned officers, open either to candidates from the military schools or, particularly, to soldiers who had risen from the ranks. The cult of the emperor had owed its survival in the collective imagination to the officers retired on half-pay dispersed throughout the country after 1815. The Second Empire also offered opportunity and promotion to a youth which was not qualified enough to succeed in the elite networks and who preferred State service or the dream of glory

8. B. Le Clère and V. Wright (254), pp. 86–7.
9. 354,000 men on 1 January 1852 but 526,000 on 1 January 1856 (because of the Crimean War) and 400,000 in 1870 (B. Schnapper (110), pp. 293 and 271, and 218 ff.).

overseas (in Algeria or foreign wars) to devoting itself exclusively to business. Lacking a real party of their own, Napoleon III and his supporters tried in this way to enlarge the political clientele formed of elements born into the middle-classes or the petty bourgeoisie. Unfortunately for them, the technical choice that this military policy involved (the creation of a quasi-professional army), however tenable for limited conflicts and against archaic armies, proved disastrous when called on to face a power such as Prussia, motivated by a strong national will and equipped with a modern military organisation.[10]

The Second Empire made more lasting innovations in the sphere of civil public office, where the heritage of the constitutional monarchy did not wield so much influence. The law of 9 June 1853 gave officials a unified retirement system, the first base of a statute which minor and middle-ranking officials had demanded under the Second Republic. Economic prosperity, by raising the product of taxes and facilitating loans, made it possible to increase the establishment which rose from 122,000 to 265,000 people. The Saint-Simonism which inspired part of the ruling groups thus brought about a break with the liberal policy of retrenchment of earlier regimes.

Concern for modernisation was also a stimulus – like political authoritarianism – to the extension of State influence over certain sectors. The Second Empire set up the electric telegraph and opened it to the public but kept very strict control over telegrams. Military discipline prevailed in this new technical administration. It was strictly hierarchical, with the country postman who carried the telegrams at the very bottom, and the managing director, whose salary was twenty-five times higher, at the very top. Almost irremovable under the Empire, the Vicomte de Vougy, an erstwhile officer and former prefect of the Nièvre, required total availability from his agents 'because their time belonged entirely to the State'.[11]

The forces of repression, particularly urban repression, were also expanded in order to cope with the expansion of the towns. The police were increased from 5,000 to 12,150 men. In the countryside in 1866, three-quarters of the communes employed a country policeman – 67,000 in all, more than the number of teachers (65,000). The administration remained mainly traditional; patronage and recommendations for entry, favouritism for promotions, the requirement of political loyalty, even pressure on behalf of governmental candidates all remained. The lower the minor official was in the hierarchy, the less did statutory guarantees protect him from arbitrary measures such as transfer rather than dismissal

10. S.W. Serman (276), vol. 3, pp. 1629 ff.
11. See C. Bertho (227), pp. 138–56, circular cited p. 137.

and absence of promotion.

However, two factors limited open conflict between the top and bottom of the hierarchy. In the central administration, the heads of departments tolerated poor results and below-normal hours of work (four to five real hours instead of seven to eight theoretical hours), well aware of the slowness of promotion and the lower level of salaries compared with those offered by better paid jobs in the Parisian commercial and banking sectors at the height of expansion. In the provinces, State employees played on the rivalries between the notables who defended their protégés and the more ephemeral authority of the higher officials of different bodies who were less permanent. Despite the prefects' routine complaints about their subordinates' lack of loyalty it is significant that in the crisis of 1870-1871, the State apparatus continued to serve the various powers which followed one another in office in a very short period of time (except for the Commune, which could only rally a minority).[12]

d The Clergy, Ally or Opponent?

Under the Second Republic, social fear had driven the notables of the party of law and order to strengthen the power of the Church over society, particularly through the Falloux law. The Second Empire, which adopted part of this programme, made a similar alliance with the clergy. The clergy represented a considerable force of numbers. In 1872, records show 52,148 members of the lay clergy, 13,102 members of male religious communities and 84,300 nuns. Members of the regular clergy controlled a large part of primary education, particularly that of girls, and also secondary education, as the Falloux law favoured the proliferation of religious colleges.

This period also saw the establishment of the structure which later, at the end of the century, gave birth to the two 'youths', a source of renewed political conflict between clericals and anti-clericals. In less religious regions, secondary religious foundations were chosen by a better established or more traditional bourgeoisie which sought for its sons a moral and more familiar framework. In very Catholic regions on the other hand, the Catholic colleges and small seminaries were open also to the petty and middle-rank bourgeoisie, and even to comfortably-off elements of the peasantry, who were looking for a cheaper and more decentralised network for social promotion than that of the *lycées* situated in county towns. Nuns filled the void in primary education for girls left by the inadequacy of public education. There were in fact half as many secular female teachers as male in 1872, and only 17 departments possessed a

12. G. Thuillier (116), pp. 326–7, 301.

teachers' training college for women in 1876.

The clergy also played a major role in the provision of welfare. Free rural medicine for the poor was established under the Second Empire, provided by nuns who illegally sold or distributed medicine and health advice, drew up lists of the poor, and in return encouraged the expansion of congreganist schools in the most deprived strata of society.[13] They won the confidence of the peasant women, whom they had often taught to read, more easily than the doctors or pharmacists who lived too far away and charged much more dearly for services which were not always effective. In hospitals and welfare institutions also, nursing nuns often attacked the medical authority, establishing a specific moral order in respect of certain categories of hospitalised patients (those suffering from venereal disease, the insane, unmarried mothers and prostitutes), urging them to acknowledge that pain and disease were punishment for sin and must be suffered rather than combated or alleviated. In a poor rural society, the administration and medical profession could not dispense with this network of medical staff, particularly when there was a need to fight epidemics or spread vaccination.

Assisted by these female auxiliaries, the priests also reached their apogee during this period. In the 1870s the ratio of priests to inhabitants reached 15 per 10,000 as compared with 10 per 10,000 when the Concordat was signed. The Public Worship budget increased substantially by almost 10 million francs for the Catholic religion alone between 1852 and 1866. With the help of the State, county councils, municipal councils, Catholic notables and parish councils multiplied the restoration and reconstruction of churches or presbyteries in most regions, as well as charitable foundations and pilgrimages. In return the expansion of the clerical educational network facilitated a rise in the numbers of those opting for religious careers, guaranteeing that the countryside would be well served. On the other hand, the maintenance of the old framework of parishes proved unsuited to the Christianisation of the migrants in the fast expanding towns.[14]

In this hierarchical society, where the town-country gulf remained deep and where the school network was incomplete, priesthood still seemed a reliable route to social promotion, and one which did not involve a sharp break with the native rural environment. At that time, positions as teachers or minor officials did not offer the same advantages, though by the end

13. J. Léonard (94), especially pp. 890-1. On the peasants' cultural lack of understanding of the principles of health and 'modern' practices, see the evidence in E. Guillaumin (7), pp. 95–6, concerning the share-croppers of the Bourbonnais faced with their master, a former pharmacist.

14. See P. Pierrard (105), pp. 66–7; P. Boutry (229), pp. 119 and 187; and M. Launay (91).

of the century their roles would be equivalent. In addition, in rural regions where the reproduction rate had remained high (a consequence both of the persistent grip of the Church and reduced contact with the towns and their 'deadly secrets'), an ecclesiastical career constituted a convenient means of controlling inheritances for peasant or artisan families, otherwise threatened with coming down in the world because of the fragmentation of their land or the contraction of outlets in the face of competition from the towns and nascent industry. For example, in the Sarthe, a strongly clerical department in the West, the majority of priests came from these two groups (30 per cent and 20 per cent respectively), with their numbers augmented by the small tradesman class (about 10 per cent).

The ecclesiastical hierarchy encouraged this recruitment from within the rural and artisanal petty bourgeoisie in the absence of sufficient candidates from the bourgeoisie or nobility. The most deprived countrymen from poor and uneducated families, who could not pay the seminary fees or dispense with their sons' labour or the money they earned, were in fact barred from such a career. According to the Catholic hierarchy, even if they overcame these obstacles, they would not command sufficient respect from their flocks. As for the sons of comfortably-off families, they had a repugnance for the country life which a clerical career involved, and had other outlets if they should wish to serve God including joining prestigious communities, taking up religious teaching posts, or enlistment in pontifical Zouaves. The inequality of the financial rewards and secondary privileges among the various categories of priesthood also contributed to the maintenance of recruitment from the masses; the majority of ordinary priests in charge or assistant priests (ten times more numerous than first and second class curate-deans), received a salary below the income of many farmers (800 francs or even less).[15]

Regarding the clergy as a specific category of officials (which it legally was by virtue of the Concordat), the regime followed much the same policy towards them as towards secular officials. It granted favours and considerations to dignitaries (cardinals were legal members of the Senate, for example, and bishops' salaries were raised), and left the bishops, the

15. P. Foucault (244), pp. 149-70, especially pp. 150 and 156. The sociological analysis summarised here was carried out by the bishop of Mans, Mgr. Bouvier himself, in 1846. This example is confirmed by data supplied by M. Launay for the diocese of Nantes (253), vol. 1, p. 276; by P. Boutry for the diocese of Belley (229), p. 191; by G. Cholvy (235), p. 264 (80 per cent of priests were sons of wage-earning agriculturists, small landowners, artisans or tradesmen); and by N.-J. Chaline (233), p. 385–405. Senior parish priests received 1,500 francs plus extras, which were very considerable in large urban parishes; curates only had a fixed salary of 300 to 400 francs plus a proportion of extras (P.Pierrard (105), pp. 37–49).

'purple prefects', much room for manoeuvre in managing their subordinates and proclaiming an official moral order reflected in the censorship or lawsuits concerning certain famous literary works (for example, *Les Fleurs du Mal* and *Madame Bovary*). However, the advance of ultramontanism and the Italian policy of Napoleon III, both unfavourable to the Pope's interests, drove part of the Catholic party into the opposition.

The clergy as a group mirrored these different developments. The pastoral letters of certain bishops and the agitation by the minor clergy under the influence of the ultramontane press marked a break between the regime and the Church. The authorities reacted with a return to Gallicanism and attacked the most extreme clerical elements. Despite everything, however, the social interests common to the two parties restricted the scale of the conflict. There was no question of losing control of the rural bases of the regime at a time when the hostility of the towns was increasing, republican opposition growing and anti-clericalism re-emerging amongst the masses.

B The End of the Agrarian Ancien Regime

a The 'Extinction of Pauperism' in the Countryside

The expression 'the golden age of the peasantry' is often used to characterise the situation in the rural sector under the Second Empire. Official optimism and the rural masses' support for the regime, demonstrated both in legislative elections and plebiscites, were justified by comparison with the first half of the nineteenth century and particularly with the crisis at the end of the 1840s. The economic and demographic indices turned upwards at the beginning of the 1850s and, if crises in specific sectors or regions occurred, they were either partial or were counter-balanced by favourable developments later.

France retained its exceptional character, with its predominant agricultural sector, despite the industrialisation then in progress. Peasants still constituted 49.8 per cent of the active population in 1866. Moreover, a slight fall in relative weight was accompanied by an increase in the absolute figures: there were 7,305,000 active peasants in 1856 and 7,535,000 in 1866. However, the continued existence of this high proportion of peasantry in the structure of the active population was no longer synonymous with overpopulation or pauperism as under the July monarchy because it concealed the shedding of the most marginal elements in peasant society, such as temporary day labourers, beggars, domestic servants and small itinerant artisans. An average of 71,000 departures annually from the countryside was recorded between 1851 and

1881.[16] Sixty-five departments were affected by this exodus compared with forty-six before 1851. The rural workers found new outlets in the great workyards of the Second Empire such as railway building, land clearance, opening of local roads, large-scale urban works and bringing new mines, quarries or factories into operation. This was all manual labour which did not require qualifications, while at the same time a greater number of small jobs appeared in the public sphere including enlistment in the army or the country police force.

This exodus improved the situation of those agricultural wage-earners who stayed in the fields and who still numbered nearly 3 million in 1862. They encountered less seasonal or cyclical unemployment, and rates of pay increased as the landowners had to be more generous to keep a workforce which could find more lucrative outlets elsewhere. In the Loir-et-Cher, for example, wage rates rose to 165 in 1866 from a base of 100 in 1852. This rise can be noted almost everywhere; the income of a couple of day labourers in the Calvados increased from an index figure of 148 in 1852 (1811=100) to 184 in 1862; in the southwest, the increase was 66 per cent and in the Hérault from 60 to 90 per cent, between 1845 and 1872, much greater than the cost of living.[17]

Though they were still limited, these departures have been interpreted as facilitating access to property and explaining the increase which *Enquêtes agricoles* recorded in the number of farming landowners (340,000 more farming landowners between 1862 and 1882) and assessments on land. Very small holdings of from one to five hectares increased slightly by 2.7 per cent between those two dates, while the workforce on holdings of between five and ten hectares was a quarter higher.

It is very hard to find a coherent general explanation for these movements, given the diversity of the agrarian structures and farming systems in force in France. Alongside access to property by the best paid wage-earners, this extension of small landownership could equally have come from the division between heirs on succession, from the resumption of direct farming by *rentier*-landowners of domains formerly leased or farmed by share-cropping in order to take advantage of the favourable agricultural situation, or from the purchase of farms by tenant farmers or vine growers who had made enough money. There is one last standard case: the migrant who settled back on his native soil after having saved enough money while he was a wage-earner in the town to buy or lease

---

16. M. Agulhon et al.(31), p. 223.
17. G. Dupeux (241), p.264; G. Désert (63), p. 942; A. Armengaud (124), p. 275; G. Cholvy (292), p. 870.

sufficient land off which to live.[18] Nevertheless, this golden age was only relative.

In fact, despite this shedding of rural pauperism, demand for land still exceeded supply as the rise in the price of agricultural land shows. Even in a poor department such as the Haute-Loire, the price of rural dwellings rose by nearly 50 per cent in thirty years (1851–1881), or faster than rural income (over 40 per cent).[19] This limited access to larger property to the category of peasants who were already equipped with a minimum of capital.

Agricultural prosperity also brought a rise in rents. Ronald Hubscher has analysed these phenomena of mobility in the Pas-de-Calais during the period of prosperity by rural category. Overall, 62 per cent of the individuals observed were static between 1851 and 1872, and 29 per cent experienced a rise in status, whereas 9 per cent came down in the world. There was no improvement in the social position of 63 per cent of the day labourers (above the average) while 37 per cent were better off (also above the average). Amongst *ménagers*, or small tenant farmers, 46 per cent entered the higher stratum of farmers; on the other hand, 29 per cent did not change status and a quarter fell back. The position of farmers remained stable at 80 per cent, with 7 to 9 per cent reverting to *ménagers* or moving into the ranks of non-farming landowners. A study of two generations (father and son) confirms this stability in the hierarchy of rural society, accompanied by a general incline upwards.[20]

Although these social data tend to confirm contemporaries' impressions, the extent of the disparities which still existed among the French regions must not be forgotten. Here too the process of modernisation and opening up to the market corresponded with the initial differences, since advanced agricultural regions were the first to be affected; they were the first to be connected to the railway or to specialise in marketable crops. Even on the scale of a limited region such as the Beaujolais, uneven prosperity is perceptible between the vine-growing sector, which received the most benefits thanks to the new urban outlets for wine, and the more distant mountains or plateaux, which remained loyal to more traditional and unprofitable mixed farming. Comparison between the two Frances of the early nineteeenth century is complicated by certain specialisations directed towards the most lucrative agricultural products such as meat and wine. It was in this way that islands of rural wealth came into being in the midst of a countryside clinging to traditional mixed farming to support populations, which were still excessive through

18. A. Corbin (170), vol. 1, pp. 214–23.
19. J. Merley (153), pp. 593 and 566.
20. R. Hubscher (84), pp. 793–803 and 816–20.

lack of emigration or an above-average birth rate. In the Gard, for example, the sericulture region was hit by a crisis linked with silkworm disease while the vine-growing areas were at the height of their prosperity. Neighbouring Hérault was orientated towards the same monoculture and could claim the highest income per person active in agriculture in France. Yet not far away, the Lozère, Aveyron and Tarn lived under a prolonged agrarian ancien regime remote from progress.[21]

The map of departmental incomes in 1864 clearly delineates the contours of advanced rural France (which was often also urbanised France) and of the France which still belonged to the agrarian ancien regime. The white patches are the Breton departments, the North (the Limousin) and the south-east of the Massif Central, the Alpes, the Pyrénées and the Vosges. In these regions it was difficult to establish complex crop rotations because of the poverty of the soil, lack of manure and the need to maintain the wastelands or commons indispensable for the survival of the poorest peasants. The comfortably-off departments were on the contrary those where the discoveries of the agricultural revolution were widely practised by large landowners, dynamic tenant farmers, or farming landowners who possessed enough working capital to abandon standard practices.

In fact, the new agriculture involved increasingly large capital sums. For example, sugar beet cultivation, already established in the North, spread after 1850 in the Soissonnais. Comfortably-off tenant farmers adopted it, abandoning fallow or secondary cereals. With the by-products (pulp), they could raise beef cattle in permanent stabling in place of the less remunerative sheep. But the pre-requisites of this complex and more intensive system of farming were new buildings, deep ploughing (therefore requiring improved ploughs and strong draught animals) and secondary material to prepare the soil. In addition, farms had to have enough funds to buy seed and cattle and cover the waiting period until the beetroot was sold to industrial sugar refiners and the oxen to cattle merchants.[22]

Obviously all these conditions were absent from the poor regions which suffered, as they had in the first half of the century, from lack of credit. This was always obtained by usurious means or mortgage credit from notaries, or even from big landowners. Small farmers felt less choked by debt than before 1851, because of the favourable economic situation which lessened the burden of loans. As a result, the curve of house repossessions, which reached a maximum in the middle of the

21. G. Garrier (70), vol. 1, pp. 371–86; R. Huard (184), pp. 143–5; G. Cholvy (292), p. 871.
22. From P. Goujon, in J.-P. Houssel (83), pp. 287–8.

century, showed a constant fall until about 1865 not only at a national level but also in poor regions such as the Limousin which profited from the higher price for cattle and the repercussions of temporary migrations in the building trade.[23]

However, the scourge of debt remained because, despite the creation of the *Crédit foncier* in 1852, the State did not set up specific institutions. In the *arrondissement* of Brioude for example, the sum of mortgage credit per inhabitant fell from 313.02 francs in 1840–1849 (the maximum for the century) to 297.02 francs (1850–1859) and then to 247.07 francs (1860–1869). This figure still represented four times the net agricultural income per inhabitant. In these circumstances it is understandable that the notables' complaints about peasant routinism evaded the problem. For the small peasant, the purchase of land was the only means of realising a marketable surplus, surety for obtaining the liquidity necessary for any agricultural investment or improvement. This created something of a vicious circle, since these tactics damaged future prosperity in that the additional income gained from expansion was reduced by the burden of the loans.

b *Nouveaux Riches* Peasants?

Contemporaries, trusting monetary indicators or studies of peasants only in wealthy regions, tended to spread the image of *nouveaux riches* peasants satisfied with their lot. As evidence, they cited peasant support for the imperial regime which contrasted with growing working-class or urban discontent and with the rural agitation at the end of the July monarchy and the Second Republic. Despite an increase in the number of regional works, it is hard to give a precise average picture because of the co-existence of peasant societies integrated to a greater or lesser degree into the monetary economy. The departure of the poorest automatically resulted in a rise in the average standard of living of those who remained, though not to the level of urban life.

The rise in the standard of living can be measured indirectly by the consumption of manufactured or artisanal products such as textile products. According to Le Play, the sharecropper in lower Brittany spent 12.3 per cent of his budget on clothing (or almost the same proportion as the town worker) out of an annual income of 460 francs; a farming landowner in the Pyrenean Midi set aside 18 per cent of his 2,000 francs income. After adjusting these figures to allow for their inclusion of clothing produced at home, Maurice Lévy-Leboyer and François Bourguignon have calculated by a process of extrapolation that, on the

23. Graph in A. Corbin (170), vol. 1, p. 175.

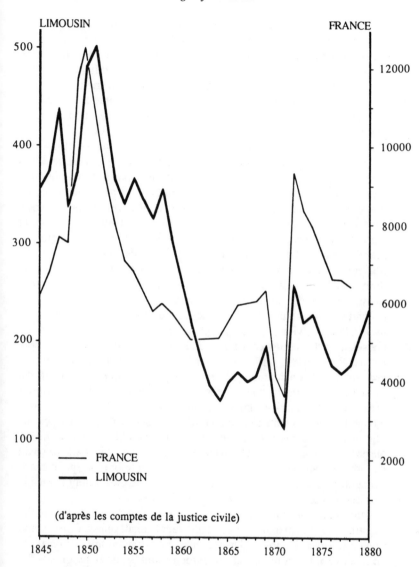

Source: Alain Corbin, *Archaïsme et Modernité en Limousin au XIX siècle, 1845–1880*, Paris, Marcel Rivière, 1975, p. 179.

FIGURE 1: Showing peasant prosperity: the number of repossessions in France and in the Limousin, according to the accounts of the civil legal authorities.

basis of a theoretical average of 28 francs per head in the 1860s, peasants in fact accounted for no more than 20 to 25 per cent of total textile consumption, for 50 per cent of the active population and for 40 per cent of disposable income.[24] The growth of the peasant clothing market was therefore real (shown indirectly by the reduction in industrial crises induced by agricultural crises) but it primarily benefited the producers of cheap textiles, which it was harder for the peasant household to produce.

The increase in fairs and peddling was also a sign that articles which had not been produced locally had arrived in the village. Therefore, when contemporaries talked about the spread of luxurious habits among the peasantry, they were exaggerating on the basis of the new trend whereby the peasants were now buying products from outside which were not basic necessities. Thabault's monograph on Mazières-en-Gâtine, a small rural market town in the Deux-Sèvres, dates the opening of that region of traditional agriculture to the outside world from this period. Before 1850, trade was limited, at best; work was paid in kind, bread was made on the farm, wooden tools were made by the peasant himself and were therefore rudimentary, and there were no specialist building workers. Under the Second Empire, on the other hand, new opportunities were possible with the arrival in the village of permanent masons, who built or rebuilt peasant houses, and the settlement of new craftsmen and merchants, who now had a clientele with a sufficient demand for goods which were sometimes brought from considerable distances, thanks to the opening of the railway.[25] Conversely, the impression of poverty shown by literary evidence concerning dwellings or clothing (Zola's *La Terre* for example, though this deals with a rich region) does not necessarily contradict this 'optimistic' evidence if the savings realised were used for other invisible purposes such as reducing indebtedness, purchase of land, balances paid to co-heirs, daughters' dowries, purchases of cattle or tools, payment to a substitute to avoid a son doing military service or, more rarely, to enable children to continue their education.

Putting the evidence in perspective in this way does not exclude the fact that peasants, small farmer landowners, small tenant farmers and sharecroppers as a whole had least access to the commodities which these optimistic mid-century decades regarded as the fruits of progress. The peasant house rarely had more than two rooms. In southern Brittany, for example, the main room was used for all domestic purposes, kitchen, bedroom, reception room and dining room. The adjoining room was

24. M. Lévy-Leboyer and F. Bourguignon (39), p. 33, quoted by P. Verley (43), p. 53.
25. R. Thabault (277), pp. 53–109.

reserved for preparing the animals' food or for a second household. The stabling, on the other hand, was completely separate, unlike the situation in the Massif Central where the partition between accommodation and stabling was only 1.5 metres high in order to benefit from the heat from the animals. Because of the tax on doors and windows, openings were kept to the minimum, hence there was poor light, and the air was permanently tainted by charcoal or cooking. The sharecropper's house in the Bourbonnais, described by Émile Guillaumin, was better designed and had two separate rooms, the kitchen or common room and the bedroom, in addition to the barn and stable; but the floor was still made of beaten earth, the ceiling was falling to pieces because the stingy landowner had refused to repair it, and the windows were very small. The advantages of this lesser degree of overcrowding were counterbalanced by strict subordination to the manager and landowner of the domain, which had to be put up with. The other factor in the insalubrity and poor health of the population was the absence of reasonable drainage of waste water and refuse, aggravated by proximity to dung and animal droppings, while practices of bodily hygiene continued to be non-existent, particularly in isolated regions such as the Limousin.[26]

Access to water, which varied from region to region, signified an important physical *corvée* everywhere, carried out by the women who also assumed responsibility for doing the washing. Because of this, folklorists claim that the wash-house constituted a female area of sociability and a counter-power for keeping a check on the whole population through swapping tittle-tattle. The centres of male space were twofold, the smithy and, increasingly, the tavern; more sporadically, there were also the nearby markets and fairs which were proliferating as products became more commercialised.[27]

The overall health of the peasantry showed some very limited signs of improvement, stemming more from the alleviation of food crises and epidemics than from real progress in medicine or food. Inadequate medical facilities continued to exist in poor regions. Doctors and non-graduate medical practitioners (*officiers de santé*, i.e. doctors of the second class) preferred to practise amongst an urban or rich clientele than amongst peasants who still had confidence in alternative healers – nuns, bone-setters, charlatans – or even relying on providence or the natural resistance gained from a life of unremitting toil. In Haute-Loire for example, the number of doctors fell from 58 in 1849 to 46 in 1869 and

26. M. Segalen (319), p. 264; E. Guillaumin (7), pp. 160–1; A. Corbin (170), vol. 1, pp. 77–80.

27. M. Segalen (111), pp. 151–4; on peasant sociability at fairs, see A. Corbin (236), pp. 70–7.

the number of non-graduate medical practitioners from 22 to 8; only the number of midwives rose slightly, from 20 to 36. This means that the majority of inhabitants in that rural department (over 300,000) used no medical service at all. On the positive side, however, the number of conscripts exempted for lack of height (less than 1.56 metres) decreased from 16 to 10 per cent, and the average (and therefore peasant) food ration rose as a result of better harvests and improved communications between regions which imported crops and those which exported. On the other hand, infant mortality remained high and even increased in the 1850s.

The statistics of military recruitment for 1868, drawn up by Emmanuel Le Roy Ladurie and his collaborators, gives a similarly qualified picture of the relative position of the peasants within the social structure. The index of relative affluence, represented by the possibility of purchasing a substitute, shows three unequal strata. Amongst farmers, a quarter possessed the 500 to 700 francs necessary to pay for the security of avoiding service, 59.8 per cent did not have this sum, and 14.5 per cent, even more poverty-stricken, served as substitutes for the more affluent. For agricultural and domestic (mainly agricultural) wage-earners, the least poor fringe was half the size (11 per cent and 8.8 per cent respectively).

There is also a strong correlation between indicators of educational backwardness and the economic hierarchy; 28.8 per cent of farmer conscripts were illiterate, as compared with 34.5 per cent of agricultural wage-earners and an average rate of 25.5 per cent for France in 1866. These initial educational advantages in turn determined equally divergent social careers. The less well-off were forced to be more mobile. From the age of twenty, their place of residence was different from their parents': 11.1 per cent of farmers who did not have substitutes and 18.4 per cent of vine growers, 22 per cent of day labourers, and 39.6 per cent of domestic servants were in this category, against 3.89 per cent of those active in agriculture who found substitutes.

These percentages are reinforced when illiteracy is added to poverty (with which it is already correlated, as has been shown). The index of illiteracy shows the persistence of an old society of interchangeable workers in which poverty and ignorance were a cause of mobility. The same thing had happened in the previous generation; unsettled, poor and uneducated conscripts came from unsettled (and equally poor and illiterate) families. These unequal conditions of survival also determined anthropological features like stature. Despite progress in agriculture and food supplies, this imprint of the social hierarchy on the physical hierarchy of individuals at the end of the Second Empire shows itself in the military statistics; there were twice as many short men (less than 1.59

metres) amongst poor and illiterate farmers than amongst the more affluent and literate.[28]

c The Return of the Notables?

Did the notables' power in the countryside contract as a result of the increased strength of the central State and the emergence of a category of better-off peasantry? It has been seen that the Second Empire had to depend to a large extent on notables connected with preceding regimes in order to establish its central and departmental authority. At the local level, even if the pre-eminence ensured by the traditional components of the notables' power (financial means, level of education, old social networks), were not as undisputed as before 1848, they still retained all their former importance so long as new groups had not emerged to organise the rural masses. The retrospective fear of 1849 and the imaginary fears of the 1852 elections stirred the old ruling classes to use any means to prevent the return of similar dangers. Alongside the utilisation of the clerical structures already mentioned, the most enlightened notables had faith in the virtues of agricultural innovation which they sought to spread among the affluent sectors of the peasantry.

In the Sarthe as well as in the Mayenne and Manche, the notables pressed tenant farmers on their domains to opt for stock-raising in order to economise on manpower and to take advantage of the high meat prices resulting from urban demand. They thus achieved a sort of miniature 'green England', where social relationships were tinged with deference and where the high profits of both parties, resulting from the favourable situation and judicious investments, smoothed out social tensions. Their social power as well as their financial affluence found material expression in stone, with the fashion for building or re-rebuilding châteaux surrounded by English-style parks and rationally-designed farm buildings. Notables became county councillors or mayors; they were sometimes selected as official candidates. Whether they were of Legitimist or Orleanist descent or had supported the Empire, once they had regained, in the majority of regions, at least at the local level, the monopoly of the powers (economic, social, political and cultural power) which was their strength before 1848, they had the impression that they had stopped history and were in a fair way to achieving the ideal rural

---

28. J. Merley (153), p. 608. A. Corbin makes the same observations concerning the Limousin ((236), vol. 1, pp. 94–5); on food supplies generally, see J.-C. Toutain (278), p. 2015. The rest of the figures in these paragraphs are taken from the article by E. Le Roy Ladurie and N. Bernageau (258) or reworked from unweighted data contained in it. S.W. Serman records the same contrast between the size of officers (from middle or upper class backgrounds) and private soldiers (from rural or working-class background).

society. This ideal society was hierarchised but open to economic progress, and was protected from the noxious influences of the town.

Despite universal suffrage, the composition of county councils in 1870 was almost entirely the same as in 1840; over 28 per cent of councillors were landowners, over 15 per cent were businessmen and nearly 40 per cent were magistrates, officials and officers. The wealth of these departmental notables increased even further, aided by the favourable agricultural situation and the rise in strength of industrialists; 43 per cent of notables derived over 20,000 francs in income from the land, as against 30 per cent thirty years earlier. Lastly, the nobility would always be well placed on any honours list drawn up on the basis of this sample (noble county councillors were always wealthier than average, with 31,000 francs average income against 19,000 for commoner landowners). In the 'who's who' of this landed notability, the old families were being closely followed or overtaken by the new financial or industrial barons, but they still made a good showing; out of the ten highest known incomes, five belonged to titled families (the duc de La Rochefoucauld-Doudeauville, the marquis de Talhouet, the comte de La Rochefoucauld, the baron de Graffenried and the marquis de Voguë).[29]

C An Urban Society in Motion

When all is said and done, what most undermined the notables' social power was the growing influence of the towns over the whole of society. This influence was direct in that an increasing proportion of the population was concentrated in towns or was flowing towards them; it was also indirect because the driving forces of the economy and the beginnings of social change came from the towns; they were centres for railways, industrial investment, international trade and price and wage-fixing mechanism. Socially, these developments made their first appearance within particular groups in the industrial society, which was then in process of making its presence felt; these groups included employers and workers, but also intermediate groups connected with the tertiary activities which were increasingly important as the national market became unified.

More intensive studies of these groups have qualified this classic, overly simple, model. Contemporaries and novelists (led by Zola), followed by early historians, tended to emphasise the social innovations which appeared under the Second Empire: large modern or modernised towns, big shops, big banks, joint stock companies, financial and

29. G. Postel-Vinay (313), especially pp. 42-5; A. Guillemin (179); M. Denis (173); L. Girard, A. Prost and R. Gossez (248), pp. 48, 57, 81–2. .

economic conglomerates and large factories. This is a classic delusion which overestimates unaccustomed and unprecedented phenomena without trying to measure their real effect on society as a whole. Without minimising their effect, what needs to be known is whether or not these innovations changed prior social relationships and the dynamic of social change: were they the products of existing mechanisms or on the contrary exceptions in an unchanged landscape, and what checks did they encounter from older structures?

a The Employers

The 1872 census records the diversity of the composition of the employers group at the end of two decades of growth; for example, slightly more than 14,000 persons ran mines and quarries and employed over 164,000 male and female workers. This general heading includes both joint stock companies developing coal mines with thousands of wage-earners and micro-enterprises dispersed over the countryside, since the ratio of workers to business owner is only 11:1. Fifty-one thousand are described as factory owners with more than one million male and female workers (an average of 19.6 workers per employer). The concentration is higher here but still shows that small industrial (urban or semi-rural) workshops co-existed with large factories; the spinning mills in the North, in the Rouen region or Alsace are examples. It has been calculated that the big cotton mills in Normandy employed 708 workers on average.[30] Lastly, more than 231,000 'manufacturers' were registered as employers, along with 75,000 contractors and a mixed category of 'working chiefs' (nearly 200,000) which probably covered 'home-workers', artisans and the dispersed or semi-dispersed workforce employed in small workshops or at home. They were a survival of the proto-industrial organisation of work, with its cohorts of middlemen (manufacturers and commission agents) managing bespoke work, sub-contracting, semi-cottage industry or production carried out by a rural workforce. Including these, the average number of workers per employer then falls to slightly above six.

Without attributing over-much precision to these figures, these contemporary classifications have the virtue of showing the imperceptible transition of the artisan and worker described as 'workshop-chief' (the classic case being the Lyons silk-weaver) to small sub-contracting entrepreneur, then to semi-trader and manufacturer giving orders, and finally to true industrialist and founder of a lasting enterprise. On this subject, Jeanne Gaillard notes: 'Contemporaries of the Second Empire did not have a very clear idea where being an employer began and

30. D. Barjot (226), p. 219.

ended'.[31] The myth of the 'self-made man', originating in this period, was based on the notion that the different groups of employers listed above represented rapid stages in a career culminating in entry into the great class of dynasty-founding employers.

The Self-Made Man, Myth or Reality? — Nonetheless, despite the favourable economic situation, it was rare for a single generation to be time enough to enter the new bourgeoisie of the industrialists. Recurrent crises, particularly the very serious ones in the mid-century, overseas competition (after 1860), distance from the sectors of innovation, lack of credit, family misfortune (premature death, absence of heirs) and successful concentration by the luckiest of their number, regularly ruined a proportion of entrepreneurs on their way up; unless they opted for early retirement to enjoy their income without risk.

Jean-François Cail is quoted as the classic example of a self-made man of the Second Empire, apart from the owners of the department stores. The son of a wheelwright of Chef-Boutonne in the Deux-Sèvres, he was apprenticed to a cousin as a boiler-maker at the age of fourteen. After his *tour de France* and a period working in his native region, he went to Paris and in 1824 was taken on by Derosne, which constructed equipment for sugar mills. Twelve years later he became a partner. The business prospered but narrowly missed going under in 1848. Cail re-established it on new foundations in 1850 and by about 1860 the company was one of the two largest manufacturers of locomotives in Paris, employing 2,000 workers in three factories.[32] However, this success must be viewed against the overall pattern and comparison shows that Cail was an exception.

The biographies of the employer elite which are beginning to appear suggest that the classic routes to social ascent were most common and that their pace was less rapid. The textile sector was the prime jumping-off ground and, to a lesser degree, metallurgy, because these sectors did not require too much capital and could grow by self-financing. Even in the case of this elite, the firms were recent creations (dating from the end of the July monarchy and before the mid-century crisis). These employers were not very well educated; school at the most, followed or replaced by apprenticeship to the business or to another company. Although over a quarter of a sample of 180 employers in the Normandy-Maine-Anjou region began in subordinate positions (clerks, employees, workmen, book-keepers), the majority held positions as director, deputy

31. J. Gaillard (245), p. 132. See also the comments by G. Noiriel (103), p. 22.
32. G. Duveau (242), pp. 151-2. J.-P. Chaline also cites the case of Auguste Badin in Normandy as a former worker who became a wealthy and 'social' employer, but he also shows that Badin was an exception and, for that reason, all the more often quoted by devotees of the established order; see (56), pp. 74, 299, 319.

director, partner or manager. 51.5 per cent had actually founded their business (the figure is the same for employers in the North), 38 per cent had inherited, and 10.5 per cent had purchased the business.

But the founder himself was rarely one man on his own; three-quarters were in partnership with relatives or outside partners. The importance of these family networks appears right across the board: for the heirs (68.8 per cent succeeded their fathers, 17.2 per cent their fathers-in-law); for general social origin; and for marriage (73.7 per cent of fathers and nearly 70 per cent of fathers-in-law were bankers, merchants or industrialists).[33] These parents were probably less highly placed in the hierarchy of wealth than their sons, but success without the starting capital was increasingly improbable as industrial equipment became more expensive.

The illusion of contemporaries that they were witnessing the birth of a new class come up from nothing arose from the very rapid pace at which wealth was acquired, itself linked to the very high profits of the period. Heirs to fortunes on a middle-class or petty-bourgeoisie scale found themselves twenty years later or even sooner possessing several millions. They were therefore on an equal footing in terms of capital with the upper bourgeoisie or aristocracy, while still retaining the ascetic behaviour and vulgar tastes of a man of no breeding. For example, 34 per cent of the employers in the North studied by Frédéric Barbier possessed more than a million francs, while only a third (and not necessarily the same ones) had inherited more than 100,000 francs.[34]

These family employers had varied degrees of success in founding dynasties. In Normandy, logic of maintaining a patrimonial system impelled a large number to abandon or sell the business rather than attempt to mechanise when the cotton sector faced difficulties caused by trade treaties or the War of Secession. In the East and North on the other hand, the great textile families because of their high reproduction rates were forced to find means of survival for their firms. The strong religious convictions which inspired them (Protestant on one hand, Catholic on the other), which was the basis of a not entirely altruistic paternalism (the owners hoped to attach the workers to them by good works in order to avoid conflict), inculcated the idea of their responsibilities to their wage-earners. In Normandy on the contrary, 45 per cent of the businesses belonging to the employers studied were sold in the short term and 15 per cent had to file petitions for bankruptcy.

Other French regions produced other variations. Despite its traditionalism, the Lyons factory system also gave birth to new bourgeois

---

33. D. Barjot (226).
34. F. Barbier (224), p. 19. See also F. Codaccioni (59): the average inheritance of Lille industrialists was 758,852 francs in 1856–1858 (p. 65).

dynasties which re-invested in the new sectors (chemicals, the gas industry, mines, big business, banking, metallurgy and transport). Some of the best example are Henri Germain, founder of Crédit Lyonnais, born into a silk-manufacturing family; Arlès-Dufour, a Saint-Simonian and a manufacturer of silk goods; Jean-Baptiste and Émile Guimet in the chemicals industry; the Bonnardels, who began in a shipping company; and the bankers Aynard, Côte, Saint-Olive who, like the great Parisian businessmen, entered the world of boards of directors from the 1860s.[35]

In Marseilles, growing specialisation and a break with past diversification can be noted in business circles. For example, the number of men who defined themselves solely as shipowners went from 7 in 1846 to 21 in 1868; as insurers, from 49 to 56; and as bankers, from 38 to 20 (this decrease was a symptom of competition from large foreign credit organisations or joint stock companies).[36] Large-scale merchants and manufacturers connected with harbour industries (soap works, oil mills, etc.) also separated off. When we look at employers linked to tertiary industries, we are approaching the financial or speculative sector which epitomised (erroneously) for contemporaries the whole logic of imperial capitalism.

Speculators and the Two Hundred Families — Under the July monarchy lampoons were already calling to account the hidden responsibilities of a financial oligarchy manipulating power and the economy. Renewed expansion and the creation of large companies through stocks and shares and the emergence on centre-stage of big businessmen, often connected with members of the ruling faction, gave definitive credibility to a favourite theme of social critics over the past hundred years: the 'two hundred' (at that time critics called them the '183') families.[37]

What shocked contemporaries were the partly artificial and intangible bases of their power. The millions they owned did not come from the sale of industrial products or from visible commercial activity, as was the case with department store owners. They were the result of acquiring capital, primarily invested in service, finance and transport activities, or into industries which they did not run themselves or which were situated overseas. This mystery surrounding speculation was fascinating and alien to the predominant artisan or shopkeeper mentality. The other change (or impression of change) introduced by the Second Empire was the democratisation of these money-making mechanisms by expanding the

---

35. P. Cayez (232), pp. 335-9, J. Bouvier (231).
36. R. Caty and E. Richard (133), pp. 341 and 344.
37. Figure given by an associate of Proudhon in *L'Empire industriel. Histoire critique des concessions financières et industrielles du Second Empire*, Paris, 1869, quoted by A, Plessis (265), p. 108.

number of shares quoted on the stock exchange, issuing stocks and shares available to a larger number of people, founding deposit banks alongside the high financial institutions reserved for a select few, and extending the network of the activities of the Bank of France to the provinces.

In addition, a whole new and more or less lasting generation of businessmen came out into the open alongside the already long-established bankers (the Rothschilds, Mallets, Hottinguers, etc.) who were also company directors. These new men were genuine and creative, like the Pereires, Talabots, Benoist d'Azys, Schneiders, or remained ephemeral and on the borderlines of speculation in the pejorative sense, like Mirès. They were not, however, entirely new. Socially, they came from sometimes provincial but mainly Parisian families of merchants or industrialists, little different from the family employers mentioned earlier. What distinguished them was their interest in national or even international expansion, their refusal to specialise in a single sector, their disrespect for prudent deliberation or over-strict accountancy rules and their utilisation of a social capital which was constantly enlarged by their friends' entry into company directorships and their connections with politicians. They won their attachment by providing easy profits for the aristocracy and a grateful share-holding bourgeoisie.

The romantic image of the duel between the Pereires and Rothschilds (imagination against cold reason)[38] is replaced by another picture which shows the emergence of networks of liegemen or of cohorts of company directors, giving growing economic power to other groups, now allied, now competing. The majority of directors of the Bank of France, who represented the peak of this financial oligarchy, hailed from old finance. They took an equal part in the development of big business, also forming groups similar to those of the Pereires and the Crédit Mobilier. The financial capital of the companies they administered rose from 100 million francs in 1851 to 2.5 milliards in 1870, while that of the Crédit Mobilier represented 1.5 milliards, but the directly productive sector was of little account in these new companies.[39]

The infatuation with speculative stocks was not as strong as contemporaries thought. For example, most of the famous two hundred biggest shareholders in the Bank of France were still great notables or aristocrats as in the past. Despite their wealth, they kept the major part of their assets in traditional investments (stocks, government annuities, foreign bonds, land and town property). Overall, the total amount of

38. This was the basic plot of Zola's novel, *L'Argent* (1891), which merges several figures of business tycoons of the Second Empire and the early days of the Third Republic (Pereire, Mirès, Bontoux) in the character of Saccard, contrasting him with Rothschild/Gundermann, entrenched behind his 'milliard'.

39. A. Plessis (266) and (267) and R. Locke (259).

stocks and shares held by French investors rose from 117 to 204 million francs between 1852 and 1868, but this was only a rise of 1 per cent of total wealth (from 5 to 6 per cent). The authorities themselves, despite the close relationship between some leaders and financiers, sometimes restricted the excesses of this over-venturesome capitalism. They prevented excessive concentration in mining and coal, refused the necessary permits when the Pereires were in difficulties, and only belatedly liberalised the law on joint stock companies in 1867.

In all, the Second Empire laid the foundations of modernity in this area of society as in many others. But it is far from being true that these new actors influenced or profoundly changed the functioning of an economy where industry and business remained in the hands of small family groups, largely unstable and strongly impregnated with pre-industrial values. The principal visible change in the behaviour of the various employers lay in their adoption of a distinguished lifestyle and ostentatious expenditure.

A Distinctive Lifestyle — Following a classic process in social history, the emergence of these founders of lasting enterprises was accompanied by their imprint on social space. The urban changes of the Second Empire were partly a response to earlier causes and to the State's wish for social control of the towns. Nevertheless their success, which varied from one great town to another but was always visible in the landscape, resulted from their coincidence with the new needs of these bourgeois groups. These groups sought to separate themselves from the masses and the middle classes. They were therefore attracted to new districts or to new avenues opened up in old districts.

Workplace and residential area were thus increasingly dissociated. In Lyons part of the business bourgeoisie left the peninsula, the trade and finance centre, for the Brotteaux, near the Tête-d'Or park which was then in process of development. In Marseilles, the port district was partially abandoned for the new southern and eastern districts. In Paris, the old centre on the Right Bank lost its bourgeois elite which settled in the new districts in the west near the Champs-Elysées. In Rouen and Lille, the richest manufacturers and merchants moved to the new boulevards, where they built themselves individual mansions. In the small towns or in regions of rural industry, the industrialists' adoption of the symbols of aristocratic residence (purchase or reconstruction of a château or a gentleman's home) was a symptom of the first generation's wish for distinction. On the other hand the most paternalistic employers, particularly in Mulhouse or Le Creusot, had dwellings specifically built for their workers.

This growing attachment to appearances also explains why this new wealthy bourgeoisie adopted the particularly ostentatious Second Empire fashions in clothing and interior furnishings, as well as the syncretism of styles which the aesthetes of the day identified with 'bad taste', which was in fact no more than the index of a still uncertain position in the space of lifestyles. This must be further qualified by reference to region (the bourgeois employer class in the provinces was more austere than in Paris) and level of wealth. The richest, who had often been in the upper class longer, had already assimilated part of the aristocratic lifestyle or possessed friends or arbiters of taste who shielded them from vulgar errors. All these social or symbolic evolutions in the lives of business leaders emphasised the gulf between them and the workers, day labourers or clerks they employed.

b The Workers between Field and Town

Blurred Boundaries — The difficulty in estimating the proportion of workers in the social structure in the period under consideration is the same as in the first half of the nineteenth century. Official surveys suggest a paradoxical reduction in the workforce, despite two decades of industrial growth. According to the 1856 and 1866 censuses, the population active in the secondary sector fell from 4,418,000 to 4,384,000. The decline is even clearer as a proportion of the active workforce, from 31.1 per cent to 28.9 per cent. In addition to the figures themselves, which vary according to sources, year and authors' definition,[40] this paradox suggests that the boundaries of the concept of worker were still blurred.

First there were spatial boundaries; a large proportion of workers were still part-time peasants, agricultural day labourers or temporary migrants. They would be assessed as falling under one heading rather than another depending on the date of the census, the nomenclature used or their own choice at the time. There were boundaries of age or sex as well, and the continued importance of child labour or intermittent female labour also involved discrepancies. Work by women was inadequately recorded (depending on the age of their children, state of health of companion or

---

40. G. Duveau (242), on the basis of E. Levasseur, *Histoire des classes ouvrières*, A. Rousseau, Paris, 1903, vol. 2, p. 576, again quotes different figures from those reconstructed by demographers: 4.7 million people in industry, including 1.6 million employers and 116,000 employees, some, but not all, of whom were quasi-workers (p. 196). The decline, even clearer than that which he observes on the basis of the 1872 census, is explained by the crisis the country had just experienced, the loss of industrial Alsace, the under declaration of workers connected with the anti-worker repression which followed the Commune, and by the inevitably botched nature of a census in a country which had just suffered defeat and foreign occupation.

husband or economic position) because they alternated between activity and semi-unemployment, working in sectors which were least skilled and most subject to cyclical fluctuations. Child labour was also scarcely recorded since it was regulated by the 1841 law, which was applied badly if at all, since the wage paid to the child went to the parents and was not a whole wage, and since the status of an apprentice was still dubious. Lastly, the boundary of status, already apparent in the classifications mentioned above; the frontier between the dependent or semi-dependent artisan, the wage-earner, the small employer and the head of a workshop or team was permeable.

Several alternative but compatible conclusions can therefore be drawn from the decline recorded in the number of workers. The surveys could have coincided with a boom period in one case and a depression in the other. The fall in rural pauperism, mentioned already, might have enabled the workers/peasants to become full-time farmers again. A considerable number of workers in skilled trades might have changed to the status of craftsmen or even small employers. Lastly, and conversely, a 'new' unskilled working class linked to large industry and formed of day labourers, bankrupt rural craftsmen or poor peasants might have been under-recorded because of their mobility according to the economic situation. These occasional workers periodically tried to return to the land or to escape into unskilled but less exacting jobs in urban tertiary industries or in transport, which proliferated at the time. The overall figures freeze and conceal these manifold patterns of internal and external development.

Sectors and Typology — The structure by sectors and the uneven process of mechanisation also explain how the changes wrought by industrialisation were blurred inside the vast traditional overall heading of 'crafts and trades'. The coal mines, for example, symbol of the industrial revolution in progress, experienced rapid real growth in terms of jobs and production. Numbers increased from 448 mines in 1852 to 610 in 1867, and from 32,900 workers in 1850 to 84,900 in 1868.[41] But what weight did these latter carry in the working-class population compared with nearly 2 million textile workers in 1866?

A mixed situation typical of French industry already prevailed in the iron industry. The slowness of the transition to coke smelting and the fact that deposits and blast furnaces were dispersed led to the co-existence of a few major giant businesses (Schneider's Le Creusot with 10,000 workers, de Wendel at Hayange with 5,000 workers, the Maubeuge blast furnaces, the Denain-Anzin ironworks) and a multitude of minor sites

41. G. Duveau (242), pp. 139–40.

in rural France. These smaller undertakings gradually found themselves out of their depth when faced with innovations and had to convert to metallurgical specialities. But they still retained a semi-artisanal dispersed structure (for example the Thiers cutlery works, the pin factory in the L'Aigle region in the Orne, the small ironworks in the Périgord and the Haute-Marne or the Ariège).

Textiles, the leading sector, was probably the only one where the gap between the types of workers and the organisation of labour was reduced rather than enlarged. Mechanisation was more advanced there and the process of concentration, along with the more rapid collapse of the artisanal textile trade and the old production systems, was perceptible by the end of the period. In the cotton trade, however, although spinning had moved over to the mechanical system and was expanding (there were 4.5 million spindles in 1852 and 6.9 million in 1867), many industrialists were reluctant to invest in the 'self-acting' mule-jenny for fear of losing money. There were 200,000 handlooms still employed in the weaving industry in 1867, compared with 80,000 mechanical looms. As far as other fibres were concerned, industrialisation of the processes for wool, and particularly for silk and linen, was still partial. The system whereby production took place in units scattered over the countryside or was carried on in urban workshops on the one hand, and in factories in town and country on the other, therefore co-existed and even expanded. Moreover, the two were not necessarily in competition because they often handled different fabrics and qualities.

The trend towards concentration can nevertheless be noted, as only large establishments could utilise the most modern machines or steam-power. But this was far from being the general rule; in areas a long way away from sources of supply (the Rouen region, for example) or mountainous zones (such as the Mazamet basin, tied to wool), hydraulic power was infinitely preferable to importing combustible fossil fuel from afar, while in the towns, small workshops joined up to use one steam machine between them. Because of these heterogeneous technical conditions, it was in the textile industry that the full ambiguity of the workers' position under the Second Empire was most evident. A large proportion of the work was carried out by a rural workforce, very often female, as a source of supplementary income. Urban operations were also sub-divided to the maximum extent, a system which economised on fixed capital and enabled production to be adapted to fluctuations in demand in a consumer industry where demand in fact varied considerably, particularly in sectors verging on luxury (ribbon manufacture, lace, furnishing fabrics, silk).

The interests of these types of male and female workers involved in these disparate methods of production were sometimes more at variance than convergence. The embroideresses in the Meurthe or the Vosges, for example, suffered from competition from the workers in the machine-made lace industry in Saint-Quentin at the end of the Second Empire. They found that they had stronger links with the merchant manufacturers who distributed the work to them than with those unknown workers who reduced their earnings. Employers used female labour in some sectors to bring down wages in areas where mechanisation diminished the need for physical strength. The entry of women into the printing trade, a particularly proud guild, was regarded as a challenge and provoked hostile action by militant workers. Taking advantage of differences between age-groups was another divisive tactic that increased profits; apprentices were often used in place of wage-earning adults to get simple tasks done at the lowest cost, without yielding any real training for the apprentices concerned.[42]

The same heterogeneity, while affecting a smaller workforce, was typical of other sectors of industry. As in 1848, the sectors where a strong corporative worker identity was expressed were those where there was still a tradition of skilled trades, in artisanal forms of work but also in some new factories through the transfer of technical skills for certain operations. There was also a very wide internal gap between those described as 'day labourers' (the equivalent of unskilled labour), who were an interchangeable population going from one job to the next without definite specialisation, and real workers, possessing knowledge inculcated by family tradition or by apprenticeship to an elder brother or a parent. This gap, in a network of corporative mutual aid which sometimes existed on a national scale, remained significant in the mentality of the time and even, as has been seen, in official nomenclature.

However, these two worlds of workers were not entirely enclosed. In large towns, where the social segregation of districts was clearcut, they lived in the same parts of town. In businesses and workshops, the division of labour necessitated the use of both types of worker. Cail, for example, employed in Grenelle a ratio of 78 per cent specialists to 15 per cent day labourers or odd-job men in 1870. These latter were older, came from the provinces and were less militant. The skilled workers came from departments where heavy metallurgy was carried on (Saône-et-Loire, Nièvre, the East), and were trained by circulating through different businesses.[43] Glassmakers had a preference for endogamy within the trade and skill. On the other hand, the least skilled workers (manual labourers or weavers, for example), or those of rural origin (miners, for example) rarely married girls whose fathers had trades higher up the labour

42. See J. Gaillard (245), pp. 410 and 415 ff.
43. J. Gaillard (246), pp. 37–9.

hierarchy.[44]

These enclosed labour worlds also reflected socio-cultural differences, such as different literacy levels between one and the other, greater or lesser degrees of demographic limitation, earlier or later arrival in a town or rural roots preserved to a smaller or larger extent. Temporary migrants or people who opted for permanent relocation first turned to work where physical strength rather than qualifications counted, unless they had a traditional village speciality which they could re-employ in a market town, town or factory. However, there was not an impregnable barrier between these groups, as a result of the variety of different forms of organisation of labour. The shortage of skilled manpower opened up prospects of promotion to the unskilled, while the misfortunes inherent in contemporary working life (disease, physical disability, failing strength with age, unemployment in times of crisis or of recession in one sector or financial problems arising from bad budgeting connected with the illusions created by good pay) or the period of apprenticeship sometimes obliged workers in trades to accept unskilled jobs. For example, Jean-Baptiste Dumay spent time in Paris during his *'tour de France'* and, because of a period of unemployment, had to sign on as an unskilled labourer at Cail. He subsequently endured the brutalities of a puddler whom he served as assistant while waiting for a better post to become vacant, although he had already been trained as a turner at Le Creusot.[45]

Standard of Living — The workers, as urban consumers, benefited from the reduction of the crises of high prices whenever harvests were bad. On the other hand, the advent of the industrial economy introduced other fluctuations, cyclical crises, crises connected with international events or trade and competition between modernised and traditional sectors. The urban changes, either deliberately brought about by the regime or as a result of industrial developments, also had negative effects on the workers' standard of living with rises in rents and reduced supply of workers' accommodation.

Calculations of averages from this point of view are fairly meaningless because of the segmentation of the labour market (between sectors, between town workers and semi-rural workers and between regions, and dependent also on status, the family's situation or the point in time), and because the masses reacted on the basis of nominal figures and in the short term, not on a 'real' invisible wage. Further, particularly in large towns, the different rates at which various types of income grew, which were perceptible in the display of luxury by the ruling class already

44. Y. Lequin (98), vol. 1, pp. 224–38; J. Scott (275), pp. 33–7.
45. J.-B. Dumay (5), pp. 85–8.

mentioned, created a subjective impression of pauperisation in popular opinion despite an objective real improvement.

In any case, the rise in wages throughout the Second Empire did not eliminate three basic features of working conditions in the towns; instability of the labour market, particularly in the predominant textile sector and most of the consumer industries, cuts in wages made by employers at times of depression, and the structural impossibility, except on the part of the most highly skilled, of building up a financial reserve in the face of unexpected misfortunes, so that the frontier of the minimum living wage was never very far off. After compiling detailed descriptions, George Duveau was able to distinguish four levels of workers' wages: an above-average privileged group (earning more than 4 francs), which comprised only decorative sculptors; a 'fortunate' group who earned a daily wage of between 3.20 francs and 4 francs, made up of skilled trades (stone-cutters, metal-turners, clockmakers, carpenters, sawyers, tapestry makers, printers, stove-setters and smiths); a 'normal' group (earning from 2.50 francs to 3.20 francs), which included the miners and most of the iron-workers; and an 'unfortunate' group containing some unskilled workers, most of the weavers and spinners, wool-combers, drapers, etc. But unlike today, the hierarchies were blurred depending on region, the balance between the sexes, labour supply, the quality of the cloth worked, the type of fibre and urban or rural work.

In these conditions it is very hard to calculate precisely what proportion of workers were above, below and level with the basic minimum of the day, since it varied according to multiple parameters. Social theorists, obsessed with worker improvidence, drew up detailed budgets and encouraged the masses to open savings bank accounts. Monographs by Le Play and his disciples concluded, in accordance with these premises, that the provident pulled through better than the rest because they respected a certain 'moral order'; they did not suffer from alcohol abuse, or have tastes above their station, and they had regular work. For example the Paris water-carrier, with only 1,858 francs annual income drawn from two 'industries', saved 162.6 francs (or 8.8 per cent of his expenditure), while the tailor living in the same town and with a considerably higher income (3,271 francs) put no surplus by. The only items in their expenditure which differed were the meals the tailor ate out and his drinks at the tavern, which accounted for nearly half the total.[46]

46. See P. Verley (43), p. 59 for a handy summary of these two examples. The overall structure of expenditure is classic and confirmed by all other known examples. For the first, almost 60 per cent of income was spent on food, 9.8 per cent on rent and 7.1 per cent on making their own clothes. For the second, 'the ne'er do well', unnecessary expenditure forced him to cut down on necessities: 143 francs was spent on rent (against 182 francs for the other) with double the income and 26.4 francs on laundry (against 86.3 francs) but 1,434 on taverns and restaurants (taken from *Les Ouvriers des deux mondes*, vol. 2, 1858).

On the other hand, overall figures show that economic functioning involved hard times even for the 'provident', and even degradation at the end of life except for a few privileged people or the most ascetic or determined who managed to make the leap out of the wage-earning class. For example, the number of savings bank accounts held, particularly by workers, paradoxically increased (they tripled nationally) and pawnshops prospered. In an apparently contradictory fashion, although 120,000 of the 416,000 Paris workers held accounts, from 200,000 to 250,000 of them were regularly reduced to borrowing from pawn-shops. Duveau concludes from this that half the Paris workers were in debt, a quarter were able to save and a quarter spent what they earned.[47]

If individual behaviour is comparable, well-balanced financial management depended in the last resort on elements over which the working man or woman had little control. Unmarried textile workers came through respectably: 625 francs annual income for 460 francs expenditure in Roubaix, for example. The same was true of a married miner in Anzin whose children worked; with three wages, the family possessed 2,580 francs income for 2,000 francs expenditure. But as soon as one element of the budget was missing, the family moved towards debt and poverty; the birth of too many children (but it was generally the most poorly paid, the more ignorant or those who counted on their children to increase the family income who had the most children), the death of a member of the family or loss of a job, or high prices of food and lodgings could tip the balance. That was also why the most flagrant phenomena of chronic poverty were in the large towns; the rural worker's safety net of supplementary sources of income disappeared, the family self-help network slackened, and the paternalism provided by some employers or charitable institutions was almost non-existent. There were only the voluntary institutions of the worker elite (mutual aid societies, etc.) to replace them, and then only for a minority. Most vulnerable in this liberal society were people who lived alone; single women, widows, natural children or orphans, migrant day labourers, old unmarried working men, worn out, the under-paid and the under-employed. But the high worker death rate multiplied the number of these cases; a third of the conscripts facing the army medical board in Paris did not have a complete family.[48] It was these groups on the edge of the basic minimum wage who periodically tipped over into marginality: in 1866-1869, for example, 278 paupers and 294 arrests, i.e. of delinquents, were recorded per 1,000 Paris day labourers (against 55 and 71 respectively for skilled workers).[49] As

47. G. Duveau (242), p. 404.
48. J. Gaillard (246), p. 224.
49. J. Rougerie (270), p. 133.

for women workers, it was well known that popular jargon described prostitution as the fifth quarter of their day.

Hours and Conditions of Work — The persistent uncertainty of the standard of living was not offset by a reduction in the length of the working-day or an improvement in working conditions. From this point of view the Second Empire continued the regressive policy begun by the party of law and order, after the timid attempt at regulation by the government of February 1848. As in the first half of the nineteenth century, at least twelve hours were therefore the general rule in the provinces and eleven in Paris. But this average does not take into account seasonal fluctuations and differences in the organisation of work. Home-workers, very numerous at that time, had to work far longer in order to honour orders when they came in. In sectors which were introducing machines, the employers pushed for intensive use in order to squeeze a profit from the investments which burdened the first years of utilisation. Conversely, a home weaver had to work longer (from 14 to 15 hours) if he wanted to withstand competition from the factories.

The conflict between employers and workers concerned the boundaries of work rather than its duration, and whether to deduct or not to deduct time for meals eaten on the job, additional cleaning work, the observance of the Sabbath and the struggle against the tradition of 'Holy Monday' (receding except amongst the best paid urban workers), taking Monday off for drinking with one's friends. The difficulties of the 1860s, linked to international competition, drove both large businesses and small old-fashioned works to increase the intensity of labour in order to cope. Piecework or task-work became the general rule in several sectors, and the introduction of fines or warnings on the English model serve as numerous indications of this.

The picture of working conditions and life for the worker scarcely changed from the early days of industrialisation. However, with the extension of industrialisation, a growing number of wage-earners were naturally exposed to the dangers or discomforts of mechanisation or of intensified exploitation of labour. Mining accidents in particular were more frequent as concessions proliferated and deep deposits were reached: 151 deaths in 16 years (1842–1858), or nearly 10 a year, were recorded in Montceau-les-Mines, for example. Six to nine fatal accidents a year were reported in Blanzy between 1868 and 1870. Technical processes (in forges and foundries), still at the experimental stage, as well as the shortage of skilled manpower and the abuse of alcoholic beverages to 'hold back' fatigue, also explain many accidents connected with the lack of caution, inexperience or thoughtlessness of recently-engaged workers. In addition legislation, unilaterally favourable to the employers at that period, removed all compensation for the victim who was always assumed responsible and delivered up to the goodwill of his employer. Slowly, however, after the successive defeats of 1848-1851, the workers re-invented a strategy of social resistance which could be either spontaneous and passive or organised and conscious.

Strategy of Social Resistance — Together with the form and level of wages, the variable intensity of the supply of work was a factor discriminating between male and female workers. A mechanic or carpenter who could earn between 1,300 and 1,500 francs a year in Paris, in other words, a high income, was structurally unemployed for three or four months. A Paris milliner could hope for 640 francs a year, with four or five months unemployment. A dressmaker's earnings fell to 340 francs, with a dead season of four months. In order to pull through they therefore had to build up reserves, work harder at good times or sell their skill more highly, and if possible find a partner either in marriage or concubinage, or a company in a different sector. The constraint of this cyclical under-employment was therefore a factor in the great mobility of the workforce. Changing employers or moving to another district or town was one way of bypassing a local employment crisis or of negotiating better pay elsewhere. But these solutions were scarcely practicable for women who, given their specialities, were heavily dependent on an urban environment and large towns.

In a country of small businesses, this mobility was part of normal life. According to Denis Poulot, a small employer and critical observer of the skilled working-class elements in Paris, 60 per cent of workers had between three and five employers per year.[50] These Brownian movements could be caused by problems in human relationships (quarrels with employers or foremen, brawls between workers), hope of a higher wage, the wish to leave an expensive or isolated district, or the need to escape from pressing debts or an unpaid bill. Theoretically, the institution of the worker's registration book by Napoleon I and its re-introduction by Napoleon III was meant to control this workforce on the military or domestic-servant model, as it was considered too fly-by-night by those responsible for order. But even contemporaries realised that the registration book had become a dead letter, particularly for those with specialist skills, or only affected the least skilled who needed certificates to get a job in the face of harsher competition.

On the other hand, with the concurrent expansion of large businesses, it was becoming difficult to manage this employee turnover, and employers began to devise means of stabilising a fixed nucleus so that

50. D. Poulot, *Le Sublime* (16), quoted by G. Duveau (242), p. 256.

production would not be constantly disorganised by departures and absences. The point at issue in the first version of this invisible class struggle was control of attendance. Fines for absence or unpunctuality were only effective when the worker had no possibility of other employment. But, given the favourable agricultural situation, farming even a small piece of land could, for the miners in Carmaux, for example, or for many other part-time workers, be more profitable than overtime in mines or factories as long as it enabled the family to live or provided additional income, free from the arbitrariness of the employer and his intermediaries.[51]

Before the 1860s and particularly before strikes were made legal, workers' means of resistance remained limited and indirect. Their best weapon was to take advantage of the economic or seasonal situation. When a job fell vacant or when rural and urban, industrial and artisanal work was available, employers, particularly the less desirable large factories, had to grant some benefits. But many other prototypes co-existed with this ideal model of a labour market conforming to the theory of economic liberalism. Large sectors of the working labour-force retained a peasant mentality; seasonally employed, the peasant-workers regarded their industrial wages or jobs as day labourer as supplements, a spare wheel or a preliminary period for accumulating money before turning to a different profession. Some silk spinning-mill employers in the Lyons region turned this career-pattern to the advantage of their convent-factories set up in the countryside where young peasant girls boarded and saved all their wages to accumulate a dowry before returning home.[52]

Methods of collective remuneration, which blurred individual wage rates, were continued or extended during this period. For example *marchandage*, a system whereby a middleman recruited a group of workers for a job, was in use in workyards in the building trade; or else a collective allocation was made for an interdependent team, which divided payment between its members. Likewise, sub-contracting spread in the building trade after 1860 under the influence of Belgian masons. This collective wage-earning could react to the workers' disadvantage if prices were lowered competitively to win a market but it could also secure them greater autonomy in their work, with self-discipline replacing external discipline.

The end of the Second Empire was marked by a deterioration in the social climate resulting from a time-lag between wages and prices, pressure from employers facing international competition, greater

51. R. Trempé (279), vol. 1, p. 224.
52. B. Plessy and L. Challet (107), pp. 40–56.

liberalism in matters of social administration on the part of the authorities, heightened awareness of the gap between bourgeois prosperity and the persistent insecurity of the working-class situation. Here, as elsewhere, imperial stabilisation which aimed to reconcile classes had actually accelerated the maturing of latent antagonism by imposing measures on the ruling classes which they would probably not have accepted under a parliamentary regime. This democratic drive was not limited to workers' activities. It was a more general expression of new aspirations, suppressed by the absence of free political and social expression and engendered by the new open urban society, itself a product of the imperial modernisation process.

D The Democratic Thrust

a The Failure of Social Bonapartism

The Second Empire was the first nineteenth century regime to have a voluntarist social programme. The first man to be elected by the whole nation, Louis Napoleon Bonaparte claimed to be above class and claimed the right to solve the social question by authoritarian methods which were repugnant to the traditional ruling classes. This 'social Bonapartism' proposed correcting the blind play of economic forces by State action but also liberating these forces so that they increased the well-being of all. As far as agriculture was concerned, this programme had for the most part been fulfilled, as has been seen; but there were as many rural proletarians as workers, if not more, in the towns at this period. In the industrial cities, on the other hand, the contradictions in this one-sided gamble were glaringly apparent. Whereas after the disappointments of the Second Republic, Napoleon III had seemed to constitute a remedy for a section of the workers facing the party of law and order, the notables and the employers, the political opposition of the towns grew ever stronger and ultimately showed the failure of this policy.[53] This failure originated in three causes: the ill-will of the elites whose mentality, stamped with Orleanism, was totally opposed to this policy; the budgetary constraints resulting from a foreign policy of prestige; and the hostility of working-class leadership to any caesaro-socialism on principle.

The balance sheet was not completely negative. In addition to a few charitable achievements (orphanages, workers' cities built by the State), the large-scale works policy had eliminated the chronic under-employment of the first half of the nineteenth century and anti-worker legislation had gradually been emptied of its content. Evidence of this

53. G. Duveau (242), p. 101.

could be found in the attempt to calm social relationships through the conciliation boards (reorganised by the law of 1 June 1853), *de facto* tolerance of workers' associations, the 1864 law on unions, the June 1868 law on public meetings which facilitated the concerted cessation of work by workers, and the abolition of the article in the Civil Code which sanctified the unequal position of master and worker before the law. But these belated measures did not compensate for the suffering and discomfort caused by the urban policy which primarily affected the masses.

b The Towns and Paris, Social Laboratories

If contemporaries then, more than under any other regime, had the impression that they were living through a change in society during the Second Empire, it was primarily because of the rapid and deliberate change in the urban landscape and framework of life, particularly in the capital. For the first time in the history of France, a State authority supported by the dominant economic and social forces, but sometimes also fighting against them, attempted to remodel an urban society of several million people. A distinction must however be made between the urban policy pursued in the provinces and in Paris, because the situations were different even if the movement towards urban growth was general.

In the Provinces — From the time of the Second Empire, the complexity of the economy and the advances in communications gave towns, particularly large towns, a new function which explains why their powers of attraction were stronger than the medium-sized or small towns of the old urban network. The populations of Lille and Saint-Étienne for example doubled in twenty years, that of Roubaix tripled, Marseilles grew by 70 per cent and Lyons by 85 per cent, although it is true that in the last case the territory of the commune was enlarged. In a concurrent development, towns which had sprung up around industry reached a respectable size at that period, competing with some urban metropolises. Rive-de-Gier, a metallurgical, textile and glass-working town, grew from 15,000 to 30,000 inhabitants in ten years; Mulhouse, specialising in cotton, recorded 20,000 additional inhabitants and with a total of 60,000, overtook Nancy, the capital of the Lorraine, which only added 9,000 souls over the same period (for a total of 50,000 inhabitants).

It was also during this period that urban growth was at its fastest, with the result that the municipal authorities faced problems they barely mastered, a difficulty hitherto only experienced by administrators of great metropolises. The policy of large-scale annexation of mushroom suburbs was one response to these problems. But even in Paris, where the central authorities were past masters at that strategy, an additional trauma was caused because the change in boundaries, apart from affecting material interests (payment of *octroi* by merchants and industrialists, and therefore by consumers), accelerated the sociological transformation of zones that were still semi-rural, thus causing new tensions between populations of different origins.

The enlargement of the large towns extended the pathological features of Parisian urban life of the first half of the nineteenth century to the provinces: a high death rate caused by conditions propitious to epidemics; an imbalance between the sexes (the industrial towns were more masculine); a concentration of young adults and floating populations in furnished rooms; the appearance of 'shanty towns' on the peripheries for the most deprived wage-earners; and the proliferation of dilapidated ghettos overcrowded with wage-earners who could not find accommodation to meet their standard of living. Even in a town like Le Creusot, which was not restricted by old building and where Schneider tried to cope with demographic growth by new construction, one room was the norm for a family. The municipal authorities were solely concerned with combating the collective social evils; they worked at supplying drinking water and improving sanitation to limit the spread of epidemics, opening up new means of communication and institutions for the most deprived, and building up food reserves to combat bad harvests and avoid disturbances.[54] All the rest was left to private initiative, with the result that urban progress only benefited solvent demand; housing, as has been seen, was the only item in the budgets of the masses which could be cut and food and clothing absorbed the main part of incomes.

The result was a deterioration in the 'framework of life', even compared with the countryside from where the new inhabitants had come: dwellings frequently had no fireplaces, and were in high-level buildings, which aggravated daily fatigue (in Lyons and Saint-Étienne, for example), or deep down (as in the *courées* of Lille and Roubaix or Rouen), which caused an accumulation of polluted air; there was inadequate drainage of dirty water and refuse; the forced promiscuousness of too-thin partitions was a source of conflict between neighbours and of strain because of noise. The only space where the man could feel free was therefore the street or the tavern, or through flight to the outskirts of the town, on Sunday, for example. Thus, by its economic laisser-faire policy which benefited the richest, as well as by its repressive policy towards associative life and places of amusement, which were suspected of being hot-beds of subversion, the Second Empire was acting directly contrary

54. O. Voilliard (281), ch. 4; J.M. Merriman (99) and (100); J.-P. Chaline (56).

to the needs of the urban working classes born of this brutal transplantation.

In Paris — In Paris, all these problems of urban society had already existed for a long time and were aggravated by nearness to the seat of political power. An authoritarian power based on the cult of law and order could not exist in proximity to a social powder-keg, where every fifteen to twenty years the class struggle turned into street warfare and endangered the regime. The policy was therefore to control space, direct the flow of change and drain the abscess of poverty, the sources of the dangers. The lesson of the events of 1848-1851 had also been learned; the working class only became dangerous when it was not occupied. Urban re-organisation ensured full employment and must therefore eliminate poverty, the evil councillor.

But the authorities' Saint-Simonian utopia ran into two barriers; opposition from established interests (the bourgeois in particular), and resistance from the proletariat who refused to let themselves be dispossessed of their sole collective possession, urban space itself. Jeanne Gaillard has shown in detail how the remodelling of the city aimed to clear it of the sub-proletariat who threatened the historic centre, the seat of power, which was where the wretched floating population of the rented rooms was also concentrated. Building railway stations on the peripheries tended to keep new arrivals in the less crowded outside districts, which grew with the annexation of the *'petite banlieue'*. The opening of the second and third railway networks aimed to draw land speculators and industries outside old Paris to reduce crowding.[55] However, a section of the poor population, driven out of the new streets, merely resettled in nearby areas which had remained dilapidated because only the city centre provided small tradesmen with the means necessary for their survival. The housing crisis produced by the demolition also multiplied the number of new furnished rooms, which was an opportunity for landlords to invest profitably in blocks of flats earmarked for reconstruction in the short or long term. These provided accommodation for all the day labourers, attracted by the workyards, who had to live on the spot.

At the same time, shanty towns appeared in peripheral districts which still had empty space.[56] Here, the working class driven out from the old districts by the demolition sought refuge side by side with a new population of recent immigrants; in Belleville, for example, 80 per cent of the population was proletarian. Various social classes therefore still co-existed in the old districts in the east because of the 'back-yard'

55. J. Gaillard (246), pp. 30–58 and 206.
56. Ibid., pp. 207–13.

phenomenon where dilapidated areas existed at the rear of well-to-do apartment blocks. In the new districts in the west on the other hand, social segregation in space was much more clear-cut because of the homogeneity of the houses erected which left no room for working-class categories.

The impressive aspects of the renovation of the centre must not eliminate the memory of the relative failure of the annexation of old suburbs. Public monuments were initially created there in order to mark out the space, before the road system was reorganised on the same principles as the new centre. Urbanisation was thus anarchic, based on criteria of short-term profitability. Large factories or insalubrious establishments were directed there (to the La Villette section, for example) and this lowered land-values and attracted an almost wholly working-class population.[57] The least rich landowning bourgeoisie, the bourgeoisie from the periphery, therefore felt cheated of the rewards from which the bourgeoisie of the centre had benefited.

But the principal failure of Haussmann-isation lay in the new social tensions created by the rise in rents for workers' lodgings (at a rate of 3 per cent annually, clearly more than wages). This caused stronger antagonism between lodger and landlord than that which existed between employers and workers, the frontier between the status of the last two categories being less impervious than the frontier between the first two.[58] In addition, workers could act collectively to improve their wages, whereas they were helpless against a speculative mechanism linked to the imbalance between supply and demand for workers' lodgings. But proximity to a bourgeois clientele was an essential ingredient of survival for all craftsmen or home-workers. The growing difficulty of finding lodgings in the central districts was an additional penalty in relation to the instability of the market.

The combined effect of the forces of resistance to urban change and of the authorities' inconsistencies therefore produced an ambiguous social result. Certain urban ills from the first half of the nineteenth century were reduced, but more from being diluted in a larger space and as a result of an improved economic situation than because of the authorities' policies. The number of paupers decreased during the Empire according to official figures (1 per 11 inhabitants in 1831, 1 per 16 in 1869), but these statistics also reflect the greater selectivity of the criteria for aid, which was increasingly limited to the aged and infirm. The Haussmann-ian city was in fact harder on the most deprived because the traditional poorhouse system of relief reduced its residential function for the homeless during

57. Ibid., pp. 110-3; G. Jacquemet (251), pp. 118 ff.
58. J. Gaillard (246), p. 133.

crisis periods; residential facilities were considerably reduced when the Hôtel-Dieu, situated in the City, was reconstructed, while the number of new beds in other poorhouses did not keep pace with urban growth. The policy was to divide and disperse the poor or make them responsible by encouraging mutual aid societies.[59]

However, the general state of health improved because the immigrants were the product of physical selection; only the most robust ventured forth from their home areas. In addition, the new town planning had partially eradicated the hotbeds of contagion which the overcrowded districts in the centre had constituted. A fall in the death rate in Paris compared with the rest of France in the 1850s has been attributed to this rebuilding; the death rate of 31.1 per 1,000 in 1846-1850 fell to 25.7 in 1861-1865. This trend was reversed after 1866, because of the slowing down of immigration, the ageing of the population and an upsurge in the cost of living which was unfavourable to the poorest; as a result, the Paris death rate remained above the death rate for France or London, and this indicates the limitations of the urban transformation.[60]

c The Demand for Education and Culture

Along with urban change, the other symptom of the democratic drive was the demand for education at all levels. Progress in eliminating illiteracy at this period came less from new government measures (apart from the belated law of 1867 conceived by Victor Duruy) than from the specific dynamic of mass, particularly peasant, demand and the long-term effects of the 1833 Guizot law. Almost every commune now possessed a school (in 1863, only 818 did not) but considerable imbalances continued to exist in rates of school attendance depending on the wealth of the population, the characteristics of its habitat and, in particular, sex. Within the peasantry, the poorest could be exempted from school fees, but this extension of free education, accelerated by the 1867 law, was not enough to convince those who needed their children's labour or did not see the benefit of education, often having none themselves. The same process of internal social division was found amongst the workers, where it was aggravated by a time-lag in the provision of facilities in the rapidly growing industrial towns.

The social dynamic of the demand for education is therefore a good index of democratic emancipation, and it prepared the ground for opposition by the politically inclined in the early days of the Third Republic. The notables, particularly in regions dominated by the Church

59. Ibid., p. 313.
60. Ibid., pp. 215-6, and L. Chevalier (136), p. 543, and (26).

and where the structure of property demanded a large wage-earning workforce, were in fact hardly in favour of universal education which threatened to breach their social domination and make it easier for poor peasants to leave for the town. The Falloux law, favouring congreganist schools, was the first response found. It is this law which was responsible for the long delay in eliminating illiteracy amongst girls (39 per cent of wives did not know how to write in 1866, against 26 per cent of husbands). The regime's partial break with the Church at the end of the 1860s and the rise in anti-clerical movements in favour of education (such as the Ligue de l'Enseignement) were two new threats to this strategy for keeping the people under the influence of the notables.

In large towns, and particularly in Paris, popular demand for education had two aspects. There were social contrasts between the various types of school in these early centres of anti-clericalism. The crush of manpower in the poor districts drove the petty bourgeoisie and the middle classes towards either the private secular network or the religious schools, according to their ideological choice and convenience; the congreganist schools were sometimes less expensive than the state schools, and were therefore more popular. The absence of regular attendance, linked to the constraints of working-class family life, and the maladjustment of teaching methods to a heterogeneous and uprooted population, made the education dispensed less effective. In Paris, judging by attendance statistics and not by registers, a third of children in working-class districts were in actuality not educated. For this reason the working-class elite which wanted to safeguard its educational position preferred to look for specific schools and secular evening classes. In Paris and Lyons for example, evening classes in draughtmanship were very successful under the Second Empire.

The other symptom of this specifically popular demand was the expansion of adult classes and educational reading rooms. In 1867–1868, 684,092 students attended adult classes, 11.9 per cent of whom did not know how to read or write when they began. The government's introduction of educational reading rooms was more ambiguous. Its aim was to guide the people's reading in a moral and conservative direction and protect it from contagion from political pamphlets, which were credited with the spread of socialism in 1848. The number of these reading rooms increased from 4,833 in 1865 to 14,395 in 1869, and loans increased from 179,267 to 955,121. True, this considerable expansion only affected a minority of the population but it was a sign that popular education was no longer limited to the bare rudiments and no longer consisted of reading in the evening the volumes of the 'Bibliothèque Bleue', circulated by pedlars. These pedlars had been persecuted during the initial phase of the Second Empire because they were held responsible for the democratic contagion. Their role in circulating printed matter now declined irreversibly thanks to competition from the railway system, permanent bookshops, station reading rooms, the popular press and the changed taste of this new reading public which was beginning to consume products derived from the dominant culture.[61]

The same differentiation in the demand for education occurred in secondary education, with the success of special education, already existing locally but officially organised on new bases in 1865. Special education offered a ladder of social ascent for the middle classes, who were no longer satisfied with primary education alone but could not afford to envisage their children embarking on the classical education which led to the bourgeois professions. Available data on the social origins of pupils in the various streams of secondary education do in fact show a continued prevalence of the bourgeoisie, particularly the *capacités* (officials and members of the liberal professions), in the classical stream of *lycées* and colleges. Special education opened its doors to the petty bourgeoisie (39.6 per cent of pupils) and even to a rural elite, with comfortably-off farmers and tenant farmers accounting for 21.4 per cent and rural landowners 13.5 per cent of pupils in small towns.[62] The enquiry from which these data are taken reveals that these pupils, if they wished to 'change class' or in current language, rise in the social hierarchy by learning, were aware of their handicaps and aspired to humbler professions than their comrades in the classical sectors. This reform by Duruy thus met the aspirations of those whom Gambetta, speaking later in 1872, called the 'new strata'.

The expansion of the press when the Empire relaxed its supervision and the high print-runs which the new technical processes made possible, also demonstrated this deep-seated demand for living culture at every level of society. The cultural duality which characterised French society in the past was beginning to fade away and prepare the conditions for a real and in-depth democracy. Some papers deliberately aimed at a popular readership, for example *Le Petit Journal*, which made its fortune with various stories such as the Troppmann affair, while a more decentralised, quality press quickened the political discussions permitted by the new liberalisation of the regime.

61. J. Gaillard (246), pp. 273-5 and 427; A. Corbin (236), vol. 1, p. 336; J.-J. Darmon (238), especially p. 229; R. Gildea (34), ch. 6.
62. P. Harrigan (250), tables 3, 4, 5, pp. 21, 24, 26-7; see also the data collected in C. Charle (359), p. 39. For regional analyses, see also R. Anderson (222), pp. 121–46; A. Corbin (236), pp. 367–9, and R. Gildea (34), ch. 5.

d The 'New Strata'

As has been seen, one of the characteristics of society in the first half of the nineteenth century was the weakness of what today are called the middle classes. Preceding developments (urbanisation, the expansion of large-scale capitalism, the development of tertiary activities and the extension of vocational education) prepared the way for the enlargement of these 'new strata'. They formed the classes for whom the republicans were the self-elected spokesmen at the end of the Empire, and who rejected the social vision of both the traditional notables and the working-class trends in the socialist movement. The lack of precise vocabulary is a good indication that what existed so far were only the bases of a new social category, which would only be fully legitimate later when political democracy had become an actuality.

In fact the traditional ruling classes as well as the urban and rural working classes regarded these new professional groups as suspect. They did not owe their social position to any landed or personal capital worthy of note, nor to visible material work. They therefore did not employ other people, or at least very few, and did not have the advantage of the traditional prestigious labels of 'employer' or 'landowner'. If they were wage-earners, they could certainly not be confused with classic manual labourers. They owed their position solely to their 'merit', and therefore to an education above the average of the working classes (which was still very low) and equal to or even higher than that of the bourgeois classes.

These educational ladders which upset the old hierarchies came in several forms; community colleges, special education, engineering schools, agricultural schools, on-the-job training of auto-didacts helped by evening classes, in short all the expanding educational streams that have just been mentioned. Apart from public office, they led to employment in the offices of large companies, on the staff of the big shops which followed a policy of promoting internally their most successful employees, in trading firms, as commercial agents, in transport, banking, administrative posts in industry and in all the minor liberal professions which could find a large enough clientele in the prosperous countryside: pharmacists, notaries, bailiffs, road surveyors, land surveyors and local officials.

It is very difficult to estimate the numbers of this class because there is a time-lag between the census categories and the actuality, and the census categories are also mixed up with categories which relate much more to the masses. In the 1872 census, the heading 'employees', which encompasses the largest number of them, actually lumps together employees in business, trained on the job, who proliferated in the towns, and skilled wage-earners working in the offices of major companies. Another attempt to distinguish them can be made indirectly through the proportion of the population who employed a male or female servant; this gives a figure of less than 30,000 people.[63] If this figure is added to all the other non-identifiable groups included in public office and on the periphery of the most elevated liberal professions, the figure arrived at is the electorate of the *monarchie censitaire*.

Their relatively small number, strengthened by a strategic position in the new social networks born of modernity, gave these new strata the choice of two possible directions for their future in society. They could either blend into the better established bourgeoisie, although the notables' exclusivism made this a hazardous operation; or they could direct the democratic and popular drive towards equitable power-sharing, by identifying with other groups benefiting from prosperity and also aspiring to liberty. The general spread of education could only strengthen their own function and the foundations of their social position.

This was the programme of the new republican generation, whose elite was made up of bourgeois members of the liberal professions but whose rise was recent, particularly in the case of those surrounding Gambetta.[64] Studies of the local leadership of the republican party at the end of the Empire also show the considerable proportion of militants who came from the breeding-ground of a petty and middle rank bourgeoisie of trade, industry and education. In the Gard, for example, 20.8 per cent of republican leadership belonged to the liberal professions, 10.1 per cent were officials or employees, 20.8 per cent were traders and 16.5 per cent were artisans and workers; the rest emerged from a classic capital-owning bourgeoisie and, more rarely, from agriculture.[65]

e The Militant Movement

However, this republican inter-class political plan ran into an obstacle in the concurrent emergence of a new working-class movement, which intended to preserve its autonomy vis-à-vis the bourgeois or petty bourgeois leadership of the opposition, even if after 1848 it shared with the latter some of the same demands. This new generation of militants was mainly recruited from amongst workers in skilled trades who considered themselves qualified to play a political and social role without bourgeois or petty bourgeois intermediaries, thanks to the spread of education amongst the masses and the self-education movement of the

63. Total obtained as follows: according to the census, 45.6 per cent of employees, engineers, administrators and transport staff (or 8,691), 21 per cent of their equivalents in industry (or 10,102), but only 0.6 per cent of those in trade (or 9,987).

64. See P. Sorlin (343), or the study of the prefects in the government of National Defence by V. Wright (283).

65. R. Huard (184), p. 385.

working-class elite. It was also based on the growing working class and urban discontent produced by the deterioration in the economic situation at the end of the Second Empire: the time-lag between wages and prices, constantly rising rents, cyclical crises increasing unemployment, and international competition which caused industrialists to establish work discipline and a remorseless chase after profits were all to the detriment of the workers. The liberalisation of the regime and the greater tolerance of organised labour activities also facilitated the explosion of militant movements after 1864.

The great wave of demands broke between 1868 and 1870. An important new feature appeared: the regional extent of the movements and the reverberations, sometimes on a national scale, when events took a tragic turn. For example, the miners of Firminy downed tools in June 1869, followed by those in Carmaux, then by the women silk workers in Pélussin (Ardèche) and the silk throwers (silk winders) in Lyons at the end of the month. Other guilds also swung into action during that hot summer, including the carpenters of Vienne, the weavers of Rouen and the spinners of Elbeuf and Champagne. Another important feature was the beginning of workers' organisation. In the Loire, for example, 5,000 miners belonged to the *Société fraternelle des ouvriers mineurs*. In Paris, the trade unions federated under the aegis of the Socialist International and mustered some 40,000 members in 1870.[66]

This outbreak and the boldness on the part of hitherto submissive groups (particularly female workers) rested on the illusion that the authorities, who were called in as arbiters, were impartial. But employer intransigence, particularly by the large mining companies and in Le Creusot where the employer, Eugène Schneider, was also a leading figure in the regime, quickly demonstrated that the two powers were in collusion. Intervention by the army ended in massacres, as in La Ricamarie, next to Decazeville (13 dead and 9 injured on 16 June, 1869), or in Aubin (14 dead and 20 injured). Repression did not stop there; the employers wanted to decapitate the movement and intimidate the workers. A hundred and fifty former strikers were sacked, for example, after the strike by the spinners of Elbeuf in September 1869, despite the semi-success of their claims. This did not prevent a resumption of the action, notably with two strikes at Le Creusot in spring, 1870, which created an outburst of national solidarity thanks to a press campaign inviting support.

The increasingly important role of the International and the climate of political crisis at the end of the reign explain the rebirth of social fear amongst the bourgeoisie, which revived memories of June 1848. In Paris

---

66. F. L'Huillier (260); C. Auzias and A. Houel (223); J.-B. Dumay (5).

and other large towns the disturbed electoral climate of 1869–1870 and the numerous meetings where revolutionary sentiments were given free play resurrected the spectre of 1793 in prevailing public opinion. The attempted outbreaks in Paris (in May 1869, the beginning of June 1869, January 1870, then in May 1870) which punctuated this last year of the Empire also gave substance to this phobia which became a reality with the Commune.[67]

Table 1.1: Comparative composition (in percentages) of those arrested in May 1871, those charged with insurrection in June 1848, and the demographic strength of the various sectors in the working-class population of Paris.

SECTORS	MAY '71	DIFFERENCE*	JUNE '48	POPULATION**
Day labourers and manual workers	14.9	(+)	13.4	20.0 (–)
Wood and furniture	8.0	(–)	10.9	5.3 (+)
Building	15.7	(+)	12.4	10.0 (+)
Metal and engineering	11.9	(–)	14.8	8.0 (+)
Leather, boot and shoemaking	5.4	(–)	6.3	
Textiles and clothing	3.9	(–)	6.5	
Books and printing	2.7	(+)	0.6	
Craftwork and fancy goods	6.9	(–)	8.5	10.0 (=)
Retail trade	4.3	(–)	4.1	
Employees	8.0	(+)	6.7	
Liberal professions	3.3	(–)	3.2	
Agriculture	1.1	(–)	2.1	
Domestics	4.9	(?+)	?	
Itinerant merchants	?	(?–)	4.8	
Various	?	(?–)	5.7	
	(1)	(2)	(2)	(3)

* Difference: the difference between May 1871 and June 1848.

** Population: the proportion of the category in the population of Paris (the sign in brackets indicates if the population of insurgents was different in comparison with this percentage).

For leather, boot and shoe and textiles, clothing, as well as for books, printing and craftwork, fancy goods, the percentage is the sum of the two sub-groups. The liberal professions refers to these professions in the broadest sense.

Sources: (1) Rougerie (271), p. 127; (2) P. Caspard (169) and M. Agulhon (163), p. 35; (3) Rougerie (271), p. 129.

67. A. Dalotel, A. Faure and J.-C. Freiermuth (237), pp. 327–55. The authors have counted 933 'non-political' meetings between 1868 and 1870 in Paris. There is constant reference at them to 1793 and to June 1848 and also a constant yearning for the 'commune', that is to say a socialist and decentralised organisation.

f The Commune

The well-known story of the Commune does not come within the province of this book. Its social significance, on the other hand, does. For a long time the classic discussion between historians has centred on whether the communalist uprising arose out of an obsolete revolutionary cycle on the part of an urban people heir to the French Revolution, or was the forerunner of a new type of revolution. Social analyses by Jacques Rougerie have shown the unquestionable continuity between the communard personnel and an old type of working class, reflecting the specific industrial structure of the capital – which is hardly surprising. The conclusions of this pioneering work can be extended on the basis of data available on the two main nineteenth-century uprisings.

The general balance was roughly the same after an interval of twenty-three years. Workers, in the strict sense of the term, constituted almost exactly the same proportion, 79.1 per cent and 78.1 per cent, of those charged with insurrection during the two periods. Non-worker participants also came from the working-classes (petty traders, employees, servants, farm labourers), and a small minority came from intellectual, even bourgeois circles. The balance between the professional sectors was fairly constant despite the industrial development of the capital; moreover, the changes came from these overall developments as much as from variations in the militancy of worker groups. The sectors which show a relative decline (wood, construction work, textiles, clothing and agriculture) were those which had a reduced worker population. Those which show an increase also employed a larger workforce under the Second Empire; they include day labourers, workers in the building and book trades, employees and servants.

But the position taken in the Commune was not just a passive reflection of earlier economic developments. It also reflected the urban evils newly-born out of the savage transformation of the capital. The most militant were not the youngest but those who had lived through the urban trauma or remembered the example of earlier resistance to the bourgeois order (only 11 per cent, those aged twenty or less, had known only the Second Empire). Similarly, if the least skilled workers or the most unprivileged sectors (day labourers and building workers) were better represented than in 1848 (a sign that they were better qualified for emancipation as a result of the long period of revolt and political effervescence since 1868), the first group remained under-represented in relation to their demographic importance. The number of metal-workers is the result both of their skill and of the high level of organisation they had gained in the past. However, the number of workers from this sector shows a relative decline from June 1848, probably because their ranks had been swelled by unskilled elements from the provinces or the countryside working in the new large factories on the periphery of Paris and who were, as has been seen, less politicised or less integrated into the trades of the capital.

There was a predominance of people born in the provinces, as there was for the whole population of Paris, but there were probably fewer than in earlier uprisings. It would be more useful to know how long they had lived in Paris and the proportion of those who intended to settle permanently there. Given the predominant ideological themes in the communard movement (to win back the city and make it fit for all to live in) and the sociological distortions listed, it is probable that the most militant were those who felt the most Parisian and the most dependent on Paris as the only town in France; they were victims of the unpleasant effects of Haussmann's urban policy, which explains the over-representation in the leadership of the National Guard of the most educated workers (such as workers in the book trade) or employees.[68]

Despite this social continuity between the two movements, the Commune did not solely repeat the June Days for a three-months period with an additional seizure of power. The June Days were a desperate uprising stemming from black poverty. Despite its divisions and weaknesses, the communard government ran the city and carried out a few reforms (reforms moreover of a progressive republican rather than socialist programme). The seizure of power aside, the movement prefigured a hitherto undreamt-of municipal socialism and held promise of a great future. Its leaders' out-dated ideologies (particularly the reference to 1793) in fact concealed a modern practice of urban development which provided an answer to the inadequacies of the class policy of the authorities. From this viewpoint therefore, the continuity with the Commune claimed by the organised labour movement of the Third Republic – later administrator of the red suburb – was not merely a pious exercise, even if in the minds of its leaders it was concerned with other themes.

g Conclusion

The Second Empire had been founded on the fear of a mythical revolution, prevented by the coup d'état of 2 December, then simulated by resistance to the coup. It ended in the blood-bath of real revolution. In short, this regime based on reconciliation of the classes would be

68. Ibid., p. 129 and J. Rougerie (271).

bounded, as it were, by a Jacquerie at the beginning and a repetition of 1793 at its end. French society therefore, seems to have returned after twenty years to its recurrent head-on conflict between a divided ruling class insecure in, and obviously unequal to the exercise of, its power (as the defeat and the conduct of the civil war show) and an old type of working class centred in a disrupted capital. However, to reduce the period to this simplification would be to neglect all the seeds of long-term change which the Republic, that is to say the political regime, utilised to put an end to the era of revolutions by allowing democratic developments free play instead of restraining them or opposing them. This policy had permitted the country to emerge from the agrarian ancien regime and allowed the peasantry to become a fully fledged social actor without armed disturbances. It had led to the rise of the middle classes linked to a capitalist economy, open to the outside world, and to an increasingly educated population; it had led to a progressive change in style of rule thanks to the replacement of the traditional ruling classes by new elites, which if not actually more open then at least successfully persuaded people that they were; and finally it had led to the emergence of new working classes which no longer depended solely on stimuli from the urban centres or the capital and which were beginning to abandon violence in favour of organisation, with the result that political divergences were diminishing their powers of opposition. All these developments towards a 'democratic society' will be the subject of the second part of this book.

II
The Emergence of a Democratic Society, 1870–1914

–4–

A New Class: The Peasants

The images of the peasantry under the Third Republic fall somewhere between two extremes. At one hand there is the idyllic version of the official school text-books in which the Republic rested on the unshakeable rock of the peasant democracy of little men. At the other extreme is the tragedy of the countryside, where the new, accursed peasant paid for his passion for property and incarnated all the failings of eternal France – Malthusianism, routinism, archaism, and the mediocrity of the 'stagnant pools' policy of the constituency poll.

These caricatures indirectly disclose one of the difficulties faced by social analysis of the French peasants. It is practically impossible to reduce them to one social model because of their diversity. The farmers were reputed to be backward, yet they succeeded better than any other social category in preserving their interests in the framework of the new regime and limiting to the maximum the decline in their position in general society. Their success in this direction emphasised the unique nature of France in a Europe in the grip of industrialisation and a long-lasting agricultural depression.

Aggressive individualists, the peasants also formed the group which managed to obtain the greatest benefit from the opportunities for association opened up by the Republic. The government endowed this first economic lobby in the country with its own minister (Agriculture, created in 1881, whereas the minister of Labour only became autonomous in 1906), and its own specific programmes, both educational (the Jules Ferry school), and railway (the Freycinet project).

In short, for obvious electoral reasons, the peasants in some ways constituted the first class to be born of representative democracy. The very great majority of those elected (deputies, senators, county councillors and town councillors) depended on their vote. If a class can be defined by its contrast with other social groups and its relative internal unity, the peasants in that period were closer to being such a class than any other social category; the divergences within the elites or workers were much greater, as the ensuing chapters will show.

The adherence of the rural classes to the Second Empire was based on administrative pressure and economic prosperity. Support for the Republic by the majority of peasants, on the other hand, was maintained without external constraint and despite economic difficulties. The adherence therefore corresponded to a calculation of the advantages to be derived from the new political situation. While there was no shortage of other political forces, from the old conservatives to the socialists, trying to capture this mass electorate for their own ends, they only had limited success in a few regions and sometimes on the basis of a misapprehension. To understand this political alliance requires, therefore, a description of the mechanisms of integration at work, the social effects of the gloomy economic situation at the end of the century, and the regional development of the hierarchies in the peasant societies which co-existed in France.

A Integration in the Nation

a Peasant France: An Overall View

The success of this integration resulted from both specific political, economic and social measures, and changes peculiar to peasant France. First and foremost of these was the rural exodus.

The Rural Exodus — The contrast between the French evolution and the development of other comparable European countries is well known. The rural population and the active agricultural population decreased, but to a much lesser extent than in Germany or, *a fortiori*, in England. Agriculture remained the prime source of employment (42 per cent were employed in this sector in 1911), and the rural population (those living in communes with less than 2,000 inhabitants, according to the legal definition) was still in the majority three years before the war (55.8 per cent of the population). This contradictory situation of relatively sustained strength and inexorable contraction accounts for the peasant state of mind and the tone of Republican discourse. Faced with this graduated evolution, politicians, like farmers, could believe in the possibility of controlling the decline.

In fact, the 100,000 to 150,000 countryfolk who left the land and the villages every year between 1881 and 1911 were not all peasants. They were more often rural craftsmen whose products were meeting competition from urban industry or whose trade was losing its *raison d'être* because of the rural exodus, day labourers attracted by the higher wages in the towns or young people taking up temporary or permanent positions as domestic servants or entering the service sector. Sometimes owning a few ares, the migrants would sell their land at the same time.

The number of craftsmen in the Loir-et-Cher for example, fell by nearly a half between 1871 and 1914; the workforce in the Somme fell by a quarter between 1872 and 1911. The rate of rural exodus by rural craftsmen's sons in the Beauce was also above the average.[1]

These departures were often a godsend to the small landowners who remained, giving them the opportunity to buy additional plots or lease more land. The migration to the towns also put those day labourers or domestic servants who did not leave in a strong position. The increasing scarcity of labour made it possible to negotiate wages, and even gave the hope of buying a few patches of intestate land and thus changing status. The proportion of 'proletarians' amongst those active in agriculture in the Hérault, for example, fell from 32.2 per cent in 1872 to 27.9 per cent in 1892, whereas the proportion of independent landowners rose (from 28.5 per cent to 33.9 per cent) and that of landowners obliged to supplement their income by working for other people fell slightly by a little over 1 per cent. In another department where large property was predominant, such as the Loir-et-Cher, the number of agricultural wage-earners fell by 10 per cent between 1871 and 1914; the Somme and Seine-et-Marne recorded comparable movements. In France as a whole, the number of full-time agricultural wage-earners fell by 150,000 and of domestic servants and farm servants by 120,000 between 1882 and 1892.[2]

Malthusianism — The exodus to the town or to other industrial jobs was not solely responsible for the decline. An early restriction of births practised by the French agricultural population, which was at first a response to the fragmentation of the land, re-enforced the weakening of the rural world in this period of exodus and depression. However, here again a national picture veils the real dynamic of the phenomenon because a 'squeezing' process took place between regions. Zones which remained demographically very fertile tipped their surplus peasants into depopulated zones so long as these did not suffer from insurmountable economic disadvantages. Brittany, for example, served as a labour reservoir of new agricultural workers for the centre-west, the south-east, Normandy and the western fringes of the Paris basin. Temporary migrations, so important in the first three-quarters of the century, had prepared the ground for this transfer movement from overpopulated to underpopulated regions. The same phenomenon, which restored equilibrium, sometimes went beyond frontiers: for example, Belgians

1. G. Dupeux (241), p. 501 (from 9000 to 5000); P. Pinchemel (106), p. 106; J.-C. Farcy (294), p. 589, n. 13.

2. G. Cholvy (292), p. 871; G. Dupeux (241); P. Pinchemel (106); P. Bernard (288), p. 66.

settled in departments in northern France and Spaniards and Italians
became seasonal agricultural workers in departments of southern France.

Over Lap of Social Status — The French peasants therefore gained in
homogeneity and relative social strength during this phase of
demographic decline, since their ranks had been reduced by the poorest,
weakest and most dependent elements. However, available statistics on
a national scale convey contradictory pictures. When viewing the official
picture, one can be led to the conclusion that France was a country of
small landowners owning and working their own farms, since 75 per cent
of the farms were of this type and farming landowners or landowners with
a composite status formed more than 51 per cent of the agricultural
population in 1882. But although these farming landowners were
numerous, they farmed only 53 per cent of the agricultural area, with a
derisory average of 4.37 hectares per farm. The remaining 47 per cent
of the land was rented out to tenant farmers or sharecroppers in the form
of far larger farms (slightly more than ten hectares), clearly because they
belonged to bourgeois or noble landowners.

These averages conceal even larger differences in distribution. Official
records show that there were still 142,088 farms of more than 40 hectares
in 1882, with farms of more than 100 hectares (less than 50,000) alone
comprising a quarter of the country's land. Conversely, there were
1,865,878 farms of between one and five hectares. Moreover, this latter
block tended to decline whereas the 5–10 hectares block increased at the
expense of the larger blocks, which it did by 24 per cent between 1862
and 1882, and by 2.5 per cent during the crisis phase (1882–1892).

The agricultural crises were even able to push farmers who were most
dependent on the market to withdraw into self-sufficiency and family
mixed farming. Viticulturalists and cereal-growers, who sold their
surpluses, and farmers with large properties were worst hit by the
vicissitudes of the economic situation. In two regions as far apart as the
Pas-de-Calais and the Pyrénées-Orientales, the small farm gained ground
in response to the commercial problems: in Pas-de-Calais small farms
accounted for 22.6 per cent of the total in 1881 and 30.4 per cent in 1911,
and in the Pyrénées-Orientales, 79.4 per cent in 1910 against 66.9 per
cent in 1820.[3]

The disparity between these figures, despite the general trend,
indicates the differences in farming methods in different regions. The
north-western quarter of France was the realm of leased lands. This was
the country of urban, *rentier* bourgeoisies or resistant rural nobilities
(Brittany, the lands of the Loire, Normandy, Maine-Anjou, the great Paris

3. R. Hubscher (301), p. 10.

basin and Nord-Pas-de-Calais and the Côte d'Or). The areas where share-cropping prevailed should also be included here (Landes, Allier and part of the south-west). But the rural France of indirect farming was heterogeneous, as has been seen. Tenant farming could go hand in hand with advanced open-field agriculture as well as with the technically backward agriculture of small farms or unstable *métairies* (as in Brittany, the centre and the south-east).

The small owner-farmers, on the other hand, were to be found in central, eastern or south-eastern France, in the lands of vine-growing and specialised crops, but also in the poor mountainous lands of subsistence mixed farming which attracted less investment in land by the upper classes.[4] These zonal divisions are still misleading in every respect; every canton, even every commune presents variants, in which these ideal models of peasant societies co-exist in infinitely varied patterns. Not status, nor property, nor the area owned, nor the employment or non-employment of wage-earners is sufficient to distinguish these variants fully. It is just as useless to place them on a scale of modernity, as the agricultural situation could ruin lands which were previously prosperous.

Large properties still accounted for almost half of French soil but large farms were crumbling, unless the landowners abandoned sharecropping or cultivation by managers for tenant farming, or even sold up at the time of a division or an excessive drop in income. Georges Dupeux has calculated that the area of large noble property in the Loir-et-Cher decreased by 18 per cent between the beginning of the nineteenth century and 1914. In the valleys, it was small property which increased on the richest soils, and in the Beauce it was medium-sized property, with tenant farmers gradually buying the lands they leased.[5] The same phenomenon can be found in an area of small farms such as the Var. The number of farming landowners increased from 15,300 in 1862 to 25,300 in 1892. Conversely, the number of landowners farming with the help of a manager or farm foreman halved in the thirty years between 1862 and 1892, whereas the number of tenant farmers and sharecroppers also declined; another sign that big *rentier* landowners were withdrawing from the land.[6]

Overall figures register similar changes but show them less clearly because of the perplexities of official classifications, which vary from one investigation to another, and errors arising from the different meanings of words in different regions. The multiplicity of composite

4. Figures taken from R. Price (314), p. 350–3, T. Zeldin (44), vol. 1, p. 180, and maps of tenant farmers and sharecroppers in 1892 (p. 184) and of share-cropping only in A. Moulin (101), p. 147, taken from G. Dupeux, *Atlas historique de la France contemporaine*, p. 48.

5. G. Dupeux (241), pp. 577–9.

6. Y. Rinaudo (316), p. 142.

statuses (farmer and craftsman, tenant farmer and landowner, day labourer and micro-landowner, etc.) also makes any rigid valuation dubious, more especially as, depending on the stage in his life, the same peasant could change status not by rising or falling on the social scale but solely through the family cycle.

In fact, a combination of activities often went hand in hand with the small farm. In mountainous regions, the women continued with artisanal activities in order to bring in income in cash. For example, from 50,000 to 80,000 lace-makers were still active around the Puy in about 1900, and 20,000 peasant women made gloves in the Isère. The peasants could also play on wage differences between sectors or regions. The Breton tenant farmers discharged their rents from their wages as temporary day labourers in Normandy or the Beauce. In the Loire, some vine-growers signed on in the Bully mines in order to meet the cost of replenishing their phylloxera-stricken vines.

It could also be more profitable to send children or a spouse to find temporary work in the town, even if this in turn meant hiring in help from a less highly-paid day labourer. A monograph published by Le Play on the soap-maker from Marseilles shows this process in action: the wife managed the farm with two day labourers with a wage-bill of 940 francs, while the father earned 1,490 francs as a worker in Marseilles (in 1859). However, the rise in agricultural wages at the end of the century forced them to employ family labour.[7] In the Finistère, in the Pont-l'Abbé region, the young son was frequently sent as a servant to a neighbouring farm before returning to help with the family farm or, if there was sufficient labour there, leaving again to work as a seasonal wage-earner on another farm. With this training, he could then obtain a farm of his own if he married. Depending on the date of the census, his parents would appear as small family farmers, tenant farmers, employing wage-earning manpower or farming landowners or semi-*rentiers*.[8] There will be more discussion of these long-lasting complex structures later. Nevertheless, they went through changes determined by the centre precisely in order to locate them in an overall universal structure, 'the Republic in the village'.

b Insertion in Republican Space

The School — The cultural contrast between the two peasant Frances separated by the Saint-Malo/Geneva literacy line was still very visible

---

7. Monograph by A. Focillon, published in *Les Ouvriers européens*, 2nd edn., vol. 4, pp. 390–444, quoted by R. Hubscher (301), p. 15.

8. M. Segalen (319), p. 259.

at the end of the Second Empire, even if it tended to diminish with the rise in demand for education in backward departments. The contrast was definitively wiped out under the Third Republic. This well-known development in the history of education had a particular consequence for the peasants. It concerned them essentially, since the establishment of an education system in the towns had already been achieved before this date. The growing unification of all the peasants of France through their minimal education ceased to make them a separate category of Frenchmen, either as a professional group in general or regionally.

Eugen Weber speaks of the transition from 'peasants' to 'French citizens' in this period. 'Frenchmen' has a double meaning here: it implies that the citizen was bound to the French nation by a number of rights and duties (education, conscription, the vote), and that he was above all imbued with the official French culture, particularly in the younger generations. In 1863, the inhabitants of 8,381 of the 37,510 communes, in other words a quarter of the total did not speak French, and this does not include local patois derived from the dialects of northern France. If this too is taken into account, it can be estimated that half the French, comprising an overwhelming majority of peasants, were foreigners in their own country at the time the Republic was proclaimed.

Heirs of the Revolution and its battle against patois, the Republic made the new school the weapon in its struggle against this isolating factor which separated the peasants from the regime. This dual linguistic and educational integration of the peasantry was all the more difficult because it occurred in zones where conditions were the most unfavourable, in poor regions with dispersed habitation, bad communications (where the need for a 'national' language was less apparent, as the notables served as intermediaries) and sometimes strongly clericalised, where the secular school had difficulty in becoming accepted.

Morbihan is a good example of this scenario. Most of these disadvantages facing the establishment of schools were concentrated in this department. In 1850, 17.6 per cent of agricultural labourers and farmers in Breton-speaking cantons were literate compared with 35.3 per cent of those in Gallo (that is to say, French language) areas. Forty years later, literacy rates in the two regions had risen by 33.7 and 40.2 percentage points respectively. Rural Breton-speakers were clearly less under-educated than before, but their disadvantage compared with French-speakers remained and had even increased.[9] Paradoxically, contrary to what happened in other rural regions, this minimal educational integration went hand in hand with greater religious indifference and less political submissiveness to the conservative notables.

9. F. Furet and J. Ozouf (143), vol. 1, pp. 332 and 335.

In general, however, the countryside which had been won over to the new enlightenment of the Republican schools was a bastion of support for the regime. Roger Thabault's classic book on Mazières-en-Gâtine draws an ideal model of this support. The peasants recognised the school as a necessary institution from the moment when all material progress, that is to say the entry of agriculture into the market economy, caused education to be regarded not as an imposed and gratuitous culture but as an instrument of social promotion, whether one remained a peasant or not. The rich peasant France of literacy and advanced schooling realised this as early as the first half of the century. The poor peasant France of the West, South and the mountains gradually came round to the idea as these areas became integrated into the market and the nation, or as the school could become a means for the younger generations to escape the poverty or degradation of their status in the face of the crisis by enabling departure or a change of job.

This development engendered new local or family tensions, or tensions between village groups; between market towns and remote hamlets, for example, where the children had difficulty attending school, and between parents and children. The illiterate father was now dependent on his literate son who could claim a new independence; the daughter could advise her mother; the eldest son had to leave school early to help on the farm while the younger could attend school more regularly. Farmers could dispense with their children's labour more or less easily depending on their level of affluence, a factor which made school attendance variable according to season.

As schooling came to form part of the peasant community's general baggage, its non-possession became an additional social stigma, even a disadvantage, a reversal of the old situation where education was a slightly suspect privilege. 'It became shameful not to be educated', notes Thabault, writing of that period.[10] But school attendance, if pushed too far, also reacted against the peasantry. The most outstanding children then left the peasantry for other trades or the town. The Republican school represented the introduction of both France and the towns into the heart of the village, just at the time when its textbooks were giving an idealised image of unchanging peasant France.[11]

Roads which Led Somewhere — The end of cultural isolation was accompanied by the expansion of the peasants' spatial horizons. The first railways and new roads were still remote indeed from most of the villages let alone from the hamlets. The new lines, on the other hand, aimed to

10. R. Thabault (277), p. 118.
11. R. Ponton (312).

open up the hinterland and feed the main lines by branches much better distributed through the depths of the French countryside. Railways increased from 19,746 kilometres to 26,327 in 1882 and 64,898 in 1910, including 12,000 kilometres of local line.[12]

Concern for economic profitability and natural barriers did of course mean that the design of this secondary network maintained inherited inequalities. For example, the density of the network in relation to area was 3.9 kilometres per 10,000 square metres in the Basse-Alpes, against 9.7 kilometres in the Tarn, 26 kilometres in the Rhône, and a national average of 11.5 kilometres. But in actual fact no *arrondissement* was without a railway-cutting, whereas the railway map of the Second Empire had been limited to the major strategic axes, ignoring almost every mountain range, intermediate hilly area or plain remote from towns. Now, there was always a line that could be joined from a main road or byway and thus lead to the whole country.

Internal migrations were assisted, but it was primarily the sale of produce, arrival of new products from the town, departure for the army and visits from migrant relatives which now became commonplace. Specialisation by agricultural regions was directly connected with this new relationship with the outside world, even if various types of agriculture were only very unevenly affected. The closer link with the rest of the country changed the peasant condition, one of the main features of which had been isolation and withdrawal. Even the family farm of subsistence mixed farming had to take account of the new environment which external communications facilitated. The gradual decline of crafts to the advantage of industrial products actually made at least a minimum of trade using these new means of communication a necessity.

The appearance of real business in the new products of the town especially benefited market towns which were best situated in relation to the exchange network. It did so to the detriment of older, more direct, sales methods such as fairs and peddling. The end of the subsistence crises reduced price fluctuations and product availability through a better adjustment between markets. On the other hand, the peasants faced a crisis of over production (particularly in viticulture) because of the arrival of rival products from overseas or other French vineyards. The new communications therefore created the same ambiguity as the school or the introduction of technical progress. They removed the old problems (climatic uncertainties, ignorance, endless work with mediocre yields), and introduced new ones (loss of cultural identity, the race for profits, heavier expenses, division of labour between land of varying fertility).

This general information must obviously be qualified according to

12. E. Weber (320), p. 300.

region, type of agriculture and agriculturalist, and the prevailing situation and period of the Third Republic. It is probable that the slow rate of change and the continuation of local contrasts stemmed partly from the peasants' perception of the threats that technical progress concealed and its unsuitability for the very small family farm. It has been calculated that only 800,000–900,000 farms, or a quarter of the total, were really integrated into the market.[13] The miscalculations of people who were involved in the market during the crisis period were an incentive to withdrawal on the part of those who had held back. The preference for buying land rather than tools and the persistence of old reflexes in an environment which was not sufficiently changed to make them ineffective were therefore not only the effects of Malthusianism or sheer habit, but a form of semi-rational calculation and choice between controllable and uncontrollable disasters.

News From Elsewhere: The Newspaper, Mail and Army — The peasants now had points of outside comparison as a result of the spread of daily papers and letters from sons in the army or relatives who had left to try their luck elsewhere. All the components of this modernity obviously sustained connections of circular causality. These snowballed to culminate in real political participation in the new Republican arena.

These new connections can be measured by statistics or by more everyday indicators. Postal traffic grew from 9 letters per person in 1869 to 14 in 1880 and 40 in 1914. The French sent 14.5 million francs to each other by postal order in 1881, compared with 789 million francs in 1898.[14] On the other hand, Daniel Halévy notes that the limitations on rural postmen's rounds, particularly on Sundays – which the post office workers had fought for and won before 1914 – deprived peasants of what had become a necessary distraction; the arrival of the newspaper or a letter, or the opportunity to send a postal order.[15]

Popular national dailies or local papers also reached their apogee in these years. A rural department such as the Haute-Savoie had no less than five weekly or pluri-weekly periodicals before 1914: *L'Écho des Alpes* in Annecy, *L'Allobroge* and *Le Mont-Blanc républicain* of Bonneville, *L'Écho du Léman* in Thonon and *Le Progrès de la Haute-Savoie* in Annemasse. They were mainly sold by subscription in the villages. In addition, there were the more committed departmental or regional dailies which came from Lyons or Grenoble and were sold by issue. Consulted in cafes or at home and very local in their scope, these newspapers created

13. R. Price (314), p. 362.
14. E. Weber (320), pp. 319–20.
15. D. Halévy (8), p. 184.

a village public opinion which was involved in both local problems and the political life of the department.[16]

The introduction of universal conscription was also a factor which helped to modify the socialisation of the peasantry. In the first three-quarters of the nineteenth century, military service was resented as an intolerable burden to be avoided and was reserved for the poorest, who were paid to be substitutes. From 1889, when most of the preferential systems disappeared, the peasants shared the same fate as townsmen. For two years they even experienced a quasi-urban life, since garrisons were in market towns and small villages. Despite the harsh discipline of the period, barracks life was the opportunity for a series of learning experiences which would have been impossible in the countryside, including a minimum of hygiene, a more varied diet and a different relationship to time and space.

This break, which corresponded with the end of adolescence, convinced a not inconsiderable number of countrymen to extend military service by permanent exodus; some 100,000 youths did not return to work the land after service.[17] For example at the beginning of the twentieth century, 43 per cent of conscripts from the Lozère region and 13 per cent from the Hérault broke away from their families at this time. Those from the poorer department turned to viticulture, jobs on the railways, low-grade public office and mining. Those from the Hérault aimed higher (the post office, the railway and the gendarmerie headed the list).[18] The national integration aimed at by the army resulted in a partial change in the social aspirations of peasants who had served in the army, all the more so as their way of life was more archaic than that which they had experienced as soldiers.

Power in the Village — The first part of the nineteenth century and even the first half of the Second Empire (the last important subsistence crisis was at the end of the 1850s) were, as has been seen, characterised by the existence of at least two Frances, one largely integrated into the market economy, the other deriving from an extended economic ancien regime. Deliberate or involuntary changes, already mentioned, narrowed the gap. But the most striking phenomenon was that the whole countryside came into the orbit of the predominant towns, and the majority ultimately into that of Paris. Peasants in Aveyron knew the capital, through their expatriate cousins, better than they knew the next prefecture. The Ardèche

16. J. Raymond (315), vol. 2, pp. 857–77.

17. J. Dupâquier (32), p. 266.

18. J. Maurin (306), p. 319. R. Thabault attributes social and political effects to the first law on conscription in 1872 to explain peasant emancipation and the rallying to the Republic (277), p. 118.

and the Savoies lived in as much of a symbiosis with Lyons or Paris as with Privas, Chambéry or Annecy.

Traditionally, the land provided the ruling classes with their means of existence drawn from ground rents. Because of the agricultural crisis this was decreasingly so. The proportion of rural property in every bourgeois or noble inheritance fell, and was replaced by stocks and shares. The countryside and peasants were therefore no longer solely dead land dominated by the town and the bourgeois or the châteaux. What was, or aspired to be, an autonomous rural space took shape, and it was to this space that the Republic, both in its opportunist and then in its radical phase, addressed its message.

Therein lies the full ambiguity of agrarianism. This conservative ideology, in response to modern economic threats, wanted to protect a unanimous society from the liberalism of the towns. But the same ideology was also revived by the Republicans because it ensured the support of the small peasants recently won over to the regime. It is probable that the people concerned did not see the ulterior motives that drove the promotion of this ideological trend, regarding it as a lever to defend agricultural interests at the highest level. The return to protectionism, which also suited many industrial or urban interests, was not only the sacred union of vested interests. It was also in a certain sense the delayed application of the 1849 socialist-democrat ideal of a republic of small independent producers protected by the state. In the long term this was an illusory solution, which led to the forced economic progress of the second half of the twentieth century. But it did show that the interests of the small peasants were taken into account at the highest level and here again contrasted with the unilateral domination by the towns and notables under the earlier regimes.

The Republic permitted the introduction of a real local authority with the election of the mayor, and the establishment of real communications between the village and the department and, further afield, the nation. The deputy became the member elected by one *arrondissement* and was therefore relatively close to the countryside, while the men who sat in the Senate were even more closely connected with landed interests. The political driving force in this relatively decentralised regime worked in both directions since the elector had more means of action than ever before, whereas the administration with its new local branches was no longer a distant entity but an important social factor which dispensed subsidies, compensation, small jobs, various favours and, inevitably, dispensed more to some or the same people. Truly great politicians had to have rural or local roots in order to have smooth and successful careers, even if their tastes and education were very different from those of their electors. There will be more discussion of this in Chapter 6.

At the local level, control of mayoral office was more consistently in the hands of comfortably-off peasants and no longer of notables or mainly urban families as had largely happened in the past. The rise in the level of education, as well as electoral freedom, accounted for this. According to a national enquiry, the proportion of farmer-mayors rose uninterruptedly between 1866 and 1913, from 37 per cent to 46 per cent. If communes with more than 1,000 inhabitants are excluded, in 1913 this percentage varied between 78 per cent for the smallest communes (less than 200 inhabitants) and 44 per cent for the largest (500 to 999 inhabitants).[19]

However, this was an incomplete democracy, where the oldest, most established peasant families, who had a network of connections, wrangled over power from generation to generation. The agricultural difficulties made small farmers and day labourers dependent on large employers or people who had funds available and gave loans to the most deprived, creating an equivalent number of people with an obligation to them. Political contests were therefore no more than struggles for primacy between rival clans in a different guise. In the village of Minot in the Côte-d'Or for example, the two main farming landowners contested the office of mayor. One of them, Villerey, who owned 118 hectares, controlled the small farmers through the money that he had lent them during the period of agricultural difficulties. Although the other, Potey, who had bought the residence of the lord of the manor, had previously been a Republican, he went so far as to defend clerical standpoints, relying on the resentment of his rival's dissatisfied debtors who blamed not only their creditor but the regime for their blighted economic hopes.[20]

B Crisis as a Social Indicator

This period of the Republic's national integration was also a period of economic contrasts. The Republicans' assumption of power coincided with the beginning of a difficult economic situation, whereas the return of prosperity at the end of the century went hand in hand with an exacerbation of political tensions (revival of militant anti-clericalism at the time of the Bloc des Gauches) and social tensions (large-scale peasant movements in 1907 and agricultural workers' strikes).

19. M. Agulhon et al.(31), p. 84. The predominance of peasant mayors was all the greater because this was a region of owner farms and small landownership; for example in Haute-Savoie, there were 516 farmer-mayors as early as 1881 against 58 non-farmers (J. Raymond (315), p. 717).

20. M.-C. Pingaud (311), pp. 191–206.

a Readjustment to the Crisis

France, like every European country, was hit by the great agricultural depression at the end of the nineteenth century. The fall in prices which ensued and the natural disasters which accompanied it (silk-worm disease, mildew, phylloxera, etc.) engendered deep-seated unrest which nevertheless culminated neither in violent revolt nor in as strongly marked a social change as in neighbouring countries; there was no massive wave of emigration as in Germany, no accelerated urbanisation, no final triumph of exclusively capitalist agriculture as in England.

According to retrospective assessments, the gross physical product of agriculture stagnated in the two decades between 1875 and 1894. In the following decade (1895–1904 compared with 1885–1894), a slow recovery appeared (an increase of 0.8 per cent, whereas industrial growth was 2 per cent), which was confirmed on the eve of the war (with growth of 1 per cent). This stagnation in terms of production was particularly serious because it was accompanied by a fall in prices; there was a decrease of 34 per cent in the price of a quintal of corn between 1875 and 1896–1900, and similar decreases of 26 per cent for rye, 19 per cent for barley and 30 per cent for potatoes. Livestock prices were less affected, which impelled some farmers in western regions to change over to stock-raising. Overall, net agricultural product expressed in money terms fell by 10 per cent.

Net revenue is harder to assess, as the idea of agricultural accountancy only existed in the somewhat rare large farms. Only indirect assessments are therefore available on the basis of regional examples, and it is always difficult to generalise from these in view of the diversity of French agricultural and geographical structure. The deterioration in terms of exchange between agriculture and industry (which Maurice Lévy-Leboyer places at between 5 per cent and 10 per cent from 1880 to 1895) affected costs to a greater or lesser degree depending on the extent to which advanced techniques were in use. In the Loir-et-Cher, real profit was reduced by 21 per cent for the farming landowner and 29 per cent for the tenant farmer. In the Calvados, non-farming landowners saw real income from their land tumble nearly 30 per cent between 1883 and 1905, which impelled many of them to sell. The decline was less for cereal-growing farming landowners; they lost 19.6 per cent of their income between 1879 and 1893 but recovered 16.6 per cent between 1893 and 1905. On the other hand, tenant farmers, whose situation deteriorated earlier (income fell by 64.2 per cent between 1862 and 1888), recovered and went much further ahead at the end of the century (an increase of 230 per cent).

Hardest hit by the crisis were small farmers who were more dependent on the sale of corn to obtain money and who saw the disappearance at the same time of the supplementary artisanal industrial activities which they or their families carried out. In addition, they were often burdened by debts incurred when they extended their property in the period of prosperity and found it increasingly hard to honour their commitments when their products sold less well. The French mortgage debt was assessed at about ten milliards in 1900. In the Pas-de-Calais for example, there was a proliferation of repossessions, principally amongst farmers and *ménagers*, or small farmers who had to do additional work for other people.[21]

In viticulture, the agricultural crisis had a chronology and character all of its own. Viticultural production reached its apogee in 1875, with a record harvest from at least 500 hectares of vines in 72 departments out of 87. Requiring a great deal of work but giving high profitability from a small area, viticulture was the most frequent form of agricultural speculation in the zones of rural democracy by small farmers. Its development was therefore electorally sensitive, particularly as the Republic took root early in the Midi, and as the State drew a sixth of its income from viticulture through indirect taxation. It was the realm of big interests in high-quality vineyards, which were major exporters, and also in the mass vineyards of the Languedoc which were very dependent on traders and the national market.

The crisis caused by the spread of phylloxera therefore took on the appearance of a national disaster, but its resolution by action at every level permanently transformed viticultural society. Phylloxera spread slowly but inexorably throughout the period. It appeared in the Gard in about 1863 and reached lower Languedoc and Provence later in the 1860s. Vineyards further north and further west were still prosperous during this period, and even profited from their rivals' misfortune. But by the time the early victims had found the remedy in flooding or replanting, the disease was affecting the others in their turn (the Bordelais, Charentes and Beaujolais were hit by phylloxera in the 1870s, the province of Burgundy and the Loire valley in the 1880s and in the East in the 1890s), which increased the prosperity of the first group.

The radical solution of replanting was only adopted slowly because the small vine-growers lacked the means to survive without returns for several years. They therefore delayed the moment by using chemical products of varying degrees of efficacy, or they abandoned the land or changed specialisation. Despite the financial blow it dealt to viticulture, phylloxera, by making it necessary to rationalise cultivation or to move

21. P. Barral in F. Braudel and E. Labrousse (24), vol. 4/1, pp. 364–73; G. Dupeux (241), pp. 492 ff; G. Désert (63), pp. 992–1015; R. Hubscher (84), pp. 583–8.

some vines, was even beneficial in the long term from the point of view of economic productivity though not from that of social equilibrium. The Languedoc, first to be affected and first cured, increased its lead in total production and became a region of fully capitalist viticulture. The marginal vineyards or the weakest farmers, on the other hand, were wiped off the map. In the Loir-et-Cher for example, the number of vine-growers fell by a quarter between 1871 and 1914. In Charente and Charente-Inférieure, the area planted with vines fell from 265,000 to 60,000 hectares in fourteen years (1875–1889). In the Toulouse region and in the vineyards north of the Loire, half of the area under vines was destroyed; in the Haute-Garonne, the drop was from 66,000 hectares in 1879 to 30,000 in 1900. In the Beaujolais, the vineyards were only maintained for the better crus because the yield from one hectare under vines was the same as that of a century earlier, whereas expenses had quadrupled. The new vines, more widely-spaced and treated with fertiliser and chemical products, required more equipment, implying local mutual help. Some people therefore, preferred to return to mixed farming.[22]

b Social Effects of the Crisis

The crisis in cereals also had contradictory effects. After the difficult years, it impelled the most venturesome farmers to change over to more remunerative crops or to diversify. In the Toulouse Midi, small peasants were little affected by the fall in corn prices because they sold little. Their condition actually improved; they could supplement their income by working on other people's land at a higher price because the rural exodus caused agricultural wages to rise. The small rural bourgeois, with a diminished income, had to seek means of complementing his income in the town, in public service for example, and to lease or sell his land.

The small peasant landowner also did better, to the detriment of the sharecroppers of absentee landowners who invested elsewhere or changed their method of administration. The small farmer abandoned hitherto remunerative cereal cultivation for mixed farming, combining stock-raising, cereals and specialised crops in order to spread the risk over several products. The economic and social balance of the region was transformed: 'The class of corn barons was replaced by the class of small peasant landowners' (Roger Brunet).[23]

In a period of declining agricultural returns, economising on labour is one solution to the crisis. In the large farms of the Paris basin, increased

22. G. Dupeux (241), p. 501; M. Lachiver (87), pp. 449–58; R. Brunet (291), p. 406; G. Garrier (70), pp. 433–2.
23. R. Brunet (291), pp. 403–11.

mechanisation was directly linked to this policy. Half the mechanical harvesters in France were concentrated in the twenty departments situated around Paris. For example, Ephraïm Grenadou's father, who farmed 25 hectares in the Beauce, bought his first mechanical harvester-binder shortly before the 1914 war and thereby saved on four workers' jobs.[24] The fragmentation of the land in other regions caused increased recourse to family labour at the expense of outside jobs.

In regions of demographic decline or those least favourable to cereals, the solution consisted of putting large areas under grass. This was a further incentive for day labourers and domestic servants, who were finding fewer job opportunities, to join the exodus. In Normandy in particular the crisis accelerated the final predominance of the more remunerative specialisation in pasturage. For the same reasons, milk and cheese production expanded in moderately hilly areas. But in order to succeed, these ventures implied that the peasants had to combine to form 'cooperatives', which centralised cheese production. In Haute-Savoie, nearly every commune had one; there were 207 in 1872, 310 in 1890 and 420 in 1911, or more than one cooperative per commune. National approval for these cooperatives was obtained after the 1889 World Exhibition, where Emmental from the Savoie was offered on the Paris market. This gave the Savoie village a new centre of collective life, which was linked with a mutual aid or agricultural credit society. In this case, the decline in mixed farming in favour of specialisation did not demand inaccessible technical modernisation but a form of cooperation which protected the interests of the small peasants, where once the individualism of small owner-farmers had been predominant. The success of the milk and butter cooperatives in the Charentes and Poitou were a reflection of the same mental evolution; in 1899, 96 societies were listed with a total of 47,120 members managing a herd of 112,948 cows. They were federated in 1893.[25]

c The Response to the Crisis: Unionism and Agrarianism

More generally, the principal innovation which changed the overall situation of the peasantry beyond these local social developments was its organisation into pressure groups at a national level, or into self-help groups at a local level, through the rise of agricultural unionism after the Waldeck-Rousseau law was passed in 1884. This unionism was profoundly ambiguous since it was led from the top by the large landowners. Their aim was to use the small farmers to put pressure on

24. R. Price (314), p. 387; E. Grenadou and A. Prévost (6), p. 40.
25. J. Raymond (315), vol. 1, pp. 220–31; P. Barral (286), p. 123.

the government to further their own interests and, beyond that, to use the organisations as a force to win the countryside back to conservatism in the name of a paternalist and Catholic conception of class unity. The first policy was fully successful since the Republican leaders, some of whom were also landowners, rallied to the cause of a return to protectionism as a means of saving agricultural income from land during the fall in prices. The second hung fire, except in places where the notables were already in a strong position, because the republicans in their turn based their own national organisation on the same agricultural unanimist ideology but with a contrary political orientation.

This resulted in the paradox of two inter-class federations of unions: the *Société des agriculteurs de France*, founded in 1868, which in 1886 took the name of *Union centrale des syndicats agricoles de France*, the conservative 'rue d'Athènes'; and the *Société nationale d'encouragement à l'agriculture*, launched by Gambetta, the republican 'boulevard Saint-Germain'. What divided them was not the agricultural policy to be followed, but the non-agricultural reasons for the policy. Their combined membership rose to some 600,000 in 1896 and to over 900,000 in 1911 which, even taking the formal nature of basic membership into account, made it the first real modern pressure group with political and economic influence far above the employers' or industrial workers' unions.[26] The innumerable functions of these unions and the multiplicity of interests they represented made them comparable with a modern version of a corporation.

The best use of the resources of this unionism was made by those vine-growers confronted with the gravest crisis. The landowners, often of conservative and Catholic bent, were behind the origin of the first 'union shops', charged with pooling purchases to replenish the vines. The largest associations emerged from this process, for example, the *Union du Sud-Est des syndicats agricoles*, founded in 1888, 'the first union in France' (with 125,000 members in 1911 in ten departments). It combined a defence and provisioning function with a role as a mutual insurance company (providing insurance, pensions and credit), indispensable to surviving difficult years, as well as with a training function at a local level. The inclination among the various groups of peasants to join can be seen from the distribution of union members; 12.7 per cent were land *rentiers*, 58.84 per cent were farming landowners and 28.4 per cent were workers and vine-growers working on other people's land or cultivating vines on the basis of *vigneronnage*, a variation on sharecropping in local viticulture.

In the Var, the traditions of Provence made the communal scene the

26. P. Barral (286), p. 341.

predominant focal point of the unions. Their main expansion occurred at the beginning of the twentieth century in response to the crisis caused by the slump in sales which followed the replenishment of the vineyards. Their membership rose from 1,280 in 1890 to 11,000 in 1913 (about 30 per cent of all farming landowners), but only a minority belonged to larger groups. Political schisms created rival organisations right down to the village level, while the social composition was equally diverse; a fifth of non-agriculturalists (minor officials, small traders) stood alongside small farmers (less than 5 hectares) whereas the leaders were landowners, minor notables or teachers of agriculture, depending on the organisation's political slant.

In a region of high education such as the Beauce, the moving force behind the republican-orientated *Syndicat de Chartres* was the modernist faction of the tenant farmers or comfortably-off farmers who wanted to convert more humble farmers to agricultural progress and urban enlightenment. Their activity succeeded through close connections with republican elected members and officials and through the manifold services they rendered; these included agricultural credit, popularisation by bulletins and lectures, and the presentation of a united front to dealers to bring down prices.[27]

The crisis therefore obliged farmers to emerge from their traditional passivity under the leadership of old or new notables. The tendency for peasants to organise into separate groups, equipped with all their own institutions, continued when prosperity returned. Particularly after 1900, farmers could have access to agricultural credit, mutual insurance companies, even to some forms of pension fund, as a result of legislation brought in by the republicans. These institutions did in some ways accentuate the integration of agriculture into the modern urban world, but they also underlined its irreducible uniqueness and its formulation of a social model of its own. The end of the nineteenth and the beginning of the twentieth century in particular were disturbed by diverse types of large agricultural movements. Some were in accordance with the Marxist analyses of the socialists of the day; others, clearly functioning more as an agency of mobilisation, marked the triumph of agrarianism as a basis for protest. Contemporaries interpreted these conflicts as new Jacqueries, the first since the mid-century rural movements, but they were born in the regions most integrated into the capitalist economy or most open to revolutionary political culture.

27. G. Garrier (297), p. 31; R. Leveau (304), pp. 61–78; P. Goujon (298), p. 15; Y. Rinaudo (316) and (317).

d The Agricultural Proletariat's Intermittent Class Struggles

The paradoxes of the situation and the social attitudes of the agricultural wage-earners were a part of the problems contained in the socialist vision of peasant society. They were authentic proletarians, exceptionally underpaid and exploited and poorly housed; theorists saw in them the possible seed of a class struggle, which would lure the small farmers into breaking their solidarity with the large farmers or landowners on whom they depended for their survival through the permanent or temporary work that these latter provided. Agrarian ideology on the other hand claimed to protect the peasantry from these noxious germs of class struggle and socialism by uniting landowners and wage-earners with common interests against the town. The rare but intense episodes of class struggle inspired by the agricultural proletariat therefore made the challenge they represented to landowners all the more intolerable.

However, some aspects of the objective situation at the time favoured those nourishing the first vision. The demographic weight of day labourers and agricultural domestic servants was not negligible; there were more than 1.2 million day labourers and more than 1.8 million servants, or 22 per cent of all wage-earners, in 1892. The weaknesses in this vision are just as obvious. These do not prove that agrarianism was right, but they do account for the inability of wage-earners in the fields to shuffle off their dependent relationship. Almost half the day labourers were also landowners, and were therefore tied to the land or living in hopes of moving up into the category of independent farmers by dint of saving and enduring hardship.

If these labourers were distributed equally over all the farms in the country, an average of less than one per farm would emerge. This obviously conceals the fact that there were concentrations of labourers at some points (the Paris basin, wooded mountains and viticultural Languedoc) and other areas with no, or only temporary, wage-earners. They were a younger than average population since for some their status represented an apprenticeship period before setting up, or going into a partnership, in a farm of their own. They were more illiterate (because they were sent out to work at a younger age). Their numbers also consisted partly of women – over a quarter of domestic servants were farm servants – or of people of foreign origin; as early as 1891, 3 per cent of the agricultural workers of the Brie were foreigners. The rural exodus, which primarily affected wage-earners, obliged the landowners to bring over a less demanding workforce from Spain, Italy, or Belgium. Their overall power to strike was ten times less than their demographic size and very uneven in time and space.

The movements were therefore very localised, very intermittent, and organised poorly or from the outside. They constituted mainly a response to an offensive coming from landowners who cut wages rather than a primary and positive initiative. Other, more individual, solutions were faced with a costly struggle because of the shortage of financial reserves and was often sabotaged by other unemployed or more wretched day labourers ready to take the strikers' places. Rather than try to obtain higher wages by striking, it was better to go and look for better-paid work elsewhere, outside agriculture. This was the thinking of 1.6 million agricultural wage-earners who left the countryside between 1862 and 1892. Moreover, this trend was of indirect benefit to the least venturesome; there was a clear upward trend in wages despite the depression. In Seine-et-Marne for example, the purchasing power of wage-earners, who received neither their food nor housing, rose from an index of 47 in 1852 (510 francs a year) to 69 in 1892 and 100 in 1914 (1,170 francs a year).[28]

The first large-scale action came from woodcutters in the Cher in November 1891, in response to an attempt by the wood merchants of the Meillant forest to lower wages because of the sales crisis in their industry. Republicans hostile to the reactionary wood merchants supported the strikers at first, but the woodcutters soon encountered repression by the administration when their actions took too much of a socialist or organised turn (including violent pressure on strike-breakers). Despite phases of demobilisation, this was the only group of agricultural workers to succeed in founding a lasting organisation, distributed over six departments and sometimes forcing its employers to observe hiring conditions.[29]

Paradoxically, the vineyard workers of the Languedoc, the other group of day labourers which initiated large-scale conflicts, were much less successful in winning autonomy or powers of collective bargaining, although they operated in conditions much more propitious to mobilising their forces; the region was strongly urbanised and open to the outside world, the vineyard workers lived in grouped villages and the product concerned was entirely dependent on market forces. A strike did not break out in Languedoc until 1903, after the foundation of the *Fédération générale des travailleurs agricoles*, in response to a wage cut of 50 per cent in three years imposed by the employers to cope with the slump in the wine trade. From November 1903 to October 1904, 46 strikes broke out in the Hérault. They generally ended successfully. But here too the action ran out of steam because the government increasingly acted on behalf of the landowners, and when overproduction and slump recurred

28. P. Gratton (299), p. 62; P. Barral (286), p. 29; P. Bernard (288), p. 79.
29. C. Pennetier (310), pp. 41–56; P. Gratton (300).

the landowners withdrew what they had conceded. They called in foreign manpower or counted on the convergence of interests with small landowners who were partially day labourers and needed the supplementary income derived from working for someone else.

The same intrinsic weakness marked the strikes by day labourers in Seine-et-Marne in April 1906 and June 1907. All in all therefore, although unionism was in existence among agricultural workers in the Belle Époque (20,000 woodcutters and 15,000 viticultural workers belonged to unions in 1904–1905), it remained very marginal and did not represent a promising plan for the target group, let alone for the small peasants who viewed their status as one to be shed, or only accepted temporarily.

e Agrarian Unanimism: The 1907 Vineyard Workers Movement

Peasant society therefore did not completely escape the class struggle, but it did not become the regular expedient in conflicts that it did in labour circles, because the categories capable of taking up the struggle were constantly declining or defenceless in the face of much more powerful adversaries. On the contrary, as the 1907 movement shows, they were carried along by the agrarian wave when it managed to recreate the old town/country antagonism within commercial agriculture.

The strength of the 1907 movement in Languedoc has nourished several myths to which historians have done justice against the pious remembrance of legend. There is, for example, the myth that this was a purely popular movement, whereas in fact all classes participated. There is also the myth that it was an *avant la lettre* 'Occitan' regional movement struggling against Parisian hegemony, whereas demand for governmental and parliamentary arbitration was a permanent factor.[30]

Faced with the crisis of overproduction, not only the small farmers and the rural petty bourgeoisie but also the big landowners and the agricultural workers, and sometimes the socialist militants, joined forces on the strength of a misleading catch-phrase (the struggle against fraud), containing all the ambiguities of unanimist movements. The trader was attacked as the symbol of parasitical capitalism, of the middle-man linked to the interests of the North (the sweetening of wines was favourable to beetroot production), of money as opposed to labour, of the artificial and adulterated against authentic nature, and of the 'fat cats' confronting the '*gueux*', a nickname adopted by the Languedoc rebels. This battle order was not specifically agrarian, since it had nourished some of the battles of the French Revolution, from the taking of the Bastille to the cry of 'Hang the hoarders!'. This old scenario also made use of the most recent

30. See the resumé by G. Cholvy (292), J. Sagnes (461), and M. Lachiver (87).

democratic methods such as organisation, mass meetings, appeals to public opinion and Parliament and reliance on the municipalities and their mass resignations.

Paradox pervades this movement; despite its mass and pacific character (80,000 demonstrators in Narbonne on May 5, 600,000 on June 9), it began to take a dramatic turn thanks to the government's brutality and to collapse as fast as it had blown up, partly because of the inexperience of its extempore leader, the cafe-owner and vine-grower Marcellin Albert. He is reminiscent of the avatars of Boulangism who concealed the same catch-all ambiguity, or of the middle-class movements of the inter-war period. The peasantry partly succeeded in adapting itself to all the challenges of a difficult economic situation, providing it relied on the State, and submitted to market forces or, on the contrary, protected itself from them. By challenging the first and denying the second, which is what the vine-growers of the Languedoc Midi were doing, they risked suffering the fate of the people of Paris at the time of the Commune. They were digging their own grave by cutting themselves off from the rest of the country, the ultimate trap of agrarianism taken to its logical conclusion.

C Rural France and Peasant Societies

The mid-century agricultural crisis had opened out into a serious social and political crisis and the development of a wide-scale social confrontation. As has just been seen, the overall social effects of the end-of-century crisis were limited, even if the crisis permanently changed the peasants' image of themselves and of their relationships with society as a whole. This limitation stemmed from the specific features of that crisis and the fact that the republican State made partial attempts to meet it. But it also resulted from structural disparities between the various types of peasant society co-existing in the French countryside. It is patently impossible to draw an overall picture of peasant France, showing all the nuances. The best t. it can be offered are examples drawn from areas dispersed over the land surface and representing contrasting types, from the most old-fashioned to the most modern, from the most to the least egalitarian.

One common feature does however emerge, which illustrates the thesis of this chapter. Despite the tensions and inequalities, each sub-group, because of its individual structural characteristics, cannot be integrated into a pattern of general social confrontation, since the purely peasant components in internal solidarity remained stronger than the links with the corresponding urban components. Like the early American workers, French peasants who could not tolerate their subordinate situation always had the solution of blending into general society by abandoning the rural way of life. The manner in which this way of life evolved must first be described.

a Overall Improvement in Way of Life

Almost every category of society had benefited from the prosperity of the Second Empire. The end-of-century difficulties and then the advances of the Belle Époque increased variations in ways of life between people who succeeded in surviving or reaping advantages from the challenges of the market, those who tried to isolate themselves from the modern world, and those who flocked to the town or tried their luck there. Endemic pauperism tended to disappear, as is shown by the disappearance of the category of professional, officially recorded, beggars from the lists of inhabitants in the poorest regions such as in Brittany or south of the Massif Central. Not that there were no longer any vagabonds; but what was regarded as normal in a poor economy became aberrant at the end of the century, the sign of a refusal to integrate socially or the effect of permanent disability.[31]

However, quantitative assessments are always unreliable when they concern a situation where a way of life which is partially integrated into the market co-exists with one which is partially self-sufficient. An optimistic or pessimistic picture of the peasants' lot emerges, depending on the choice of examples, the bias of the sources or the sample year (whether it is a year of crisis or prosperity). In short, every indicator can be turned around. The growth of wealth revealed by declarations of inheritance do in fact reflect the elimination of the poorest peasants, who had left the land or changed jobs, and were therefore not counted.

Differences in levels of fortune bequeathed remained large. In the Calvados, for example, the median fortune in about 1895 was calculated at 800 francs for day labourers, 6,619 francs for farmers (eight times higher) and 11,855 francs for *rentier* landowners (less than double that of farmers). In this region of rich agriculture, the farmer formed the foundations of a new middle class which could hope to become *rentiers* of the land, while the proletariat of the fields, whose mode of life, culture and work still resembled that of the farmers' had practically no chance of crossing the property barrier.

The differences in level were smaller when there was a predominance

31. See the comments by Antoine Silvère in Toinou (18) on peasant victims of accidents or incurable disease, obliged to live on charity; in the first three-quarters of the nineteenth century, there was an over-lap between begging, temporary migration from the mountains to the plains and delinquent gangs.

of small farmers cultivating their own land. In the commune of Passy in Haute-Savoie in about 1890, the 450 farmers who cultivated 1,000 hectares of land – an average of slightly more than 2 hectares per farm – consumed three-quarters of their own wheat production, sold half of their cider and, above all, their output of dairy products. They shared 670,000 francs of gross commercial production which yielded an income of 1,500 francs a year. With some secondary income, this amounted to double the wage of a provincial labourer (900 francs a year). But this average conceals an actual disparity, half the peasants only had the equivalent of the labourer's wages, while the other half had two or three times more. In various other communes in the same department, peasant incomes ranged from 600 francs in Abondance, to 1,400 francs for the mayor of Saint-Gervais and even 5,000 francs for the richest peasant in Thorens. An agricultural wage-earner in the same department could hope to earn 420 francs a year. Here, the notion of the rural democracy of the little man came closer to the objective economic situation.[32]

The way in which income was used also changed. Subsistence farming was probably still predominant in reality, but external purchases by the new-rich minority introduced the innovations of the urban way of life. People gave their flour to the baker who baked the bread, whereas they had formerly been satisfied with a few oven-loads made on the farm and poor-quality stale bread. The decline in poor cereals, or in chestnuts in the mountains, together with the fall in wheat prices enabled more peasants to gain access to white bread, hitherto reserved for sale or for the well-to-do. The prominence of livestock-raising made increased meat consumption possible, although it was still less than in the town. In 1882, Parisians on an average ate nearly four times more meat than countryfolk (79.3 kilograms against 21.9 kilograms); the Bretons ate half the rural average (10 kilograms a head).[33]

The consumption of ordinary wine, facilitated by liberal republican legislation, the proliferation of village taverns and the fall in prices replaced the sporadic drunkenness associated with major occasions (fair days, feast days and social rites) by chronic alcoholism. This was the time when the Breton departments began to break consumption records in this respect.[34] In country areas nearest to towns, new foods were eaten or became a sign of distinction. It seemed normal after 1880 to serve milk, eggs, cheese, sugar and coffee to the most deprived members of society in the shelters and poor-houses in the Limousin. In about 1900, a poor

32. G. Désert (63), p. 1163; J. Raymond (315), p. 771.
33. E. Weber (320), p. 212.
34. T. Fillaut (295) and (296). R. Hubscher notes the same phenomenon in the Pas-de-Calais (84), p. 784.

peasant woman in the Ambert region in the Puy-de-Dôme dreamed of buying these last two items: 'It is good! But it is so dear!' she said.[35] The poorest peasants felt the need for these new products which had come from outside before they were able to satisfy it.

Better connections with market towns and the diversification of the commercial apparatus brought the most refined urban products within the reach of more affluent peasants, such as un-traditional industrially-produced clothing, for example, as sewing-machines made it possible to imitate urban styles. The rise in the standard of living of one section of the peasantry was also reflected in external signs of wealth hitherto reserved to the ruling class, including the replacement of thatched roofs by tiles or slate, more rooms in houses, a greater variety of furniture, or the purchase of personal, non-utilitarian, means of transport (horse-drawn charabancs in Brittany, bicycles in north-east France). It was not so much the value of the objects, which varied greatly, but their resemblance to urban models which mattered. The inventories of ten peasant families in Saint-Jean-Trolimon in the Sud-Finistère, between 1871 and 1911 show that furniture represented betweeen 6.5 per cent and 14.4 per cent of assets at death, whereas the gap between the value of the highest and lowest assets was much larger. Affluence was indicated more by the replacement of the kneading trough, a table-cupboard which was also used to knead bread, by the more comfortable flat table. Dressers and sideboards also became more common; grandfather clocks, rare objects in the middle of the century, were found even amongst the poor in 1900.[36]

On the other hand, what is today understood as comfort remained on the threshold, or far removed, from peasant homes. Diseases connected with food deficiencies or the quality of the drinking water remained an important cause of death in the countryside. The communes in the Var, however, increased water supplies (with cast iron-pipes) in order to put up a town fountain, ceremonially inaugurated. Medical conditions also improved as a result of better compliance with vaccination requirements and the imposition of municipal regulations to combat traditional carelessness with regard to waste and drainage of dirty water.[37] There was however barely any increase in the ratio of doctors; the abolition of the *officiers de santé* (non-graduate doctors) by the 1892 law actually reduced

35. A. Corbin (236), vol. 1, pp. 72–4, and A. Silvère (18), p. 139.

36. M. Segalen (319), pp. 271–3. The same basic elements can be seen in the Baudoins' poor farm in the Ambert region described by Toinou (18), p. 137); at the home of the parents of the latter, the wardrobe and the bed were the starting-point of the household, brought as dowry by the wife (p. 5).

37. Y. Rinaudo (316), pp. 222–6. This obviously presupposes grouped habitation and a civic spirit, which strengthened regional differences, the republican Var being a favourable example compared with the archaic blockage in the Centre and the West.

the numbers of medical staff in poor regions where they had been mainly found.

The classic indices record the signs of improved standards of living *a posteriori* with a decrease in the number of conscripts discharged for being too short or malformed and change in causes of death; but the improvement was limited and modest, with very strong regional differences depending on the type of peasant society. There was in fact a strong hysteresis of the inherited structures which determined acceptance or non-acceptance of the end-of-century crises as well as adaptation or non-adaptation, and a more or a less favourable response to them. The development of peasant societies was affected by the systems of bequeathing possessions (egalitarian or non-egalitarian), demographic behaviour (Malthusian or traditionally prolific), openness to the outside world (with large or small-scale migrations), professional qualifications (the length and extent of literacy, connections with the towns) and the importance of religion or, on the contrary, the extent of de-Christianisation. Two examples, described as 'archaic' from a current standpoint, have been selected to illustrate the combination of all these factors; the south of Brittany and the south of the Massif Central. These two regions are similar in some basic respects but differ in their customs of bequeathing land. One modern example has also been chosen on the same economic and cultural criteria: the great plains of the Paris basin.

b Antiquated Egalitarianism: Brittany

In western Brittany there was an egalitarian system of bequeathing possessions which had no particularly unfortunate consequences before the end of the nineteenth century. Landed property was handed down by the system of domains held under tenancy at will, which distinguished two different types of ownership. Ownership of the land primarily fell to nobles or bourgeois; the *domaniers* only owned 'reparative rights', farm buildings, hedges, bushes and improvements that they had added to the land. At the end of the lease, the *domanier* could be dismissed upon payment of reimbursement for the reparative rights. On the other hand, the *domanier* could sub-let his reparative rights and take advantage of the demographic pressure to exploit the poorer members of society.

This complex system was very unfavourable to the farmer. It involved insecurity, which could be reduced by advance payment of an 'ex gratia allowance' to the landowner, dependence (reparative rights were regarded as personal property and could be sold by the landowner in the event of non-payment of rent) and economic uncertainty. The owner could set the price of the land as well as the rent, given the demographic imbalance between supply and demand for land, whereas any surplus cleared was primarily used to make additional payments, pay dowries or buy out the shares of brothers and sisters, conditions required by the egalitarian system. Inherited capital did not cease to melt away, even in the case of families who were privileged at the beginning of the nineteenth century, because of the persistence of old-style demography.

A series of counter-tactics were employed to combat the overpopulation which the slow fall in the death rate threatened. One of these was the 'chaining up of marriages', that is to say, preferential marriage between families having two pairs of ancestors in common, which permitted plurality of reparative rights. The poorest individuals resorted to multiple activities (fishing, crafts, working in the canneries or temporary migration). They developed abandoned or communal lands by the sea shore (*palues*), which were still extensive in the first half of the century, and pooled resources with other farmers in order to have enough horses to draw the more modern ploughs. At the end of the century, they practised the demanding cultivation of green peas, which the canneries required during the dead season for fishing. But failing the rapid spread of contraceptive practices, as in southern regions (the Church's hold as well as cultural backwardness remained strong), the maintenance of a high fertility level and the sale of land by absentee landowners who were turning towards more profitable investment, brought in their train accelerated fragmentation of farms and the impoverishment of even middle-rank peasants.[38] Depending on the date at which this process reached its critical point, the various regions of Brittany saw their traditional, long-standing peasant society succumb in its turn to rural exodus.

c The South of the Massif Central: Unegalitarian and Antiquated

Technical and agrarian conditions were just as unfavourable in departments south of the Massif Central, a region characterised by poor mountain agriculture based on stock-raising and secondary cereals, low yields, unequal distribution of land and a high proportion of non-peasant ownership, the maintenance of common rights to enable the poorest families to survive, latent overpopulation which made temporary and, more and more frequently, permanent migrations necessary. However, the structure of peasant society was very different because possessions continued to be bequeathed to children unequally, despite the Civil Code. The eldest was chosen to maintain the 'house', the *ousta* in local language, as it stood. In the best cases, those who did not inherit received a bequest and could then marry and set up in their own right on a vacant

38. M. Segalen (319), and G. Augustins (285).

farm or on their spouse's parents' farm, forming an enlarged family.

This favourable fate was limited to children of comfortably-off peasants. For the majority of peasants, the endowments given were insufficient or even non-existent, which condemned a large number to remain unmarried and to find work either outside the village community or on the land of more privileged elder children. This resulted in a proliferation of family tensions and frustration. The high rate of religious careers was a consequence of the strong hold of traditional clericalism (the region is a 'Vendée of the South') since the rejection of the Revolution, but it was also a mechanism for absorbing out-of-work bachelors. Parish priests watched all the more closely over the maintenance of moral order in that the ordinary social order gave birth to a whole range of deviant sexual behaviour in response to sexual frustration; late marriage and large numbers of single people explain in particular the high rate of pre-marital conceptions or abuse by masters of servant girls who were disinherited younger daughters.

This society, close to the traditional model dear to Le Play's heart, was challenged by its exposure to the outside world earlier than the Sud-Finistère. By about 1880, cohabitation between generations was tending to disappear in the Aveyron, while demographic pressure following the fall in the death rate was an incentive to apply less inegalitarian rules (such as the emergence of part-bequests). Younger sons began to claim their rights instead of submitting as hitherto. The arrival of the railway, the forced secularisation of schools, the introduction of officials from the interior of France and the Republic's use of patronage to benefit its supporters also destabilised old relationships of dependence or domination. Emigration on an increasingly vast scale was making it possible for people leaving the region to build up savings in Paris, which were sometimes reinvested locally. The hierarchies of the old *oustas* were overturned. Poor peasants, who had emigrated and made money in Paris, could take the place of the old ruined families who formerly dominated the countryside. Archaism thus depended on modernity, with innovations from outside serving to maintain or restore peasant society by bringing in new capital and subsidies from the central power in the form, for example, of retirement pensions or officials' salaries.[39]

d Unegalitarian Modernity: The Paris Basin and the Pas-de-Calais

As has been seen, the regions most integrated into commercial agriculture

39. P.M. Jones (302), ch. 9; E. Claverie and P. Lamaison (293); Y. Pourcher (108); F. Raison-Jourde (109), p. 183 and ch. 5; J. Merley (153).

were hardest hit by the crisis. Here, visible peasant society, village society was distinct from actual society. Small landowners, small tenant farmers, a few larger farmers whose farms were often in hamlets, and a decreasing number of landless day labourers and domestic servants all co-habited the regions of grouped habitations in the Paris basin and the Nord-Pas-de-Calais. Particularly in the Paris basin, large landowners most frequently lived at a distance from their lands mainly in Paris. Breaking a tidy pattern, there was not necessarily a correlation between rate of profitability and size of farm, with large farms having increasingly heavy labour costs due to the decreasing number of agricultural workers and the early fall in the birth rate in these regions. Describing peasant society in the Beauce at the beginning of the century, Grenadou recalls big farmers, in particular, the largest landowner in the country, the marquis de Roussy de Sales, owner of 200 hectares going bankrupt. Some landless peasants benefited from this by borrowing in order to lease or buy land; the grandson of a shepherd and the son of a carter who became a landowner, Grenadou managed to raise himself into the ranks of the big farmers.

As opposed to these small surviving or reconstituted properties, the peak was formed of large farms where military discipline prevailed. Agricultural wage-earners were hired by verbal contract twice a year at *louées*, a sort of human fair. An internal hierarchy, based on length of settlement and specialities, existed within this proletariat. Large tenant farmers held the real economic and social power since the noble and bourgeois landowners lived in the town and hardly had the choice of finding buyers who possessed large operating capital.[40] The farmers had possessed power locally since the Second Empire or even before. The same families monopolised municipal mandates and acted as representatives of the humbler peasants, forming what has been called a "farmocracy",[41] strengthened by the expansion of agricultural unionism, as has been seen.

Despite this strongly-marked economic hierarchy, peasant society in these regions had some degree of fluidity. According to Ronald Hubscher, there were more rises than falls in the social hierarchy in the Pas-de-Calais, with real proletarianisation being expressed in the scale of departures. This homogenised the internal structure, while the local agricultural proletariat was too weak or too dependent to pose a genuine challenge. The climate of social relationships in this type of agricultural society, which was compartmentalised but without strong tensions, is

40. E. Grenadou (6), pp. 24 and 49–51; P. Bernard (288), pp. 172–9.
41. J.-P. Jessenne (147). From the Second Empire, top-rank tenant farmers were invited to receptions at the prefecture of Seine-et-Marne (P. Bernard (288), p. 73).

summed up by Grenadou: 'Everyone was poor. Everyone was friends. There were a few semi-rich who lived amongst us and did not have much to do with us. They went first class. Their daughters did not come to the ball. And then there were the real rich, they lived in another world. We, the poor, lived amongst ourselves'.[42]

e Conclusion

Pierre Bourdieu has defined the peasantry as a 'subject class', that is to say, a pawn in the play of external political and ideological manipulations by the real holders of the capacity to rule.[43] Some of the developments described in this chapter suggest that this definition is correct; they include agrarian ideology, the structure of agricultural syndicalism, the dependence when faced with the market and the new type of crises and the ambiguous eulogy of return to the land and the small farm by the republicans, frightened by the rise of the labour movement. But other features established under the Republic contradict this definition and prove that the peasants could also be the subjects of their own history and benefit from the new areas opened up by political liberalisation.

It is usual to emphasise the growing hold of the town on the peasant way of life and behaviour. But the demographic, and therefore political, weight of numbers maintained in the countryside, as well as the selective process of the exodus, combined to give the French peasants an overall social weight which was unique in Europe. The ideal of a France of little men, which was their own ideal, deeply impregnated the mentality of the middle classes. The divisions on labour strategies (integration, establishment or secession) partly resulted from the arrival of rural or artisanal elements from the countryside in the new urban proletariat. The Malthusian economic choices by old or new elites were also connected with their continued relationship to the land and the need to take account of peasant opinion. The analysis of these diverse groups in the ensuing chapters will attempt to confirm these hypotheses.

---

42. E. Grenadou (6), p. 60; see also J.-C. Farcy (65).
43. P. Bourdieu (289), p. 4.

–5–

The Rise of the Middle Classes

Under the ambiguous banner of the 'new strata', the Republican ideal sought a social base outside the peasant classes in the France of the petty bourgeoisie; retail tradesmen, small craftsmen, employees and minor officials. At a higher level, the liberal professions, whose position rested on their qualifications, also identified with this group, since they largely supplied the political cadres of the regime. In the inter-war period, before radicalism became the favourite political expression of those classes which were not yet called middle, sheer numbers and political and social influence made these groups one of the major pivots in every important crisis of the regime. Yet everything seemed *a priori* to combine to divide them. One category put its faith in economic capital as a basis for its social ascent. The second placed its hopes on education to equip it with the qualifications to enable it to reach a better social position. The first was very close to manual workers; the second carried out intellectual tasks. The first were employers, the second were wage-earners, with the liberal professions having a composite status.

Consequently, their unity was partly negative: nearly all of them lived increasingly in towns or market towns and not in villages, which distinguished them from peasants. Both were strangers to the factory world, even if their income was lower than skilled workers' and they had to work excessive hours. Although they followed different paths, the pattern of their careers was homologous; both sought to break away from their original environment. This negative unity, like the many internal differences that this chapter examines, explains their political instability. Depending on region and period, they were able to support xenophobic movements or provide the cadres for socialism, plunge into Boulangism, participate in Catholic defence movements or support the radicalism of Combes, adopt unadulterated Republican legitimism and then, gradually, through embryonic unionism, transform themselves into forces challenging the State's authority, such as the post office employees or the teachers of the Belle Époque.

A The World of the Petty Bourgeoisie, or How to Escape from the Proletariat

a The Retail Tradesmen

The retail tradesmen underwent a contradictory evolution at the end of the century. Some socialist theorists predicted their disappearance or denounced them as parasites. On the other hand the politicians in power favoured them, regarding them as a guarantee of social stability in the face of labour disturbance. The urbanisation movement created a new market for their services but the parallel appearance of giant entrepreneurs in trade and industry directly threatened their independence, while their working-class consumers, by creating cooperatives, shed doubts on their usefulness. Lastly, the crisis of 1880–1890, which slowed down activity and consumption, could not be other than unfavourable to the weaker businesses.

However, despite this gloomy climate, overall statistics show a positive balance sheet for the development of this type of commercial organisation. The number of licensed traders rose from 1.3 million to 1.5 million betweeen 1881 and 1905 in standard trade. Judging by the censuses, the number of 'employers' in the statistical sense rose from 2 million in 1866 to 3.5 million in 1896, but 2.5 million had no paid employees and were therefore traders on their own account, independent artisans or home manufacturers rather than small industrialists. Even if these figures, because of their imprecision, probably conceal part of the reality, they are evidence of the vitality of this social group which resisted both proletarianisation and crisis.

However, this sustained, even increased, demographic weight in contemporary society went hand in hand with symptoms of malaise or relative decline. The average value of the licences to trade, which these independent tradesmen paid, at first grew much more slowly than those for big business or industry, by 0.9 per cent (1881–1905) against a rise of 1.8 per cent for big business and 1.1 per cent for industry.[1] This relative decline in the average value of the taxes levied on capital reflects both the successful defence of the interests of the retail trader or the small business against the income tax which surtaxed big business, with concessions made in order to retain the electoral support of the retail trade, and the lesser prosperity of this sector affected by the depression. It is also probable that the proliferation of these businesses in certain sectors or in certain districts condemned the majority to stagnation, with a cheap

---

1. Figures taken from *Enquête parlementaire*, 1912, quoted by A. Daumard in F. Braudel and E. Labrousse (24), vol. 4/1, p. 404.

retail trade or a micro-workshop sometimes presenting itself as a solution to unemployed wage-earners from other sectors.

b The Struggle to Live

Public houses are the most obvious example of this trend. Their numbers rose from 364,875 in 1870 to 367,825 in 1881, after the new Republican majority had passed a liberal law. They reached their peak with more than 482,000 in 1911, or 1 public house per 80 inhabitants or, if women and children are excluded, 1 per 36 adult consumers, an average which conceals the disparities between regions and between town and country.[2] Even if urbanisation, the increase in exchanges, and the rise in the standard of living expanded the number of potential purchasers and the quantity of goods consumed, the concurrent pressure of competition always made survival problematic.

The process of setting up an independent business can be reconstructed with the help of a number of monographs. For example, wine dealers or cafe-owners, particularly in Paris, were most often migrant Auvergnats who had built up a small nest-egg while working as waiters. After a few years, and generally at between the age of twenty-five and thirty-five, thanks to a relatively high wage of eight to ten francs a day in a second-rate establishment and by dint of hard work, they were able to buy first businesses in a peripheral or low-grade district. If things went well for them, by combining trade in two commodities, for example (wine and coal, or a cafe with lodgings), they sold up in order to move nearer the centre where profits were even higher and businesses more expensive. The risk of failure did not go away; business failure was often caused by making excessive improvements to attract customers, by cyclical crises which reduced popular consumption, or by default on the part of a debtor who was not covered by the family solidarity which was so strong amongst migrants.

The thought of founding a dynasty never entered the heads even of the most prosperous. With this primitive accumulation of capital, the 'Cantalous' invested it in the land of their birth or retired there as *rentiers*. In this pattern – particularly in this region – retail trade in the capital was a temporary substitute for land which had not been able to yield a living. It was also a means of avoiding permanent descent into the wage-earning classes or unskilled factory work, the only other outlets for these countrymen with no qualifications.[3]

---

2. J. Lalouette, 'Débits de boisson et discours bourgeois', in L. Murard and P. Zylberman (263), pp. 346–7.
3. F. Raison-Jourde (109).

Understandably, there was a considerable turnover in these small businesses. This was as much a consequence of the business death-rate as of the temporary nature of the establishment's policy. In Paris in about 1900, for example, one grocer's shop in five changed ownership every year.[4] This was dictated by the changes in the demographic balance; the working-class clientele migrated to the suburbs and outskirts, whereas the centres became less remunerative for the retail trade in consumer goods because of competition from big or multiple department stores (Félix Potin in Paris, for example). Thus, 573 grocers' shops disappeared in central Paris between the Second Empire and 1914. On the other hand, in the XXth *arrondissement*, where the population doubled between 1861 and 1891, their number rose from 196 to 392, with the result that the number of inhabitants per grocer's shop remained constant.

These new retailers were generally former wage-earners or grocers' assistants who served their apprenticeship on the job. In Paris, businesses were bought with money from dowries and marriages, from obtaining credit or from savings, while in the provinces, many single women were grocers. Only the large central shops, which had a longer life-span, were handed down from father to son.

These career patterns show just how much this area was a transition zone between classes and also a battlefield between middle-rank and small traders and between established traders and new comers. Thus study of the electoral lists of the Niort commercial court[5] shows that an oligarchy composed of the longest established and most prestigious merchants of the highest social standing, continued to exist. Although the republican laws of 1874 and then of 1883 had opened up the electorate, good care was taken to rule out all the little shopkeepers who were too new to the trade or were the more fortunate victims of the bankruptcies that the court had to handle. Even when the electoral lists came near to real commercial universal suffrage, the little men were hardly part of it (only 15 per cent of Niort voters in 1883). The workings of the economic system, like the power mechanisms within commercial society, thus made it a milieu which, beneath its apparent openness to free enterprise, was based on a hierarchy of notability and had no compassion for the weak, since it was creditors (the affluent tradesmen) who would judge their debtors.

c The Financial Balance Sheet

All that is available to draw up a genuine balance sheet of the contribution

4. A. Faure (326).
5. J.-C. Martin (335).

of retail trade to social mobility are rough and always biased data. The bankruptcy files partially reveal the other side of the picture and the importance for survival of credit networks, which were more or less free because they consisted of the family, but also the importance of an intuitive knowledge of the market which was aimed at. Contrary to appearances, statements of inheritance do not provide a true financial balance sheet. They do not actually record any of the cases of return to the countryside with a fortune made, or rapid failures before death. They therefore present a more favourable picture than the reality, except in cases of early death. The inventories of commercial fortunes they contain only record the partial successes of businesses which had lasted for a certain length of time.

Even with this enhancement, the total amount of the ultimate fortune of retail traders, like the total for their accumulation of wealth, shows how limited was their access to the ranks of the real bourgeoisie by this route. In Lyons in 1869 and also in 1911, for example, half or more of the retail traders whose bequests have been analysed left less than 5,000 francs, or barely the cost of a mediocre business. In Paris in 1911, calculations show that 21 per cent of shopkeepers had become poorer, 27 per cent had virtually neither gained nor lost on their capital, 38 per cent were moderately richer, and 14 per cent had actually made a significant amount of money (an increase of more than 50 per cent).[6] Likewise in Lyons, half the butchers left no fortune.

These data, adjusted downwards to allow for the aforementioned bias, make it possible to understand the extreme social inflexibility of the individuals involved in this process. As Heinz-Gerhard Haupt shows, the tardiness of social legislation in France was due to the utilisation by the larger businesses of the body of opposition and pressure from these micro-businesses, which were more liberal than the liberals. Any legislation was an obstacle to their growth and therefore to their potential success. In this individualist milieu, the formation of employers' unions was always a reaction to censure by the administration, threats of regulation, or the perception of a threat from larger businesses in the sector. This is also why small-scale business was never able to establish itself as a real group, except as a body of opposition.

d The Political Balance Sheet

Under the Second Republic, the little men – traders and artisans, it being hard to distinguish between the two – had provided the extreme Left with troops and leaders in the direct sans-culotte tradition which dreamed of

6. P. Léon (93); A. Daumard (24), p. 404.

a democracy of small producers. Under the Third Republic, this preferential link tended to be broken or even be reversed in large towns where conflict and competition were keenest. The retail trade's transition from Left to Right was most obvious in Paris. It happened as a response to a dual threat; from the department stores – exaggerated, because these only affected a few districts and a few sectors – and, above all, from the change in the capital's centre of commercial gravity. Life was ebbing from the old centre as the bourgeoisie migrated westwards, and this harmed the economic prospects of the over-crowded traditional businesses which had set up there.

As a consequence, in 1888, the *Ligue syndicale du travail, de l'industrie et du commerce* was created; it claimed 140,000 members at its peak. The traders who founded this league felt threatened both by the ready-made clothing revolution and by the industrialisation of some consumer goods. They lost both their bourgeois clientele, who were going to the department stores or to the luxury shops situated on the boulevards, and their working-class customers who were leaving the centre and turning to the large working-class stores or, increasingly, to cooperatives. These traders appealed to the liberal heritage of 1789 against the social decline (the new Bastilles were the big businessmen), but in an outmoded sense; the economy had to remain autarkic and be formed of small producers and small consumers, without intervention from foreigners or financial capital. Boulangism, like end-of-century nationalism or antisemitism, attempted to utilise this body of discontent against the Republic. Although the first failed, the second owed its municipal success after the Dreyfus affair to its convergence with the business sector's discontent with rising socialism and the 'Jew-ified' Republic.

However, viewing this type of balance sheet would only be simplistic. To begin with, the political commitment of these groups was always intermittent. The individualist, customer-orientated viewpoint ran counter to any continuous and unfailing collective commitment. The traders could change their vote if the moderate Left or Centre were able to adopt the slightest measure to allay their fears for the future. Even in Paris, the turn to the Right was not total. In the provinces, where tensions were less, loyalty to the Republic lasted longer because the conflict between Blues and Whites maintained the gulf, inherited from the Revolution, between the 'aristocrats' and the heirs of the third estate; here the petty middle classes still kept their full place.

Here also, radicalism found part of its social base. The small draper from the Deux-Sèvres, 'Blue' from the West, who cursed at paying the highest licence in town, was typical of this composite ideology, which was unknown to the Marxist viewpoint developed by the socialist trend. Despite everything, he was a good republican who was not above singing in Church. He was the son of a farrier; his son was the historian Ernest Labrousse, a professor at the Sorbonne and, intermittently, a militant socialist.[7] This point of arrival makes him an exceptional case but he does illustrate a general law. Unsure of its future, this group often guided its descendants towards more secure careers as employees or officials, which proliferated at this period.

B The Employees: A New Proletariat

a Attempts at Definition

The meaning of the word 'employee' changed during the nineteenth century. For the first three-quarters of the century, 'employee' implied 'State employee', as it did in Balzac's novel, *Les Employés*, where the title really meant 'the officials'. However, census terminology indicates that the word quickly took on central importance as a form of classification in the eyes of contemporaries and was extended to employees in the private sector. The three-part division of the censuses, employers/employees/workers, was a clear symptom of the buffer-function that this new category was to have in the social pyramid.

The employee was not an employer since he was not independent, but he was not a worker, less because his work was not manual than because he fitted into a complex division of the tasks of business organisation and operation without influence over production. According to a distinction made by the sociologist Maurice Halbwachs, the employee had to do with men and not, like the worker or artisan, with things. On the railways, the employee was said to be 'in contact' (with the public, with management, with the customers).[8] Through the accounts he kept, the sheets of paper he filled, his keen salesmanship and the statistics he drew up, the employee was the intermediary between the business and the world, between the upper and the lower reaches of the hierarchy, between the material and the immaterial, between policy and final result. If the proletarian was the child of industry, the employee was the son of capitalism.

There was therefore a time-lag between the increase in the numbers of employees and industrialisation, when the large companies emerged and when banking, finance, transport and big business became elements in the unification of the national market. The employee was therefore

7. This is the father of Ernest Labrousse, who has painted an affectionate portrait of him which smacks very much of the time; see 'Entretiens avec Ernest Labrousse', *Actes de la recherche en sciences sociales*, 32–3, pp. 111–25; on the unrest among Parisian tradesmen, see P. Nord (338).
8. H. Vincenot (348), p. 89.

primarily urban and concentrated in the metropolises, while the worker could be scattered over rural zones or in small mono-industrial towns. He was the most complex social product of the new society which came to maturity at the end of the century. That is why there were so many employees in Paris, where numbers of 'white collar workers' rose from 126,000 in 1866 to 352,000 in 1911.

Clerks and shop-girls, supporting or helping their male or female employers, did probably exist in the first part of the nineteenth century. But the relative smallness of establishments, the employment of younger workers who were frequently replaced and the absence of the possibility of promotion except in the paternalistic fashion of integration into the employer's family, made them little different from a specific category of domestic servant or, at the best, associates like those young men of good social position who did their apprenticeship on the job in a friend's firm.

The bureaucracy of the large joint stock companies, the staff of the department stores and the restricted management of expanding middle-sized businesses created large numbers of new employees. The numbers of employees at Bon Marché increased from 1,788 in 1877 to 3,173 in 1887 and 4,500 in 1906. The twelve largest Paris stores employed a staff of 11,000 in 1913. The railway companies also mustered impressive armies. The majority of railwaymen were 'commissioned', that is to say, benefited from some guarantee of promotion and pension which set them apart, even if the work they did was the same as an ordinary worker's. However, the staff of the 'operations' branch, the 'messieurs' in railway jargon, were employees in the strict sense. They remained distinctive thanks to their uniform, the fact that some of them were accommodated in the stations, the link with the public and the administrative hierarchy, and their better educational qualifications.

The banks, financial institutions and large firms also began to be considerable employers. In Paris in 1881, 50,000 men and women were clerks or employees in the banking and commercial sector, 11,000 worked on the railways and in transport (in transport this was as many as workers and manual labourers).[9] The Longwy steel-works had 45 employees for 2,800 workers in 1896; Le Creusot took on 319 employees between 1887 and 1895 for a workforce of 10,000 workers. In the latter case the labour force did not expand after 1895 but employees were engaged at a gathering pace; 41 per cent of them had managerial jobs connected with production while the remaining 59 per cent were in the offices as book-keepers, articled clerks and employees to carry on the correspondence

9. 1881 census, *Ville de Paris*, Table F, p. 217.

arising from the close links the firm of Schneider had with ministers.[10]

The new employee, more perhaps than the worker in the same period, worked within specialised structures which resembled the State administration. The railway companies proliferated grades and jobs on military lines, probably due to the fact that a large number of the managerial staff were educated at the *École polytechnique*. The large banks and department stores invented hierarchies in order to develop a team spirit within the firm and a keenness, which would be rewarded by a rise to a higher grade, even if the work demanded no increased initiative.

b Paternalism and Bureaucracy

Bon Marché, whose history has been the subject of an exhaustive monograph, was the largest shop in Europe, perhaps the world, under the Third Republic. Its management made every effort to create a staff policy in which paternalism, bureaucracy and competition embraced the employees uninterruptedly from morning to evening and even outside of work. To be recruited was already an honour because the rewards were more substantial than in small shops, the working-day was less long, there was a chance of promotion, and there were social advantages unmatched elsewhere; this first barrier could be crossed only after a preliminary enquiry and the submission of references. But the hard hand of dismissal fell mercilessly on offenders. In 1873, for example, out of 400 appointments, 39 per cent were dismissed in less than five years and 43 per cent left voluntarily, in the case of new recruits because of inability to adapt to the environment.

The basic wage was actually fixed at a relatively low level, and the salesperson was assumed to be able to double it through his tact in handling people, thanks to the principle of commission (from 1,200 to 1,500 francs, thus making a total of 3,600 francs). If the individual proved his ability, he could become a 'second' (from 2,400 to 3,600 francs basic salary and 9,000 to 12,000 with profit-sharing in the turnover). Heads of departments were head and shoulders above the highest officials since, with bonuses, their salary was the same as a prefect's (12,000 francs), or even that of a leading presiding judge at the supreme Court of Appeal (25,000 francs).

Although there were theoretically no *a priori* barriers to promotion, as there were in State employ, length of service to the firm and appointment during the early days of the shop were major assets. As the firm expanded, the probability of rising through the ranks became almost nil. That was why Madame Boucicaut, before stepping down, established

10. P. Bourdelais (324), p. 439.

a contingency fund for employees, with no deduction from wages, which provided a bonus which was only received at the end of twenty years service, in order to keep staff. With this system, and then with the introduction of pensions and various welfare schemes, the managers came to think of the business as a sort of family of which the individual became a rightful member, whatever his level in the hierarchy. But the benevolence of paternalism was not sufficient to guarantee attachment, nor the bonuses to guarantee efficiency. That was why measures such as a body of inspectors, niggling regulations that had to be scrupulously observed, a tight hierarchical chain of succession, and a division between status groups complemented the family spirit with the team spirit of the firm, which various collective ceremonies relentlessly inculcated.[11]

This model for employee management recurred to a greater or lesser degree in other tertiary businesses whose only source of productivity was an efficient staff. Employers tolerated the spirit of collective protest even less than in industry. The benefits conceded aimed at dissociating the employees from any solidarity with other categories of wage-earners and making them feel different because they were slightly privileged. The strong asymmetry between a few large employers who granted favours to their staff and a mass of small employers who were unyielding because their survival depended on the absence of social measures was both a strength and a weakness for the two parties. It was a source of strength for the general body of employers since the employees working in the most concentrated groups, capable of taking effective action, considered themselves privileged and were therefore more submissive. It was also a weakness because, however sparse their membership, the unions which were formed – and more so in the non-concentrated sectors – could argue on the basis of these measures to demand parity with their more favoured colleagues. The conciliatory paternalism of large-scale capitalism thus risked introducing a ferment of class struggle into the former solid front that had existed between small employers and their clerks.

c Employee Unrest

The development of employee unrest at the beginning of the twentieth century was the result of their proliferation. As primary and intermediate school, and even curtailed secondary school education spread, the low-grade qualification that gave access to white collar jobs lost its scarcity status. The hierarchy of wages then collapsed, particularly when compared with the workers. It has been estimated that three-quarters of employees' wages in Paris were below 1,800 francs a year, or less than

11. M.B. Miller (262), pp. 83–111.

a skilled worker's.[12]

The only advantages the employees retained were greater security and the absence of a cut in wages as they aged. However, the urban life of the employees and the dress-requirements imposed by their superiors increased expenditure on prestige items (such as dress, housing and entertainment) which made them all the more sensitive to their relatively low wage-level. Practice of a second trade and the tendency for employees' wives to be forced to work, contrary to petty bourgeois ethics, made the worst-off feel that they were going down in the world. This increased with the employment of women in offices or the use of assistants in order to cut down on the benefits gained (in the Gas Company their numbers increased from 6 to 12 per cent of the total employees between 1881 and 1893).

This internal tension between the dream of entering the bourgeoisie and the dominant trend towards a status approaching that of a small wage-earner accounts for the employees' personal conduct. Late marriage, restricted births, and the value set on manners and education reflect the pursuit of the plan of ascent, at least for the next generation. However, out of a sample of 168 sons of employees in the XIIIth and XVIIIth *arrondissements* at the end of the Second Empire, only 3 per cent gained liberal profession status, while 31 per cent returned to manual labour.[13] Others, still full of illusions about their real status, took the easy road towards imitation of bourgeois life by cheating, thanks to buying on credit or restricting food consumption in order to spend more on leisure activities. These divergences recur in collective attitudes.

Overall, the employees were only organised into unions to a very small extent and they were very submissive (two strikes in fifty years at the Bon Marché, a few partial movements in the BHV (Bazar de l'Hôtel de Ville) in 1909, at Dufayel in 1905, and at Galeries Lafayette in 1907). They did not make common cause with the workers even when they acted collectively. Like the small employers, they rejected collectivism. Some drifted into the end-of-century nationalism. The main employees' union, Christian-inspired, was close to Le Play and advocated cooperation. Its membership expanded belatedly after 1900 and was still only 13,000 on the eve of the war.[14]

On the outskirts of Paris, on the other hand, a not inconsiderable number appear on socialist lists – but the employees there had probably lost all hope of personal rise or else were municipal employees. The once solid alliance between employers and employees was broken because of

12. L.R. Berlanstein (413), p. 65.
13. Ibid., p. 148.
14. M. Launay (333), pp. 16–9.

the intransigence of small employers over social demands. This was precisely the logic of the distinction between employees and the workers, who were urging the former to obtain advantages (shorter working hours, holidays) which wage-earners in industry had earlier extracted.[15] The same tension, with the aggravating circumstance that the other party directly concerned was the political authority, was gradually going to shatter the harmony between the State and its officials.

C The Officials: Servants or Rebels?

a From the Old to the New State

In order to understand not only the officials' growing importance under the Third Republic but also the crucial changes that affected them at that time, some aspects of the State's powers need to be recalled. Opponents of the State incessantly denounced officialdom as one of the plagues of democracy. From a wish to please their electors, politicians proliferated public posts in order to find places for their strings of election workers. This phenomenon probably had some marginal effect, but there were much more fundamental reasons for the massive growth in the number of State employees. Growth was connected with the appearance of new State functions, including the State as educator, the State unifying the nation by a postal, telegraph and telephone service, roads and general conscription, the State as coloniser and the State protecting the economy and, timidly, society.

Louis Fontvielle has reconstructed statistics of the changes in the State's operating expenditure between the end of the Second Empire and the end of the century. They show stagnant budgets for old State functions, whereas the budgets for the new functions mentioned above rose markedly. Thus, budgets for foreign affairs, general administration, justice, police and prisons and religion varied within small limits between 1869 and 1899. The budget for education, on the other hand, rose from 27 million francs to 209 million francs; for economic activity, from 79 million francs to 206 million francs; for social activity, from 9 million francs to 23 million francs; and for the colonies, from 115 million francs

---

15. See the answers to the enquiry on the regulation of employees' work conducted by the *Conseil supérieur du travail*. On all the topics (work by women, children, reduction in the working-day, breaks in the day's work and weeks off), although there was always a minority of employees' unions in favour of adopting a point of view hostile to change in imitation of their employers, a majority of wage-earners were in favour of overthrowing the customs inherited from paternalism (*Bulletin de l'Office du travail*, 19, 1912, pp. 905–12).

to 173 million francs.[16]

It is clear that these new expenditures implied new staff. Fontvielle also points to the contrast between the stagnation, or slight rise, in staff numbers at the old ministries and the proliferation of new officials in external services or the new State functions. In the Ministry of Public Education, for example, the number of persons employed rose from 47,509 in 1858 to 120,988 under the Méline ministry (1896). During the same period, the workforce attached to the Post Office, soon enlarged by the telegraph and telephone to become the PTT, increased considerably from 27,486 to 67,949.[17]

Overall estimates differ depending on author and sources, as the definition of who should be considered an official was no longer the same at different periods. Members of the clergy were officials under the Concordat but were not after 1905, whereas the teachers' status changed in the opposite direction as a result of the education laws. But above all the State for a long time and in increasing numbers employed men – and women too – without giving them an official status based on their roles. All factors taken into account, it can be estimated that the number of officials doubled between 1858 and 1896, from 217,000 to 416,000 (excluding the army).[18] In the same forty year period, the average wage remained mediocre; 1,350 francs in 1858, 1,490 francs in 1896. This apparently respectable average conceals a more dismal reality; a third of officials received a salary below 1,000 francs, and half the workforce received between 1,000 and 2,000 francs a year. Taking only civilians, the three large sectors of State employment were finances (20 per cent of the total), the PTT (18 per cent) and public education (31 per cent). As for officers, their manpower was between 20,000 and 25,000.

b Administrative Unrest

This administrative system which was spreading its branches wide, became increasingly heterogeneous as new categories appeared. The employee depicted by Balzac lived in a large town, nearly always Paris, and almost never changed his job. This classic figure still existed but he was now in a minority. The new services were increasingly set up outside of towns, even in the smallest villages or hamlets in the case of primary teaching, when teachers too became officials. This geographic diversity introduced a new problem, that of finding suitable candidates for the available positions and their needs. The multiplicity of job descriptions

16. L. Fontvielle (327), pp. 2113 and 2115.
17. Ibid., p. 1847, and V. Turquan (346), p. 7.
18. From V. Turquan (346), p. 11.

involved increasingly formalised and strict recruitment procedures. The growing numbers made promotion increasingly desired and increasingly difficult to ensure without competition. That is why this period of growth in numbers of officials was also the time when unrest developed and gradually challenged operating rules inherited from authoritarian regimes.

The crisis in the relationship between the State and its employees was all the more serious and prolonged in that the political leaders refused to question those ideas inherited from Bonapartism. These included first the absolute authority of heads over subordinates which formed the basis of their right to weed out staff, change their function or more or less arbitrarily suspend them. The second of the Bonapartist legacies was centralisation which implied a national, and therefore complex, administration of careers. Lastly, there was the hierarchy which widened gaps in salary between the lowest and highest levels of posts or between categories, and multiplied friction and discontent at any suspicion of favouritism.

Whereas the republicans had an education policy, they never took the time to reflect on the State or to reform it. They preferred to imitate their predecessors and make the administration an instrument of their political power. This explains their slowness to face up to the real problems and the manifold expedients found, such as assigning women to certain positions.

c Officials in the Central Administration and the Crisis of Confidence in the State

The central administration was the most unwilling to develop and adapt to the new social realities because it was closest to the centre of political power. As portfolios were the main issue when forming political majorities, the division or combination of ministries in each new cabinet depended more on personal issues or political colouration than on any purely technical concern for an efficient division of labour between services. However, the dominant tendency was towards division, which changed former directorates into full ministries, departments into branches or directorates, etc., following a classic process of bureaucratic inflation. The Republic created five new ministries, all very typical of its general orientation: these were the Post Office, freed from the guardianship of the Ministry of the Interior as a pledge of liberalism; Agriculture, separated from Commerce in 1881 by Gambetta in order to seal the regime's alliance with the peasantry; the Colonies, given autonomy from the Navy in 1894 in order to organise the Empire, which was increasingly spreading its red stain over the world map; and lastly, the Ministry of Labour, in 1906, charged with soothing conflicts with workers whose hostility to a regime they had at first supported was growing by the day. Although the divisions in the services permitted promotions, they complicated administration and politicised hitherto technical positions. The basic employee thus felt that he was at the mercy of fluctuations in parliamentary majorities more than in the past.

The central administration remained a small world; there were 2,256 officials in 1870 and 3,800 in 1914, a much slower growth-rate than in the rest of public office. Divided roughly into ten ministries, themselves subdivided into three to ten directorates, the members of these services formed groups of at most some fifty State servants. Relationships therefore remained very personal, with no collective consciousness except of the neighbouring service or competing body. The authorities deliberately employed assistants or supernumeraries, winning their loyalty by dangling the hope of establishment before their eyes, and this also served to divide the employees.

This world was still close to the structure inherited from the Napoleonic departments. There was little division of labour and promotion on the basis of length of service took precedence over recruitment on the basis of specific aptitudes. As a rule, and in the absence of political accident or too flagrant lack of ability, the same people who began with the purely mechanical tasks of transcribing, entrusted to copying clerks, then rose to more lofty positions drafting material, and were finally promoted to supervising other employees as deputy chief clerk and then chief clerk of a department. After considerable resistance from the 'old' employees had been overcome, an attempt was made to differentiate between the lower and upper cadres by creating competitive examinations for drafters, involving higher educational qualifications.

After 1887, the most unrewarding tasks were primarily reserved for female typists. At first, they were assistants, paid less and barred from the possibility of promotion by a rigid hierarchy between the sexes. Later, in the 1900s, they were recruited through a specific competitive examination.[19]

This organisational revolution was facilitated by the arrival on the labour market of new generations who had emerged from the intermediate schools or colleges. The old system of supernumeraries recruited from employees' sons, who were given a routine training on the job, could thus be replaced by selection on the basis of education. On the other hand, what did not change, and was the cause of the unrest and crisis, were the hierarchisation of salaries and the discretionary rises to stimulate enthusiasm. The fact that there was no actual division within the body of employees in a ministry considerably expanded the salary range. A

19. G. Thuillier (116).

clerk, depending on the administration, could begin at 1,500 to 1,600 francs a year and receive 9,000 francs if he became head clerk. The administrative pyramid was such that hope of promotion or a rise in salary was statistically illusory for the vast majority. Most were condemned to mediocre or average salaries; consequently their enthusiasm declined with age, loss of illusions and the development of political favouritism, which was particularly advantageous to members of ministerial *cabinets*. Maupassant, an erstwhile official who became a journalist, faithfully depicted the straitened circumstances of these employees, comparing the advantages of State white collar staff to workers who, according to him, were better paid. But collective expression of the employees' grievances took time to appear.

In the first decades of the Republic, political authority was exercised unilaterally. An easy-going attitude towards discipline was tolerated, reflecting the presence in departments of several men of letters, who cultivated the muse more than public service. Any manifestation of politics, on the other hand, was immediately penalised. Employees who were Boulangists or who showed sympathy with the far Left were dismissed out of hand. The idea that an official could have any political freedom appeared as heresy, even to the republicans, who had previously been persecuted by the imperial administration or during the period of Moral Order. Later, the idea of the State's servants forming unions seemed an equal heresy.

A commission of enquiry appointed by the National Assembly in 1871–1873 had already drawn up a list of the officials' basic problems. Poor division of labour implied a mediocre return in the absence of material incentives. Unduly low starting salaries had not kept pace with the cost of living and employees were tempted to take up a second trade. Despite relative job-security, the typical budget of a State servant only just balanced and debt and deficit lay in wait when it came to setting up a home. The idea was also widespread at this period that French Malthusianism, which demographic statistics show was particularly strong in this group, was a consequence of the expansion of bureaucracy.

But this parliamentary commission did not go beyond the report stage. The two conflicting ideological models, the liberal and the military, for solving the administration's social problem were impracticable for opposite reasons. The liberal view proposed laying off staff, increasing productivity and raising salaries in proportion to quality of work. But politicians would then lose their prerogative to promote their protégés at their discretion or find posts for their supporters. The neo-corporatist attitude, on the other hand, gave civil officials a quasi-military status, with rights and duties analogous to those of officers and non-commissioned officers. This would limit the margin of power of politicians and heads of departments even further, and the flexibility of administration allowed by the employment of assistants and women would be lost.

Budgetary difficulties connected with the unfavourable economic situation in 1880–1890 and the growing weight of pensions of officials recruited under earlier regimes, as well as the republicans' 'opportunist' desire not to tie their own hands, were therefore incentives to take the easy solutions. The administration left the structural problems in abeyance or solved them as they came up when pressure from below was too strong to be ignored. The general introduction of assistants, women or new categories to cope with new needs not covered by routine administration was the result of this hand-to-mouth approach.

However, the seeds of the open explosion of the crisis were contained in democracy, both in its freedoms, notably in the freedom of the press and in questions in parliament, but also in its defects, such as the evils of recommendations and ministerial instability which diminished the official's prestige in the eyes of those he was supposed to command. Associations of State employees, such as friendly or mutual aid societies, were created; corporative publications, often very liberal in tone, proliferated; petitions circulated which disputed the authoritarianism of minor department heads. The first large-scale action occurred in 1887. Before leaving office the Post Office minister, Granet, had appointed numerous protégés in an irregular way. A petition signed by 230 employees challenged this abuse and prompted a question by a conservative deputy. Although the new minister, Rouvier, publicly maintained a firm approach against this insurrection, he backed up the employees in practice by rescinding his predecessors' measures.[20]

The officials could not but form a favourable opinion of the effectiveness of forming a pressure group, if not a trade union. The second factor in this sudden awareness sprang from the new methods of recruiting draftsmen by competitive examination. Strengthened by the rights their success conferred on them, these officials, generally graduates, no longer tolerated the old methods of administration based on acquired advantages or protection. The new unionists came from their ranks after the Dreyfus Affair, which revealed all the defects in the executive authority. These officials were in an uncertain position between non-qualified officials and protégés of the cabinet or members of the *grands corps* (i.e. the *Conseil d'État*, the *Cour des Comptes*, etc.) who monopolised the most interesting promotions. Now, anxious to apply the Dreyfusard ideal to the administration, they challenged the traditional principles of

20. S. Bachrach (321); C. Bertho (227); O. Beaud (322); D. Bertinotti (323); J. Siwek-Pouydesseau (342).

administrative management. In their discussions and conflicts they pleaded for a statute for officials, which was obtained half a century later; an aspiration shared by the Republic's new officials, the teachers and post office employees and their female equivalents.

d Newcomers

The School-Teachers, a New Clergy? — The social image of the school-teachers, men and women, is contradictory. The pride of the regime, the incarnation of its own social philosophy, the school-teachers retrospectively became the centre of the myth formulated at the time when the school of the Third Republic lost its substance during the twentieth century. Contemporary evidence, particularly when the parties involved dared to speak out, is less rosy. This contrasting perspective is not only the effect of the comparison between the idealised memory and the teacher's disenchantment when confronted with the harshness of everyday life. It was also contained in the republican educational plan and its effects on the actual status of those charged with implementing it.

Unlike schoolmasters in preceding regimes, whose status was uncertain, the men and women teachers of the Republic were gradually endowed with all the attributes of a new corps, a secular version of the traditional clergy. Their training was unified by the *École normale*, the college of education which corresponded to the seminary. They received a diploma testifying to their knowledge, which corresponded to ordination for the priesthood. They had a specific place in which to carry out their duties and to live, the school built by the commune and often part of the town hall, which corresponded to church and presbytery. They possessed a functional monopoly thanks to progressive secularisation, even if congreganist schools continued to offer stiff competition in certain places.

Paid by the State, housed by the commune, controlled by the prefect and the departmental inspector, the schoolmasters were situated at the point where the three power-levels of democracy met. The products of specific training – primary school, intermediate school and college of education – the men and women teachers were moulded by a different culture from the dominant culture of the *lycées*, the high schools. It was dispensed to them by former teachers, holding the *brevet supérieur* (higher school certificate) and soon by former students of the *Écoles normales supérieures* of Saint Cloud and Fontenay.[21] This apparently regal path to promotion for the most gifted children of the people, according to the official ideology, was also a ghetto to prevent

21. A. Prost (41); J.-N. Luc and A. Barbé (334); J. Ozouf (339); F. Muel (337).

materialisation of the fear that haunted conservatives – whether Republicans or not – that semi-scholars might be 'de-classed' upwards.

Existing data on social origins confirm the part played by this expanding profession in bringing about relative social promotion. At the *École normale* in Saint-Lô for example, peasants' sons formed 53 per cent of one class list in 1880–1884, against 28.2 per cent for artisans' and traders' sons, and 3.4 per cent for the sons of workers and employees. This preponderance of peasants was connected with the rural nature of the department concerned, and diminished in any case during the Third Republic to the advantage of the other two groups mentioned. In more urban, more working-class or more southerly departments, it was the higher reaches of the masses (artisans, skilled workers, shopkeepers) and middle classes in difficulties (small employers, retailers experiencing financial problems, or with too many children) who guided their most gifted children towards this stable profession. Whereas workers constituted 62 per cent of the active population in the Nord, for example, only a quarter of the teachers during the Belle Époque were of worker origin. Similarly, in the south-west, farmers' sons and daughters only constituted 18 per cent of teachers against 30 per cent who were the sons and daughters of petty offficials, employees, retailers and artisans.[22] The school-teachers often came from families threatened by economic developments (agricultural crisis, disappearance of small rural industries, or the fall in status of certain artisanal trades). This profession gave them the security and the reassuring structure of a clearly delineated culture.

But the profession's prestige with the petty bourgeoisie did not make the role of cultural intermediary any less difficult in an often hostile peasant or worker environment, since the first posts or the new posts were by definition in the remotest villages where the tradition of education was least well established. For women, there was also the new problem of replacing – with a greater or lesser degree of facility – a well-established and respected religious staff. In the countryside, the schoolmaster and particularly the schoolmistress, often from a superior social background, was intellectually isolated, with barely anyone locally to whom they could talk except a few minor notables. The Republic had reviewed salaries (they rose from 800 to 2,000 francs) but they still involved outside work if a family was to live off them.

The isolation of the countryside was, however, counterbalanced by the lower cost of living, the opportunity to play a role as advisor to the villagers, the possibility of exercising some influence through adult classes or classes in agriculture, and the chance to act as public letter-writer or secretary to the local administration. Joseph Sandre has left a

22. F. Muel (337), pp. 24–5.

published account of his early days in Montceaux-l'Étoile in Saône-et-Loire. In order to support his small family, he combined a post as secretary to the local administration (60 francs), singing in the church choir (100 francs) and various bonuses (20 francs). This 980 francs was reduced to 805 francs through debts contracted during the period when he did not receive a full teacher's salary when he was settling in. According to his calculations, this gave a final figure of 1 franc 10 per person per day on which to live.[23]

In the town, the mediocrity of salaries was more glaring and working conditions were harder. Classes were too large in popular districts and teaching methods often ill-adapted to difficult working-class pupils. As with the employees however, the latent discontent, expressed in some enquiries at the end of the century or which the literary evidence deliberately exaggerates, was slow to be expressed. The schoolmasters were dependent on their superiors, who had absolute power over them, and were caught up in political conflicts during periods of anti-clericalism. Isolated and scattered over the countryside, they scarcely had the means to make their voices heard. Moreover, the closed system, in which they formed one cog, proved efficient on the whole, and the limited chances for social promotion which the republican school system offered (and of which they themselves were the best example) were enough to offer a way out to the small fraction of the masses who followed the primary curriculum to its conclusion. The popular elite thus formed moved into the increasing number of minor public posts which, despite the fact that these qualifications had lost their scarcity, nevertheless constituted a true promotion.

On the other hand, perhaps it was the fact that the culture which they passed on, their secular faith and their adherence to the system corresponded too well that made the schoolmasters more republican than official republicans. How could they tolerate their superiors' arbitrariness, permit promotion on length of service, or discretionary selection on the basis of political recommendation, when they were teaching liberty and advocating merit and its reward? The first friendly societies indicate the birth of an *esprit de corps* and an attempt to conquer rural isolation. These societies were at first held in check by the authorities who feared contagion from working-class unionism. However, the return to strict secularism and anti-clericalism after the Dreyfus Affair and the need to remobilise the 'black hussars' (Péguy) against the nationalist and clerical threat led to growing tolerance of the profession under the Combes ministry, and to a progressive social and political emancipation of this secular clergy which was escaping from its social hierarchy.

23. Bertrand, Baptiste, Joseph, Marie Sandre (17), pp. 347–8.

After the salary review, quickly absorbed by the rise in the cost of living on the eve of the war, the struggle against the authoritarianism of some headmasters or inspectors and the denunciation of political favouritism became the principal themes of the schoolmasters' protest. But, except in a minority of cases, this growing organisation did not go so far as to become a real trade union organisation or to resort to strikes as did the workers. Whatever their sentimental solidarity with the 'people', the 'proletarians in jackets' set themselves out to be individual and different, a symptom of a sort of middle-class consciousness; to serve the Republic was not to be dominated by an employer, contrary to what revolutionary syndicalism or radical socialist factions wanted to inculcate in potential customers for their ideas.

However, this emancipation did not put an end to inequalities between the sexes within the profession. These were even less justifiable than in other public offices, given the absolute identity of the duties prescribed. Lower salaries, exclusion from posts as principals or inspectors, a greater probability of remaining single; this was the fate of the secular schoolmistress, whose moral distress was undisguisedly expressed in the enquiries at the end of the century.

Caught between the old female image, which was prevalent in the society where they taught, and the new, of which they were the avant-garde but which shut them up in a social cul-de-sac, the schoolmistresses felt torn in two. As surrogate mothers, they had to put too much into their profession ('I regard my profession as a priesthood', wrote Marie Sandre, daughter of Joseph Sandre, mentioned earlier)[24] and struggle against isolation by creating an ideal intellectual world of their own. Only later, with the spread of 'pedagogical marriages' and the growth of professional heredity and of associative or militant life, were they able to become full members of the teaching society. The same tensions can be found within the other group of officials which was employing women at this period, the PTT.

PTT Employees, Corps Conflicts and the Sex War — The unrest which developed amongst employees in the PTT administration was directly related to the increasing employment of female staff, much more so than in the case of school-teachers. The opposition between employees of the two sexes did not however involve the bottom of the hierarchy, which was occupied by postmen. As the postal network extended outside the towns, these jobs – and there were some 36,000 in about 1900 – provided a new outlet for countrymen with a minimum of primary education. Wages were between 650 and 1,150 francs around 1880 and were

24. Ibid., p. 433.

reviewed in about 1900 following a series of social movements. They then ranged from 1,100 to 1,600 francs in towns and from 700 to 1,150 francs in the country. These sums ensured a living standard comparable to that of the teachers but for a much lower level of qualification, though with much heavier hours (a day off on Sunday was granted only in 1902) and considerable physical fatigue in areas of dispersed habitat. Not until the Waldeck-Rousseau ministry were rounds limited to 31 kilometres and the working-day to nine and a half hours.[25]

Tension was primarily generated at the intermediate levels of post office employees in market centres, towns in particular and Paris above all. They faced a considerable increase in business and more complex duties with the creation of the post office savings bank, the integration of the telegraph and then the nationalisation of the telephone system. Women were traditionally postmistresses in small provincial offices. This responsibility was often handed down in a family or given to an official's widow to provide her with a living. But under pressure from male employees, these first women employees were gradually excluded from the most lucrative offices.

The second wave of female employees arrived in 1877 in the Paris telegraph system, then in 1884 in the post office savings bank, and lastly in 1892 with the opening of the first women's post offices in Paris. The female post office officials' level of qualification was identical to that of the men but their salaries were systematically kept down in order to economise. A postmistress received from 800 to 1,400 francs in about 1880, and from 1,000 to 2,000 francs in about 1900. The wage bracket for a female employee at the same dates was between 800 and 900 francs, and 1,200 and 1,800 francs; the figures for a male clerk were 1,200 to 2,700 francs then 1,800 to 3,600 francs.

In the provinces, very young girls were recruited as the assistants and helpers who now backed up the official postmistresses in combined post and telegraph offices. These temporary positions tended to become the first stages in a career as a postmistress. But the main reason why the employment of women became general was the contradiction between the blockage in careers of new employees appointed during the prosperous phase and the government's wish to reduce budgetary expenditure during the period of recession. Rather than resort to assistants, who demonstrated their discontent at the end of the 1880s and whose wages were lower than those of workers (three francs a day against six francs), it seemed preferable as in the telegraphs to create a specifically female body of employees. There was no lack of candidates, given the shortage of professional outlets for women of a certain

25. G. Frischmann (328), pp. 95–105.

education. Most often from a petty bourgeois background (daughters of employees, artisans or retailers),[26] these women needed work because they did not have a dowry and were not able to continue with their studies.

It has been calculated that the employment of women resulted in economies on salaries of 30 to 40 per cent in the budget. Male salaries were calculated on the basis of a bachelor employing one domestic servant or being able to support a wife without her needing to work. The female employees, in the view of the times, fulfilled both jobs (office and home) and were most often fated to remain single. Without dowry, since they were obliged to work, they could not marry a man from the same milieu and they were too educated to accept a husband from a lower social level. Their time was also very much taken up by an unlimited schedule, particularly in the provinces where they might work from 15 to 17 hours a day, and in effect had neither Sundays nor holidays as days off.[27] In addition, the regulations made marriage subject to express authorisation from superiors. This explains why nearly three-quarters of postmistresses in 1880 were single women or widows as still were two-thirds by about 1900. Men were promoted more rapidly and could expect to marry and keep a distance between themselves and their profession. The number of marriages of women employees did in time rise, but it remained well below the French average. This category therefore, illustrates a general law; for a large number of people, any social rise in contemporary society was paid for by the inability to ensure that the advantage gained was retained in the next generation.

The opposition between the sexes did diminish however, because the government did not persist in its policy of employing women. The object was to remove additional grounds for discontent on the part of post office employees, whose social pressure mounted relentlessly from the end of the 1890s. Thus, two women sat on the administrative council of the *Association générale des agents des PTT* in 1902. Despite the foundation of a purely female association, the *Association générale* could claim 2,800 women employees and postmistresses amongst its 11,673 members in 1904. At the height of the wave of protests in 1909, women participated in the strike called by post office officials against new promotion procedures.

The proliferation of these movements and the formation of corporative associations by the various categories of the post office, telegraph and telephones, which were becoming radical without taking the plunge into unionism *stricto sensu*, except at the level of State workers or postmen, demonstrated both the failure of republican employment policy for the

26. S. Bachrach (321), pp. 51–2.
27. D. Pézerat and P. Poublan, in A. Farge and C. Klapisch-Zuber (67).

reasons mentioned above, and a sudden consciousness similar to that of the teachers, even though it was not impregnated to the same degree with secularist idealism. When the administration, which was not yet called the 'employer State', utilised the classic methods of business leaders to divide their workers – rivalry between groups of different status, use of certain bonuses as a bait to the most submissive or dismissals – it was caught in the trap of its own contradiction. Could it treat its employees as eternal minors when groups, theoretically at a lower social level, obtained greater advantages in the private sector? On the other hand, did the dignity of State service still mean anything in sectors which closely overlapped with economic forces or social processes? The contradiction also appeared amongst the officials themselves. Like the other classes, they certainly discovered the virtues of collective action at this period, but they utilised this action in a way to indicate that in other respects they were a category apart from the common wage-earner. In this fashion they expressed their middle-class consciousness in transition between the world of need and the world of liberty; a characteristic also of their secret models, the middle and upper rank officials and the liberal professions.

e A Protected World: The Officers

The officers were protected not only by statute, a protection acquired as early as the Restoration, but also by memories of nineteenth century political history. The army leadership was the principal body responsible for maintaining order as the police, except in Paris and a few large towns, were weak. The officers were feared by the authorities, who remembered the coup d'état of 2 December, but also coddled, since they were the incarnation of the hope of the Revenge. The introduction of general conscription also gave them the social role of 'knocking the corners off' the youth from the countryside and supplementing the shortcomings of the educational system.

The pact made with the army after 1871 – autonomy in return for political neutrality – was not only based on the pragmatism of opportunist republicans, as was thought after the scandals of the Dreyfus Affair. The officers enjoyed genuine prestige in the eyes of the political class and bourgeois opinion. Contrary to the nobiliary legend wrongly espoused by earlier studies, work by Serge William Serman has shown the social function fulfilled by promotion within this corps of officials.[28] Before 1880, the majority of officers were promoted directly from the ranks, thanks to the massive promotions the wars of the Empire permitted. After 1880, officers were promoted indirectly after passing through schools for

28. S.W. Serman (341).

non-commissioned officers. This democratic body therefore allowed social mobility perhaps even more than public office, since it was more independent of pure book learning.

Paradoxically however, the republican peace narrowed this channel of social promotion. The general increase in education raised the level of the various competitive examinations for officers and non-commissioned officers, whereas the end of the wars lessened chances of promotion via military campaigns (except in the colonies). At Saint-Maixent, the school for non-commissioned officers, for example, 78 per cent of those who passed in 1887–1888 had only an elementary education. This was true of only 33 per cent of students in 1901–1909; in the same period, the proportion of students who had passed the baccalauréat rose from 21 to 57 per cent (1892–1907). The preparatory classes of Catholic colleges competed successfully with State high schools to prepare officers for Saint-Cyr. This caused the authorities some concern and later became a political issue (with the case of the officer trained in the 'Jesuit houses' in the Dreyfus Affair).

Lower in the social scale, the officer corps, in its desire to imitate Prussia, set up its own specialist school in the form of the *École supérieure de guerre* (founded in 1876), the 'generals' school' as its critics called it. However, this nascent meritocracy still contained a very strong element of social connivance, particularly in certain branches (such as the general staff and the cavalry), given the specific ideological or sociological characteristics of the upper echelons which were inherited from conservative regimes and co-opted because of their affinity. The correlation between social background and rank was not only the result of mechanisms of educational reproduction (there was only one general who had risen from the ranks in 1901), but the conscious product of the tactics of leading cadres or regulations, as was shown by certain practices revealed by the Dreyfus Affair.

For example, one regulation decreed (before it was abolished by General André) that officers had to obtain authorisation in order to marry, accompanied by an investigation and the furnishing of proof of a minimal dowry for the bride. Although these rules were bent and although the less affluent remained bachelors, those officers who founded families still had to find worthy consorts within the bosom of the bourgeoisie, frequently the traditional bourgeoisie. Only then could their sons follow in their footsteps, given the growing professional hereditary nature of the corps. A rich or 'well placed' wife in her turn was the guarantee of a successful social life, an indispensable asset for access to the highest and most prestigious posts which demanded that a certain position be kept up, not always possible on pay alone.

Despite the fall in the proportion of nobles (they comprised 24 per cent of sub-lieutenants in 1825 but only 11 per cent, primarily in the cavalry, in about 1900), the aristocratic model continued to determine officers' conduct, as is indicated by the practice of duelling. This anachronistic rigidity of a military society deprived of political rights partly resulted from the corps' isolation in a society which offered more lucrative careers in the economic sector. It was also a defensive reaction to successive waves of anti-militarism, which could be expressed freely for the first time including bourgeois anti-militarism against compulsory service for everyone in the 1880s and anarchist and socialist anti-militarism against the army's repressive function in 1890–1900. The cadres of the armies of the Republic were increasingly linked to an older France, even if they did not all originate from it socially. This France found a substitute for its nostalgia for the monarchy and State Catholicism in revanchist nationalism and the cult of the army.

f A World Apart: Secondary School-Teachers, between Elitism and Utopia

Secondary school-teachers were in a position corresponding to that of officers within public service and the middle classes. They differed in a number of ways – particularly in their ideological or political choices – but, sociologically as well as functionally, they were similar in many ways. Their status remained largely determined by the Napoleonic heritage. Like the officer's career, the teaching role was very clearly defined and framed in a rigid hierarchy. But, unlike other state professions, it enjoyed fairly wide autonomy – which was further increased by the Republic – which partly explains why corporative unrest, identical to that of the other types of officials mentioned earlier, did not develop within its ranks. Other explanations can be found in quantitative evidence. The group only experienced moderate growth; 6,318 teachers and assistants were employed in secondary education in 1873 and 10,014 in 1896. There was neither the massive increase in numbers that there was in primary education, nor the improvement in quality as in higher education. The scarcity value of the most highly-prized qualifications, guarantee of the best positions and the best promotions, was also maintained. Thus the number of candidates who passed the *agrégation*, the competitive examination for admission to posts, rose without causing its selectivity to slacken, primarily because of diversification into new disciplines or the creation of its equivalent in secondary education for girls. The average level of qualifications for secondary school-teachers was forced up without there being any deterioration in their working conditions, thanks to a fall in the staff ratio and the creation of more modern *lycées* in large or new towns.

On the whole, the majority of high school-teachers in 1910 held the *agrégation* certificate. This raised the profession's prestige in the eyes of parents but it also resulted in a financial gain, since the new graduates of the *agrégation* could expect a longer career at a higher grade. They no longer came principally from the *École normale supérieure* as in the past, but also through scholarships for degrees and *agrégation*, established by the Republic in order to provide a professional role for provincial arts and science faculties. However, the *agrégation* remained a selective and prestigious examination because the number of potential graduate candidates was simultaneously rising faster than the number of positions to be filled.[29]

Similarly, the creation of a female version of the secondary teacher's position had the political aim of snatching bourgeois girls from the clutches of Catholic teaching, and was accompanied by manifold fences to prevent any correlation with the male role. The diplomas conferred were not equivalent; forms of training were heterogeneous, and specific subjects were still assigned to women (economic and domestic hygiene, needlework and morality). The pupils at the *lycées* were meant to be Republican mothers, not blue-stockings; their teachers, educated in the secular convent of the *École normale supérieure* for young girls at Sèvres, were quasi-nuns, often the daughters of Protestant ministers, and rarely married.[30]

This controlled and partly deliberate expansion which aimed to checkmate the quasi-preponderance of Catholic secondary education, explains why the social characteristics of the recruitment of secondary school-teachers remained stable. Studies by Paul Gerbod, Gérard Vincent and Victor Karady demonstrate a predominance of lower sectors of the middle classes. In 1877, and also between 1900 and 1914, most secondary teachers came from craft and trade backgrounds; sons of employees and of primary and secondary school-teachers formed the second largest category. The upper echelons of the bourgeoisie, on the other hand, hardly ever guided their children into secondary school or college teaching because in their eyes the profession represented a fall in social status or salary level. A job as a secondary school-teacher therefore constituted promotion, playing a role at a higher level, analogous to that of jobs as primary school-teachers or petty officials for more working-class elements.[31]

However, this very tempting image of mobility must be put in perspective. What must be borne in mind is the size of the workforce in

29. V. Karady (330) and (331).
30. F. Mayeur (336).
31. P. Gerbod (75), G. Vincent (349) and (350), V. Karady (330).

this group. As only a few thousand jobs were involved – not hundreds of thousands as in the previous case – and as they were very unevenly distributed in space and presupposed access to the classical secondary channel, these social elevators had only very narrow doors. Moreover, the teachers had no intention of opening them because of the elitism which was so widespread in this milieu. As social selection increased, the further the teacher rose in the hierarchy, but chances of promotion were closely dependent on the scarcity value of the qualifications possessed and on geographical origin. Progress in the hierarchy involved uprooting, the teacher's desire to return to his native department being largely counter-balanced by the attractions of Paris where high schools offered considerably higher salaries.

However, the new advantages which the Republic granted secondary school-teachers to counter Catholic competition were in marked contrast with the government's inability to make deep-seated changes in syllabuses, examination procedures and the balance between disciplines. The improved status of previously subordinate disciplines (languages, sciences, history and geography) breached neither the predominance of classical subjects in timetables, nor the predominance of teachers of these disciplines in the demographic balance of the teaching body. The majority of them regarded the timid advance of modern education as regression or as a way of fortifying private education because of the social distinction that study of Latin conferred. Although the State's secondary school-teachers had increasingly enjoyed the benefits of scholarships, they still regarded the idea of 'democratising' their institutions as alien lest they lose the battle against competition from private institutions. They were more worried about falling standards (educational but also social) than about the fall in the size of the workforce. This emerges from the *Enquête sur l'enseignement secondaire* (1899), carried out in preparation for a reform which materialised in 1902, and which did not make a clear distinction between classical and modern education.

The secondary school-teachers saw themselves much more as guardians of a threatened culture in the modern world. What bound them to the elites was precisely the education which they shared with the real holders of power; in preserving it, they had the illusion of holding the keys to social success. By establishing a certain degree of democracy within the university, the Republic could not but maintain the *status quo* this majority of teachers desired. Innovators, who understood the social issues behind this traditional dialogue, did exist but, when faced with the inertia within the profession, preferred to turn towards the better-paid administration or towards higher education, which was expanding and where intellectual innovation was at least acknowledged as a value. The only goal that many other secondary school-teachers set themselves was to mould their own successors in an identical fashion through the medium of classes which prepared pupils for the entrance examinations to the major colleges (*grandes écoles*), and such classes proliferated at this time.

The teachers' ideal republic was therefore a sort of island protected from politics, from the deterioration of falling standards, from the rising tide of the modern humanities and from the religious quarrels with the rival religious education. There was also a reactionary side to this idealism – hence the strong representation of secondary school-teachers amongst the anti-Dreyfusards. It also had its progressive side – hence the militant role of young school-teachers, particularly graduates of the *École normale*, in the opposite camp. Neither side thought of themselves as a social group, but rather as guardians of the temple or awakeners of the masses. For a long time, therefore, they rejected the corporatism which was being born amongst the other categories of officials.

The teachers often fulfilled a general cultural role – particularly in the provinces or in the upper classes of the high schools – and thought of themselves as closer to the other elites than as the servants of the State. They were respectful of the hierarchies, which could act to their advantage, and protected from the too-flagrant injustices which were commonplace in primary education. They could therefore feel that they were free, particularly in comparison with their predecessors in earlier regimes, who were subject to close supervision. Possessing social rather than financial privileges, they held more aloof from their functions than did other members of the middle classes or holders of public office, and they could always hope that their children would obtain the qualifications or positions which they themselves had not yet been able to acquire.

In fact, all the indices of the probability of educational success place these children amongst the best in most bourgeois careers. The expression 'the republic of professors' is beyond a shadow of doubt untrue if it meant that the secondary school-teachers had an important share of power under the Republic. On the other hand, it is true if it meant that the professors belonged to an Athenian republic where the hierarchy of ranks remained open, where power was amicably divided and where there was the greatest possible autonomy in relation to a State which remained partly Bonapartist and to a society which was hardly permissive.

D The Liberal Professions: The Dream of a Classless Society?

However, it was indisputably the members of the liberal professions who most enjoyed this professional freedom in the society of the day, so much so that a number of other middle-class groups used them as a reference point. Three reasons explain why these professions experienced their golden age at this period. Access to their ranks still remained selective but their social influence was extending thanks to a controlled expansion and the conquest of new social functions. The liberal professions therefore combined the virtues of scarcity (without the weakness of marginality) with the attraction of an expanding market (without the risk of loss of value or popularisation). But, above all, the political system put these professions in a strategic position. By restoring the strength of provincial life the Republic placed these decentralised professions in the position of intermediaries, indispensable to every type of representational process, political, associative and cultural. By developing an ideology based on knowledge, it stamped the liberal specialists with a quasi-official label as general practitioners in social therapy. Only later did experts in administration or professionals in representation (unions, political parties and pressure groups) rob them of this role.

This intermediate function appears in contemporary official classifications which isolate them as a social category *sui generis*, grouping together certain public professions (the most qualified officials, members of the clergy, etc.) and private professions (doctors, lawyers, intellectual and artistic professions). The discussion here will be limited to the second body as conceived in present-day terms, though the contemporary concept, whereby there was no real gulf between the status of a high-level official and the medical or legal world, will still be borne in mind.

Other factors explain this blurred boundary. For example, many liberal general practitioners held secondary official appointments as experts attached to the courts, workers in institutions or on charitable boards, or teachers. Similarly, the massive purges of the magistracy at the end of the 1870s and the beginning of the 1880s allowed a large number of barristers to enter the ranks of the law, whereas those purged returned if they were still young enough to the bar. There was also all the ambiguous status of legal officials, a profession in the service of private interests but strongly structured and regulated by the State, which delegated semi-public functions to them for certain documents. Lastly, socially and culturally, this was the same world of the middle-rank bourgeoisie, possessing a culture which was not yet widespread.

a Overall View

Depending on the definition adopted (elitist or broad, hierarchical or functional), a correspondingly different view of the overall growth of these liberal professions at this time is obviously gained. According to the censuses, which give a broad view, the legal professions grew from 30,341 members in 1876 (including barristers, solicitors, legal officials and general agents) to 45,512 in 1906, or a growth of over 50 per cent in thirty years. The corresponding figures for doctors, including the diminishing category of non-graduate doctors (*officiers de santé*), officially abolished in 1892, are 16,500 and 20,673 (an increase of about 25 per cent). This overall growth conceals a phase when the availability of medical services regressed at the time when there were not enough new doctors to compensate for the fall in the number of *officiers de santé* in 1880–1890.[32] Similarly, while the number of barristers increased, the number of notaries fell; there were 9,765 notaries in 1855 and only 8,164 in 1912.[33]

This overall growth in the professions may seem small by the yardstick of twentieth century trends but contemporaries found it striking and tended moreover to overestimate it. In fact, it followed on a period of stagnation or decline under the Second Empire, linked to the complaints about the congestion of the liberal professions which had marked the July monarchy. The trend of numbers of people studying for medical and legal examinations shows a clear break at the end of the 1880s. This has been explained by young people's desire to profit from the exemption from military service which only graduates enjoyed; but it was above all a general movement by bourgeois, and sometimes petty bourgeois, youth to gain qualifications, reflected in the number of students who passed the baccalauréat. According to Fritz Ringer, the percentage of the age-group studying law rose from 0.2 (1875–1876) to 0.7 (1910–1911), with the figures for medicine being 0.2 and 0.4. The corresponding rates for Germany were 0.2 for law at both dates, and 0.1 and 0.3 for medicine, which emphasises the link between the attraction of legal jobs and the existence of a liberal regime in France.[34]

The other liberal professions grew at a faster rate, but without reaching the demographic strength of the traditional professions. These primarily involved careers in journalism and literature, which benefited from the rise of the national, popular and provincial press, and every type of artistic career, in this period when Paris was the artistic capital of the world. Numbers engaged in the first category more than doubled (from 4,173 men of letters and journalists in 1876 to 9,148 in 1906), bearing in mind the limitations of misleadingly precise figures for professions with variable boundaries; the second category showed a rise of nearly 60 per cent (from 22,615 to 35,593 at the same dates). Alongside these prestigious professions, which could bring, if not wealth, at least fame

32. J. Léonard (96), pp. 87–9.
33. T. Zeldin (44), new ed., vol. 1, p. 60.
34. F. Ringer, 'Education and the middle class in modern France', in W. Conze and J. Kocka (367), p. 120.

and social esteem, there was an increase in the ranks of all the intermediate professions that a population which was becoming urbanised and a service economy required, such as pharmacists, dentists and financial agents.

This confusion was further increased by the disparity in the geographical distribution of these groups. The map of the legal professions is the map of urban France. The map of the density of the medical professions does not match so closely, since the industrial departments with their proletarian populations did not offer adequate numbers of patients, while the concentration in the Midi, so strong today, appears already on the 1881 map drawn by Jacques Léonard. This map shows both the appeal of the rich and leisured clientele staying in the Midi and the solution found by small rural notables to find jobs for young men of good social position whose inherited income from land was not by itself enough to live on. On the other hand, the bourgeoisies of mercantile or industrial France hardly ever guided their children into these professions.[35] The contrast is even stronger in the other liberal professions. Lawyers and doctors were already heavily concentrated in Paris but the majority of people engaged in the intellectual professions followed suit. This generated a climate of competition and conflict, even a struggle for life, reflected in literary evidence such as Maupassant's *Bel Ami* and Zola's *L'Oeuvre*.

The disparities inherent in the liberal professions were not solely spatial, and were in fact primarily social. A rough idea of these can be gained from the enquiries into wealth in the various towns in France, as well as census data on the proportion of servants employed in this milieu. In 1911 in Lyons, out of 48 inheritances deriving from the liberal professions, half left less than 50,000 francs and half left more. In Paris, differences in wealth were even clearer; 49.6 per cent of inheritances were below 50,000 francs, but 16.6 per cent exceeded great wealth with 500,000 francs, a non-existent, figurative case in the provinces. In Bordeaux and Toulouse for example, the average wealth of this group at death was clearly lower at about 145,000 and 78,000 francs respectively.[36]

Their incomes ensured all members of the higher-grade liberal professions of a bourgeois standard of living (almost all notaries, advocates and doctors employed domestic servants). On the other hand, the status of the new, rapidly-expanding, liberal professions was already more insecure. A minority of their members could afford domestic servants. The bohemian life, popularised by Henry Murger in the first half of the nineteenth century, may represent an extreme case or a

35. J. Léonard (96), p. 87.
36. A. Daumard (29), p. 149.

temporary phase in literary or artistic life. But discomfort, obscurity, the need for a second trade or the degradation of liberal status by the mercenary versions of these trades (free-lance newspaper work, penny-a-line journalism, jobs as reporters, regression to the decorative, industrial or popular arts, etc.) were the ransom extracted by the structural congestion in these professions which, unlike the preceding ones, were unregulated.

b The Doctors: Paths to Success

It will be recalled that the doctors went through a similar situation in the first half of the nineteenth century, a period of 'medical congestion'. The over-lax laws of Ventôse, year IX (1803), by recognising all the unofficial doctors spawned by the Revolution's absence of regulation and by establishing two orders of doctors (doctors for the rich on the one hand and *officiers de santé*, doctors for the poor, on the other) created a difficult situation for this profession. The existence of *officiers de santé*, trained more quickly or primarily on the job, helped to lower the social prestige of the legal medical practitioner in the eyes of a population whose mentality was impregnated with religious fatalism or various superstitions, particularly in the countryside. Until late in the century, countryfolk often placed more confidence in bogus doctors than in the bearers of a knowledge which did not prove effective until the end of the century, thanks to the discoveries of Pasteur and his followers and, above all, to progress in hygiene.

The rise in doctors' prestige during the second half of the nineteenth century and particularly under the Third Republic,[37] was the result of a four-fold process. The first element was increasingly effective corporative action aimed at freeing the profession from the poor image of the *officiers de santé* by gradually abolishing the position; this was sanctioned by law on 30 November 1892. Secondly, doctors' incomes increased as a result of general prosperity and the rise in the standard of living, particularly in the towns where the majority of them were concentrated. Thirdly, the majority of doctors were gradually absorbed into an associative movement which obtained better guarantees from the administration against unfair competition. Lastly, belief in the efficacy of medicine became more widespread amongst the general public, a belief itself based on support for the ideology of progress and science encouraged by the Republic.

All these political, social and psychological developments were interconnected. The decline in competition between the two orders of doctors

37. J. Léonard (96).

extended the clientele and raised the standard of living of the most highly qualified doctors. The doctors' associative movement made it possible to establish standard minimum rates and prevent the drastic undercutting indulged in by doctors with no patients in the first half of the century. Expenditure on medical services, particularly those which involved more expensive operations or examinations, increased as the public's belief in medicine grew. Lastly, the doctors' internal organisation gave them greater weight when decisions had to be made which recognised them as influential social intermediaries. Evidence of this is found in the growing number of doctors in the Chamber of Deputies: 10 per cent of the deputies had taken the Hippocratic oath, some forty sat in the Senate, a dozen even held a ministerial portfolio. It can be gathered that this lobby which had now reached maturity had not done badly from the 1892 law.

Whereas at the beginning of the century an *officier de santé* earned between 600 and 800 francs a year and a doctor around 4,000 francs, by the century's end there was a clear financial improvement; a good doctor in Brittany could make from 5,000 to 14,000 francs from his patients in 1870–1880. Sticking to average examples, a medical journal estimated the income of a doctor in the west at 5,750 francs a year, but at 8,500 if he practised in wealthy Normandy. The disparities were much larger in towns. According to a contemporary essayist, half the Paris doctors earned 8,000 francs or less but the other half exceeded this threshold of a comfortable income, while big specialists, particularly surgeons, succeeded in amassing real fortunes even without personal inheritance. The professorial body of the faculty of medicine in the Belle Époque therefore included several millionaires flaunting all the external symbols of high bourgeois lifestyle; individual mansions, second homes, art collections, and leisure activities which brought them into contact with smart circles.[38]

These fashionable doctors had sometimes achieved this success in one generation. Sons of small doctors or of provincial petty bourgeois, they had broken into good society after successfully fighting their way along the rough path of a large number of competitive medical examinations. This career-pattern therefore made them mediators between the classes; doctors to the poorest in the public hospitals, to the richest in the town, advisers to administrations or the legislator, they were the incarnation of the virtues of science, of republican meritocracy and of a society marching towards progress.

This success on the part of a profession and its elite must not conceal its failings and contradictions, which exploded at the beginning of the twentieth century. The liberal or moderately progressive ideology, which

38. C. Charle (359), pp. 361–2.

was the main basis of the doctors' political culture at the end of the century, was slowly faced with varied challenges. The first came from within the ranks of the profession itself; some doctors were going too far in the pursuit of profit. The doctor in a hurry who made innumerable house-calls, doctors who collected public sinecures, offered thermal cures or clinics for rich patients, or recommended miraculous medicines, all these new social types from social novels or newspaper publicity were typical of the variety of products of industrialism contained in corporative claims. The rush to raise the scientific level of studies was not socially neutral. By prolonging studies, it added to their cost and preserved the imbalance between leading faculties (particularly the Paris faculty where half of France's aspiring doctors clustered) and lesser schools. Big specialists, haunted by the fear of a return to former mediocrity, did everything to make the curriculum more selective. And, in fact, the percentage of doctors in relation to the number of medical students fell from 16 in 1889–1890 to 13 in 1907–1908.

Without going as far as the pharmacists' *numerus clausus*, the reforms tended towards a new elitism which restricted this now very popular profession to people who were best equipped socially and culturally, that is to say, the heirs to medical dynasties in process of formation. In 1909, for example, training was extended to five years. These schemes provoked a series of disturbances in the faculties which the extreme Right tried to turn to their advantage. The medical unions were also opposed to them and denounced the mandarins cut off from patients. They also demanded the abolition of the *agrégation*, the medical elite's hidden tool for co-option to the ranks.[39] Thus the profession, beacon of this century of science, in its turn gradually experienced new internal tensions. These were sharpened by the renewed expansion of the medical workforce and by fear of losing their liberal status in the face of collective patients who increased in number as mutual assurance societies multiplied. Lawyers were better protected from these challenges, which were the ransom to be paid for the spread of medical services in society.

c The Legal Professions

While the doctors were winning their bourgeois credentials, the legal milieu completed its professionalisation and managed to adapt itself to social demand without losing anything of its sociological uniqueness. The partial, and therefore questionable, statistics available on social recruitment to this milieu show how closed it actually was. In legal professions involving full higher education (barristers, magistrates,

39. G. Weisz (351), pp. 359 ff.

professors), only 10 to 15 per cent of parents came from the petty bourgeoisie.[40] With the bourgeoisie holding 80 to 90 per cent, these professions recruited their members in a way that was balanced between the economic bourgeoisie (40 to 50 per cent depending on the region), identical reproduction (20 to 25 per cent for the descendants of legal professions), and sons of officials or members of other liberal professions (the same order of magnitude).

These social data show that jurists stood at the crossroads to numerous possible jobs. A post as a law officer was one means of promotion for the petty bourgeois who had a small amount of capital available from inheritance, marriage or a loan from a close relative. The bar and the magistrature served as a transition to the strata of power or culture for a newly-promoted economic bourgeoisie. They also served a purpose in maintaining an old type of bourgeoisie of the robe, thanks to a strong hereditary element or to two-way exchanges between public and private jurists.

This general sociology has to be qualified according to place and types of predominant activity. Membership of the body of clerks attached to the courts of justice (*basoche*, solicitors, small-town notaries, process servers, etc.) was, like small business, one of the most effective social elevators in places where the modern economy had so far made little impact. In large towns on the other hand, because of the cost of offices, this level of the profession was restricted to bourgeois of good social standing, or even the high bourgeoisie. The chambers of a small rural notary thus represented a capital of about 15,000 to 20,000 francs. In a prefecture however, the required capital was 100,000 francs, and in Paris 700,000 francs plus security, which itself varied with the type of town.

The yield from these posts was also very unequal. Although some in Paris brought in more than 100,000 francs a year, only 10 per cent nationally produced more than 30,000 francs. The majority fell below the 10,000 franc line, and more than a fifth below the 5,000 franc line.[41] The least lucrative offices were situated in rural cantons which suffered from the end-of-century agricultural crisis. Their holders were the least qualified and the most tempted to resort to dubious speculation or fraudulent use of their clients' funds in order to round up their incomes. The period 1880–1890 was thus marked by a new outbreak of dismissals of notaries who had failed or been involved in scandals; there were nearly 500 such cases between 1882 and 1895, or over 5 per cent of the

40. From P. Harrigan and V. Neglia (249) and the findings of as yet unpublished personal research into the legal professions in Paris. See also my article (325), p. 118, which assembles existing data.

41. T. Zeldin (44), p. 63.

profession's workforce.[42] But the various projects to reform or to challenge this survival of the Ancien Regime in the heyday of the Republic failed because of the problem of compensation for the cost of the notaries' offices and goodwill (estimated at more than 950 million in 1911) and the fear of displeasing the rural clientele, whose interests were managed by notaries, in the absence of a decentralised and efficient credit structure.

The profession of barrister, on the other hand, ensured a prestigious position in middle-sized towns, where it was not possible to set up at will and where people relied on local men they already knew. The career of Waldeck-Rousseau is typical in this respect. The son of a Nantes barrister who achieved only average success, the future president of the Council first tried to set up in Saint-Nazaire, but the town proved too small to yield him a living. He then tried his luck at Rennes, relying on his republican friends, who were also barristers but with strong political interests. He specialised in defending economic interests and, after a few years, he was arguing 150 to 200 cases a year which yielded him 25,000 to 30,000 francs, or more than double his father's fees.[43] Moreover, personal talent and a feeling for which cases would be profitable (financially or symbolically) were as important as the locality of the office or professional heredity. The case of Waldeck-Rousseau's elder brother demonstrates this; he started from the same basis but was never able to make a breakthrough and finally retired to his property and became a police court magistrate. In Paris or the large towns, new men won fame through major cases which hit the headlines and enabled them to build up a clientele more rapidly than usual. Although this profession was a seed-bed for politicians, particularly republican politicians, those who succeeded in Paris came more from the milieu of the new bourgeoisie; such as Gambetta, son of a Cahors grocer, and his friends in the Republican Union.[44]

Those not bold enough or talented enough to try their luck in the capital could still find an outlet in public office, and particularly in the magistrature or the prefectoral corps, if their clientele was inadequate. The discretionary recruitment, openly based on political recommendation, to these two bodies found jobs for more than fifteen hundred barristers or graduates at the beginning of the 1880s. Not all of them had good careers, but they were still a godsend to a whole generation which could not have acceded to these positions ten years earlier when recommendations went exclusively to young men of good social position

42. E.N. Suleiman (344), p. 72.
43. See P. Sorlin (343), pp. 150 ff.
44. Ibid., p. 194.

from the local notability. Louis Lépine, for example, the future – and famous – prefect of the Paris police, was one of those lucky enough to be promoted by the republican administrative revolution. In his *Souvenirs*, he reveals how he saw no future in his first profession as a barrister.[45] Other future high judges owed their rapid promotion or the end of a lack-lustre existence in small provincial towns solely to these events. But, as always in such cases, the result was to worsen congestion at a later date, because these new young magistrates or officials blocked their juniors' entry or promotion.

At the end of the 1880s, as has been seen, the number of articled jurists rose considerably at the same time as the economy entered a dull phase and the State restricted expenditure and therefore recruitment of qualified officials. Careers in both public and private law were therefore less open than before. A few figures reflect this increased competition; the number of barristers at the Paris bar rose by 110 between 1873 and 1883 (from 643 to 753), but by 250 between 1883 and 1893 (from 753 to 1,003), and again by 122 in the following seven years. At the national level, although a perceptible rise can be observed in the number of law students (an increase of 44 per cent between the averages for 1876–1880 and 1894–1898), the rise in the number of graduates was much lower. Professors, faced with increased numbers, therefore reacted by raising the level of selection for entry to the higher grades.

This effort to maintain the scarcity value of the qualification did not prevent the situation deteriorating in the capital where the most ambitious jurists were concentrated. With the closing down of administrative posts and economic stagnation, provincial opportunities were limited to the heirs of the best-established families who were able to profit from an already existing social capital. Moreover, a comparison of official data and the census figures shows a fringe of jurists on the periphery of this recorded legal world who utilised the title of barrister not in order to plead but in order to play an intermediate role in various types of business, as they did not have sufficient funds to open a real office or wanted to escape the disciplinary control of the bar.

The first signs of this deterioration in the social position of a protected bourgeois profession explains why its elite hardened itself against the threats taking shape at the end of the century. Measures were instituted such as the refusal to allow non-Latinist candidates to enter the faculty; maximum limitations on entry by women (whereas this had already come about in medicine), and restrictions on entry by foreign students who, as

---

45. The son of a Lyons accountant, he became secretary to the republican deputy of the Rhône, Louis Andrieux, who recommended him to Gambetta for appointment as sub-prefect in 1878 (L. Lépine, *Souvenirs*, Paris, Payot, 1912, pp. 21–39 and 43).

was seen in medicine, might stay in France and increase competition with native-born.

d Conclusion

The expression 'middle class' was synonymous with bourgeoisie in the first half of the nineteenth century but took on a quite different meaning, by acquiring a plural, at the end of the century. It was used to embrace everyone who tried to escape from the masses (workers or peasants), without being sure that they would attain undisputed bourgeois status. The diversity of the list drawn up in this chapter emphasises this tension within all the groups sharing this dual concern. The small grocer or the draper's assistant dreamed of being a new Boucicaut or Félix Potin, but in greater probability risked bankruptcy or dismissal. The doctor or barrister, whose secret role-models were the big specialists, habitués of the salons, or the glamorous future minister, might be no more than legal or medical practitioners with no clients, peddling miracle cures or wonder-working investments. Petty or middle-rank officials were divided between the illusion of the respectability which a certain degree of job-security provided and the collective claim for a place in the sun in respect of a State with no rules. The only areas less gripped by this tension were the worlds apart constituted by the cadres of the army and the members of the University, coddled by the regime and living in a closed world.

The balance between categories of status which improved and those which deteriorated was fairly equal from one milieu to another. Although the artisans and shopkeepers, and the employees, suffered from the mediocre economic situation at the end of the century and from growing competition, they also profited from the liberal climate introduced by the Republic by establishing a collective defence (unionist or political) of their status. Similarly, although the entry of women into some branches of public office involved an objective deterioration in some administrative sections, it also contributed to the mobilisation of men and the rejection by officials of the State's authoritarian paternalism. Lastly, the liberal professions as a whole had now won full rights as bourgeoisie and therefore served as models to the petty middle classes. Precisely for this reason they became more and more attractive to the new educated generations of petty bourgeoisie. These in their turn had to take care not to fall back on the invisible social ladder of liberal society. These internal and external struggles were the price paid for the decline in the old forms of domination and of the loss of prestige of the royal power, and were therefore linked to the divisions at the top between old and new elites. These fault-lines are the subject of the next chapter.

–6–

Old and New Elites

There have been a variety of contradictory interpretations of the character of the ruling groups in the Third Republic. The classic image, borrowed from political history and from the first essays on the subject, is of a transition from an old ruling class to 'new strata', to use Gambetta's phrase, or to a republican bourgeoisie formed mainly of lawyers who had moved into the ranks of professional politicians. This purely parliamentary image is very inadequate. It omits the fact that, in a liberal regime, a large part of social power lies outside the parliamentary and State arena. It also neglects the confused mixture of various forms of power which defined the elites: economic power, which was largely autonomous; and the administrative power of certain corps; cultural and religious power at the centre of a number of contemporary political discussions. Lastly, it simplifies social contrasts by freezing them in the mould of the ideological debates of the 1870s, which themselves date back to earlier regimes. This chapter will thus aim to couple traditional analysis in terms of ruling class (which involves using the terms nobility, notable, bourgeoisie) with a transverse approach in terms of elites. This makes it possible to apprehend other types of divisions within the dominant milieu as well as the internal dynamics of the contrasts between them, the source of reclassifications and changes in the political scenario.

Although these two ways of perceiving the summit of society were born of two opposing sociological traditions (that of Marx on one hand, and of Pareto and Weber on the other), they are not really incompatible. They are to a large extent the theoretical expression of how contemporaries saw the society under consideration. They reflect in scholarly terms the ideological conflicts which divided the old and new ruling classes of the period and, because of this, correspond quite well with the social evolution that has to be taken into account. The contrast between old and new elites does not imply a value judgement, such as Gambetta's term 'new strata'. Despite the reforms introduced, the new republican elites very rapidly proved powerless to cope with certain serious national crises or were compromised by scandals.

Challenged from the Right, by the old notables who held on to many strong positions in the provinces or in some administrative bodies and, from the Left, by new movements expressing the aspirations of social groups who were claiming a share in power (the workers' movement, the petty middle classes and the 'intellectuals'), the 'republican aristocracy' still lasted longer than the old ruling classes. This was due to the processes of integration of both the middle classes and part of the working-class elite, through education, colonial and administrative expansion, the return to protectionism and the first social measures. While pressure from below was thus partially defused, pressure from above also served to reinforce periodic revivals of republicanism, cementing the alliance between the elites in power and the working-class electorate at the time of the Défense republicaine and the Bloc des gauches, for example, after the Dreyfus Affair.

A Nobility and Notables: Decline or Adaptation?

A The Causes of the Decline

A large part of the power of the nobility and, more generally, of the notables in France before 1870 derived, as has been seen, from their occupation of important positions in the State apparatus or the representative institutions. Even the Empire, which claimed to be partly the emanation of the will of the people, systematically chose its high officials, deputies, senators, general councillors and mayors from amongst men privileged by birth and wealth. The 1871 elections gave back to the nobility and the notables the illusion that they enjoyed wide powers of influence over the population, even without the support of a dictatorship. In fact, numerous rural regions had voted for the old ruling class not on the basis of its actual programme (a return to the monarchy) but on its official programme, a return to peace. The whole of the republicans' political strategy had been to convince the peasantry that this programme of order and conservation was the programme of the Republic and that a return to the monarchy would be a new source of disorder and revolution. The series of electoral defeats suffered by the old parties showed that this message had got through to the small peasantry; it was no longer the red rag of socialism that was waved at them but the white flag of the Ancien Regime and its privileges.

But the defeat of the old notables was not solely the result of poor political tactics; it had wider social foundations which need to be understood. The 1885 elections only just failed to give power back to the old Right; Boulangism, supported by some aristocrats, endangered the regime. Later republican majorities were never overwhelming. In short, the notables retained a wide social influence until before 1914.

It remains to be understood why, despite these local foundations, these encroachments were never able to become unequivocal successes at a national level. How this society in transition between on the one hand the Ancien Regime and on the other hand a social organisation based on individual relationships and the laws of the market, came to collapse can be understood by studying the example of the western regions, where the notables and nobility had succeeded in establishing close relations with the peasantry based on patronage.[1] In the Mayenne, for example, at the end of the nineteenth century, royalist notables gradually lost the focal points for the exercise of their influence that they had patiently built up since the Restoration. They withdrew from the few industrial enterprises in which they still had interests because, in the period of agricultural prosperity, they preferred to place their liquid financial assets in prestige investments (building or rebuilding châteaux, or restoring churches) or in land, in order to keep intact their domains which were still threatened with division in every generation. The industries were therefore now managed by new men, most often supporters of the Republic, who thus influenced the workers' vote in the most highly developed regions of the department. Two of the republican leaders in Mayenne were industrial dyers; one of them would later be mayor, senator and deputy.

The basis of power, the land, in its turn betrayed the notables at a time of agricultural crisis. The level of income from land tended to fall, sometimes below the cost of farming the land. In Normandy the problem was solved by specialisation in livestock-raising which cut labour costs. In the Mayenne, the notables refused to enter a fully capitalist agricultural economy out of loyalty to polyculture and the practice of sharing their farm produce with their tenant farmers. They claimed that this type of social relationship avoided any seeds of a class struggle between landowner and lessee. They then entered into competition with the comfortably-off peasants who did not enjoy the same enchanted relationship with the land. But this independent peasantry no longer had any reason to remain under the protection of nobles and notables, and it too increasingly supported the Republic.

These notables were not only economically, but also socially, diminished. The advances in commercial life and in primary education reduced the notables' role as intermediaries between society in general and the once isolated rural regions. Demoralised by their political defeats, tending to leave their lands which yielded less and to invest in stocks and shares, the old notables failed to develop modern means of influence

---

1. M. Denis (173), pp. 339 ff, and 'Le renforcement du patronage aristocratique sur les paysans de la France de l'Ouest au XIXe siècle', unpublished contribution to the colloquium on *Les Noblesses Européennes*, Rome, 1985.

over the countryside. Republican or Catholic unions competed with their agricultural unions; the livestock-raising companies or agricultural banks also tended to avoid coming under their control. Whereas enlightened large landowners had been the instigators of agricultural innovation under the July monarchy and the Empire, their withdrawal to the towns and to other investments made them increasingly conceive the land as a place for leisure activities, as a symbol of a lifestyle, not as the centre of existence.[2] As a result the peasantry escaped from their patronage and their political directives, more especially as the notables were deeply divided over political tactics between loyal followers of a hopeless legitimitism, proponents of conservatism, and enthusiastic supporters of the Catholic cause against the excesses of anti-clericalism at the beginning of the century.

The last cause of the decline in the notables' power lay in their very world view. Their ideal was an unchanging hierarchical society, where inferiors naturally acknowledged the guardianship of their superiors in exchange for the services these superiors rendered the peasants.[3] This ideal was still tenable in some increasingly rare isolated regions. It was no longer tenable in a market economy, dominated by the towns, where a quite different model of social mobility and of challenge to the old hierarchies was spreading. The government of Moral Order had been an attempt to re-establish the old order by artificially isolating all the revolutionary elements. But this therapy implied massive recourse to State power, a method which ran counter to the Legitimists' liberal and decentralising ideals. For them, the State bore the real responsibility for the social crisis because of its levelling role.

Conservative governments therefore used power hesitantly. Their repressive measures did nothing but alienate the new strata, without having the necessary strength to be effective in the absence of social networks. Split into centralisers and decentralisers, liberals and authoritarians, men who rejected the whole revolutionary heritage and men who wanted to retain part of it, those who counted on the Church's support and those who mistrusted it, the notables did not succeed in pursuing a coherent policy despite their unifying ideology. Their sole achievement was to unite their adversaries against them.

These divisions also stemmed from internal schisms in the notables' world between the most provincial and the most Parisian, with the first having less chance of changing and adapting to the modern world. This explains their political impotence and their differences as to strategy.

2. Ibid., pp. 444–95.
3. See R.R. Locke (392), ch. 4.

b The Provincial Notables

The map of legitimism in 1876, drawn up by Robert Locke, highlights the areas that were most resistant to the modern world which the Republic symbolised. Comparison with the map of the Legitimist vote in the 1837 municipal elections shows the extent of the ground covered in forty years and the change in social relationships in rural France between the two periods.[4] Whereas under Louis-Philippe, domination by the old elites was accepted almost everywhere except in the great Paris basin and the East, in 1876 only Brittany and a few departments in the interior of the West, the Nord Pas-de-Calais and, less decisively, the south of the Massif Central and the Franche-Comté held fast.

As has been seen, the question of homogeneous regions either economically or completely dominated by Catholicism does not arise. André Siegfried's model of rural societies retaining feudal features has since been criticised by Paul Bois in its application to the Sarthe. Bois places greater emphasis on more historical data, such as the scars left by the Revolution, the presence or absence of social intermediaries such as artisans, and the town-country conflict.[5] To the peasants in the north-west of the Sarthe, the mainly republican bourgeoisie in this traditionally Royalist land seemed to be exploiting them more than the old remote or absent nobility.

In the infinite social and political diversity of rural France, which has been glimpsed in a previous chapter, it would obviously be simplistic to give a synthetic view of the manifold factors accounting for the survival or decline of the dominance of the notables. The same changes as in Mayenne are found again in the Deux-Sèvres village of Mazières-en-Gâtine; as the commune expanded and modern ways were introduced, the old large landowner lost all his social and political attributes and ended up leaving the countryside and selling his lands.[6] In the Morvan, long since infiltrated by the new breeze from Paris because of migrations, the most coherent explanation for the peasants' opposition to the republican vote was the link between large property and a dependent relationship; hence the vote for the notables, on the lines of Siegfried's thesis.[7]

The basis of power remained land which provided the means of

---

4. Ibid., pp. 82 and 258.
5. A. Siegfried (407) and P. Bois (51).
6. R. Thabault (277). The Manche provides a comparable example: the loosening of the links of dependence between landowning peasants, who were in the majority, and large landowners derived from the peasants' conquest of cultural autonomy and their perception of the Republic as a regime which genuinely defended agriculture. See A. Guillemin (181), especially p. 60.
7. See M. Vigreux (221), pp. 450 ff.

exerting influence over small farmers, through leasing it to tenant farmers, the distribution of work to day labourers or domestic servants, common rights and charitable activities. But despite the crisis in agriculture and forestry, the proportion of great domains was not significantly reduced in regions where they predominated. The nobles or notables refined their propaganda, posing as defenders of agriculture as a whole against the Republic which, they claimed, would betray peasant interests by leaving the frontiers open and by placing a heavy fiscal burden on the land. This agrarian argument, mentioned earlier, and inspired by the *Syndicat des agriculteurs de France*, dominated by large Right-wing property, made it possible to restrict the decline of the notables' influence over a peasantry relieved of its weakest and therefore most dependent elements.[8] Nevertheless, it was only sufficient if a siege mentality on the part of the rural community solidly united behind the old authorities was nurtured via the medium of the Church and religion. In the normal case, that of the majority of rural regions won over to the Republic, the old notables only retained positions at a local level in places where their physical presence, that is to say their properties and their agents (guards, stewards and people under an obligation to them), was powerful enough to combat the new mediators of modern society such as school, the press, fairs and markets, roads, railways, officials, etc. At a cantonal level, it would have needed a concentration of land rarely achieved in France (unlike England) and the absence of a large urban centre to counter-balance peasant support. Even in places where the element of domination continued to exist, the use of visible means of pressure underlines the fact that the traditional deference was no longer acceptable even in the old 'fiefs'.

However, it would be simplistic to see the position of the old notables solely in terms of their loss of political power and influence. Some of them tried to fight back by creating new institutions for patronage or intellectual activity. In particular they adapted the theories of Le Play, which continued to guide the thinking of many notables. Faced with the challenge from the workers and the socialists, some moderate republicans, who identified more with the notables than with the democrats, drew closer to these most innovative members of the old elites.[9]

But the remedies these theorists suggested essentially consisted in adapting the patronage relationships which the large landowners had practised to the industrial world (the world not only of medium-size

8. P. Barral (286).

9. S. Elwitt (372), especially ch.2. Examples of the overlap between the old world view and the handling of relationships within industrial society can be found in the Musée social group, the work of the Catholic worker circles of A. de Mun, the paternalism of Léon Harmel, and the various types of paternalism in the North, the East or the large-scale businesses in the Massif Central.

enterprises where relationships were still on an individual basis, but also that of large enterprises, which they hoped to make more humane). In villages or market towns dominated by one enterprise, the employer, who was sometimes also a landowner and sometimes a noble, regained the same conditions of domination over his wage-earners as did the rural notables.[10] He had to introduce a revived form of paternalism if he wanted to avoid outbreaks, such as those provoked by the hardships brought on by the depression, as at Carmaux, or by contagion from the workers' movement and the desire for emancipation which the Republic had disseminated in its early days. This paternalism took a variety of forms but was directed more fundamentally towards re-creating the enterprise as a new community welded into a family, as legitimist rural ideology depicted the large domain and the peasants living round it, than towards political influence. These policies will be discussed further in the later chapter dealing in detail with the workers. Here, it is important to show how the modern world was impregnated by the re-actualisation of social relationships inherited from a world in decline. The same interaction between the old and the new characterised the integration into contemporary society of the highest aristocracy, that of Paris.

c The Paris Aristocracy

The great notables and the aristocracy who normally lived in Paris were in a very different situation from the old notables who did not have the means to emigrate to the large towns. The dazzling picture that Proust has left was certainly embellished but does partially correspond to the reality which the social and economic indicators convey. In the sample of large Paris fortunes analysed by Adeline Daumard, the titled nobility more than maintained its ancient splendour. The landowner-*rentiers*, of which the nobility was mainly composed, were probably now outclassed in wealth by the great businessmen of the Belle Époque, but they still enjoyed comfortable incomes with an average capital of more than three million francs.[11] More even than the provincial notables, they had converted part of their inherited property into stocks and shares; 38.8 per cent of their wealth was in property in 1911, against 60 per cent under

10. M. Pigenet (456), especially pp. 37–43. The manager of the iron and steel factory situated in the hamlet of Rosières (Cher) was at the same time the village mayor and general councillor. The policy of social patronage made it possible to maintain a low wage level and preserve social peace until 1892. But after that date, this protection was no longer enough to prevent contagion from unionist and socialist ideas.

11. A. Daumard (29), pp. 257–67. The noble officials were clearly less rich (540,108 francs), like the *rentiers* (303,779 francs) and the members of the liberal professions (1,104,363 francs).

Louis-Philippe, and almost equally in Paris and outside Paris, whereas fifty years earlier land investments in the provinces were twice as great. The percentage was even less amongst nobles involved in business; 34.1 per cent of their wealth was invested in land.[12]

The noble origins of this aristocracy dated from different periods (including a declining number of old nobility, men ennobled before the Revolution and the nobility of the Empire and the nineteenth century). All, however, tried to keep the distinctive signs of their social identity: a fashionable lifestyle, imitated by the high bourgeoisie since the July monarchy; charitable works; leisure activities which were expensive in both time and space (hunting, riding to hounds); and two homes (ideally, a family château and a mansion in the Faubourg Saint-Germain but also Saint-Honoré).[13] But to keep up this role in the face of the decline in income from land – even when it was drawn from extensive lands – and divisions of inheritances – even with the addition of the eldest son's extra share – made it imperative to adapt to the modern world. In addition to the property investments already mentioned, seats on boards of directors, obtained thanks to the society network, were a respectable way of increasing income without stepping too far from the image of a man of independent means. Some 10 per cent of the company directors mentioned in the 1901 *Annuaire Chaix* belonged to titled nobility.

These connections with large-scale capitalism did not date solely from this period, but were strengthened in comparison with earlier regimes. From 1871, for example, a not inconsiderable minority of businessmen figured amongst the ranks of both Legitimist and Orleanist deputies. They were quite often men who had left State service after their administrative or political careers were interrupted when the notables were swept back after 1877. Unlike other businessmen, as will be seen, these men's movements into the private sector were mainly effected by utilising the society and family assets of the nobility, which often already had relatives or friends on boards of directors. This lesser degree of professionalism was accompanied by a preference for certain sectors where the aristocratic presence was traditionally strong, such as insurance, mining, railways, safe stocks or those close to a public utility, far removed from the hazardous speculation of the *nouveaux riches* or the new companies. The prince d'Arenberg, a large landowner in the Cher was also chairman of the Suez Canal Company after the retirement of Ferdinand de Lesseps, while the duc de Broglie was at the head of the

---

12. C. Charle (365), p.426.
13. This type of aristocratic life is described in detail in respect of the d'Harcourts in P. Chabot (4), pp. 42–118; it had scarcely changed from that described by A. Martin-Fugier (193) for the period 1815–1848.

Saint-Gobain board from 1872 to 1901.

For all that, the nobility, even the old nobility, did not abandon State service, even republican State service, when it could. In 1901, a quarter of the upper ranks of the diplomatic service, a fifth of the councillors at the *Cour des Comptes* and over 15 per cent of major-generals belonged to the old or more recent nobility. On the other hand, the corps purged by the republicans or based on strong educational selectivity were almost entirely in the hands of commoners. Similarly, the nobility only pursued intellectual activities in marginal sectors, those that were more traditional, or in an amateur way; for example at the *École des Chartes*, at the *Collège de France*, in some provincial academic societies, or through patronage of literary salons. The *Académie française* was unusual in that it had a strong minority of aristocrats in its ranks.[14]

The Parisian nobility cannot therefore be reduced to the status of a leisured class, even though it was this aspect which exercised the strongest indirect social influence on bourgeois 'snob' elements who wanted to ape it (the word 'snob' came into common use at that time). The oldest or the richest noble families had no hesitation in coming to terms with the enemy when it was to their advantage. The son of Albert de Mun married a Mademoiselle Werlé, heiress to a great champagne firm; his daughter married a Hennessy from the cognac firm. Henri Schneider, king of Le Creusot, married his daughters to genuine aristocrats, as had Pouyer-Quertier, the cotton king, before him.[15] Society chroniclers may have exaggerated the manner in which impecunious nobles married rich American heiresses (as in the case of Boni de Castellane), but examination of the matrimonial alliances of aristocrats from various milieus and the fate of their children proves the astute adaptation of the old rules to modern imperatives. Young titled girls continued to marry nobles so as not to lose their noble name, whereas young nobles could marry well-endowed commoners. But the level of the husband's wealth or the sector of the activity he engaged in also influenced the decision in these *mésalliances*. If he was already in business, he sacrificed self-interest to his prejudice in favour of a title; if he was in the less lucrative administration, the bride's dowry or her father's social position carried more weight than the family's crest. Whereas in the provinces the castes remained tightly closed, because of political divisions and the narrowness of the ruling class, Parisian nobility, above all concerned with maintaining its membership of the social elite, had no hesitation in effecting a compromise with its aristocratic customs and taking advantage of the fascination it exercised over would-be nobles or high bourgeois.

14. C. Charle (365).
15. M. de Saint-Martin (406), p. 7; P. Levillain (388), p.207; J.-P. Chaline (56), p. 117.

B The Bourgeoisies

The analysis here will be limited to the bourgeoisie in the limited sense, that is to say the landowners and/or the men running industrial, commercial or financial concerns or the more important agricultural enterprises. Other groups, privileged by their office or cultural level, continued to be encompassed by this generic term in accordance with the usage of the first three-quarters of the nineteenth century. But the spread of socialist ideology tended to make the economic bourgeoisie the most important group in the general view of contemporaries, since it was the worker's enemy, the peasant's parasite, or the author of the downfall of part of the middle classes. The defenders of the established order also contributed to this change in the meaning of the word, justifying the employer by his irreplaceable social role. He was the creator of wealth, defender of national greatness, an example of the social ascent possible through work or ability, and a benefactor in his paternalistic incarnation.

For all that, this contracted meaning of the word 'bourgeoisie' must not conceal the diversity within the milieu, which explains the use of the plural in the title of this section. The plurality of bourgeoisies derived from the hierarchy of wealth, their location, their division into sectors and the degree to which the employer class was open in relation to the length of time the branch had existed and its degree of concentration. This plurality also arose from the strength or weakness of links with the land, distance in relation to the financial capital, i.e., Paris, and also from more ideological factors such as religious affiliation (Catholic, Jewish or Protestant employers did not have the same political options or the same social orbits) and the relationship with politics. Depending on the size of town, the degree of industrialisation of the region, the dominance of one sector or the existence of a more diversified economy, the employers, notably those in middle-sized businesses, a modal case in contemporary France, might or might not reinforce their economic domination with wider social and political influence. Their relationship with the working-class population was then based on their role as notables.

a Overall View

While the great traditional notables were beginning to slide down the scale of prestige and wealth if they remained loyal to the land, the largest industrialists and traders continued the rise they had begun under the Second Empire, despite the crises at the end of the nineteenth century. In Lyons, inheritances in 1911 show that their wealth grew at the most scandalous rate; by 291 per cent for traders, and by 219 per cent for industrialists. In Lille, where industry was even more predominant, the average sum bequeathed by manufacturers in 1891–1893, and these were hard years, was nearly 1.4 million francs, or twenty thousand times the average level of a worker's inheritance. In a wider sample from the North, the average fortune at death at the beginning of the Third Republic was also between one million and 2.5 million francs.[16] Under the Second Empire, the great fortunes might still have originated from the land; on the eve of 1914, financiers and great industrialists reached peaks that a landed fortune could no longer approach.

What struck contemporary imagination was the rapidity with which wealth was acquired at least as much as the scale. In one generation, entrepreneurs, like others, pulled themselves up to the level of high society and out-stripped the old aristocracy. Boucicaut, son of a hat-maker, was an employee and then the owner of the Bon Marché; he left 22 million when he died in 1877. Ten years later his wife had doubled this inheritance.[17] These are, of course, exceptional cases but they come within the range of real possibility and serve as a window on the new bourgeoisie. The self-made businessman was the model of the new society and the Republic deliberately extolled him as an illustration of its desire that class barriers disappear. He was favourably compared with the parvenu, the upstart, who also rose very fast but lost the sense of his own limitations and went bankrupt. Jaluzot, the owner of the Printemps and a deputy was an example of this phenomenon; his fortune abruptly disappeared in the sugar crash in 1905. Boucicaut went on to found a dynasty; Jaluzot was only a one-off.

b Closure or Openness?

The contrasts produced by the economic situation at the end of the nineteenth century and the Belle Époque placed the employers in situations which were favourable to varying degrees. The great depression was hard on the traditional sectors sired by the first industrial revolution (textiles, consumption goods and engineering). On the other hand, the recovery at the end of the century gave birth to new sectors, electricity, automobiles, chemicals, cement, petroleum and new metallurgy in the east. On one hand, therefore, the ranks of the business bourgeoisie tended to close in on themselves, since only the most stable businesses could withstand the unfavourable economic situation. On the other, the new branches of industry gave some self-made men their chance and they

16. P. Léon (93), p. 385; F. Codaccioni (59), p. 171; F. Barbier (224), p. 191.
17. V. Bourienne (228), p. 281.

could hope to pull themselves up to the level of the triumphant bourgeois of the Second Empire on the basis of the businesses they founded.

Statistical data which is beginning to become available on the social origins of the heads of the large joint stock companies, principally based in Paris, and provincial employers in the main industrial regions confirm this dual phenomenon of closure in the 1880s and opening up in the 1900s. According to Maurice Lévy-Leboyer, the proportion of second-generation employers in 1855 was 41.5 per cent of employers in Normandy and the East. This percentage rose to 55.7 in 1885, an indication of the closed situation resulting from the crisis. In 1913, at the end of the new growth of the Belle Époque, a slight opening up can be noted, with only 47.4 per cent of employers being heirs.[18] Although a small majority of the managers of the most important businesses were not heirs from established business families, these others still came mainly from a privileged milieu, such as the liberal professions, high public office, or lesser businesses. Large employers from a working-class milieu remained as few, or even fewer, than in the early days of the industrial revolution; they account for less than 10 per cent of all existing samples.

Thus the economic bourgeoisie who reached a certain status were usually at least one generation away from any roots in the masses. There were two reasons for this; the size of the capital needed to start up in the new sectors which involved more expensive techniques, and in the case of employers who came via a meritocratic channel, the acquisition of secondary and higher education which remained limited to a few per cent of any age-group. In both cases therefore, a family background or bourgeois social relationships were essential to move from the small business created by saving or borrowing to a middle-sized business, and then on to self-supporting growth or growth sustained by external financing.

Only sectors with small capital investment, large financial turnover and a high death rate of businesses avoided this iron law whereby capital accumulation was restricted to elements of the bourgeoisie in the broad sense. These included department stores, public works, publishing and the press. The self-made man was not impossible in bourgeois society in the Belle Époque, but he was the product of a different type of selection than before. On the other hand, he had difficulty in forming a real dynasty unless he married into an existing bourgeois dynasty or big joint-stock capitalism. In that case, he lost much of his autonomy and romantic aura.

18. M. Lévy-Leboyer (391), p. 4, and the article by M. Hau (384) in the same issue of *Mouvement social*, and his book (385).

c The Bourgeois Dynasties

Within the richest business bourgeoisie, the geographical gulf between Paris and the industrial regions and between joint-stock structure and family structure was obvious. For the railways, the large deposit banks, insurance companies, public utility companies (transport, gas, town transport), mining and part of the metallurgy industry, the size of the capital invested, the national scale of activities and the age of the businesses explain the structural difference. But there were companies within the same sector which had retained a family structure and recent companies which adopted a joint-stock model from the beginning. The division therefore primarily derived from the specific history of each firm, and movements of personnel between the two worlds of employers reduced the apparent social gulf.

The Financial Aristocracy — Contrary to the stereotypes depicted by contemporary polemicists, the managers of the great joint stock companies did not all come from the great financial families of the July monarchy or the Second Empire. As at the time when the joint stock companies were first established, the commercial bankers or those who emerged with the creation of the deposit banks probably always held a number of seats on boards of directors on the basis of the formation of groups between banks, industrial companies and public utility companies with over-lapping interests. This financial aristocracy, whose most prominent members were regents of the Bank of France, came from an even more privileged milieu than the industrial employers. For example, 46 per cent of the chairmen or vice-chairmen of a sample of joint stock companies in the Belle Époque had inherited more than a million gold francs.[19] But the strength of these joint stock employers lay in their ability to open their doors to managers, who were certainly bourgeois but whose families did not belong to big business. These large companies had increasing need of senior staff, engineers and administrators, a minority of whom, if they gave satisfaction or possessed the assets of proficiency or relationships which were indispensable to the firm, rose to the rank of managing director or even joined the board of directors and sometimes, more rarely, became its chairman.

It is for this reason that on the whole, these managers had an increasingly high educational level which broke with the old model of apprenticeship on the job within family employers. The size of these companies inevitably meant that they had dealings with the State, possessed international influence and had to cope with problems of

19. C. Charle (359), p. 89.

organisation for which the technical or legal education of engineering and business faculties or schools was useful. The most popular institutions at this period were the *École centrale*, the *École Polytechnique*, and the *École des mines*, and less frequently, the *Arts et Métiers*.

These two educational types (the less qualified heirs and the less affluent graduates) were correlated with three career-patterns leading to entry into big business. The first, the classic route, resulted from the phenomenon of centripetal attraction over the most enterprising provincial employers in banking, trade or some sectors which needed Paris capital. Part of the Lyons patriciate (Germain, Aynard, Cambefort and Bonnardel), a few textile employers from the North or East and a few merchants from Marseilles or Bordeaux were thus co-opted to Paris, unless the new scale of their business did not oblige them to settle there. For example, Émile Guimet moved from a family firm established near Lyons to the management of Péchiney which he turned into a joint stock company. The Fabre family, later Fabre-Luce of Marseilles, ship-owners connected with the colonies, moved into the management of Crédit Lyonnais with the marriage of one of its sons to the daughter of Henri Germain.

The second and newer type of career profile derived from the size of these businesses which created a hierarchy of differentiated positions which could be reached by upward mobility, as in the civil service. Certain of these 'technocrats' *avant la lettre* might become the intimates of the real owners of capital if their talents brought success to the firm. But their position remained precarious lest they were unsuccessful, particularly if they did not hold major university qualifications. Louis Dorizon, for example, who started from the bottom of the hierarchy, had no major educational qualifications and became chairman of the Société générale, but lost his position following imprudent dealings. But this self-made man of the technostructure was an exception.[20]

However (and this is the third route), the majority of the new men who entered big business possessed rare qualifications (such as engineers from the great State university colleges – *les grandes écoles d'État*) or had been trained within several business or administrative departments. These positions had given them experience on which they cashed in while working in large companies which promoted them to the highest levels. However, these 'managers' *avant la lettre* had no real autonomy. Although they prevented the financial oligarchy from becoming a caste, they were often more inflexible in their management than old established employers. Their more varied experience was a valuable asset in moving into the era of international capitalism and coping with State intervention

20. R. Girault (380), p. 344.

and the workers' social movements, but their awareness of belonging to the elite, their worship of authority and of family connections with long-established businessmen make it impossible to see them as the first fruits of a new class of employers.

Provincial Employers — Some of the directors of joint stock companies were born into the most important families of provincial employers. These men retained a large degree of autonomy from the decision-centre in Paris, particularly in the traditional sectors (textiles, consumer goods industries with regional influence, engineering or old chemicals firms). In fact, the firms kept a family or para-family structure (with limited partnership or limited partnership by shares), even in large companies in the basic sectors such as Schneider or de Wendel.

As Louis Bergeron has emphasised and a number of monographs demonstrate, the family remained the primary cell which governed the business, as in the early days of capitalism. Laws of succession, matrimonial customs and marriage strategies were practised as a function of the interests of the firms owned. It has even been maintained that the contrast between the Normandy employers ('with no dynasties', according to Jean-Pierre Chaline) and the employers in Alsace or the North derived from their basic demographic behaviour. The Malthusian families on the one hand retired from business once they had made their fortune and their heirs became men of independent means living off their inheritance, as divisions of the fortune at death still left enough to live on without working. On the other hand, a large number of descendants in every generation would dictate a judicious choice of sons-in-law from the same milieu in order to match inheritances, stimulate incessant expansion of the firms in order to fight against the fragmentation of capital, and to appoint the heir to the title from amongst the most able children by providing for his education and directing the rest of the offspring towards other professions.

The family did not necessarily consist of blood descendants. It could be elective when the employer co-opted a son-in-law. For example, the mining engineer Georges Rolland married the granddaughter of the founder of the Société métallurgique de Gorcy. He was engineering adviser to the company and became managing director in 1893, then director of the Aciéries de Longwy, in which his father-in-law owned a large interest, and finally vice-chairman and then chairman of that company in 1901.[21]

Even joint stock companies deeply entrenched in regions (for example, the mining companies in the North) established personal economic

21. J.-M. Moine (396), p. 91.

connections with the family alliances of the northern employers who had founded them. Inheritance of blocks of shares was reinforced by the inheritance of positions as directors or co-chairmen. Léonard Danel, for example, a major Lille printer, succeeded his uncle Louis Bigo as chairman of the Compagnie de Lens; he himself brought his son-in-law Émile Bigo-Daniel on to the board.[22]

These general features of provincial employers' social reproduction obviously varied with religious affiliation, demographic behaviour, relationships with the outside world, and the rural or urban nature of the industrial enterprise. For example, the mentalities of traders and businessmen in port towns did not comply with common characteristics. These men were open to the outside world; they were reinvigorated by both provincial and international migrations and they had no hesitation about investing their resources in faraway places or speculating on national or international alliances. The most dynamic businessmen under the Second Empire, the Pereires, already came from the Bordeaux region. Large-scale Marseilles capital also gambled on the colonial and international opening up of France, to counter mounting protest from the protectionist employers in the textile or metallurgical industries of the interior. Jules Charles-Roux, from a Marseilles oil and soap manufacturing family, succeeded in being elected as a deputy in order to defend free-trade and colonial positions. After an apprenticeship in London, Henry Bergasse, from a family of wine merchants, went into naval shipbuilding, and helped found the Société Marseillaise de Crédit, the Saint-Louis sugar refinery, and the Société des grands travaux de Marseille.

In Normandy, the opening of Le Havre to 'outsiders' contrasted with the timidity apparent in Rouen, backing on to the lands of Caux and preferring reinvestment in land to the new industrial ventures. The metallurgical centre of Lorraine showed all the distinctive features of the insularity of employers in the *pays haut* (i.e. the Longwy region) with its frontier position, local entrenchment, the aristocratic origin of some ironmasters, the closed nature of families by inter-marriage, and suspicious patriotism.[23] Among active family employers in a relatively backward sector of an under-developed region, like the shoe manufacturers in Fougères, some of whom were very prosperous, the harshness of exploitation left no room for any weakness towards an unskilled workforce with close rural roots. There are in fact innumerable examples of different types of employer and bourgeois mentalities: the

22. M. Gillet (379), p. 95, and F. Barbier (224), pp. 147–8.
23. D. Barjot (353), vol. 1, p. 531; L. Bergeron (50), p. 91; J.-P. Chaline (56), p. 332; J.-M. Moine (396), and G. Noiriel (446), pp. 105–16.

wool-pickers of Mazamet, for example, Republican Protestant employers of a Catholic workforce who voted Right; or the employers of the silk manufacturers' convents in the Lyons region, which supplied religious accommodation to a workforce of young peasant girls building up dowries for future marriage. These mentalities were all the more inflexible where employers had to face less favourable conditions.[24]

However, there were common features such as those arising from opposition to the 'other side' (the worker, petty bourgeois or aristocrat) and also from the competition amongst these bourgeoisies and from their desire for distinction, in both senses of the term, or imitation. The business skeleton in the cupboard must only be betrayed by lifestyles symbolic of success and as the individual rose in the hierarchy of augmented inheritances, these lifestyles increasingly approached those of the aristocracy.

d Lifestyles

The main elements of the bourgeois lifestyle remained the same as in preceding decades. What changed was the level of wealth which the dynasties of employers acquired. No longer was it only large-scale financiers or industrialists who could obtain those attributes which separated them from the common run of mortals. In the provinces, the bourgeois owned châteaux and country houses; in Paris, they had enormous apartments or individual residences. In provincial metropolises, they inhabited villas or large houses in select districts solely populated by their peers, each with a large domestic staff. Other symbols of distinction were pursuit of a sport, hunting in particular, which was a measure both of free time and of sociability, intercourse with a circle which became increasingly select the longer membership of the ruling class lasted, and the ostentatious collection of objects, curios, furniture and souvenirs in the case of the less affluent, and art collections for the most prominent. Even death and family ceremonies (big weddings, employers' golden weddings and burials) became means of celebrating the family, the employer who led it, and the business he caused to prosper.[25]

The women in these milieus played an essential role in establishing this lifestyle. It has been shown that the rise of the textile firms in the North gradually excluded women from direct participation in

24. B. Legendre (439), pp. 21–5; R. Cazals (417), pp. 184–90; B. Plessy and L. Challet (107), pp. 56–9.
25. On collections, see J.-P. Chaline (56), pp. 234–8; A. Boime (355); J.-M. Moine (396), pp. 308–9.

management, still customary in some small enterprises, as well as in trade. But the bourgeois women in the North and elsewhere were in charge of the whole of private life, the biological reproduction of the family and its spiritual perpetuation, and the inculcation of the manners and morals of the milieu into the heirs. In groups of employers most impregnated with religion, the wives controlled charitable activities – an indispensable supplement in the absence of any social policy in the modern sense – and encouraged the workers to participate in cultural and religious activities. In short, they were in charge of providing a link with elements which there was a risk might break away at any moment as a result of the effects of the exclusive pursuit of profit, and thus ruin the business of husband, father, brother or cousin. Were they therefore, the exact antithesis of the male, rationalist, industrialist mentality of the employers?[26] Were they the element of tradition in a world which was quickening its pace towards what it regarded as progress? There are actually examples of employers who were traditionalist in both politics and religion and who accepted the indispensable modernisation out of sheer necessity even if it destroyed the foundations of the society with which this ideology best accorded.

To counter-balance the risks they ran, even when they had reached the highest levels of wealth, these employers, these demi-urge businessmen extolled by the theorists, needed all the trappings of stability which made it possible to cope with the uncertainty of daily life, such as the cult of the clock and ceaseless work, and the cosy world of family life in protected places. Perhaps the elegant districts, the residences or châteaux, were not so much indications of an imitation of the nobility but of a reappropriation of protection which prominent individuals adopted against threats from below or contained in the future. The old-fashioned decor of their houses would confirm this. Similarly, the universal passion for hunting simulated the quest for survival in a framework where profit was certain at every turn. Even the building up of collections was a way of making the inheritance eternal; this was capital which gained value of its own accord, since time added to its rarity.

The novelists clearly perceived this split in the employers' mentality, divided between the old and the new. Forced to accelerate progress in order to meet competition, the employer was at the same time tempted to halt it to prevent the loss of the wealth he had acquired. Both an individualist and a strong family man, forced to make alliances with his peers while still retaining a certain degree of autonomy, the employer

26. This was the thesis propounded by B. Smith (115), from which we earlier summarised the description of the role of the bourgeois women in the North. It is confirmed by the table for the first half of the nineteenth century drawn up in P. Delsalle (172).

had increasing difficulty in preserving a pure liberal framework in an economy in the process of concentration at the end of the nineteenth century. This explains the contradictory attacks directed at him: Malthusian and tormented by the *rentier* mentality on the one hand, unscrupulous exploiter on the other, these caricatures were both stereotypes corresponding to the temperaments of various employers who, in their different ways, resolved the contradictions outlined above.

e The New Men: Self-Made Men and Engineers

The new sectors which appeared in the provinces as much as in the Paris region (automobiles, cycles, modern chemicals, metallurgy with coke in the Lorraine, electricity, rubber and petroleum) began from the same social bases. The proportion of new men was larger, as is seen from the examples of Marius Berliet in Lyons, a self-taught man, son of a satin manufacturer and at first a silk-weaver himself but with no fortune, or of the Lumière brothers, whose photographic business began on an artisanal scale. In accordance with the old patterns, these small businesses functioned on family capital and on partnerships or were self-financing, re-investing the quick profits earned by every sector which was starting up. But these sectors were still marginal. When it came to moving up to a regional or national level, the door had to be opened to outside capital and therefore to large-scale, well-established capitalism; this was the case in chemicals, gas, alpine hydro-electricity and metallurgy in the north-east. Only a few of the founders of enterprises held out; the other companies passed into the hands of engineers, technicians or directors from overseas, other regions or the capital.[27]

The increase in the power of the engineers was the direct result of the growing technical advancement of the new sectors. In the first three-quarters of the nineteenth century there were only three channels for training engineers. The first two, the *École polytechnique* and its practical schools (*Mines, Ports et Chaussée, Génie Maritime*) and the *École centrale* for senior positions. But the only outlets for graduates were in State enterprises, the largest businesses and positions in management. The third channel was the *Arts et Métiers*, which trained only the middle ranks, technicians or foremen. The type of engineer who occupied an intermediate position, still in contact with production or the organisation of work but sufficiently separate from the purely technical routine was not trained anywhere except on the job by the internal promotion of the best *gadzarts* (former students of the *Arts et Métiers*).

27. See the articles by P. Cayez (pp. 191 ff.) and H. Morsel (pp. 201–8) in M. Lévy-Leboyer (389).

The period between 1890 and 1900 saw the birth of new schools to cope with the needs of industries nurtured by the most modern applications of science. The *École de physique et de chimie de la Ville de Paris* was founded in 1882 to train the best students from the technical schools in the City; the *École supérieure d'électricité* was founded in 1892; and a series of institutes for the applied sciences were attached to science faculties in university towns where these recent industries were expanding (including Lille, Grenoble, Lyons, Nancy and Toulouse).[28] The advance between 1870 and 1874, when 190 engineers trained by the most prestigious schools entered industry, and 1910–1914, when the average figure had risen to 351, is obvious.

At the same time, this socially inconspicuous profession became organised. Membership of the *Société des ingénieurs civils* rose from 1,500 members in 1882 (when there were over 11,500 active graduates of the *École centrale* and the *Polytechnique*) to 3,000 in 1894 and then 6,000 on the eve of the war. This new profession, linked to the industrial boom of the Belle Époque, had to fight on two fronts; against competition from State engineers who were moving into the private sector more and more frequently for reasons which will be examined below, and against the *gadzarts* who refused to be relegated to less elevated jobs for want of a certificate demonstrating a secondary or higher classical education.

Although they were the product of modernity, the engineers reacted in the same way as the other liberal professions, some of them even practising their trade as engineering consultants from private offices. But the largest number, from a middle-class background, worked in industry and particularly in the bigger enterprises, which were the only ones where senior staff were not drawn from the traditional employers, that is to say from the owners' families. They therefore began to resent the contradictory effects of their intermediate position in the business hierarchy. In accordance with Lyautey's theses on the social role of the officer, or the theories of Le Play, who was an engineer himself, many of them looked for roles as intermediaries and mediators between the classes. But their community of interests with the employers was by far the stronger. In certain extreme cases, the engineer even became the scapegoat for the workers' wrath; the engineer Watrin, for example, was thrown out of a window in 1886 during a social protest in Decazeville. In a period when the upper echelons were still thinly populated, many engineers, even those at factories, were quasi-substitutes for the real employer, who remained anonymous or living elsewhere on another site

---

28. T. Shinn (113), pp. 204–16; C.R. Day (62); R. Fox and G. Weisz (374).

or at the head office of the company.[29]

No longer was the possibility of reaching the power of strategic decision-making a utopian dream, even without capital and without family connections with the real owners of companies. The best known, but probably isolated, example of this is the Pont-à-Mousson company. Xavier Rogé left the *Arts et Métiers* in Châlons-sur-Marne and was in succession a skilled worker, draughtsman, head of works, and then the manager of a foundry. Thus trained, he was engaged by Pont-à-Mousson, which he put back on its feet, and where he rose to the rank of partner and then to sole director. He went further when he redeemed part of the capital and even named his successor, Camille Cavallier, whose training was strictly identical to his own (*Arts et Métiers* and a succession of different posts within Pont-à-Mousson). Thanks to Rogé's patronage and his own commercial ability, Camille Cavallier became co-director in 1899 (at the age of forty-five), then sole managing director (1900) and finally chairman (1917).[30]

Engineering could thus provide a source for supplementing the ranks of employers, but without upsetting the pre-eminence of initial capital and founding families. In fact, the heirs to dynasties of employers in preponderantly engineering sectors were increasingly often equipped with engineering degrees, which put them on an equal footing with the senior technical staff. These latter only became real employers when families fell out or had no heirs of an age to exercise power. But even if power was completely delegated to the engineer, he rarely succeeded in founding a dynasty (and from this point of view, Cavallier was an exception). The process of identification with a firm and of building up a capital of confidence had in practice to start again with each generation. However, this new life-time elite, which was a pre-figuration of the twentieth century technocrats, played an irreplaceable role within employers' lobbies and organisations.

f The Lobbies

The last innovation which marked the entry of the business bourgeoisie into a new world under the Republic was its gradual organisation into pressure groups. In the preceding period, the big businessmen were on an equal footing with the government elite because they belonged to the same world or held political mandates giving them direct access to the

---

29. See in A. Thépot (410) the articles by Georges Ribeill (pp. 111–25) and Étienne Dejonghe (especially p. 173: 'Temps des grands vassaux' about the mines of the Nord-Pas-de-Calais) and Claude Beaud on internal careers at Le Creusot (p. 50–9).
30. J.-M. Moine (396), pp. 83–5.

central power. The extreme example of this was the presidency of the Senate which the ironmaster Eugène Schneider held at the end of the Second Empire. The separation of the recruitment processes of the economic and political elites made this figurative case rarer after 1880. The economic depression, the struggle by some individuals for protectionism, by others against its adoption, the rise in workers' protests and attempts at social legislation were so many factors driving the traditionally individualist employers to form groups on the basis at least of some common interests.

Faced with the workers' trade unions, a series of unions of employers were set up. Their membership varied with the strategic position of the sector concerned, internal discipline and the ability of the men appointed to be the industrialists' ambassadors to the political power. The *Comité des houillères*, for example, was definitively organised in December 1892; the *Comité des forges* was founded as early as 1864 but was really effective from 1887–1888; and there were also the *Syndicat des constructeurs et fabricants de chemins de fer* (1899), the *Chambre syndicale des constructeurs de navires*, and the *Union des industries métallurgiques et minières* (1901). The driving force in most of these groups were new men who were not employers, but polyvalent 'senior staff', with access to several elites and versed in Le Play's elitist doctrines; Robert Pinot and Paul de Rousiers are examples.[31] Contemporary polemicists have tended to build up a myth around these lobbies, making them secret centres manipulating the apparent holders of power.

Monographs on the groups in the biggest sectors have challenged this conspiracy view of history. The employers' unions did not avoid internal divisions or the refusal by some to join or obey general instructions, any more than did the workers' trade unions. United against the workers, all the business leaders were also competitors, since concentration was still weak and permitted dozens of enterprises or companies to continue to exist in one sector, even ones where heavy fixed capital was necessary. The opportunity for these unions to produce a strategy adapted to all circumstances was limited by regional contrasts and divergent interests between enterprises, according to which stage of production they occupied; although it is true that the milieus which they confronted or aimed to influence were just as divided and fragmented, whether these were workers or political elites. Like the parliamentary majorities, the employers' lobbying was the fruit of compromise, temporary alliances, contradictory pressures between groups and sub-groups, and defensive rather than offensive power but which, on those grounds, remained a

31. M.J. Rust (405); J.-M. Moine (396), pp. 178–92; M. Gillet (379), pp. 171–212; C. Charle (359), ch. 8.

position of strength.

Despite everything, with the more or the less active complicity of the political leaders, it succeeded in delaying to the maximum possible extent the social advances which formed part of the initial republican programme and in obtaining a protective customs policy and the most favourable budgetary and fiscal conditions. Admission in the role of representatives on bodies for concerted action set up by the Republic (all types of advisory boards) permitted the big industrialists to participate in the formulation of regulations, to bend them or make them meaningless, and they remained as permanent experts in contrast with an ephemeral political elite.

C The Elites of the Republic

The elites of the Republic is defined here as the men occupying the top positions in the administrative and political hierarchies. They constituted a population of less than 10,000 people, comprising the personnel of government, the highest officials and the politicians with the longest careers, as well as the university elite. Although these elites were as limited in number as they had been during earlier regimes, their status had changed as a result of the political and administrative changes the Republic had gradually introduced.

The proportion of elected to appointed men had considerably increased in accordance with the revolutionary tradition. Mayors were elected and not appointed as in the past; the official candidatures of the Second Empire had been ended; the co-option of irremovable senators, conceived by conservatives as a brake on universal suffrage, had been abolished; the elimination of multiple candidatures and of the practice of voting for several members from a list had put an end to the entrenchment of deputies in their constituencies. These institutional changes theoretically helped to open up competition for political mandates by restricting the prerogatives of the central power or pressure from above. On the other hand, the republicans were much more timid in their relations with the administration. The proportion of higher officials selected by competitive examination was increased, but the opportunist government rejected a return to the democratic innovation of the Second Republic, i.e., the creation of a school of administration. Every corps retained its individual characteristics and, behind appearances of competition, the absence of a common training facilitated the continuation of more or less visible co-options, as well as only a minimal widening of geographical origins.

Two considerations explain this republican timidity towards reform of the higher administration, which has already been observed in their conservative management of junior staff in public office. Democracy was the triumph of the political over the administrative, and must therefore not confer too much prestige on a caste of mandarins whose competence, proven by competitive examinations, would be an obstacle to the wishes of the assemblies. In the second place the flexible system, combining partial competition and discretionary appointment to the most political corps or to sensitive positions, left the new government free to find jobs for its followers and to exclude suspect higher officials, either by massive purges as at the beginning of republican rule or by marginalising men currently out of favour. Senior administrative positions were thus more precarious than in the past, but this was the price to be paid for the growing instability of political functions.

a The Political Elite

Members of Parliament — The members of Parliament are thought to be the best-known elite since they were under the spotlight of political history, but in fact systematic research into them is only just beginning.[32] Socially, studies still in summary form show that the end of the power of the notables was reflected by a decline in the proportion of nobility among the deputies from 34 per cent in 1871 to 10 per cent in 1919. On the other hand, deputies of modest origins could scarcely have increased their influence in the years before the 1914 war (it is calculated that 5 per cent of deputies were workers in the 1893 Chamber, the year of the first significant rise in the number of socialist deputies, and 10 per cent in 1919). Before the First World War, two-thirds of the members of the Chamber came from upper or middle-rank bourgeois backgrounds. The same intermediate position in the social structure is indicated by the presence of a majority of members of the liberal professions. They were headed by advocates (149 in 1881 and 144 in 1906 out of 560 and 580 deputies respectively) and doctors (62 in 1881).

These liberal professions formed the backbone of the republican groups in power, whereas they only constituted 18 per cent of representatives classified as Right or extreme Right. These activities, combined with public life, therefore became a means of social ascent for the provincial bourgeoisie. Doctors and barristers who were deputies captured the best clients and assumed a national stature in their town. Although there were clearly fewer higher officials amongst the elected members than under the Empire or the July monarchy, they still constituted a considerable presence, forming 17 per cent of the 1893 Chamber. Lastly, although the active economic bourgeoisie was under-

32. See the research under way into the parliamentary personnel of the Third Republic, directed by A. Corbin and J.-M. Mayeur.

represented in relation to its demographic size within the elites, it still formed the second largest body, particularly if the comfortably-off farmers and landowners are included.[33]

Even if the French were beginning to elect a few individuals from working-class backgrounds, on the whole they placed their trust in the upper ranks of society or the well-to-do as a hangover of old habits; a political career presupposed an independent income, given the absence of modern political parties, or a 'hidden *cens*' (Daniel Gaxie) prevented the other social groups from putting candidates forward. For each Jean-Baptiste Dumay, formerly a worker for Schneider in Le Creusot, or each Martin Nadaud, formerly a mason from the Creuse, there were many industrialists, large landowners and bankers. The marquis de Solages, Jaurès's opponent in the Carmaux constituency, land and mine owner; Jules Siegfried, great cotton merchant of Le Havre; Eugène Motte, Lille textile industrialist; and Jules Jaluzot, owner of the Printemps, elected in the Nièvre in dubious circumstances; these were again incarnations of this direct transformation of economic power into political power.

It is true that since national representation went from one end of the political spectrum to the other, it presented the full range of all the varieties of bourgeoisie; and it is also true that nowhere else in Europe could the masses be so easily represented by their own. Nevertheless, the impression that the republican victory had introduced a breach did not correspond with any deep-seated sociological upheaval amongst political leaders but rather with a slight reduction in the length of membership of the ruling class. Moreover, political or social barriers could be removed thanks to the system of joint committees defined in terms of the defence of certain interests and which served as ready-made intermediaries for the external lobbies, which were organised at that time as has been seen above. These general comments are confirmed by the characteristics of the ministers, which are known in depth thanks to the thesis by Jean Estèbe.

The Ministers — The governmental elite was in fact the product of a selection process within the parliamentary group, which was a partial break with earlier practices when some ministers came from the higher administration. The aim was generally to find stable members of Parliament. Whereas 40 per cent of deputies sat in only one legislature, the same was true of only 10 per cent of ministers in power between 1877 and 1899 and 3 per cent of those in office between 1899 and 1914.[34] Another asset which was a condition for certain re-election was

33. M. Dogan (369) and (370), p. 472.
34. J. Estèbe (373), vol. 3, p. 689.

possession of local mandates (to the general council rather than in a municipality). Lastly, admission to government involved a specific social selection. The fact that the ministerial personnel at this period came predominantly from the Centre and the moderate Left meant that modest backgrounds (mostly to be found amongst the extreme Left-wing deputies) and the richest (predominant amongst the Right) were at a disadvantage when compared with graduates and high-ranking officials.

The republican ministers were men who were established in society and came from a middle-rank bourgeois background. They were also mature men when they came to power. Although their median age when they took office was forty-two, the overall median age of ministers appointed between 1877 and 1899 was forty-nine, and during the period 1899–1914, forty-seven. This difference reflects the process whereby a small group of men who swapped portfolios gradually obtained a monopoly of the most important positions (despite frequent crises). Estèbe's calculations show that fewer than 20 per cent of the total number of ministers had occupied 52 per cent of ministerial positions. A hierarchy of ministers did actually exist, based on their technical ability, length of service and political importance. Agriculture, Finance and Foreign Affairs head the list for the stability of their incumbents because they affected the three pillars of the Republic, the peasants, business policy and the national presence. These became the specialities of leading politicians who reassumed them in each new ministerial combination. Conversely, War and the Navy were most frequently entrusted to technical men, generals or admirals.

This club of statesmen represents the general features of the political elite, but even more markedly. The princes of the Republic were recruited from amongst lawyers; 59 per cent of leading personalities, 47 per cent of ministers and 32 per cent of deputies were lawyers. In the period between the decline of the notables, whose tutelage in emancipated regions was too oppressive, and the advent of the new middle classes, the members of the legal professions were the breeding-ground for the leaders of the moderate Republic.[35] At a time when there were no organised parties their intermediate position, the decentralisation of their distribution, and the training for the tribune that the great courts of law gave were the keys to success in a long political career.

Access to the summit of the State by this means still presupposed solid financial backing. Electoral campaigns had to be paid for, as well as a second home, travel, post, a secretary and electoral agents. Consequently, nearly 80 per cent of ministers belonged to the richest 2 per cent of Frenchmen. Moreover, social recruitment did not become more open after

35. Y.-H. Gaudemet (376), pp. 15–20.

1877, because the first opportunists were well endowed; it was only after 1900 that political life became a springboard for new men to rise up and a minimum of political associations facilitated the election of men of meagre means. The change in relationships with big business reflects this sociological evolution. Whereas 40 per cent of conservative ministers were involved in big business, the proportion was below 30 per cent after the failure of the government of Moral Order and involved quite mediocre companies. The intrusion of business into politics was limited to small active groups in touch with various lobbies; for example, Florent Guillain and Paul Doumer were recognised representatives of the big metallurgical interests and Eugène Étienne was likewise the representative of colonial affairs. But seats on boards of directors could also be a reward for a ministerial career. In short, whereas under conservative regimes the same great families with a foot in both worlds were happy to combine both jobs, the Republic tended to prefer the circulation of elites between political and economic power. This sometimes led to a few well-known blunders in the case of novices, whose need of money left them open to pressure from dubious and unscrupulous businessmen.

This provincial legal bourgeoisie, greedy for mandates or ministerial sinecures, was the subject of many lampoons both by conservatives, who were shocked by its lack of manners, and by parties claiming kinship with the workers. They alternately identified it with the plutocracy (because of the scandals or its business connections) or with a group of parasitical orators feeding off 'cushy jobs'. The attachment to liberalism, which the extreme Left regarded as a fault – at best liberalism meant the extension of freedom and enlightenment, but at its worst, business politics and the rejection of real social reforms – formed an integral part of the world view of the members of the liberal professions, breeding-ground of political elites. The changes introduced into the high administration are also evidence of this.

b The Higher Administration

The republicans who came to power had been victims of the imperial administration and then of the reactionary government of Moral Order. They were particularly heavy-handed in their dealings with certain groups in high public office. Prefects, magistrates and the Council of State were largely changed at the end of the 1870s and beginning of the 1880s. The first appointments were comrades in the political struggle, deputies who needed other jobs after an electoral defeat, or protégés connected with republican families. But this change in personnel did not necessarily mean a great difference in social recruitment or even a change in the operating rules from the earlier period. Mostly, the republicans chose individuals like themselves, from middle-rank provincial bourgeois backgrounds and with legal training. This necessarily placed limitations on the opening up of social recruitment to Gambetta's so-called new strata, which in principle encompassed a petty bourgeoisie without higher or secondary education.

The other limitation on this administrative evolution was the introduction, prior to the political change, of competitive procedures for admission to the major administrative corps and the technical corps. These competitive examinations introduced both a social and a geographical selection, to the advantage of families who lived in Paris or were able to send their children to pursue their secondary or higher studies in the capital. Scholarship holders in the generation under consideration tended to be the sons of State servants, which hardly extended the range of social origins. Lastly, the fact that some positions were now closed to traditional families led these families to direct their heirs towards less political corps, where promotion was more autonomous in relation to the authorities, such as for example the Finance Inspectorate, the *Cour des Comptes*, the diplomatic service, *Eaux et Forêts*, the State Engineers corps or some branches of the army. Faced with the danger of the continued presence of the old elites in the administration, thanks to the meritocratic selection procedures, the republican elite rejected the solution of a school specifically for training higher officials, as has been seen. It preferred to expand a hitherto secondary institution, that of ministerial *cabinets* (grouping collaborators with ministers), which became increasingly obligatory transit points for higher officials seeking the most senior careers.

The Limitations on Social Change — These contradictory factors explain the limitations and specific characteristics of the sociological change in the recruitment of the highest officials. Despite expectations to the contrary, no significant difference in 'democratisation' can be observed between the corps selected on an educational basis and those recruited on the basis of discretionary political appointment. For example, prefects from humble backgrounds formed 3.8 per cent of the administrative corps under the Second Empire and 9.9 per cent of a sample in office in 1901. Amongst Roads and Bridges inspectors, the best products of the *Polytechnique*, the proportion of humble categories rose from 8 per cent to 20 per cent between 1860 and 1901.[36] In both cases, the selectors started from a pre-selected population, i.e., students who had completed their secondary education, or even obtained certificates of higher education.

36. C. Charle (359), pp. 66–7, as well as (363), and N.Carré de Malberg (357) on the finance inspectors.

The most significant changes from the time of the notables occurred in the balance between the various groups of bourgeoisie. The political break was marked by the decline in administrative heredity in certain corps. The republican purge temporarily ended the co-option and nepotism of the time of the notables, which sometimes went back to the July monarchy and the Empire. For example, 40.9 per cent of prefects in the Second Empire were sons of high officials while the proportion was only 6.6 per cent in 1901; the percentage for councillors of State on the same dates fell from 37.8 per cent to 9.3 per cent. The purge is not the only explanation for this change, since the technical corps also showed a decrease in administrative recruitment from within their own ranks.

The enlargement of the population possessing a secondary education, and the stricter nature of competitive selection, opened up the high administration to the more brilliant elements from amongst the *capacités* or the middle-ranking economic bourgeoisie. Moreover, the proportion of inspectors of Finance, Roads and Bridges or heads of ministries from these backgrounds increased. There was thus a rapprochement with the recruitment of government personnel, strengthened by the opening up of the provinces. With the exception of the most prestigious major corps, the proportion of native Parisians also decreased, as it also did amongst politicians when compared with the Second Empire.[37]

Social Dynamic and the Dynamic of Careers — This moderate social change explains why higher officials and governmental personnel had similar attitudes to their careers and the outside world. In earlier periods the personal wealth of these elites enabled them to keep a certain distance between themselves and their jobs or mandates. Even more, the inheritance they possessed was a factor in their promotion because of the old model of the official whose income had to be spent in order to bring glory on State service. That is why there was a correlation between levels of personal fortune and access to the highest ranks of prefects or generals, for example, under the Second Empire.[38] The Republic could not require the same disinterest from its higher civil servants, more especially as the leading personnel drew their staff from amongst the same less affluent provincial bourgeoisie from which they themselves also came.

However, the rules of promotion and remuneration remained roughly the same. Apart from the members of the political corps (prefects and the high magistracy) and the higher officials who had been through ministerial *cabinets*, promotion was fairly slow and the salary scale

37. C. Charle (359), p. 56.
38. B. Le Clère and V. Wright (254), S.W. Serman (276).

extended. A fourth class inspector of finance, for example, began with 2,500 francs a year, or the salary of a post-office clerk, and at the best only reached 15,000 francs as he neared fifty. The same wage-differential of 1 to 6 or 7 is found among State engineers, at the Council of State, at the *Cour des Comptes*, in the ministries and amongst officers. This situation dictated three combined or alternative counter-balancing strategies: the quest for a bourgeois marriage to improve the family's standard of living during the period spent in the lower grades; careerism at any price in order to make exceptional progress by means of political support; and lastly, if these two options failed, the possibility of taking a job in the private sector where salaries were clearly higher. This latter approach was increasingly adopted, particularly by engineers or in certain financial corps.

These constraints account for the prevalence of the model of bourgeois marriage amongst the higher officials of the Belle Époque. On an average, their future wives brought in twice as much as they did (136,000 francs against 72,000 francs, the medians being 100,000 francs and 33,000 francs respectively).[39] Like their political prudence, this financial perspective also explains why, more frequently than under earlier regimes, fathers-in-law were non-officials and holders of economic capital. To continue with the administrative endogamy which existed at the time of the notables and formed part of the mechanism of recommendations and nepotism of that period would have been detrimental to the career-interests of the officials of the Republic. In effect, it would have implied marriage within administrative families connected with the old political teams. This indirect social control over private life therefore placed limitations on the downwards extension of the social opening-up of recruitment.

The other method of integrating higher officials who did not conform to the average image of the corps was admission to ministerial *cabinets* and to the circle of ministers who could dispense promotions in the great corps through outside appointments. These methods of selection, independent of seniority or purely technical competence, were not new but became more frequent as the qualifications of higher officials were increasingly homogeneous. The growing instability of the composition of government also increased the importance of the *cabinets* because of ministerial 'bequests' at each change of government. Before relinquishing his portfolio, the influential minister wanted to find jobs for his collaborators in positions where they would be protected from political vicissitudes. Conversely, in order to put his own men in good

39. C. Charle (359), ch. 5.

positions, the new minister found honorary sinecures for certain heads of ministries, prefects or high magistrates whom he wanted to get rid of. These hazards also blocked the progress of less well-protected senior civil servants, who were legitimately embittered. Some abuses even culminated in parliamentary debates where these unfair promotions were denounced. But the remedies which were applied were very inadequate, such as the increase in the proportion of internal promotions as compared with outside appointments to the *Cour des Comptes* and the Council of State, for example. This unrest in high public office was reflected in the fall in the number of candidates for the competitive examination and above all by the increase in the number of men who opted for careers outside State service.

In 1905, there were two *Polytechnique* graduates over forty in the private sector for every one in State service. Twenty per cent of the members of the 1870–1879 lists of appointments to the finance inspectorate resigned; the rate rose to 27 per cent in the following decade and reached a peak of 47 per cent in 1890–1899. Resignations from the Council of State proliferated after 1900, particularly amongst auditors of the first class, and *maîtres des requêtes* who had no prospects of moving to a higher level in the absence of vacancies.[40] Certain diplomats, whose promotion was overdue, also succumbed to the temptation of offers from the private sector and shared their knowledge of foreign countries in which certain companies wanted to invest.

Relationships with the Other Elites — There are therefore contradictory ways of interpreting the position of higher officials under the Republic. The unrest, to which the movement out of State service testified, was the result both of the anxiety introduced by the political personnel into normal administrative operations and the sociological characteristics of this milieu. The corps nearest to the governmental personnel had scarcely any autonomy from the government. For example, prefects could fall into disfavour at any moment, and retirement took place at an earlier age than before – similar to the shorter period for which a territorial position was held. To compensate for this, ministers of the interior had got into the habit of finding posts for their prefects as chief treasurers and paymasters of the department or in certain major corps,[41] such as the Council of State or more rarely the *Cour des Comptes*.

The senior magistracy was in somewhat the same position, but with fewer outside jobs available. The best career prospects belonged to magistrates who agreed to form part of the public prosecutor's office and

---

40. C. Charle (364), p. 1117; P. Lalumière (387); M.-C. Kessler (386).
41. J. Siwek-Pouydesseau (408); C. Charle (364); P.-F. Pinaud (403).

therefore to be beholden to the Chancellery. Nearly two-thirds of the members of the *Cour de Cassation* (Supreme Court) fell into this category in 1901. Other channels for promotion included a period in the *cabinet* of the minister of justice or a job as head of department in the central administration.

Membership of a ministerial *cabinet*, as an alternative route to promotion, competed with promotion by rank which had formerly been the main means of becoming head of a department in the central administration – in the ministry of finance, for example. The department heads who lasted longest were those in technical ministries, where ministers were often less powerful politicians or were serving their apprenticeship to the important ministries. The end of the century appears as a temporary golden age in this respect, since some great department heads held their positions for a very long time, ensuring continuity of policy over and beyond the hazards of governmental coalitions. Louis Liard for example, was head of Higher Education from 1884 to 1902, Charles Dumay was head of the Religious Affairs division for nineteen years, and Henri Monod was head of the National Assistance Board for eighteen years. Sensitive positions, such as the Police division, did not have this stability, and the turn to the Left after 1900 was accompanied by a change in the staff of senior civil servants set up by the founding fathers of the regime.

An Administrative Authority? — This unstable equilibrium between political power and the higher administration provoked some contemporary publicists (who were also higher officials) to criticise the poor distribution of tasks between the two levels of decision-making. The political leaders, with an eye to the electorate, had a tendency to meddle in the most minute matters (for example, the appointments of petty officials) in order to gain the confidence of constituents, while large-scale essential reforms did not materialise for lack of continuity at the summit of the State. Cases of conflict did therefore sometimes occur for want of a clear division of labour. Some people went even further and criticised the political personnel for incompetence or too close connections with individual interests. The higher administration, on the other hand, was regarded as the guardian of the general interest and administrative knowledge. Errors in the management of personnel, whose increasing mobilisation has been seen, financial difficulties in connection with the rejection of income tax, scandals and favouritism were all arguments in favour of the proposal for an administrative authority (today it would be called a technocracy) which would offset the failings of pure parliamentarianism. But before this trend achieved such success as it did in the inter-war period and under the Fifth Republic, a new elite had also claimed its share of power, through the crisis of the Dreyfus affair: the *intellectuels*.

D A New Elite? The *Intellectuels*

According to a pattern which can be seen at several points in the course of history, it was the republican elites who helped to extend the influence of a new elite, the *intellectuels*, which went on to constitute a permanent source of criticism of the government's mistakes. More still, it was political discussion which gave the new name of *intellectuels* to a social group which, until then, had been represented by only a few great individuals and which, from the end of the century, acted collectively and publicly to challenge the current power. However, the Republic had granted the liberal professions everything they had been asking for since the Revolution; freedom of the press and association for journalists and men of letters, a gradual dismantling of the academic system for artists and increasing autonomy for higher education, which saw its resources considerably increased.[42] Lastly, official ideology favoured the great men of culture and science as the foundation of the system of education available to all. However, this 'state of grace' did not last. To understand the reasons why, it is necessary to go back some way and examine the social effects of the new regime on the intellectual professions.

a The Intellectual Professions in a Liberal System

Two categories of intellectual profession which would serve as a breeding-ground for the mobilisation of the *intellectuels* during the Dreyfus affair, men of letters and journalists on one hand and academics on the other, saw a complete change in the conditions in which they practised their profession after 1870. The numbers of both groups doubled, between 1872 and 1901 in the case of the first and between 1881 and the beginning of the century for the second.[43] The other liberal professions managed to control their expansion, as has been seen, but the whole scale of these professions changed over twenty years. This proliferation of professional writers and lecturers corresponded to objective needs, to supply material for the many newspapers which were created when the press was liberalised, and to build up the provincial network of higher and secondary education in order to counteract competition from the German universities or Catholic institutions.

---

42. See G. Weisz (351); V. Karady (331); M.-C. Genet-Delacroix (377) and (378); M.-B. Palmer (399); M. Martin (394).
43. C. Charle (360), pp. 38 ff.

But this change in scale was accompanied by changes within the intellectual professions. On the positive side, these new intellectuals could claim to exercise a new type of authority. The journalists represented public opinion, and it had after all been the republicans' successful activity in the realm of the press that had assured the decisive electoral victory over the notables, themselves incapable of communicating with the emancipated people. Certain literary trends, particularly naturalism, proclaimed their faith in science, in democracy, in the sound nature of the struggle for literary life and success. Through its reformers, such as Ernest Lavisse or Gabriel Monod, the new university wanted to re-arm France intellectually in order to counteract the Prussian challenge, in the same way as the foundation of the University of Berlin had been a response to the defeat at Jena. The professorial chair should no longer be the centre of fashionable lectures for provincial idlers but a glowing hearth for the education of young scholars or the future elite of the country.

Official positivism believed in the virtues of knowledge both on the moral and the economic plane. The scholar became the object of a genuine cult. Not only did he reduce ignorance and therefore combat the superstition and dogmas of the Church, but he was also of assistance to everyone through the application of his discoveries. Pasteur saved whole industries or cultures, and founded a new school of medicine which preserved human life; Berthelot opened new outlets for the chemical industry. These were the real heroes of secular republican culture, to such an extent that even writers posed as scholars. Zola claimed kinship with Claude Bernard and described himself as a 'naturalist' and sociologist. Bourget and Barrès invoked Taine and Renan and called themselves 'psychologists'.

However, this new intellectual power, which Auguste Comte had dreamed of, was very quickly challenged by the actual expansion of the intellectual field. Confronted with the major newspapers of the popular press, the excessive number of small newspapers indulged in ruinous competition among themselves and were therefore dragged down in an attempt to please as many people as possible, at the expense of the aspirations of journalists. The press itself, with its serialised novels, was in competition with literature, and writers and publishers complained of a slump in the book trade in the 1890s, which was also linked to the gloomy economic situation. With the literary market going through a difficult phase, newcomers found it much harder to find a place for themselves when in competition with their seniors. Young literature consequently retired within itself, publishing in a proliferation of little reviews which ignored market forces.

Obviously nothing comparable occurred in the social situation of the academics, since the creation of posts in particular speeded up the careers of generations formerly fated to long periods of apprenticeship in secondary teaching. The discontent in this sector was more moral and political. The poor image of the elite in power, compromised by the scandals at the end of the 1880s and the beginning of the 1890s, by its dubious methods of staying in power in the face of every type of challenge, by the favouritism which sometimes went beyond the frontiers of the administration and affected university appointments, and lastly, by the rapprochement in the name of the new spirit with Catholics who accepted the Republic, robbed the authorities of part of their legitimacy. The academic reformers believed in their mission more than ever before. For example, some scientists tried to form strong connections with local bourgeoisies, and lawyers and men of letters encouraged the student associative movement. The most creative laid the foundations of new branches of knowledge in order to gain a better understanding of their times and throw light on the future; Durkheim is one example, the first incumbent of a social science course at Bordeaux.[44] Almost all of them specialised and became professional in order to emulate German 'science'. This intellectual, even intellectualist, elitism had its counterpart in the closing up of the university milieu within itself, and the abandonment of the combination of two careers – political and academic – or the failure of attempts to do so as a result of the gulf between professors and the general public.[45]

The social recruitment of intellectuals is also an argument in favour of their prestige since democracy claimed to be open to all talents. Contemporary general consciousness regarded intellectual and artistic careers as the most open professions with bourgeois status. In the university field, the social origins of professors were lower in the sciences than in law, and were also lower at greater distances from Paris in provincial faculties or when the professors under consideration were not the products of the *École normale supérieure*. Literature offered even greater possibilities for rising in the social scale, even without possession of a large cultural capital. One of the richest contemporary writers, Zola, did not obtain his baccalauréat. The other novelists of the naturalist school hardly came from families of high social standing, while some famous artists or journalists also partially escaped the laws of educational reproduction. For example, 22.2 per cent of painters who belonged to the *Conseil supérieur des beaux-arts* and were amongst the most established of their day were sons of small shopkeepers.[46] The future

44. M.-J. Nye (397); H.-W. Paul (400).
45. C. Charle (359), ch. 8.
46. M.-C. Genet-Delacroix (377), p. 104.

intellectuels therefore represented the best approximation to the possibility of success solely as a result of talent, even if these examples of success from quite modest beginnings were only a tiny minority of all the aspirants to literary, scientific and artistic glory. It was still necessary to be able to exercise this power in order to have influence.

b Intellectual Power

The men who were beginning to call themselves *intellectuels*, even before the word became widespread during the Dreyfus affair, resorted to unprecedented procedures in order to expand their audience. The literary avant-garde, the group most cut-off from the public, set out to shock through manifestos, pronouncements on the problems of the day or investigations published in its own reviews, and attracted the attention of the authorities by flaunting its sympathies with the political avant-garde, particularly the anarchists. All these texts or declarations demonstrated great contempt for official parliamentarianism and the democracy; their aristocratic elitism reappeared in early Dreyfusism. If, at the time of the Dreyfus affair, the avant-garde abandoned its traditional positions of attachment to art for art's sake, it did so because Dreyfusism corresponded both to the ideal of political intervention outside the official political channels and to the expression of the fundamental non-conformism of that section of the literary field.

More surprising on the other hand was the attraction that socialism exercised over some representatives of the younger university generations, such as Lucien Herr, Charles Andler and Charles Péguy, who would act as intermediaries to spread Dreyfusism amongst students or convert some professors. This university socialism was an extension and an expansion of the ardent republicanism of these circles, particularly in the *École normale supérieur*. It also demonstrated their desire not to cut themselves off from the masses by shutting themselves away in a narrow intellectual speciality. Knowledge for its own sake no longer meant the same as art for art's sake. In common with knowledge, Dreyfusism – and socialism – had to be based on concern with the real, the critical and the truth. As a result, the university regained a social function which was not restricted to an uninvolved mandarinate or to a defence and glorification of the established order.

Nevertheless, these avant-garde activists might well have provoked no social repercussions. On other occasions, their political activities did not go beyond the narrow confines of their literary or professional worlds. The mobilisation in depth of a section of the intellectual professions and even the other elites, to say nothing of the working-class elite, derived from the autonomous dynamic of politics and the uncertainties of the authorities in this particular crisis. Its depths came primarily from the fact that it allowed intellectual passions and conflicting interests inside the intellectual field to be invested in the definition of new opposing identities, the Left-wing and the Right-wing intellectual. This confrontation (Truth and Justice against Order and Nation) gave the *intellectuels* a public social existence.

While every profession or class tended to organise collectively at this period in order to defend its interests, the *intellectuals* did appear as a specific social group defined by its own activities, rites and hierarchies, but the only interests that it claimed to defend were disinterested interests, universal values or general institutions. They thus present themselves as obvious rivals to the elite responsible for these general causes, the political leaders. Their opponents did not fail to criticise them for appointing themselves to this role with absolutely no vote from anyone, unlike the elected servants of the Republic. However, the *intellectuels* were not a new, sociologically homogeneous, political fraction, as a party which called itself 'labour' would be. On the contrary, they were profoundly heterogeneous since the names of young and old, obscure and famous, poets and novelists, professors in every discipline, journalists and artists, members of the avant-garde and academicians appear side by side on the lists of petitions of both camps. However, the two opposing camps did not draw their strength from all these categories in the same way; the division was diagonal, not horizontal. The Right-wing *intellectuals* combined all the features of an established position in intellectual society and the Left-wing took on the opposite characteristics, with some obvious exceptions, particularly amongst the leaders whose career-patterns would require detailed analyses which have no place here.[47]

This strongly dualistic nature of the *intellectuels* is the subject of revived polemics which explain how the notion has persisted outside of the context in which it initially appeared. In fact, it goes back to the growing complexity of society under the Third Republic. The official elite managed more or less to represent the conflicting private interests of a society of small producers, even to respond belatedly to pressure from the working classes. Less and less did it look to the future beyond the short term and no longer corresponded to the deep-seated divisions within a nation which was questioning its strength and identity since the defeat by Germany. After the first burst of reforms, the new political generations, outside of the extreme Left and extreme Right-wing movements which allied with *intellectuels* in both camps, no longer had any great ambitions. The *intellectuels*, as a political and social force in critical periods, set

---

47. For details, see the last two chapters of C. Charle (360).

themselves up as representatives of these confused aspirations. By staging the Left/Right confrontation, they gave it back its mobilising strength outside of electoral vicissitudes. But because of this, they were also liable to become scapegoats for frustrations from below, the worst attacks on the *intellectuels* coming less from the authorities than from the Right or extreme Right 'people', shocked by these privileged disseminators of disorder. On the other hand, they gave other categories of the lower middle classes – petty officials, teachers, the women's movement – the strength to dare to defy the hitherto accepted hierarchies. If professors dared to confront the authority of the army or the *res judicata*, was there any reason why officials should not challenge the abuses of their superiors? If justice was eventually triumphant there, then why not everywhere?

Indispensable intermediaries in a democracy which was evolving against the grain of its ideal, the *intellectuels* also wanted, with less success and a fair number of miscalculations, to be the new teachers of a people limited to primary education. The expansion of the movement for popular universities coincided with the commitment of the *intellectuels* in the Dreyfus Affair. For them, it cemented the alliance with the masses and the promise that the educated throng would no longer allow itself to be abused by 'bad shepherds'. They forgot that fine feelings are not always enough to cross cultural barriers and social divides.[48]

However, this attempt and its relative failure were equally indicative of one of the deficiencies in French society connected with the rigidity of its education system. Here, too, the *intellectuels* found one of their long-lasting functions: on the Left, to stimulate the invention of new formulas to break down these barriers and these levels; on the Right, to respond to the threats to the hierarchies or to redefine new dominant legitimacies. The next step here must be to measure the extent of this exclusion by analysing the position of the 'working-classes'.

c Conclusion

A controversial book by the American historian Arno Mayer maintains that the Ancien Regime was still in existence in Europe on the eve of 1914.[49] Without offering any pronouncement on the general relevance of this interpretation to other European countries, there is no escaping the conclusion that some aspects of the elites of the Third Republic confirm this thesis but also that others contradict it. The end of the notables, in Daniel Halévy's sense of the term, was only partial since the

48. L. Mercier (393).
49. A. Mayer (395); see also (102).

old elites retained strong positions in a fair number of sectors. Furthermore, it was not the new strata who replaced them but a new bourgeoisie which was quick to re-utilise some of the old mechanisms to the advantage of its political or economic power, such as paternalism by some employers, governmental favouritism and exchanges of personnel between the higher administration and big business. The only disruption arising from mobility which prevented these new elites from closing up into a ruling class, as under the constitutional monarchy or the Empire, were the advances in every level of education which required the introduction of the machinery of partial meritocratic selection: access to business through the profession of engineer, competitive entrance examinations for high public office, selection of part of the future political elite through the barrister's training course, and general competitive examinations for university positions. This partial meritocracy – which was less important in the world of business than in the university field – marked the limits of the accomplishment of the Republic's political programme. Even if France was advanced compared with other European countries where the old aristocracies retained a clearly predominant place, part of public opinion, and particularly the *intellectuals*, were justified in emphasising the distance between initial ideal and social reality.

The Working Classes: Dissent or Integration?

The end of the nineteenth century and the beginning of the twentieth was a period of decisive change in the working-class world. This fundamental fact justifies the choice of the plural (the working classes) instead of the current, militant, singular term (the working class). On one hand, the rebirth of a mass workers' movement on modern foundations (party and trade union) probably helped to sanction the idea that the workers had a general social identity over and above their apparent old or more recent divisions.

However, the weakness of this movement in France compared with those in neighbouring countries and its internal divisions strongly suggest that it would be inadequate to describe the situation of a group solely in terms of the ideal that its representatives assigned it. Some components of the workers' identity as a class were unchanged from the first two-thirds of the nineteenth century (manual labour, trade, lifestyle, the precarious nature of daily life, and social and spatial incarceration). But economic changes introduced other components, which counteracted the first, including incarceration in factories, the threat of loss of job status as a result of technology and machines, deracination of new groups attracted by developing sectors, and creation of methods of enduring mobilisation, unlike the short-lived revolts of the past. Lastly, the relatively slow rate of change when compared with other nations caused a proliferation of composite situations in which old and new co-existed, when an industrial world was grafted on to populations who were loyal to different traditions, leading to what Pierre Vilar calls 'class unconsciousness'.

Reformists and revolutionaries, direct-action trade unionists and socialists, yellows (non-strikers) and reds, Catholic workers who respected their employers and proletarians won over to Guesdism or free-thinking, men and women, Frenchmen and foreigners, workers loyal to their own milieu and those who dreamed of setting up on their own: these were all members of the working classes, but only a fraction wholly asserted their class membership as a social project. It has often been observed that the workers' movement was all the more radical in France because for a long time it only represented and involved an activist elite. We need first of all to look for the morphological reasons for this situation.

A The Crisis of the Old Industrial World and the Rise of the New

a Worker Divisions

The statistical tools available for measuring the evolution of the working classes are defective in so far as they divide the wage-earning population into sectors, thus limiting workers solely to industrial workers. But, as will be seen, a whole new category of wage-earners employed in the service sector developed in connection with urbanisation, transport and commerce. They shared many of the features of the working-class condition but also resemble 'employees' in the traditional sense of 'white collar workers'. Furthermore, the specifications in the censuses vary from one period to another. This makes it very difficult to compare periods thirty or forty years apart, since the new sectors did not appear under separate headings in the former break-down into jobs, because of their insignificance. The economic situations under comparison (the downturn at the end of the century and the boom before 1914) also had contradictory effects, with changes in contrary directions cancelling each other out in a statistical total when the years observed were too far apart. Lastly, changes which can seem minor in relation to the active population on a national scale assume major significance in a local or regional framework, however little they were concentrated in time and space. All this adds up to a warning against relying solely on abstract figures and is an incentive to explore regional variations in detail when appropriate monographs are available.

The depression at the end of the century and the slowing down of demographic growth are currently advanced as explanations for the relatively low proportion of industrial wage-earners in the total active French population. In 1906, at the height of a period of very obvious prosperity, industry as a whole represented only the second largest source of employment, with 31.6 per cent of the total of the active population (32.8 per cent for men, 29.6 per cent for women), or 12 per cent less than the agricultural sector and only 7 per cent more than the service sector. In forty years the workforce had increased by 2 million people, while at the same time commercial services were growing nearly as fast. The exodus from the countryside obviously flowed almost equally into the tertiary sector and industry.

The real evolutions were of a different order. First and foremost, they were marked by the introduction of women into the working classes. The numbers of women employed in industry rose and exceeded those in other countries. In absolute figures, the female workforce doubled in metallurgy (from 20,000 in 1866 to 43,000 in 1906), and almost tripled in chemicals and the food industry (from 17,000 to 50,000 and from 34,000 to 91,000 respectively). The proportion was 1.8 times higher in textiles and clothing, where women constituted over three-quarters of the workforce in 1906 against less than 60 per cent in 1866.[1] There was therefore specialisation according to sex in various branches of activity, inherited from old stereotypes and accelerated by the faster mechanisation of the textile industry or by the advent of the sewing-machine in the clothing industry. Alongside this, a hierarchy dependent on degree of skill also appeared, with women relegated to chemicals and food which were less well paid and required less training, or again to domestic service, which will be discussed later.

The second factor dividing workers was the different degree of concentration and the dualism between old, semi-artisanal systems of production, and modern factory methods. Overall, by eliminating the weakest enterprises, the depression contributed towards the concentration of the most capitalistic branches. But the small-scale production sector – sub-contracting workshops and home-industry, either working to order or independently – continued to employ a good number of workmen and women whose status was doubtful. Some of them took these jobs after the loss of a job in a larger industry; others saw it as a step towards setting up on their own and joining the ranks of small-scale employers. In 1896, 62 per cent of establishments had fewer than ten wage-earners, while 21 per cent were middle-sized or large factories with 200 or more wage-earners. If the resumption of growth at the end of the century was favourable to the rise of new branches of industry and commerce, it also offered a new chance to heads of establishments with no wage-earners (223,000 in 1896; 363,000 ten years later), former established workers, and independent workers, whose numbers also increased by more than 300,000. Consequently, the hybrid groups on the fringes of the working class, the small employers and craftsmen, gained as much from expansion as the wage-earners (who increased their numbers by 700,000).

The emergence of the sectors produced by the new industrial revolution (heavy chemicals, electricity, petroleum, rubber, automobiles, etc.) did not challenge the old balance between branches of industry. In 1906, the textile industry employed ten times more working men and

1. J. Dupâquier (32), p. 259.

women than the chemical industry and represented over 40 per cent of the industrial population in 1911. Second largest was metallurgy (15.2 per cent), itself very diversified, followed by building, a traditional branch, (13.6 per cent). This mix of industries from different periods, to which the working classes were attached, was reproduced within branches; it was rare to find branches which showed a homogeneous distribution of manpower. The ideal proletariat depicted by theory as working in large establishments was mainly to be found in the mines (86 per cent of miners were in groups of more than 500 persons), in heavy metallurgy (80 per cent), but also in the automobile industry where there were 33,000 workers in 50 firms in 1913. The 'average' male, and particularly female, worker in the textile industry was employed in a factory of about 200 people. The small enterprise, workshop or domestic system was predominant in most other industries, such as food, leather and the ready-made clothing industry.

b Worker Geography

If the technical and economic evolution tended rather to divide the working classes, the social and geographic dynamic, the dynamic of transition to a unified national, even international, market helped on the other hand to create a new solidarity despite these internal differences. The map of the industrial geography of France had become much simpler at the end of the depression, with the collapse of whole regions of dispersed or technically backward industries. At the dawn of the twentieth century it was genuinely possible to speak of an industrial France centred on a few privileged areas, the France that would be hard hit by the crisis in the 1970s.

In 1906, 50 per cent or more of the total industrial workforce was employed in only fourteen departments. Regional specialisation was even greater in some sectors. In mining, the four leading departments contained 69 per cent of the workforce; in metallurgy, 65 per cent; in the wool industry, 67 per cent; and in silk, 64 per cent. Working-class France was henceforth basically northern and north-eastern France, the France of the very large towns (Paris and Lyons, centres of crafts and old industries, also became proletarian with the growth of suburbs or peripheral districts). There were also a few isolated cases of specialisation: industries attached to ports (naval shipyards, ironworks and canneries in the lower Loire; oil mills, soap-works, cement and food factories in Marseilles); arsenals at military ports; two departments in the south-east: Loire (mining, metallurgy, ribbon manufacture), and Isère (glove-making, electricity); and a few remote factory cities or mining basins, such as Le Creusot-Montceau-les-Mines, Mazamet, La Grand-Combe, Commentry,

Montbéliard, Vierzon, Limoges, Decazeville and Carmaux.[2]

This concentration in space had contradictory effects. It was a pre-condition for the development of an identity because the whole region depended economically on a few branches of industry which moulded the landscape and orchestrated working life and, more generally, the life of the local population. It was also a divisive factor; the employers used the argument of competition from other better-placed enterprises in order to create local social unanimity against outsiders, who could be other workers in the same industry in other regions.

c Mobility

Geographic specialisation also shaped new migratory movements should the local rural or urban population not be large enough to supply the demand for manpower. The textile industry in the North had traditionally called in foreign workers from Belgium. But this immigration now contributed to social and national division in the world of labour, particularly in the south-east and the iron and steel works of Lorraine, because at the end of the nineteenth century the foreign labour involved was no longer workers from frontier districts but Italian peasants. This new, transplanted working class was relegated to the least skilled or most dangerous sectors which native Frenchmen rejected, iron mines, chemicals, heavy work such as handling goods or building.[3] The development of xenophobia during the crisis, on the grounds of unfair competition and unemployment and later, on the basis of the pre-war nationalist climate, created a new division within the working classes. This time it was between those true to the internationalist ideas of the organised workers' movement and the traditional reaction of a mass culture which distrusted foreigners. It was very hard to put the ideal of the workers' movement into practice because the employers, in order to weaken the organised French workers, deliberately called in peasants who had no tradition of conflict and were kept firmly in their place by the Catholic hierarchy.

This new spatial distinction between workers was repeated in urban areas. Popular anti-semitism was nurtured by a whole section of the press which was not economical with untruths. Particularly in the ready-made clothing industry, the press played on hostility to Jews driven out of Eastern Europe by pogroms and now concentrated in certain districts of

2. Ibid. (32), figs. 119 and 121, and p. 262, table 24; A. Dewerpe (64), pp. 98–9, from J.-C. Toutain, 'La population de la France de 1700 à 1959', *Cahiers de l'ISEA*, no. 133, Jan. 1963, pp. 130–1, and L. Cahen, 'La concentration des établissements en France de 1896 à 1936', *Études et Conjoncture*, 9, 1954.

3. G. Noiriel (446), p. 141, and (447), p. 69.

old Paris and in certain specialities. In order to survive, they were prepared to accept greater sacrifices than would a French workforce, which was already over-exploited because it was made up primarily of women.[4]

The geographical origins of the working population as a whole therefore became more varied at the end of the nineteenth century and particularly at the beginning of the twentieth century. The proportion of Belgians amongst the foreigners fell (from 46 per cent to 25 per cent between 1876 and 1911) because of naturalisation at the end of the century, and Italians headed the list of immigrants (rising from 15 per cent to 36 per cent between 1872 and 1911). In large working-class towns, however, the diversity of departments of origin extended over and above this injection from overseas. Even quite an inactive town, such as Orléans, experienced this inter-mixing phenomenon. In 1911, only 42 per cent of its workers were born there, and only 36 per cent of its day and manual labourers.[5] In Lyons too, in the same period, the town's range of attraction was also enlarged, spreading out in concentric circles and taking in countrysides hit by crisis (Vivarais, Forez, Savoy) and more distant towns.

But it was obviously in Paris and its suburbs that the national geographical diversity of the working population could best be seen. In Saint-Denis, traditional migrants from Seine-et-Oise and Seine-et-Marne or northern France were supplemented by Bretons from the Côtes-du-Nord, landless peasants employed as day labourers in the dirty industries, men from Alsace-Lorraine driven out by its return to the German Empire, and foreigners who accounted for 6.5 per cent of the total.[6] In the Valenciennois, an old industrial region with a high reproduction rate, the growth of large-scale industry not only attracted French workers, born further and further away, but also Italians and Poles previously employed in Westphalia.

The old industrial world, where geographical mobility was governed by various traditions connected with trades, was therefore affected. As under the Second Empire, the great majority of workers still came from working-class backgrounds, but the form had changed. Identical reproduction was a characteristic of old trades, not affected by technical changes and therefore more rare, and of small, mono-industrial towns, somnolent pockets of employment. In Vienne, Givors or Saint-Chamond, for example, two-thirds or more of the married workers were sons of

4. N. Green (429). A quarter of the workers in the Paris ready-made clothing industry were foreign at the end of the nineteenth century, most of them Jews from Eastern Europe (p. 59); on the ideological context connected with this social evolution, see Z. Sternhell (466) and S. Wilson (472).

5. A. Prost (479), p. 128.

6. Y. Lequin (98), p. 235; J.-P. Brunet (414), pp. 25–6.

workers. In Lyons, a more diversified town which offered opportunities for changing jobs, they formed no more than 54.8 per cent. In the working-class districts of Paris, more detailed statistics show a decrease in the heredity of trades and even a growing movement into non-manual work between two samples in 1869 and 1902–1903. The proportion of sons of building workers who were themselves building workers fell from 77.5 per cent in 1869 to 56.7 per cent of the total in 1902–1903. Workers in highly respected trades in Paris, as well as in less prestigious branches of activity, saw a growing proportion of their sons aspiring to non-manual work. This was the case, for example, with 24 per cent of tailors' sons and 21.2 per cent of the sons of workers in the boot and shoe industry, two trades affected by mechanisation and industrialisation.[7]

Elsewhere, it was the laboriousness and danger of the work which explained the effort to escape, if not from the working-class condition, at least from the sector in which their fathers had worked. Contrary to a self-satisfied stereotype, miners' sons in the Valenciennois did not set their hearts upon becoming miners themselves, despite the companies' encouragement. They preferred to look towards metallurgy or the iron and steel industry which were less dangerous and almost as well-paid. It is true that this was a fast-developing region with a manpower shortage. In a different type of mining region such as the Carmaux basin, much more isolated and living through a period of depression, both the economic situation and company policy encouraged entrenchment in the worker condition. But, once prosperity returned, manpower turnover increased, as it did also in the North and in the iron and steel works of the Lorraine.[8]

All the indicators underline the fact that the new proletariat at the end of the nineteenth century tried to take advantage of mobility among enterprises, regions, or even trades (by moving to a rising branch from one suffering a crisis or declining). This deliberate or partly involuntary mobility was supplemented by forced mobility caused by sackings and seasonal or crisis unemployment and dismissals for militant activities, or was the result of the proletarianisation of peasants.

The co-existence of two industrial worlds, the worlds of workshop and factory, of old branches and new sectors, of traditional towns and cities born of industry, increased the differentiation of skills and therefore of workers' origins and social strategies. The relegation of foreigners to certain jobs, shown by the statistics, was actually a more general

7. Y. Lequin (98), table 25, p.418; L. Berlanstein (413), table III.1, p. 75.
8. R. Trempé (279), vol. 1, p. 159, and O. Hardy-Hémery (433), pp. 36–8. At the ironworks at Decazeville too, the number of workers who stayed less than five years rose from 28.5 per cent in 1885 to 50 per cent in 1890, and 82.5 per cent in 1900 (R. Trempé (469), p. 258).

phenomenon which also affected French workers: the hierarchisation of categories of jobs. Michelle Perrot dates the emergence of the modern OS (semi-skilled worker) from this period, even if the statistical tools did not keep pace with reality and make it difficult now to measure his demographic importance. Like the work of manual labourers, the work of the OS was barely skilled but what made it different at the time was the relationship it involved with machines. He therefore lost the autonomy that possession of a real trade conferred. It is significant that this category represented 59 per cent of strikers and 60 per cent of days lost through labour disputes in 1871–1890.[9] Tied much more to one job than the professionals and less organised, the OS's sole means of protest was instantaneous collective action to an immediate threat.

At first these workers were concentrated in the textile industry, the first to be mechanised, but they also emerged in the iron and steel industry with the arrival of modern processes which lessened the importance of know-how on the part of puddlers and laminators; in glass-works with the mechanisation of production; in de-wooling works and in boot and shoe factories. The pre-1914 'Taylorian turning-point' (Patrick Fridenson) was the rationalisation, in both senses of the word, of this process in the new branches born of the second industrial revolution. The automobile industry, which still retained the character of a luxury craft for certain operations, was not yet the realm of the OS. The division of skills can be plotted on a tripartite basis; in the De Dion-Bouton enterprise, one-third of workers were skilled, one-third were semi-skilled and one-third were unskilled. At Renault, the number of manual labourers soared from 85 out of 1,660 workers in 1906 to 1,203 out of 4,220 in 1914, after the introduction of Taylorism in 1909.

This division, determined by the enterprise, could therefore have contradictory effects depending on the career pattern of the worker. It could enable day labourers or their children to be promoted to steadier work without an apprenticeship, which was beyond the reach of the sub-proletariat. On the other hand, it could constitute a constant threat of deterioration or loss of autonomy for established trades now facing competition because of the new organisation of work.[10]

d Working Classes or Popular Classes? The Action at the Fringe

On the other hand, the probability of saving the money needed to change status was low, implying a strict selection process. The fortunes of various social categories at time of death are usually cited in order to prove that

9. M. Perrot (450), vol. 1, p. 338.
10. P. Fridenson (425), p. 71, and (427); L. Berlanstein (413), pp. 26–9.

this was impossible; mentioned in particular is the fact that 75 to 80 per cent of workers left practically nothing when they died. But this overlooks the fact that workers who changed status by becoming manufacturers, independent craftsmen or small-scale employers would, by definition, not fall into the category of workers when they died. As a consequence of differential social mortality, the workers studied from this angle were younger than the other social groups or, if they were old, had experienced the period of financial deterioration which came at the end of a working life.

The continued existence of the tiny enterprise, independent workers, and craftsmen on the edge of small-scale industry would not be comprehensible without the reservoir of skilled workers which fed this population of micro-entrepreneurs. It is in fact known that the deathrate was particularly high in these individual enterprises whose wage-earners, if there were any, were family members or poorly paid apprentices. There was therefore a whole hazy area of comings and goings between the wage-earning world and the lower fringes of the self-employed, some of whom became established employers.

But this aspect of escape into another class only applied to an elite which possessed a trade and was not in a sector where mechanisation and the increase of fixed capital forced it into sub-contracting, disguising its status as a peripheral wage-earner of a larger firm. These pseudo-employers exploited themselves through engaging in punishing price wars in order to win markets.[11] The other escape route, discussed in the previous chapter, was represented by some retail trades where it was possible to open a shop with a small loan. Here, possession of a social or family network carried more weight in the selection process. Militant workers who lost their jobs through employer repression and became publicans are an extreme example of this parallel exit, the social network in their case consisting of the solidarity of former work-mates who became regular customers.[12]

Slower urbanisation and industrialisation accounts for the continued existence in France of this composite zone, near to the masses of the first half of the nineteenth century. This in turn explains the success of the unanimist ideology of the little man against the fat cats. For some sectors this became populist anti-capitalism, sometimes veering to the Right; for others, it evolved into progressive or radical republicanism approaching a vague, 'French' brand of socialism.

11. A. Faure (175).
12. C. Willard (471), p. 237.

B Worker Lifestyles

a Budgets

In their desire to keep order amongst the working classes, which were believed to be a permanent threat, bourgeois social reformers and observers closely examined the details of the worker's daily life by drawing up typical budgets. Statisticians took things a stage further and tried to construct general indices of wage and income movements. Historians have revived these procedures, adding more direct evidence when they could. Despite these contradictory schemes and the infinite diversity of contemporary working-class France, the conclusions which emerge from these efforts point in the same direction. They disclose a slow but spasmodic improvement in the standard of living and a relatively constant choice between items of expenditure, distinct from those of white collar workers with an identical level of expenditure, for example. The improvement in standards of living consisted of qualitative changes in items more than in a different distribution.

Fifteen budgets drawn up by members of the *Société d'économie sociale* between 1878 and 1895 put the proportion spent on food at between 46 per cent and 77 per cent (the average was 62.8 per cent); accommodation, from 5 per cent to 25 per cent (average 12.3 per cent); clothing, from 8 per cent to 30 per cent (average 16.5 per cent); and sundries, between 5 per cent and 19 per cent (average 18.3 per cent). Some ten years later in 1906, Maurice Halbwachs produced figures for the Paris workers which differed very little: food, 62 per cent; accommodation, 15.7 per cent (plus 5.3 per cent for heating and lighting); and clothing, 7.7 per cent.[13] A provincial example, such as that of a Fougères shoemaker with two children, showed that food accounted for a larger proportion (two-thirds). Accommodation accounted for less (8.6 per cent, because this was a small town), which made it possible to spend more on clothing (10 per cent).[14]

As in the first part of the nineteenth century, therefore, the worker remained in the grip of the immediate need to keep up his working strength from one day to the next. Accommodation, and therefore family life and private space, remained secondary. At the best, free time was concentrated in public places, in working-class or neighbourhood sociability, the birth of associative or militant life, and the slow emergence of leisure thanks to the reduction in working hours. At the worst, free

---

13. M. Perrot (450), pp. 208–15, and M. Halbwachs, *Revue d'économie politique*, 1939, pp. 438–55, quoted in A. Dewerpe (64), p. 151.
14. B. Legendre (439), p. 32.

time was the occasion for chronic alcoholism and the abandonment of family or of intolerable work in exchange for male exclusiveness as a sign of identity.

Sometimes the difficulty of saving, because budgets were too tight, or because of the hazards of working life (seasonal or crisis unemployment or loss of skill with age), was also the result of a deliberate refusal. It could be refusal of the abstract world of the paper-money culture of the ruling classes, the desire to celebrate payday in the same way as the old peasant culture celebrated the end of the harvest, or a feeling of the futility of saving in a world which was in no way under control. The only workers who avoided what bourgeois observers stigmatised as 'improvidence', were those who had retained a connection with the land or were thinking of setting up on their own if they were still unmarried. Saving then was the promise of an investment in land, giving a small degree of autonomy compared with wage-earning, or of transition to independence thanks to a small productive capital.

b Life Cycle

However, new facts forced workers to change their attitude to money. The budgets that the disciples of le Play drew up varied mainly according to family income and size of family. There was a specific cycle of worker family life. The working man or woman managed to economise before marriage as long as he or she did not belong to a large family, in which case everything was handed over to their parents to help with the upkeep of younger brothers and sisters. Early marriage, compared with the middle classes, bourgeoisie or peasantry, was a way of throwing off the yoke of adolescent family solidarity; but small savings disappeared in the costs of setting up a first home. On the other hand, before the wife had children and could still work, the budget was less tight. When children were born and the woman frequently stopped working, the family entered the period of financial pressure which has formed the subject matter of a whole body of, unfortunately accurate, miserabilist literature. The situation was made all the worse by the fact that the contemporary urban working classes still had the highest fertility rates.

Balance was restored by sending the children out to work or by the wife sometimes going back to her job. On the other hand, the departure of the young, the premature death of one parent (statistically probable given life-expectancy and occupational dangers), and the fall in income with aging or loss of skills recreated difficult situations which generated the physical disabilities and poverty typical of the end of a working life. Other more general cycles were grafted on to this cycle, which aggravated or lessened its effects: the alternation of the 'rush' and dead season, particularly in the consumption goods sector; recurrent overproduction crises; the surge in the cost of living at the beginning of the twentieth century; arbitrary deductions from wages as punishments; the absorption of debts incurred during a period of unemployment or a strike; job loss; illness; or the decline of a trade, necessitating a change in occupation or acceptance of increasingly precarious working conditions or pay.

However, these cycles changed at the end of the nineteenth century as a result of more general social developments. The changes were too slow to alter the worker condition to any great degree, a fact which the stability of the budgets reflects, but enough to make the younger generations no longer bear any resemblance to the workers on the morrow of the Commune. Right through the nineteenth century, implementation of the law on child labour came up against collusion by employers and working-class families. Saving on wages in the case of the first and the promise of a less tight budget for the second accounted for this sabotage. At the end of the century this law was supplemented by the law on compulsory education which was expected to raise the age at which children were sent out to work to over thirteen. Like the law of 1841, it was subject to numerous violations but did eventually have social effects, particularly in large towns where primary education could offer jobs for workers' sons in some minor posts.

The correlation noted between the fall in working-class fertility and the advance in education presupposes a change in the family cycle in every case. The loss of children's wages was balanced by a longer active working-life for the wife, as well as part-time labour at home. In mining cities, homes in mining villages included a garden cultivated by the miner's wife, which made savings on certain food products possible. In the towns, it was easier to combine home industry using a sewing machine, or running a small business, with looking after young children if the size of the family declined. Improved health care, made possible by the medical revolution at the end of the nineteenth century, had the same effect. Infant mortality decreased, particularly in working-class circles, as a result of regulations governing the system of putting babies out to nurse and the movement for hygiene in suckling the child. This practice itself was connected with women going back to work too soon after birth, in the absence of maternity leave.[15]

c Hours of Work and Wages

The fact that young people were going out to work at a less early age was accompanied by a shortening of the working-day permitted by

15. L. Tilly and J. Scott (463), pp. 130–203; F. Fay-Sallois (68).

technical progress and collective resistance to the over-exploitation of the early days of industrialisation. Nevertheless, the averages conceal large disparities resulting from the co-existence of several different worlds of working-class labour. The twelve to fourteen hour working-day, which was the rule in the first three-quarters of the nineteenth century, tended to become the exception. In Paris, according to an enquiry in 1893–1897, 59 per cent of workers worked between nine and one-half and ten hours, but 38 per cent worked ten hours or more. In the Lyons region at the end of the century, the average length was between ten and ten and one-half hours, with the privileged workers (averaging below this norm) being those in mining and the book trade, as in the mid-nineteenth century; the least privileged were the women working in the textile industry and everyone who worked at home or at piece work.[16] In Fougères, home-workers in the boot and shoe industry could carry on for up to seventeen hours a day at a time of heavy activity.

Nevertheless, these general figures comprise only a part of the reality. With the creation of outer suburbs, the distance from home to place of work diminished the additional free time theoretically available. The loss of time involved in reaching the workplace increased with the greater depth of the working face in the mines and with the spatial extension of the large establishments of heavy industry. The systematic introduction of discipline based on an objectively measured schedule (bells, sirens or clocks) and controlled by the employers and their foremen put an end to the hazy boundaries between work and relaxation of earlier, rudimentary organisation. The alternation of good and bad economic situations meant days of endless work followed and preceded by complete unemployment. Payment at piece-rates, which was still predominant for jobs in the clothing industry and for work done at home; the practice of *marchandage*, whereby a sub-contractor handed over the whole of a defined task to a team of workers and paid them less than a fair wage; the introduction of payment by output in the mines; and the chronic need for a higher income in periods of financial difficulty, were all factors prompting a non-reduction in the working-day. The relative strength of the various elements, depending on the degree of skill, branch of industry, proportion of women or foreigners, and the abundant supply or lack of manpower, also set parameters which helped determine the final length of the working-day.

The fragmentation of wage rates also reflects this diversity. The usual statistical tools (averages and long-term trends) are particularly ill-suited

16. L. Berlanstein (413), p. 97; Y. Lequin (98), p. 81, and (37), p. 62; B. Legendre (439), p. 18. In home work in the Paris clothing industry, there were periods of intense work of as many as 18 or 20 hours a day at the height of the season (N. Green (429), p. 53).

to this industrial society of several concurrent worlds. The rise in average wages, slower during the depression and faster at the beginning of the twentieth century, can probably be shown from official surveys. According to Yves Lequin, for example, they rose from 4.85 francs a day for men in 1881 to 5.08 francs in 1896 and 6.04 francs in 1911 in Lyons; in Saint-Étienne, wages were only 3.94 francs, 4.32 francs and 5.41 francs respectively; and they were even lower in Privas at 3.05 francs, 3.43 francs and 3.94 francs.

These local disparities are still larger between trades and between men and women, even within a limited region. In the Fougères boot and shoe industry in 1884, a man earned 4.10 francs for twelve hours work and a woman barely half that sum (2.10 francs); in 1890, in a period of depression, wages fell and the hierarchy of the sexes become more pronounced with men earning 3.80 francs against 1.90 francs for women. Not far away, in the Nantes-Saint-Nazaire region centred on naval shipyards (for men) and canneries (for women), the highest male wage was established at 8 francs while the female equivalent was 4.75 francs (2 francs for children).[17] Wage-levels were much lower in the Mazamet de-wooling industry, a less skilled sector in a poor region, but the principle of hierarchisation remained the same; wages were from 2 to 3 francs for a man, for work in which physical strength played a large part in cutting skins, from 1 franc to 1.50 francs for women, and 0.75 francs for children.

The highly skilled Parisian workers, some of whom worked for a luxury market, could look down from great heights, even if there was nothing comparable between the cost of living there and in the rural south-west. A Paris cabinetmaker earned 8 francs in 1882 (a good economic period), but 7.75 in 1886 (a hard year); a jeweller 7.50 francs in both 1886 and 1906. Even the worst-off Paris workers (day labourers, quarrymen and navvies) still received 5 francs in the 1880s, and came close to the highest wages with the return of prosperity but also with the upsurge of protest at the high cost of living.[18] However, it is not certain that the gap between Paris and the provinces or between large and small towns really compensated for the high cost of living in large centres and the extra needs that town life engendered, such as transport, entertainment and clothing.

17. Y. Lequin (98), p. 61; Y. Guin (432), p. 242.
18. R. Cazals (417), p. 179; J. Rougerie (272), p. 102; for details of average wages per category, see Office du travail, *Salaires et durée du travail dans l'industrie française*, vol. IV, 1896. As M. Guilbert (431) shows on the basis of this investigation, the difference in male and female wages is proven even for strictly identical work; it was a weapon for the employer against the workers as much as a sign of anti-feminism since, as soon as he was able thanks to mechanisation, the employer preferred to employ women, the question of strength no longer being a criterion (p. 20).

This analysis must be taken even further because the mechanisation of processes introduced a differentiation depending on which technical operation a male or female worker carried out. In boot and shoe-manufacturing, for example, the machine-operators were most highly-paid (from 1,500 francs to 1,600 francs a year), followed by cutters (over 1,200 francs), sole fitters (from 1,100 to 1,300 francs), hand assembly workers (1,050 francs). Once again, women were at the bottom of the list, as stitchers (earning from 450 to 600 francs) and shop girls. In mining, glassworks and metallurgy, the hierarchy was more one of age, which was synonymous with strength, know-how and technical skills gained from an older man. However, the 'natural' nature of wage differentials could be upset by the industrialisation of a trade, as happened with the glassworkers.

Wage differentials sometimes hampered solidarity between trade associations but they also stimulated emulation through the contagion phenomenon (with the less privileged demanding what the privileged had already obtained). Methods of wage payment introduced specific disparities and conflicts. According to a contemporary survey, only 9 per cent of provincial workers were paid by the month; 57 per cent were paid on an hourly basis and 34 per cent were on piece rates. The figures for Paris are slightly different, 3 per cent, 59 per cent and 28 per cent respectively. But here again the breakdown into sectors was a strong deterrent to a possible claims strategy. In the majority of cases when the final product was comparatively unchanged (mines, quarries, textiles, or stone-cutting), wages were related mainly to production. Wages based on time spent working were more common for jobs done by a hierarchised team or dependent on seasonal variations (building, metallurgy, or coal-mines). Piece-wages were the lot of the over-exploited such as women in the clothing industry or home workers.

The method of payment at close intervals distinguished workers in general from other wage-earners. It explains not only the instability of employment, but also the difficulties of budgeting and the almost structural necessity of getting into debt to bridge the gap at some times; when the rent had to be paid (quarterly), for example, or for an unforeseen expense. Running up a bill at the shop, or a visit to the pawnbroker in more serious cases, were the results of this weekly or fortnightly rhythm of payment. This rhythm had repercussions on the cyclical character of the days chosen to unleash some protest movements.[19]

19. M. Perrot in F. Braudel and E. Labrousse (24), vol. 4/1, pp. 488–9. On the pawn-brokers, see Y. Marec (442).

d Anthropology: Worker Wear and Tear

Discussions about public health in the first half of the nineteenth century contributed to awareness of the social question through investigations into the health of the working classes. Restrictions on the most blatant abuses or chronic failings in the productive system (the gradual disappearance of food shortages, the retarding of the age of starting work, and a rough plan of a social policy in some enterprises) should have been reflected in the physical condition of the working classes. But here again, averages can conceal reality. The connection between diet and height has been known for a long time. Zola refers to the parable of the fat people and the thin people in *Le Ventre de Paris*, a theme which worker and socialist literature repeated ad nauseam. The contrast between 'fat cat' and little man could also be interpreted as identical with the bourgeois/ worker relationship.

From this point of view the improvement brought by the rise in the standard of living and the reduction in the working-day remained limited. In Paris in 1869, a third of working-class recruits from the XIe and XIXe *arrondissements* were not fit for service because of physical defects; in 1914, this only applied to some 10 per cent.[20] In Bordeaux, the difference in the average age at death between the bourgeoisie and the working classes fell from nineteen years six months to eleven years and one month between 1853 and 1913.[21] But towns, particularly large towns, were now special cases since the old forms of industrial work, the least geared to intensive production, were still predominant there. The lowering of the age when pension rights were available from mutual aid societies and employers' pension funds show that premature wear and tear from work increased with the extension of mechanisation, large-scale industries, strict discipline and the new forms of intensive production.[22] Some large factories used workers who were too worn-out by work as unskilled labourers to save them from poverty or unemployment.

The death rate amongst coal-miners in the 45–54 age group (in 1907–1908) was 20.7 per 1,000, against 17.1 for the active population as a whole.[23] In the case of the miners, the impossibility of continuing beyond the age of forty-five because of failing strength and chronic diseases contracted at the coal-face is explained by their working conditions (lack of air, stale air, dust, working in a bent or lying position, the intense effort involved in cutting in the absence of mechanical means and the high

---

20. L. Berlanstein (413), p. 53.
21. P. Guillaume (77), p. 143.
22. A. Cottereau (418), p. 80.
23. R. Trempé (470), p. 137.

accident rate). In textile factories, crowding, humidity, the stress of mechanised work, continual standing, the noise of the machines and the insalubrious air explain the systematic use of a very young and predominantly female workforce which changed at regular intervals, either because it was a stop-gap for young peasant girls until they married or because of the high death rate from tuberculosis amongst the women workers.[24]

The end of the nineteenth century was marked by a new desire to control working conditions and to preserve the 'race', with the aim of increasing the population. But the methods of public action – because they were timid – and of organised worker protest – because they only involved a minority – were not commensurate with the problem. Every indicator of French health underlines the fact that France was considerably behind Germany with its State 'socialism'. In the first place, the predominant world of small businesses avoided all regulation or real control. Conditions there were scarcely better than in large enterprises, even if workers preferred them because of the climate of human relationships. The factories themselves, mediocre buildings built without a thought for comfort or rationality until a relatively late date, helped to make the work more laborious; poor ventilation and an absence of heating and protection against the dangers of the machines were all problems which occurred regularly. Because their incomes were inadequate (medical expenses formed a minute proportion of workers' budgets), the workers barely took care of their health or only had dealings with public medicine, which was enveloped in an image of failure. In the provinces, they, like the peasants, preferred to consult amateur doctors, bonesetters and charlatans, such as in Mazamet, for example.

The workers' over-crowded accommodation and absence of comfort also prevented them from completely replenishing their strength to work. Initiatives by employers or social reformers (such as the construction of worker housing to keep workers attached to the enterprise in industries with a high staff turnover, and a movement in favour of cheap dwellings in the most poorly-off towns) concentrated on this point as a priority because these schemes enabled them to exercise more control over wage-earners and involved no interference in the life of the enterprise. They were also a potential means of causing a division amongst workers, between those who were more and less privileged in this respect. Short of turning the workers into houseowners, an old dream of the ruling class, it was hoped that these schemes would make them privileged tenants and therefore loyal to the established order. But the small number of achievements relative to needs was itself a result of the unresolved

24. N. Truquin (19); A. Cottereau (418).

contradiction between philanthropic initiative, desire for profit and absence of overall policy.[25]

e Workers in the Service Sector

The living and working conditions of a new category of workers, those in the service sector, require specific mention. Their numbers had increased with the expansion of the capitalist exchange economy at the end of the nineteenth century. Census data on this new sector of proletarians are imprecise. The censuses lump them together (because they belong to transport, business or management) under the general heading of 'employee' and therefore greatly underestimate their numbers. Because of this, most of them were confused with employees in business or book-keeping clerks. But although the ranks of this last category had considerably increased, as has already been seen, the greater number worked in tramways, gas companies, hackney carriages, omnibuses, railways, warehouses or in the services attached to factories.

Service workers could be less skilled than some other workers, more dependent on their wages or their employer, more uprooted because they lived in large towns or suburbs or were moved from one place to another as the job required; they earned less and had fewer means of pressure, much like the most exploited workers. Less frequently brought into contact with machines and the pressure for intense production, wage-earners in the service sector were still subject to just as many painful constraints as workers in industry; many worked standing up; workers in transport had night work, cabbies spent interminable days waiting for customers. The lesser possibility for direct hierarchical control (in urban transport, for example) accounts for the severe disciplinary measures or the employment of spies to counter any inclination for independence vis-à-vis the 'duties' of the job.

Other factors explain why workers in the service sector had taken so long to think of themselves as wage-earners, identical to production workers. This sector had often served as a transition point for rural populations looking for a town job which did not involve entering the industrial world, where their lack of skill would have relegated them to posts at the bottom of the scale. For example, if migrants to Paris from the Auvergne did not go into retailing they often found jobs as cabbies, a trade similar to their professional experience in the countryside. More generally, transplanted provincials working in this sector primarily came from poor departments in Brittany, Savoy or the Massif Central. The struggle between independent cabbies and the leading companies tended

25. S. Elwitt (372); R.-H. Guerrand (430); A.-L. Shapiro (464).

to lower the working conditions of the independents, as well as of the wage-earners. The wage-earners could only take action at the time of universal exhibitions, when they launched strikes which showed their disruptive power to best advantage; but the strikes also showed their limitations because the employers had no trouble finding new workers to replace the strikers.[26]

The same situation arising from intense pressure for productivity explains why the railway employees opted for action at the beginning of the twentieth century after disillusion with a reformist strategy. There is a clear correlation between the degree to which the various groups of railmen participated in the 1910 strike on the northern network and proximity to a classic type of worker job. Even though they had strong reasons for discontent, the railmen only dared to challenge the hierarchy in industrial stations with heavy goods traffic and in places where there was a concentration of workers and which were in a strategic position to disrupt the enterprise (in the workshops, 84.8 per cent of workers struck, while 75.4 per cent struck in haulage). The entry of this new section of workers into strike action had a strong effect on contemporary public opinion because of the strategic role of the railways in wartime. The strike itself marked the culmination of a long process of challenging the old discipline, of which the railways were the last bastion.[27]

C Employer-Worker Relations

This period was marked by the emergence of a workers' movement, organised and structured in a durable way (most present-day organisations were born at that time). This institutionalisation accounts for the belief, drawn from the theories the organisations espoused, in a growing unity of the working class. This, it was claimed, was the way to break free from the misfortune of isolation which had caused the downfall of workers' movements in the first three-quarters of the century. Nevertheless, what is striking is the contrast between this institutionalisation and the relatively low numbers of workers involved over long periods, between the radicalism of the ideal and the practical impossibility of achieving massive overall success. Also surprising is the distrust of entering the political arena which now, in theory, presented the most favourable conditions for the voice of the people to be heard.

As has already been seen, some of the middle classes had taken industrial workers as their model when they formed movements. An identical contagion had previously occurred within various working-class

26. L. Berlanstein (413); N. Papayannis (449); F. Raison-Jourde (109), pp. 206–11.
27. F. Caron (415), pp. 208–10.

sectors. This increased mobilisation cannot be compared with a steadily rising movement. Not only did variations in the economic situation create conditions which were more or less favourable to collective action but, above all, old sectors which had once been in the vanguard faded out of their leading roles. What is more, sharp flare-ups in new sectors did not always light continuous fires.

Depending on which type of literature is chosen, a variety of systems can be suggested to explain these characteristics of the French workers' movement which endured into the twentieth century. The classic explanation refers to the actual conditions of working-class life mentioned above. The workers' instability and mobility, whether voluntary or made necessary by employer repression, jeopardised the stability and permanence of organisations. The atmosphere of French political culture, stamped with individualism, is also frequently mentioned in this context. It encourages, so it is said, a tendency towards minority and radical action and a refusal to join in organised movements (as in Anglo-Saxon or Germanic countries) through distrust of any delegation of authority. There are also some interesting explanations external to the worker world, such as employer policy and its development when faced with this unprecedented challenge to its authority, and the political role of the Republic, the agent of tolerance and liberalisation, but also of division between those workers who still had faith in parliamentary action and those who only believed in action on the ground.

On the other hand, the naive theory that poor concentration of the workforce restricted concerted action is no longer mentioned. Investigations into strikes show that the largest enterprises were not necessarily the most prone to strikes. One idea, linked to the thesis put forward in this chapter, sums up these various theories: the practices which defined or marked membership of the working class – in the sense that socialist theory uses the term – were only partially and intermittently adopted in France because there, more than in any other industrial country, several types of working classes co-existed. They could be infected by contagion with collective action but found it difficult to bear its long-lasting constraints because of their manifold internal or external divisions. The main external unifying factor, general political protest, became less important thanks to the Republic. Some workers hoped that it would be more democratic and social. Others saw it only as a tool of the bourgeoisie and broke away from their comrades wedded to parliamentary action. Lastly, a not inconsiderable section still had confidence in the moderate parties; even in some regions in the old ruling classes, sometimes under coercion. Another factor, however, was the attitude of the employers, who were also not united.

a The Means of Worker Action

The Strike Movement and Its Social Significance — The strike movement grew spectacularly from the end of the Second Empire to the eve of the First World War; the number of strikes increased by 1,667 per cent, the number of strikers by 925 per cent and the number of days lost during the period 1872–1911 by 2,858 per cent.[28] The strike therefore became a familiar element in the worker's world, both in relatively small establishments (a quarter of disputes occurred in factories with less than 20 workers) and in enterprises which were large for their time (a quarter of strikes also in establishments with between 100 and 250 workers). A sector by sector analysis shows in part a hierarchy in the weight of each branch in the industry. But this picture is confused by the length of time that corporative worker action had been pursued (hence the high profile of building and furnishing), the rise of new sectors (metallurgy and transport, which held back at first and then opted for action in the Belle Époque), and by more or less favourable geographical location. For example, the miners occupied the forefront of the social scene; they come in second place behind textiles in terms of numbers and in first place in the index of propensity to strike whereas, demographically, they constituted a much lower proportion than other non-striking sectors. Rates of strikers per 100,000 persons engaged in industry in the large French metropolises (Paris, Lyons, Marseilles) during the 1910–1914 period, are also higher than in regions of varied industries and mono-industrial regions. Towns, particularly large towns, still made mobilisation, solidarity and organisation easier at the beginning of the twentieth century than in earlier periods.[29]

The other element in the emancipation from the discipline of normal work was distribution according to sex, since strikers were primarily men. Whereas women represented 30 per cent of the active industrial population, they only provided 3.7 per cent of the striking force. This is easily explained by what is known about the condition of the female worker; generally paid half the male wage, she only had small financial reserves, she was on the average younger than the working man since work was very often a stop-gap, in her life-plan if not in reality, and lastly, she was still frequently dependent on an outside authority (father, elder brother, companion or boarding-house keeper, who sometimes gave her lodgings and was often confused with her employer). Less skilled, she

28. These figures, as well as most of the following or the conclusions of this paragraph, come from the classic book by M. Perrot (450), complemented, for the later period, by those given by E. Shorter and C. Tilly (114).

29. E. Shorter and C. Tilly (114). The respective rates were 4,600 and 1,900 (1,300 without the Nord and the Seine-Inférieure) and 1,300 (1,200 without Lille), p. 292, table 11.1.

was easily replaceable and in addition worked in sectors where price competition was roughest and dismissals most frequent: clothing, home industry, or secondary stages of production. What is surprising therefore, is not that she shrank from collective action but that some women – in conjunction with men, or not – should have dared to take action at all, like the silk throwers of Lyons at the end of the Second Empire or, even more effectively, the women workers in the tobacco manufactories at the end of the century.[30]

Motives — An analysis in purely economic terms does not explain the specific factors which sparked off worker action during this period. The increase in strikes under the Third Republic extended a movement begun at the end of the Second Empire and was connected as much with the spread of revolutionary ideas as with the liberalisation of worker status. In fact, the political climate helped to expand the phenomenon of strike contagion. After the repression which followed the Commune, the success of the Republic and the improved economic situation gave the workers new hope in 1878–1882. The depression in the 1880s put a brake on the movement which then seemed mainly opposed to unemployment and falling wages and later turned more radical in conjunction with the spread of socialism and its early political successes at the beginning of the 1890s.

New worker groups appeared on the scene in the years immediately following the Dreyfus Affair, notable for the advent to power of more progressive Republicans, allied with some socialists, and an improved economic situation. In fact, every point of the curve coincides with the presence of new, previously hesitant, sectors of the working classes. In 1899–1900, for example, wage-earners in large-scale industry were definitely more active than workers in skilled trades or the old industrial branches. In 1906 the ideal of a general strike, advocated by the CGT primarily for May 1, came close to a reality. For the first time, textile and building workers, typographers and iron and steel workers were joined by metallurgical workers in their masses, especially from the automobile industry on the outskirts of Lyons and the Paris region.

This overall historical climate was not independent of a seasonal rhythm. Strikes were still a phenomenon of spring and the beginning of the month, a time when orders flowed in, when building started up again, and when the workers had some financial reserves behind them. This theoretical pattern particularly applied to offensive strikes, i.e., those which had some chance of succeeding. Defensive protest strikes against wage restrictions, increased workload or some symptom of

30. M.-H. Zylberberg-Hocquart, 'Les ouvrières d'État (Tabacs et allumettes) dans les dernières années du XIXe siècle', in (454), pp. 87–107; M. Guilbert (431).

authoritarianism did not assume this regularity. These disputes, demonstrations of offended dignity, were less frequently productive and could turn out badly as a result of mutual exasperation.

In this period of the 'strike's youth' (Michelle Perrot), wages were still the movements' main target (50 per cent of disputes had wages as sole grounds, 21 per cent as partial grounds). In second place came hours of work (13 per cent of cases); then, almost equal in proportion, protest against industrial discipline (12 per cent). This latter source of dispute showed a continual increase, particularly after 1900 as attempts at rationalisation increased pressure by foremen or engineers. Whereas the ostensible reason for 12 per cent of the strikes in 1885–1889 was the organisation of work, by 1910–1914, this applied to a quarter of disputes. In Longwy in the 1900s, for example, a shortage of manpower to develop the new iron-producing basin which, together with the boom in steel, impelled employers to introduce increasingly severe discipline. This provoked an explosion of discontent from April to December 1905, although the ironmasters had thought that their workers, partly from abroad, were under control.[31] On the other hand, few strikes show a complex collection of claims. With no procedures for industrial negotiations, strikes were the only means of fixing, changing or equalising wages between enterprises, regions and skills. They were also the only way to initiate an indirect dialogue with employers in the absence of direct channels.

From 1892, the law provided opportunity for mediation by the conciliation magistrate, but the great majority of employers did not take advantage of this; it was workers or the magistrates themselves who claimed this right. The vast majority of employers still regarded strikes, even if legal, as illegitimate; they amounted to mutiny, a unilateral breach of the work contract. Almost two-thirds of disputes in 1895–1899, and almost three-quarters in 1910–1914 (a sign of hardening attitudes) did not lead to negotiations. This intransigence on the part of employers could only be broken down if the workers managed to provoke the intervention of the public authorities. Only representatives of the State, by not promising to guarantee the maintenance of public order if the employers refused to compromise, had the means to oblige employers to go some way to meeting the claims – even if they reneged a few months later, as frequently happened. The Republic had shed worker blood and Clemenceau earned the not particularly enviable nickname of 'France's top cop' for his repressive policy in respect of the large-scale movements in 1906, made tragically famous by the shooting of Draveil. On the whole, however, the Republic's forces of law and order were not always purely

31. G. Noiriel (446); E. Shorter and C. Tilly (114).

in the service of what anarchists or extreme socialists called the employers' new 'feudal system'.

Some striking workers and trade unionists even took the possibility of pressure by the State or its representatives into account when they assessed their chances of success in the conflict. Prefects or sub-prefects were no longer the armed forces solely of the companies, as under the Empire or the *monarchie censitaire*, when strikes were illegal. They sometimes acted as men of good will out of a desire to make a higher reason prevail, such as the national interest, the general prosperity of the region, or the maintenance of public order (long-lasting strikes were strikes which were violent or marked by incidents caused by desperation). Large-scale strikes always had a greater or lesser political dimension (through the parliamentary questions they aroused and the arrival of politicians at the site) and this was another factor militating towards ending the liberal State's wait-and-see policy.

Despite all these obstacles and the predominant social non-dialogue, the record of strikes as a means for workers to make their voices heard was positive; the majority of strikes ended in success or compromise, despite the crisis period which raised the failure rate. Strikes also stimulated the organisation and expansion of trade unions, even if membership was sometimes no more than a flash in the pan. Overall, the number of trade unionists rose from 277,000 in 1884–1897 to 671,000 in 1911, with two-thirds working in mining or manufacturing and nearly a quarter in the unskilled tertiary sector.[32] This was a much lower number than in England or Germany, but what characterised the French movement was the extent to which its support varied according to trade, region, and type of worker. Figures show that 55 per cent of trade union members were in the tobacco and match industries (public sector workers) with only 2 per cent in the food industry, 4 per cent in chemicals and 3 per cent in textiles, the sectors which employed women and unskilled labour. Rates in the period 1884–1897 were only clearly above the average in branches where a strong corporative spirit could take root: mining (12 per cent of trade unionists), the book trade (9 per cent) and glass (11 per cent).

There was still something aristocratic in the attitude of French trade unionism to the strike, the safety valve of anger for the deprived. Revolutionary trade union ideology, which will be discussed later, emphasised this elitist tendency. The other significant feature of this trade unionism, related to the preceding, was its dual mode of expression by geographical location and by sector, with the first being stronger than the second in the early days. As with the peasants and artisans – and in

32. E. Shorter and C. Tilly (114), p. 150.

fact, the workers who joined unions were close to both in their origins and love of independence – the statement of worker identity through the trade union first took place locally or even regionally. This reflected the predominance of small-scale enterprises which were not always integrated into a truly national market. The movement towards labour exchanges (*bourses du travail*), an institutionalisation of this tendency, was a town workers' movement based on mutual aid by men of the 'people' in the old sense, sometimes supported by reformist municipalities; so too were the unions, which were slowly forming federations at a national level, and sometimes cancelling each other out at a geographical level, in order to preserve a close identity.

Paradoxically, these institutions which were supposed to express worker unity did nothing but reveal the divisions and sub-divisions among workers. There is even a certain logic in this; the elite militant workers dreamed of escaping from the disciplinary constraint of the employers, and therefore had a horror of bureaucratic organisation. As for those who were more deprived or more resigned to their subordinate position and who joined the organised worker movement spasmodically, lack of time, money and a tradition of organisation prevented them by definition from immersing themselves in strictly unified trade unions which would have been their strength; employer pressure was far too strong for them.

b The Policy of the Employers

From Old Paternalism to New — Business heads did not all react in the same way to this challenge to employer authority. The rise in worker organisation and challenge must first be put into perspective. What in retrospect seems like a continuously growing movement, at the time only seemed a step by step advance, with ground gained and lost. In addition, as Michelle Perrot recalls, four-fifths of establishments with more than four wage-earners experienced social calm between 1871 and 1890. Even at the peak of the pre-war strike curve, the average number of strikers per year between 1910 and 1914 (234,700) represented barely 5 per cent of the wage-earning workforce. The systematic refusal to negotiate was a reflection of the strong position the employers still held.

On the other hand, the appeals to external mediation and the verbal, and sometimes physical, radicalism of many of the strikers reflected the feeling that collective protest was a still tenuous, bright patch in a world of resignation. Michelle Perrot places a great deal of stress on the holiday atmosphere of some strikes, which were a break in the monotony of the constraint of daily work. The image of factory or mine as a prison is the counterpart of this assertion that a break had been made. Paradoxically, by daring to assert his collective identity by the refusal to work, the worker at last regained his autonomy.

Employers found this claim more intolerable than the material demands. The worker was thereby breaking the enchanted circle of the paternalistic vision in which everyone was interdependent and remained in his place. The basic theory of liberalism was also denied by this claim; the contract, freely agreed between the wage-earner and the employer, was supposed to be to their mutual advantage. Through posters, tracts, speeches, meetings and newspaper articles, strikes were also the occasion to project a different image of the employer from the one which he had the monopoly of asserting in normal times; during strikes, employers were portrayed as exploiters, feudal lords, authoritarian and pleasure-seeking. In Paris worker-slang, the employer was the *singe*, the monkey, someone who did not pay what he owed and who let people whistle for their money.[33] However clean the employer's conscience, even a rebellion by a minority reflected the failure of a relationship of trust.

Since the first half of the nineteenth century, employers had seen themselves as fathers to their workers. This was not solely an ideological ploy or complaisant hypocrisy. Several objective facts backed up this social vision of the workers as minors; their youth (the result of low life expectancy, the wear and tear of work and the fast turnover in labour), their still low educational level, particularly in newly industrialised regions where peasant roots were near at hand and illiteracy high, and the Catholic impregnation of both parties. But in the Christian religion, authority is based on the filial relationship. Economic dependence is also conceived on a family model; while the worker thinks that he is working in order to live, the employer thinks that he is enabling his worker to live, as a father supports his children.

The old paternalism, set in place during the July monarchy and particularly at the period of imperial prosperity, was an attempt to prolong that image of social relationships in the enterprise by concrete actions. It should however be noted that this system was by preference applied in the provinces, in the least urbanised regions and in places where some employers or some sectors had a monopoly of jobs. The industrialists of Alsace, Le Creusot, the mines of Blanzy and Léon Harmel in the Rheims region fall into this category. The good employer housed his workers, controlled the running of co-operatives or staff stores, founded schools, watched over their private life and church attendance, ensured their old age by pensions, looked after their health by welfare clinics and doctors attached to the enterprise, and organised their leisure activities.

However, this ideal, which the establishments mentioned above and some others approached in varying degrees, had two failings: It was only

33. See M. Perrot, 'Le regard de l'autre', in M. Lévy-Leboyer (389), p. 295.

practicable on the limited scale of a few branches or enterprises which were prosperous enough to take on this expense, and it presupposed an amenable workforce whose sole ambition was a career purely as a worker and in a given enterprise, which was the exception rather than the rule at this period. But above all, its effects belied its acknowledged aims. Some of these enterprises experienced serious labour disorders, just as did others which were less socially-orientated. The 'sublime', that is to say the hard-headed skilled Parisian worker, who claimed the right to remonstrate with his employer and was proud of his trade, had his counterparts in these supposedly amenable provinces. Le Creusot experienced two major strikes in 1870 and a quasi-Commune. The excessive clericalism of Léonce Chagot in Montceau-les-Mines also provoked rebellion in 1882 in the infectious political climate of the triumphant Republic, and Carmaux was another centre of class struggle despite an old and weighty Catholic paternalism.

Faced with this challenge, theorists and administrators (who were sometimes one and the same person, like Émile Cheysson, an engineer with the Roads and Bridges department who was called to Le Creusot to re-establish a climate of trust) tried to improve on their doctrines drawn from Le Play or social Catholicism. In their view, pure liberalism prepared the ground for socialism which, given French revolutionary traditions, would end in civil war as the Commune had shown. There was therefore, no question of abandoning either the employer's initiative or his authority, but there was a need to establish a climate of trust which would make the workers adhere to the welfare works granted them. They had to be convinced that common interest, founded on these services provided by the employer, was much stronger than potential wage claims.

The new paternalism was therefore at the start defensive; revolutionary contagion had to be averted and the recurrence of strikes, which had already taken place and which earlier repressive policy was no longer enough to stem, had to be forestalled. This paternalism also corresponded with the fears of the old elites, analysed earlier in this work, who saw the Republic as providing an atmosphere favourable to rebellion or, even worse, potentially interfering in the running of enterprises through legislation. If employers took social measures voluntarily, workers would no longer be able to press for general restrictive measures, through the parliamentary medium of the deputies. But this refurbished paternalism was also qualified by more ulterior economic motives, which varied with the economic situation and the industry concerned. In periods of depression, it was a means of attracting a stable workforce, from whom a higher output was required in return for material advantages in order to avoid wage claims. Production costs were thus reduced, since this system dispensed with the least profitable workers who were dismissed or excluded from the advantages reserved for more stable workers. The aim was always to divide the workers, with the less stable workers often being at the origin of strike movements.

In a boom, the loyalty to the enterprises created by these institutions, which only benefited workers who stayed in the job for a long time, prevented the best among them demanding pay rises or looking elsewhere for advantages they did not currently enjoy. The social engineer also assumed that humanising the worker's life outside his job (by providing a house, additional services) would make more tolerable the dehumanisation which the race for productivity and concentration inevitably involved.

It is hard to measure the extent of this new paternalism. All the agencies that extolled it, where many of the same men or the same companies recurred, obviously only constituted an avant-garde minority. But their social influence was considerable since the enterprises concerned were large or in a strategic economic position and were therefore able to serve as an example. In 1891, for example, 80 companies practised profit-sharing; ten years later, 120 did so. The *Unions pour la paix sociale*, inspired by advocates of Le Play, counted 3,254 members in 1885, including employers from large enterprises from the zinc mines of the Vieille Montagne, Le Creusot, Terrenoire, the Loire and Carmaux mines, the Messageries maritimes, Saint-Gobain, the Paris gas company, the railway companies of the East and Midi, some textile firms in the North. The membership of the *Société des participations aux bénéfices* which advocated a distinction between two forms of wages, one linked to work, the other relating to results, included employers from the North and East, and also from Lyons (Arlès-Dufour) and Paris (Magasins du Louvre, Armand Colin, and the Chaix printing enterprise).[34]

Above all, it is hard to reach any clear-cut conclusions as to the success or failure of this new paternalism. Did it succeed because it was dealing with a workforce which was in any case amenable, because it managed effectively to divide the workers into groups with opposing interests, or because it supplemented its policy by repressing the trade unions? In the minds of the employers, even those employers who took social measures, the striker was a lost sheep led by bad shepherds from outside the enterprise, or manipulated by 'politicians' or socialist trade unionists. Some employers invented other formulas during this period, in particular composite trade unions (by the textile employers in Roubaix for example)

34. S. Elwitt (372), pp. 104–11; G. Noiriel, 'Du 'patronage' au 'paternalisme': la restructuration des formes de domination de la main-d'oeuvre ouvrière dans l'industrie métallurgique', in M. Debouzy (421), pp. 17–35.

charged with managing the welfare schemes, and above all, 'yellow' or anti-strike trade unions. These latter used nationalism, xenophobia and anti-semitism to divide French and foreign workers and to fight the red trade unions. In Blanzy they managed to obtain a following of a quarter of the miners in 1900. In Carmaux, the failure of the socialist trade union also led a section of the miners to confine themselves to purely corporative action which tended in the direction of the employers' interests; in 1903–1905 a group of 400 to 500 miners, a membership approaching that of the red trade union, allowed themselves to be manoeuvred into this position.[35]

The New Discipline — However, even if a minority of employers, encouraged by the republican authorities, took the road towards a socially-oriented economy, there was still one area where compromise was impossible and which was an increasingly frequent source of conflict and worker protest: internal discipline and unilateral authority. Everything during this period promoted an increased constriction by internal regulations. The size of enterprises presupposed a growing division of labour and more and more hierarchical stages. Mechanisation lessened the autonomy of the specific task and increased dependence on the other stages of the production process. The growing heterogeneity of a more uprooted, even foreign, workforce involved closer supervision. The need to introduce technical innovations in a difficult period challenged acquired worker status, and this was achieved by new regulations. As a result of the imposition of external social legislation employers had lost the freedom of absolute liberalism, and this drove them to employ this private initiative to recover the advantages the workers had in theory gained. Lastly, faced with the deterioration in the general social climate, the regulations comprised a readily available repressive arsenal of weapons to be used against the hot-heads.

It is probable that this authoritarianism was less tolerated as general society tended to develop in the opposite direction. The image of the prison, which the trade union and socialist press made use of, reflected this contrast between political democracy and industrial monarchy, between an attempt to loosen liberal arbitrariness and a military-type internal confinement. The crisis of authority and the prolonged success of anarchism and anarcho-trade unionism in the most conscious sections of the working classes were logical reactions to this authoritarian tendency on the part of the employers. Discipline also concealed an additional means of exploitation through the system of fines and

35. Ibid., p.79, and R. Trempé (470), vol. 2, p. 778.

punishments. These could make a considerable hole in wages and contribute to the precariousness of living. Finally, refusal to obey was generally punished by dismissal.[36]

Workers in the new factories had fewer weapons to resist than in more personal, smaller workshops where a tacit agreement could permit some adjustment or passive resistance, or even the introduction of a counter-regulation through a single trade union organisation. Even small workshops were affected if they had to compete in sectors where factory production was expanding. The workers complained when employers not only urged them to produce shoddy goods to the detriment of quality in order to increase output, but also battled against absenteeism and 'porous' work. The foremen responsible for making the written regulations a reality became the first targets for the discontent created by the new discipline; one-fifth of the 3,000 workers in the automobile industry in the Paris region took part in strikes against foremen at the beginning of the century.[37] Technical arguments added their impersonal logic to human arbitrariness, with control of the workforce sheltering behind the real danger the new working tools represented.

c Rival Worker Tactics

Faced with these new constraints, strikes and trade unionism expressed resistance to this industrial order. These only involved a minority but became increasingly massive, radical to a greater or lesser degree, and prolonged to a greater or lesser extent. But even amongst the most persistent and politicised militants, the co-existence of trades, workers' groups and labour organisations, themselves distributed over a variety of environments, prevented unified tactics being perfected or the consent of the majority of workers gained. Even more serious, workers who seemed to express the strongest class consciousness developed contradictory tactics. The purpose here is not to re-write the well-known history of the worker movement, but to examine a few concrete examples of the social choices between the two extremes of dissent and integration.

The Reformist Option: The Example of the Miners — As has already been seen when examining strikes, the miners were one of the factions of the proletariat closest to the Marxist theoretical model. They had a strong propensity to strike, very hard working conditions, consolidation in large

---

36. See A. Melucci (444), p. 153. In a scheme to introduce regulations in the Société industrielle de l'Est, 'any disobedience of any authority whatsoever' would be punished by immediate dismissal (art. 22, 1889, quotation n. 38).

37. L. Berlanstein (413), pp. 174–5.

joint stock companies, real homogeneity of origins and lifestyle, large-scale expansion of trade unionism on a national scale, and political extension by the election of worker deputies in the Pas-de-Calais mining area. They were one of the first groups to call for general social reforms such as limitation of the working-day, a fixed minimum wage, protection against the scourges of worker life (accidents, illness and old age) and the introduction of a weekly or annual holiday.

However, for a long time, the miners refused to join the CGT and continued to assert their regional allegiance. They held back from membership of a confederation because they rejected the idea of overturning the social order by trade union action. The miners who belonged to unions regarded parliamentary action as their prime means of exerting pressure; even the general strike of 1902 was perceived as a way of hastening discussion in the Chamber of Deputies. This is a clear demonstration of the logical consequences of one of the trends in the strike movement, which has already been mentioned; political action was often the only means of making strikes succeed in the face of employer intransigence.

Nevertheless, in the North and the Pas-de-Calais it had been possible to establish real collective agreements with the Arras conventions (1889–1891). At the congress of Denain in 1907 the *Fédération des mineurs* went further and even advocated a sort of joint management with the employers, with one-third of seats on the board of directors being held by capital and two-thirds by wage-earners. Moreover, miners who were against this plan for class collaboration were more inclined to support the transition of the mines to State control. Yet after seeing the employers' hostility to any State intervention and their completely contrary concept of profit-sharing, such an integrated social project on the part of the workers, which the attitude of the joint stock companies scarcely encouraged, can only seem amazing remembering the tensions prevailing in the French mines.[38]

This unusual example of the choice of a social-democratic option, in the current meaning of the term, by this section of French workers confirms what the history of social democracy in other countries also demonstrates; a mass proletariat with both political and trade union organisation and with no possibility of social escape, tries to make as much room for itself as possible in society as it exists, without subverting the employers' authority. Other worker groups in France shared this reformist attitude including workers in the book trade, postmen, and railway workers – in fact, categories like the miners, who had the strong

38. R. Trempé (468); M. Gillet (379); R. Trempé (470).

corporative identity and effective disruptive power necessary to establish a durable position of strength in relation to the employers or the State. Moreover, it should be noted that when these groups allowed themselves to be persuaded to adopt the more radical tactics of the strike, they lost the slim advantages they had previously acquired.

The opposite option, Guesdism or revolutionary trade unionism, was born of different conditions. One expressed the elitism of an active minority or the impatience of insecure groups rebelling through sudden stoppages; the other, the strategy of workers whose only hope lay in a great and redeeming social upheaval.

Revolutionary Trade Unionism — Revolutionary trade union strategy saw itself as the most purely labour-oriented movement of all. It rejected political mediation, the short-term, false reforms which blunted class-consciousness, but it also rejected urban insurrection with its inherent risk of leading to a blood-bath of the worker elite, as had happened at the time of the Commune. A general strike, by contrast, opened the way to the pure revolution, in which organised workers paralysed the economy and took the place of the employers without external mediation. This movement thereby prolonged the nineteenth-century revolutionary myth, illustrated in the various Paris uprisings, but transferred it from town and politics to factory and economy. Recurrent May Days, which gained more and more symbolic and then practical importance, represented both the extension of the revolutionary 'days' and their transformation into a specifically worker factor.

To define this mixture of old and new, Jacques Julliard speaks of the ideology of a 'working class in transition' in a dual temporal and social sense. A minority and proud of it, these militants thought that at the right time their example could become infectious, as in all earlier revolutionary processes. This was the choice of the skilled workers in 1848 or 1870, who acted as leaven to raise the dough of a floating urban proletariat set in motion by old crises. But the emphasis on the productive function, on the workshop as a battleground (and not the district or town as in former times) marked the change in the centre of gravity of a new working class in process of emerging and increasingly dependent on mechanical processes and specialisation. The most conspicuous leaders of direct action trade unionism were still workers in highly skilled trades or déclassé intellectuals. V. Griffuelhes, for example, was a shoemaker like his father before him; Georges Yvetot was the son of a gendarme and typographer; Paul Delesalle was a mechanic. In the second category, Fernand Pelloutier was the son of a clerk in the PTT; he abandoned his secondary studies after failing his baccalauréat and embarked on journalism and militant action. Pierre Monatte, a former assistant teacher, became a proof-reader at a printers.[39] However, the body of their troops could come from a new proletariat suspicious of political mediation but as easily discouraged as inflamed: in Brittany at the Forges d'Hennebont, for example, or the workers in the boot and shoe industry in Fougères.

This alliance fell to pieces when the dominant centre refused to permit internal democracy in order to keep control of the organisation. Official positions were imposed from above by a non-proportional voting system, with the result that the body of trade unionists, who were actually reformist, was represented by militants propounding revolutionary maximalism. These manipulative practices led the anarchists, at the origin of this specifically French form of trade unionism, into the trap that their strategy sought to avoid; the isolation of the organised proletariat from the working masses, its penetration by police informers or *provocateurs*, and the absence of solidarity even on the part of basic trade unionists in the face of repression. In the end, the only defenders of the CGT prosecuted in 1908 were the much abused socialist leaders.

The Dominated Workers: Guesdism — In addition to differences over strategy, corporative divisions and different social ambitions, there were also marked regional divisions. The foundations of revolutionary trade unionism were in the Paris region and in a few peripheral regions; the Marxist transplant took root primarily in the North and the textile regions, among the Calais net-makers, the weavers in Roubaix and Lille or Roanne, the hosiers in the Aube and the Commentry iron and steel workers who were the first to vote for a party of labour. This was already a second-generation working class, concentrated in factories but not lost in large anonymous enterprises, the victim of low wages and poor housing in towns which had grown too fast and without prospects because the strikes, despite their frequency, brought no substantial advantages. Unlike the revolutionary trade unionists, they did not regard politics as synonymous with corruption but as the only means of obtaining, by delegation, an improvement in their lot either through the seizure of power, expected to be imminent in the 1890s, or by obtaining the minor local government jobs given to devoted and persecuted militants in socialist-controlled local administrations. Guesdism was a caricature of Marxism and, as a social project, was also partly a caricature of German social-democrat bureaucracy.[40]

39. H. Dubief (423), pp. 30 ff. J. Julliard (436), pp. 258–9, maintains that, despite its weak representation, direct action trade unionism (from 1 per cent to 2 per cent of the industrial population) still represented the aspirations of the workers whereas a schism occurred in 1906–1908 when it carried out a witch-hunt against non-strikers. See also his contribution to the colloquium *Jaurès et la Classe ouvrière* (457), p. 111.

40. C. Willard (471), pp. 223 ff.

D From Dependence to Exclusion

a Domestic Servants

The final component in working-class division was the continued existence of a lasting nucleus of dependants and people barred from society. The workers in large and small scale industry probably did not recognise them as belonging to their world; they were 'embourgeoisés', in the sense that they were caught up in a dependent relationship in respect of the bourgeois or excluded from any autonomy because they did not do 'real' work. The very notion of a working class, as defined by the organised workers, was against the imposition of this dependent role which certain forms of paternalism were trying to introduce or restore.

In practice however, there was a functional and even social continuity in the status of the two types of wage-earners. The odd-job man or day labourer did resemble the domestic servant of a factory or workshop. The retailer's assistant helped in the shop but also carried out household jobs in his employer's home. The workshop 'boy' and the apprentice were servants who were liable to domestic duties for their superiors or the employer. Likewise, the marginals were recruited from the ranks of working men, working women or dependants who had lost their human capital through illness, age, long unemployment, or because they refused the new social or industrial disciplines. Men, thanks to a trade, specialisation and better education, were more able to show how far they were from the old model of the wage-earner attached to the master's person and, early on, abandoned jobs as domestic servants (except for the most lucrative and prestigious in the great houses). For men, this job only constituted 4.7 per cent of non-agricultural work in 1866 and 2.5 per cent in 1906.

For women, on the other hand, domestic service still remained a considerable source of employment, equivalent to one-third of the work open to them. Moreover, particularly in the case of countrywomen, domestic service was not necessarily a bad option in the comparative balance sheet of constraints and rewards. At the end of the Second Empire and also in the Belle Époque, 82 per cent of non-agricultural domestic servants were women. However, there was a perceptible decline in the ratio of domestic service jobs to all non-agricultural female jobs, from 37.8 per cent in 1866 to 17.7 per cent in 1906.[41] In the Belle Époque, between 900,000 and 1 million persons still earned their living in this way.

41. J. Dupâquier (32), p. 259.

Between the Masses and the Bourgeoisie — The social importance of domestic service goes beyond these overall figures, particularly for unskilled countryfolk who supplied domestic service with its new members. In places where there was no important industry or salaried jobs for women, they found work by migrating to large or very large towns. A job as a maid, a tradition going back to the Ancien Regime, was the road to survival, to building up a dowry or to getting away from the town for good. Such work was much less necessary for men because of the appearance of new jobs in the commercial services. The male servant originated more from an urban or family tradition, except for specialised 'rural' jobs (coachman, groom, gardener or estates manager). In fact, men were only employed in the houses of the upper echelons of the bourgeoisie.

Jean Chabot, for example, was the son of a tailor from a village in the Creuse who lost his money and died young. Jean was placed with a local aristocrat and became 'general handyman' to a man of independent means in the Blanc (Indre), before being recommended for a post as 'third coachman' to the marquise d'Harcourt in the heart of the Faubourg Saint-Germain.[42] The social career of his future wife, Yvonne, was much more arduous, like hundreds of thousands of other young girls from artisan or peasant families in poor regions; placing these girls as maids at an early age was the only way their families could manage to rear them. Daughter of a Breton working mason who was over-burdened with children, Yvonne first acted as housekeeper after her mother died. Then, when her father remarried, she became a servant with the dowagers of Saint-Pol-de-Léon who took advantage of the fact that she was only thirteen to pay her no more than five francs a month.

The youth of these maids explains why the dependent relationship was so intense; 51 per cent of female domestic servants were under thirty at the beginning of the century. The first professional break occurred at about twenty-four, the average age of marriage in the working classes. After ten years or even more of domestic service, 'savings' could permit return to the land or starting a family. The failure of this strategy – analogous to that of all migrants – quickly implied relegation to the status of a single woman, so belittled in contemporary society. The masters, particularly the largest category, i.e. those who had small means and a single 'maid of all work', systematically rejected married women or made their family life almost impossible. And in fact in 1906, 62 per cent of female domestic servants were unmarried and 13.4 per cent divorced or widows. The proportion was reversed for men; 57 per cent were married because they worked in houses with several servants – their wives could therefore also

42. P. Chabot (4), pp. 9–28.

be employed there – or because they were given greater freedom as the result of a more highly valued specialisation (chauffeur, butler, valet or cook). In large houses (more than ten servants, such as those of the Murats or the d'Harcourts) it was not unusual to employ married couples as domestic servants or to arrange marriages between servants; this was a guarantee of their loyalty to the household in the style of the Ancien Regime.

The harshness and meanness of master-servant relations under the merciless rod of the petty bourgeois, who formed the overwhelming majority of 'served' people, implied a rapid staff turnover. Jeanne Bouvier, for example, began as a young millhand in Vienne. When she was fourteen she came to Paris under pressure from her mother, in order to go into service as a young maid with tradesmen. She had no less than four situations in one year, a victim of every variety of greed or abuse from a series of masters. She then preferred to work in the clothing industry.[43] As well as this instability, there was also the promiscuity of the maids' rooms on the sixth floor, or the hostels for unemployed provincials where a convent-like discipline prevailed. Whether these were philanthropic or religious foundations, their managers never forgot that business was business and extracted their dues from these dependants in distress.

In Paris, the maids formed an invisible world of more than 150,000 inhabitants concentrated in two sectors: under the roofs of Haussmann's buildings, or more rarely in the dark rooms of bourgeois apartments, and in the elegant districts to the west. In the capital as well as in the main towns, the hierarchy of wealth could be assessed by the number of servants. In Rouen under the Third Republic 11 per cent of households employed servants and the ratio was probably similar in the rest of France, except in the case of the bourgeois professions (magistrates, barristers, notaries and doctors), men of independent means, landowners, merchants and industrialists with a certain level of income.[44] These men and women who traded their lives in exchange for relative security also served the function of maintaining the distance between the bourgeoisie and the material world and particularly between the bourgeoisie and all the other groups who did not possess this index of social status. To acquire this symbol, the least affluent members of the middle classes had no qualms about devoting up to one-sixth of their income to wages, in order to have the impression of being on the side of the masters. Consequently, they eased this burden by cutting down on every non-monetary aspect of the maid's pay including food, accommodation, leisure and clothing.

43. J. Bouvier (2), pp. 65–80.
44. J.-P. Chaline (56), p. 39 and fig. 5, p. 436; P. Guiral and G. Thuillier (78), pp. 11–2.

Despite the miserabilism which descriptions of domestic servant life exude, the relatively persistent choice of this hard profession can only be understood by comparing it with what women from a working-class milieu experienced in other sectors. The condition of farm servant was just as harsh in terms of hours of work demanded, with physical fatigue, discomfort, bad weather and rural isolation into the bargain. The woman industrial worker was exposed to the insalubrity and intensity of factory work coupled with the insecurity of work and pay, or again, excessive working hours in a clothing workshop. The workers' surly attitude to domestic servants was directed at men rather than women. The men had chosen a code of values which could even lead them to identify mentally with the bourgeois or noble. The women had been led towards one form of the domination of women rather than another by the hazards of geographical chance (this was the time when Breton women, prototypes of the naive country girl, arrived in Paris, or girls from Savoy in Lyons), by ignorance (11 per cent of female domestic servants were illiterate at the beginning of the century), or family or regional networks.

Moreover, it was easier for them to go on hoping to be able to extricate themselves once they had saved enough. A young peasant girl could view the 500 franc average wage of an ordinary maid in Paris (300 to 340 francs in the provinces) for a 15 to 18 hour working-day as clearly preferable to the 450–600 francs paid to a stitcher in the boot and shoe industry, which also had to cover the cost of feeding, housing and clothing herself. The maid could save, as long as she did not let herself be 'tempted' by all the opportunities to spend induced by urban life and the 'civilisation' she was discovering.

However, domestic servants also went through the bad patches associated with the worker condition including voluntary job loss (rising in the hierarchy of masters was to gain the impression of rising in the social hierarchy), or forced loss of employment through illness, accidental pregnancy, a reverse in the master's fortune or incompatibility of temperament between master or mistress and domestic servant. The risk of a mis-match was all the more common if the woman servant was inexperienced or the employer stingy through being at the limits of his real standard of living. Finding a new job was very expensive because of the exploitation practised by the employment bureaux; a month's unemployment amounted to the equivalent of six months' wages.[45]

The other vicissitudes of a domestic servant's life arose from her lower legal status. A servant who stole was punished more severely than other people (under Article 386 of the Penal Code). Theft was less often a question of domestic theft than of shop-lifting, connected – as was the

45. A. Martin-Fugier (443), p. 74; a great many concrete details originate from this book.

case with workers – with periods of unemployment, the temptations of the newly-discovered town or to counter-balance under-feeding by miserly masters. Until 1909, a pregnant maid was automatically dismissed; after that date, the contract was suspended without being terminated. With regard to social legislation, domestic servants benefited neither from the 1898 law on accidents at work nor the 1906 law prescribing one day off a week because they belonged to the 'private world'. Moreover, the servants themselves were divided on this point; the trade union affiliated to the CGT was in favour, while the much more representative moderate trade unions were against in order not to jeopardise relations with the masters.[46]

The Crisis in Domestic Service — The image that novels and the bourgeois theatre paint of good society in the Belle Époque implies the presence of housemaid and footman in the background. In this ideal world, partly preserved in good houses (see the memories of Proust's maidservant), the master-servant relationship still had its elements of collusion and deference. Devotion and goodwill, family loyalty without blood relationship, a dream which obsessed the theorists of societies of order, prevailed there. In the more representative and dominant real world where the maid was only an instrument for work, sometimes for pleasure, or almost always for revenge for the humiliations of a mediocre petty bourgeois life, the charm subsided as the abuses were exposed by naturalist literature (cf. Mirbeau's *Le Journal d'une femme de chambre*), journalists or the small minority of domestic servants who asserted themselves.

The domestic servant crisis of the 1900s was not just the theme song of masters lamenting the end of the 'good old days' of submissiveness. It can also be measured by figures showing the decrease in manpower employed (given above), at a time when the rise in bourgeois living standards should have permitted increased employment of maidservants. In fact, the advantages of the condition of the domestic servant over the condition of the woman worker tended to disappear, in the absence of organisation and collective action. Wages were not raised in proportion to the cost of living; the length of the working-day remained the same. But above all, the supply of candidates for posts diminished as a consequence of the spread of Malthusianism in the countryside and the return of agricultural prosperity. Thanks to the higher educational level and the considerable increase in the number of jobs for women in the tertiary sector which did not restrict private life, poor young girls had an alternative solution to domestic service besides being workers.

46. Ibid., pp. 254, 264 and 268.

The emergence of trade unions of domestic staff, previously unthinkable because they were incompatible with the vision of the social order of this milieu, confirms the evidence, already shown by the example of other associations, of the way in which the Belle Époque was being shaken. When they formed themselves into a group, even those who viewed the master as a father, like the members of the yellow, non-striking, trade union founded in 1905, they moved away from the personalised, individual relationship and towards the anonymous, collective image of the employer.[47]

What the voteless and unorganised (over 95 per cent of domestic servants of both sexes, as much as 99 per cent for women) thought will never be known. However, letters sent to newspapers record their feeling of being excluded from progress. Women servants were also never far from every type of moral lapse because they were deprived of the normal life of a woman of the day, particularly in a rural environment. They were driven to secret liaisons; procreation was forbidden or outlawed, which led to abortions or infanticide and made them easy victims for illicit or organised prostitution. It is by definition difficult to measure the whole pathology of the dependent condition. There is, however, clear evidence for it. As this specific deviation came to be included in the information disseminated about the occupation (by various events, actions brought before the courts and realist novels), the powers of attraction of the condition of female domestic servant decreased and the numbers of women interested in filling the role became fewer.[48]

b Excluded Men and Women, the Hell or Purgatory of the Working Classes?

The end of the nineteenth century was also marked by a change in relationships between marginal elements and the working classes which provided them with the bulk of their recruits. In the first three-quarters of the nineteenth century, official discourse tended to identify the labouring classes completely with the dangerous classes. With the Republic, social fear became diffused and was modified. It was distributed over several groups considered to be at irreparable risk, and the aim was to make the workers more responsible through the hope or reality of liberal reforms brought in by the regime.

47. The three servants' unions had about 6,000 members, or 3 per cent of the total number of servants (1.7 per cent for women); this minority included a revolutionary unionist avant-garde and a reformist or 'yellow' majority (A. Martin-Fugier (443), pp. 273–4).

48. Thus in 1890 the majority of unmarried mothers were servants in Paris institutions; 10 per cent of the abortions recorded by the *Compte général de l'administration de la justice criminelle* were also their doing; see A. Martin-Fugier (443), pp. 321 and 339.

And in fact, if collective action did increase, uncontrolled violence diminished or appeared a thing of the past. As has been seen, the dream of a general strike lay in the hope of showing its strength sufficiently not to have to use it, in order to break the cycle of bloody defeats of the proletariat by the forces of law and order. But, concurrently, any analysis of social ideologies and legislative measures shows that, after a short liberal period following the constraint of the government of Moral Order, there was an irreversible tendency to multiply repressive measures against categories regarded as irremediably deviant and liable to disturb the social order. In vain did the supporters of public liberty denounce the arbitrariness with which the administration and the police hunted down registered or illicit prostitution in the name of public health; it remained more prevalent than under conservative governments. In 1885, Waldeck-Rousseau brought in a law relegating intractable criminals, 'rebels against any form of work', to a penal colony, and Parliament strengthened forced labour by instituting isolation at Cayenne for convicts, most of whom were sentenced 'for crimes against property'.[49]

All the evidence suggests that the most liberal nineteenth century regime was concentrating its legitimate violence on the most vulnerable section of the working classes, after having lightened the general yoke weighing on the elite members who supplied their militants. Because of this, the barrier between 'decent people' and the instigators of disorder, which formerly corresponded to the boundaries between the ruling classes and the ruled, now moved to the inside of the ruled classes by way of theory and practice based on biological stigmatisation. The degeneracy of the criminal and prostitute, the inheritance of defects and the battle against contamination were fashionable subjects at the end of the century.

The Prostitutes — This is clearly a realm where theory and 'objective' reality are so mixed up that the 'facts' cited are largely the product of the arguments they support. For example, the probable increase in prostitution can only be measured by statistics drawn up by observers who wanted to emphasise the danger that this growth constituted. This engendered greater repression which in return augmented the statistics. The anxiety came from the collapse of the old regulated system of registered brothels and prostitutes, whose share of the market fell in comparison with non-official prostitution practised illicitly or in places which defied supervision (cafe-concerts, women's beer-gardens, public houses or 'front' enterprises). For example, 10,000 lodging houses in Paris

---

49. A. Corbin (60), pp. 154–66; M. Devèze (422), p. 147. In 1890, 590 people were sentenced for crime against persons as compared with 1,085 for crime against property (p. 165); see also M. Perrot (452), p. 67–91.

and 74 taverns in Roubaix were listed as acting as places for prostitution at the end of the century.[50]

Prostitution was therefore compared to an epidemic, which was both biological (it spread venereal diseases) and social (it perverted the vulnerable social categories, with a risk that they might be distracted from honest work and towards parasitism and pleasure). In fact, this moral vision reflected a social fact; the inequality of male and female pay doomed some women to see prostitution as an answer to a structural lack of respectable income.[51] But such was the demand that the official or occasional prostitute, even when she was exploited (by the brothel-keeper, pimp or complaisant husband) was much better paid (whatever class of prostitution she belonged to) than the most skilled worker or best-paid servant. In brothels in the Var, earnings were between 5 and 6 francs a day in a working-class establishment, 15 francs in a bourgeois establishment.[52]

The proliferation of forms of prostitution which avoided supervision increased temptation, as did urbanisation, the spreading taste for luxury, and entry to more select social circles. Although the majority of prostitutes registered in Marseilles in 1871–1881 did not have a previous profession, many more of the remainder came from under-paid female trades (dressmaking, domestic service, or the service sectors) than from industry. On the other hand, illicit prostitution was most commonly combined with a regular profession, the principal professions here again being domestic service, shop assistants and seamstresses. However, any overall picture would be misleading because, like domestic service or trade, prostitution was hierarchised by geography, the clientele and the type of 'ponce' on whom the prostitute, grisette, courtesan or kept woman depended. An immeasurable distance separated the two ends of the social scale of prostitution. At its depths was the hell of the street-walkers haunting the unsavoury districts on the outskirts of the city, the barmaids in the shady taverns of the poor districts or the canteens reserved for Italian immigrants in the iron and steel region of Lorraine. At the top of the scale of 'love affairs' came the regular visitor to the assignation hotel, an almost respectable bourgeois lady simulating fashionable adultery, or the demi-mondaine, favourite of prominent men, set up in a private apartment in the fine districts in western Paris.

What aroused social fear in a hypocritical society was the very

50. A. Corbin (60), pp. 212–8.

51. For example, Jeanne Bouvier recalls the memory of two neighbours living on the same floor from her youth: one a linen maid, committed suicide at the age of twenty-two to escape the privations, so as not to die of starvation; the other made beading and spangles for braiding and earned so little that she worked as a prostitute in the evenings ((2), pp. 89–90).

52. A. Corbin (60), p. 119.

ambiguity of the prostitute's status. The prostitute represented the underside of society. It was impossible to abolish or acknowledge her but she was indispensable, given the mounting frustrations engendered by the prevailing social order. She was a social indicator which the moralists could not tolerate. And the naturalist novelists who made her the central subject of some of their most successful and scandalous works (*Nana, Boule de suif*) made no mistake. The violence of official discourse, particularly on the danger of venereal diseases carried by prostitutes, conveys anger at a social figure who was unthinkable in the dominant mental categories, rather than a totalitarian plan for confinement which the whole of social evolution and even the personal conduct of the ruling or middle classes rendered hopeless. In fact, the prostitute was the only woman except for the actress whose body was a capital asset with a higher yield than the body of a proletarian male and thus not a source of weakness in comparison with man.

The Confined — Many of the themes of the discourse on prostitutes recur in relation to the other groups excluded from society (prisoners, convicts, vagabonds, recidivists and aliens). This discourse was directed towards the same end: first, to dissuade redeemable elements from settling in that counter-society and second, more or less openly, to get rid of the irredeemables who were a permanent danger to the established order. The proliferation of mechanisms to control deviants who had managed to avoid the effects of the inculcation of the work ethic by general schooling and military conscription was in response to the first aim; these included the creation of the *casier judiciaire* (the register of police records) in 1890, the Criminal Records Office in 1893 and the application of scientific methods of identification (Bertillon's anthropometry and fingerprinting).[53] The increasingly heavy punishments imposed on recidivists, the practical effects of which (permanent exile or a high death rate) amounted purely and simply to physical elimination, corresponded to the second.

Although official statistics are imprecise, the change in the social backgrounds of those sentenced to imprisonment does show that they came from a narrower social spectrum. Under the government of Moral Order, convicts (mostly convicted of theft) included almost as many workers, even skilled workers, as members of the agricultural professions, day labourers and domestic servants, or workers mostly living from one day to the next (5,032 against 6,092). Weighted on the basis of general demographic distribution, they were even proportionately more numerous. This reflects the result of a decade of post-Communard

53. M. Kaluszinski, 'Alphonse Bertillon et l'anthropométrie', in P. Vigier (119), p. 279.

repression, when social, political or purely dissolute delinquency were mixed up together in prosecutions. On the other hand, at the end of the century as in 1909, at a time when there were fewer convicts (a symptom of an improvement in general discipline in the new, better structured society), the majority of convicts came from among the most under-privileged or least integrated workers (the 'nomad' professions, in official terminology); these represented 49.9 per cent and 49.2 per cent of the total in 1897 and 1909 respectively.[54]

Likewise, the fall in the number of prosecutions for vagabondage, a major crime in the eyes of the authorities and the law, was a sign of the relative success of social control procedures. They turned formerly unstable elements away from wandering the countryside and towards the large towns. There, they practised a variety of minor trades intermittently or swelled the ranks of unskilled workers caught up in the accelerated turnover which characterised the new industrial regions with the return of prosperity and the chronic shortage of manpower.[55] The social imagination then either painted the irredeemables who swam against the stream in the flamboyant colours of the rebels of the Bonnot band or the myth of the Apaches, gangs of youth terrorising some marginal areas; or, by contrast, in the sombre colours of a cancer to be eradicated. In either case, they were now only a subject of cultural consumption for the working classes through the intermediary of reports in the cheap daily papers or the feature stories which were inspired by them, and had less and less relevance to the social life of the majority of workers, except at the critical ages of adolescence and the time immediately after conscription. In 1909, for example, the crime rate for 18–21 year-olds (3 per 1,000) was triple the average rate.

The democratic society, because it was democratic, was less tolerant of people who ignored its rules than any other. The incarnation of reason and the majority, this society relentlessly excluded irrationality – that of crime or madness – and the non-conformist minority. It interpreted as biological pathology what was often only the maladjustment of its institutions to heterogeneous populations.

54. *Annuaire statistique de la France*, 1881, p. 11, 1900, p. 140, and 1910, p. 98. Here, I add the percentage of agricultural workers, day labourers and domestic servants and those of the nomadic occupations (4.1 per cent and 5.1 per cent at the last two dates). The fact that the agricultural sector held a minority share in the 'poor' population at the dawn of the twentieth century can be established from other data; 60 per cent of defendants in 1902 were resident in urban communes (M. Perrot (452), p. 79) and 47 per cent were day labourers in transport or industry (ibid., p. 80).

55. M. Perrot (453). In 1895 a specific census of all nomads was carried out as a deterrent. A considerable figure of 400,000 resulted, including only 25,000 real gypsies (M. Kaluszinski in (119), p. 283).

c Conclusion

Working-class dissidence – as well as integration – could take a far greater variety of directions than in the past. The theoretical dilemma of the workers' movement – reform or revolution – does not wholly account for this as both revolutionaries and reformists were, in their turn, divided over several options. The most important social change in that period, outside of the social gains in the narrow sense, was probably the emergence of the new descriptive paradigm of the working classes, whether it originated from the interested parties themselves or other social groups. Legality of collective action was an established fact, even for the least assertive groups. If they refused it, they had at least to make their position clear in relation to it. On the other hand the archaic forms of challenging the established order, because they were individualist, were increasingly rejected in the non-social or infra-social.

France of the Belle Époque, the society which contained the promise of progress, did channel rebellion, but it also engendered and at the same time generalised permanent dissatisfaction, as the overall balance sheet will now show.

–8–

The Ideal of a Democratic Society?

Because of the Manichaean logic of political debate, opponents and also supporters of the Republic always had a tendency to emphasise the failings, and also the virtues, of that regime. The tale of woe emanating from the Right and extreme Right stressed the levelling downwards that democracy implied. Not only did the latter have no elites worthy of the name, but it set out to devalue or ruin the position of the old elites or of anyone who might rise above the masses. The Left, and particularly the far Left, on the other hand, emphasised the gap between the democratic programme and social reality, the maintenance of inequalities, bourgeois control of important positions, the corruption of parliamentary government by private interest groups, the delay in social legislation, and the old-fashioned working of the State. To some extent these charges continue to influence our vision of the society of the Belle Époque.

However, the two overall verdicts are not as incompatible as might at first glance be supposed. Their divergence basically arises from the points of comparison taken by either side and the overestimate, typical of French debate, of the role of the State and politics in social evolutions. The Right wing had more faith in the effectiveness of republican reforms than did those who implemented them. They particularly deplored the exceptional character of France in a Europe where the aristocratic or oligarchical ideal remained largely preponderant, from England to Russia by way of Germany and Italy or Austro-Hungary. The Left, for its part, attacked the concealed feudal systems propped up by the State apparatus in order to thwart the democratric thrust. They cited as incontrovertible evidence of this thrust the mounting social tensions of the 1900s, but failed to note the weakness and division in the contending forces.

Retrospectively, some historians dismiss both these biased interpretations and put forward the thesis of a blocked society. In their view, by refraining from overt action, France and its leaders were seeking to maintain an old social equilibrium with a strong peasantry and independent plethoric middle classes in the name of an ideal of a democracy of 'little men', a pledge of something approaching social democracy. But this honourable mediocrity, so the argument goes, was detrimental both to fraternity with the most under-privileged and to the dynamism which would have brought greater freedom for the triumph of capitalism. To see the situation more clearly, some attempt must be made to measure the inequalities decried by the Left and, conversely, the new opportunities for social mobility opened at the dawn of the twentieth century, emphasised by the conservatives.

A Measuring Inequalities

a Wealth and Incomes

The society of the notables offered those who could aspire to be part of it the ideal of individual enrichment; this was the guarantee of access to the notability and to a superior status. Republican ethics put less emphasis on wealth than on saving and a respectable affluence, since the political advantages linked to wealth had disappeared. Nevertheless, by refusing any fiscal reform (income tax was not voted in until 1914), the regime maintained intact the classical liberal mechanisms for increasing inequalities. The doubling of the overall fortunes of Frenchmen between 1850 and 1914 reduced the proportion of the most under-privileged fringe but the gaps between the average indices of each bracket remained as large as at the beginning of the nineteenth century.

On average, between 1902 and 1913, 37 per cent of adult Frenchmen died with no declared property.[1] Amongst those who did leave something, the gap between the lowest bracket (less than 500 francs) and the category of millionaires was 1: 10,000, or a range close to the data available for the Restoration. What is more, the total value of the property possessed by the wealthiest was considerably higher and the concentration of fortunes had increased even more than the statistics show, as it was easier to cover up stocks and shares or untaxed property held overseas than at the beginning of the nineteenth century. In Paris in 1911, for example, the richest 4 per cent owned 67 per cent of total declared inheritances. Intermediate fortunes (between 50,000 and 1 million francs, allowing a more or less comfortable independent income) accounted for no more than 30 per cent of the total, against 45 per cent in 1847.

But the capital and large towns tended to emphasise the divide, since the most deprived and the richest lived there side by side. At one extreme were the marginals in the working-class districts who left nothing but debts; at the other, the barons of finance like the Rothschilds (around 250 million each for the two brothers, Alphonse and Gustave), the founders of the large stores (Chauchard, one of the founders of the Louvre,

---

1. A. Daumard (473), p. 81.

bequeathed 11.5 million francs to the minister Georges Leygues, not to mention his collection given to the Louvre), company directors (average fortune, 8.75 million), or the great aristocratic fortunes.[2] The concentration of the wealthiest people in the large towns also explains the geographical gaps. Thirty-two per cent of declared fortunes in 1908 belonged to inhabitants of the Seine and two-fifths to inhabitants of the six richest departments: Seine, Nord, Rhône, Seine-Inférieure, Seine-et-Oise and Marne. This urban oligarchy, composed of heads of enterprises and large landowners, was denounced in polemical literature, but it was barely visible to the mass of the population because of its very concentration. In predominantly rural regions the top men were the traditional groups, notaries, landowners, high officials, the elite of the liberal professions, merchants or industrialists. Consequently, the range of levels of fortune was less in the Beaujolais, the Vaucluse or the Pas-de-Calais, for example.

Income differences were obviously linked to these variations in inheritance even if the old image of the idle *rentier* only referred to a minority, most of the official *rentiers* of the statistics actually being retired pensioners. In addition, management of a large inheritance presupposes some personal activity, and it is significant that members of the aristocracy were also relinquishing complete idleness and were increasingly going into business.

Table 8.1: Distribution of French income levels in 1894–1895, from figures of the extra-parliamentary commission considering Paul Doumer's income tax plan.

CATEGORY (in francs)	NUMBER	TOTAL AMOUNT (in millions)
2,500 and less	9,509,800 (86.4%)	12,342 (54.8%)
2,501–3,000	563,000	1,597
3,001–5,000	446,000	1,735
5,001–10,000	294,000	2,109
10,001–20,000	123,000	1,798
20,001–50,000	51,000	1,573
50,001–100,000	9,800	674
over 100,001	3,000 (0.002%)	572 (0.2%)
Total	11,000,000	22,500

Source: E. Levasseur (475), p. 619, also quoted in J.M. Mayeur (477), p. 89.

2. V. Bourienne (228), p. 287; C. Charle (359), p. 61.

As Table 8.1 shows, the pyramid of fortunes, which was still relatively attenuated, corresponded to an equivalent differentiation of incomes. 86.4 per cent of French heads of households received less than 2,500 francs a year from their gainful activity. At the time this was equivalent to a capital of 50,000 francs, double the average overall salary of officials and double the wages of a good worker, equal to the income of a farmer, or one-third of the profits of small retailers.[3] The next stage is the world of the contemporary middle classes, heads of small businesses, small landowners with five to ten hectares, traders already safe from the threat of bankruptcy, middle-ranking officials, teachers, officers and members of the minor liberal professions. The really bourgeois level was situated at over 5,000 francs income, or 100,000 francs capital, which represented higher salaried public office, an average or mediocre income from a liberal profession, or a still modest profit from a business. According to these fiscal statistics, less than 500,000 heads of households fell into this category, or 5 per cent of the total, which also corresponds to estimates of the bourgeois population based on other indices of wealth; but this minority shared more than one-fifth of total income.

The distribution here is slightly less inegalitarian than the distribution for fortunes, because this group included the whole of the bourgeoisie with specific skills (engineers, salaried staff, members of the liberal professions, university teachers and high officials) who had reached a comfortable standard of living, without necessarily having a personal fortune as in the past. But this scale of incomes also explains why, despite the new access roads formed by the diversified educational channels, only a very small minority could hope to scale the social ladder by this means.

b Status

The verdict of the figures notwithstanding, republican ideology still managed to convince public opinion that France was more egalitarian than other countries. This shared illusion is in itself a social fact and, unlike the United States, it did not breed on the myth of a society open to people who started from nothing. Its main argument was political. The Republic, it claimed, had abolished discontinuities in status which obstructed social mobility. The rich were probably richer than they had ever been but democratic parliamentary power could obstruct them. Most Frenchmen remained in the social class that they had been born into, but

3. 55.6 per cent of retailers paid less than 20 francs for their patent, which represented 700 francs income; a third paid between 21 and 100 francs (income between 700 and 3,333 francs) and only 0.77 per cent paid more than 500 francs (over 16,666 francs income). See E. Levasseur (475), p. 62 (for 1895).

there was now a social conveyor belt which gave meaning to the efforts of those who wanted to change their condition. The opening of elective office to men of no rank (non-existent elsewhere or largely emptied of its content in monarchical regimes) was its clearest demonstration. Lastly, by virtue of its secular ideology, France had opened its doors to entry by elites from religious minorities – Protestants, Jews – who were discriminated against elsewhere.

This official view is the substance of set speeches and fills the pages of textbooks. It is not just a defence of the established order, since the categories who benefited least from the advantages of the system fought for the regime in all sincerity. These groups were convinced that a victory for the enemies of the regime would lead to a regression towards the same sort of class society as the society of notables or of the aristocratic countries elsewhere.

However, this feeling that things had changed for the better remained tenuous. In fact, liberalism engendered its share of people excluded from society whose negative status became hereditary. French Malthusianism made it necessary to call on unskilled foreign labour, which increased the wealth of the French but was kept apart from the society of real citizens – when it was not the object of xenophobia on the part of nationals. Conversely, the colonial empire gave birth to a new bureaucracy at the cost of savage exploitation of indigenous populations. Lastly, the social status of the groups which the law kept on leading-strings at the beginning of the nineteenth century (women and youth) showed barely any improvement; democracy and many bourgeois professions remained reserved to men, while age was still the main criterion for access to leading positions even more than in the past since selection procedures were being increasingly formalised.

B Mobility and Immobility

A sectoral or geographical presentation of the French population in terms of status or wealth tends to underline the relative immobility of structures, particularly in comparison with the more rapid evolutions in neighbouring countries. On the other hand, analyses in dynamic terms bring out social movements which go unnoticed on the usual macroscopic scale; unfortunately, such analyses can only be based on partial and limited samples, which do not cover the whole country. Moreover, these conflicting impressions of mobility and immobility explain the contradictions already mentioned in contemporary discourse. Nonetheless, the point here is not to exaggerate social mobility (which is not synonymous with social ascent) but to understand how it could go hand in hand with an overall stability of structures. Even though examples of mobility apply to a minority and were most frequently exceptional cases, their importance went beyond pure numbers because they implanted belief in the possibility of change. They were therefore an argument in favour of the established order or official ideology, unless they augmented the fears of those who denounced inter-class movements, or conversely, by their limitations, served as arguments for bolder reforms.

a Changes in Social Status

First, there were changes in the fate of the masses and particularly the working classes. Statistical data on the recruitment of the latter indicate a decline in professional continuity from father to son. Social endogamy remained predominant but diminished when compared with the mid-nineteenth century. In Lyons, for example, 78.5 per cent of male workers married women workers in 1911, against 95.3 per cent in 1850. In Orleans in the same year, matrimonial vows were exchanged between diverse groups of workers and employees, and even craftsmen and merchants. However, this mixing process remained very limited and linked to urban samples where the professional structure was more diversified.[4]

The real break is found in the upper reaches of the middle classes and above all, the bourgeois groups; in Orleans, 90 per cent of husbands practising a bourgeois profession had fathers-in-law in the same milieu and 88 per cent were born into that milieu. This margin of 10 per cent is found at every level of the middle and upper classes and even in the elites. The further one ascends the hierarchy of samples, the more changes in status were made to the advantage of new men, who were even more highly selected on one count or another. For example, sons of wage-earners, day labourers or workers were practically absent from the social recruitment of the classical section of the Rennes *lycée* in 1875–1890; on the other hand, the petty bourgeoisie and lower sections of the middle classes filled 13 per cent of places, alongside bourgeois groups proper. In other words, due allowance being made for their demographic weight, some three out of four were already eliminated from the only possibility of access by the front door to bourgeois status.

These intermediate groups, always threatened with a fall in status, preferred to entrust their children to the educational stream which was more open because it was free, in the intermediate schools (*écoles primaires supérieures*), which developed under the Third Republic. In the Rennes secondary modern school (*cours complémentaire*) in 1894–1898, sons of small tradesmen were four times more numerous than in

4. Y. Lequin (96), vol. 1, pp. 412 and 414; and A. Prost (479), pp. 679–80.

the classical section of the *lycée*, as were sons of artisans, while sons of wage-earners made a significant breakthrough with 30 per cent of the total (against 1.4 per cent at the *lycée*).[5] Social conservatives saw the threat of inter-class movements in this new stream, which offered an alternative possibility to simple reproduction of the paternal position. In reality, the republicans had specifically conceived it as a means of diverting away from college the aspirations to more advanced education being manifested within the middle classes and the petty bourgeoisie. In terms of a metaphor popular amongst contemporaries, it was a question of training the non-commissioned officers of industrial society and providing for the proliferating numbers of white collar jobs.

In reality, social and intellectual selection were such that only a minority went to the end and gained this type of job, and this group became even more conspicuous when the aspirants came from a working-class or peasant background. In the Nord, for example, 59.8 per cent of workers' sons from the secondary modern school went back into their father's profession or held a manual profession, while a third took up jobs in the tertiary sector or became primary school-teachers and 6.9 per cent moved into other schools. Only sons of employees or petty officials succeeded in maintaining or even improving their inherited social status thanks to this educational stream, but they were already the most privileged group.[6] Entry to the prestigious fee-paying stream was out of the question without a State grant, but the State gave priority to its servants; consequently, regardless of ability, the other offspring of the petty bourgeoisie and middle classes had to resort to the back door: either the dead-end paths which offered no social future (priests, monks or public office, with its concomitant pressures inducing a high celibacy rate), or the narrow road which was only a stopping-point and did not guarantee later progress or provide protection against re-descent in the next generation.

b The Narrow Door

The theoretical meritocracy to which the Republic laid claim was therefore very biased at its base. In vain did the myth of the scholarship boy take root at this period: recipients of scholarships, even without fortune, were not selected solely on scholastic criteria. In the Somme, for example, 63 per cent of scholarship boys at the *lycée* were sons of teachers or officials, against 29 per cent who were sons of workers, craftsmen, employees or farmers, that is to say, sons of the people in the

5. R. Gildea (34), table 10, p. 291.
6. Ibid., p. 298.

word's contemporary meaning. The proportions were reversed in the intermediate schools (19 per cent against 62 per cent). The State therefore deliberately promoted the mobility (or social reproduction) of its servants, only according financial grants to the elite of the people who at best would provide future primary school-teachers. By so doing, the Republic was merely resuming the methods of social promotion practised by the clergy or the army.[7]

The example of the *École normale de Saint-Cloud* shows this savage selectivity on the part of the socially most open educational streams. Out of 3,000 to 5,000 candidates, the colleges of education only admitted 1,200 to 1,600 a year between 1882 and 1913. Two hundred of them applied to Saint-Cloud and one in ten was accepted; 1.5 per cent to 2 per cent of the initial population thus reached the finishing post. Almost a quarter were farmers' sons and 35.2 per cent sons of craftsmen. But what weight did these 340 social miracles carry, compared with the millions of boys from the same background?[8] They became a 'super-elite' but which did not have access to the real elites because of educational barriers which prevented the 'primaries' from pursuing genuine higher studies in the years preceding the 1914 war.

There were other means of mobility concurrent with this educational and State route. Some of them have been mentioned in relation to the analysis of one or other social group: migration, setting up an independent business, or making money through a shop or workshop. But the financial balance sheet drawn up above, and the general facts of the situation, both show that these means were just as highly selective as the new educational channels, if not more so. The latent and growing discontent of the 'little men' in the society of the Belle Époque (minor officials, small-scale tradesmen, small-scale employers and minor employees) reflected the confused perception of a theoretically open society which was still made up of visible and invisible barriers. There was the barrier of Latin at the summit, defending the elite of power and knowledge; the barrier of the increasing amount of capital required to survive amongst entrepreneurs; the barrier of opportunities which divided the middle classes between dead-ends and promotion; the barrier of uncompleted or unsuitable education which excluded workers from the feast from the start; and the barrier of poverty and isolation of peasants integrated into the nation too recently.

Paradoxically, as a society claims to become more and more open, people are less and less prepared to tolerate surviving differentiating mechanisms. The more strictly partitioned society of the notables only

7. C. Lelièvre (255), p. 410.
8. J.-N. Luc, A. Barbé (334), p. 20 and table 6.

gave an opportunity to express frustrations to the most deprived victims of poverty during crises, and, in a more positive way, to an elite of the people, privileged in comparison with the mass of the working classes because it was skilled and urbanised. On the other hand, the democratic society demanded a balance sheet with respect to the illusions created by the semblance of equality. Those who tried to lift the barriers, the 'little men', were precisely those who had a relative chance of benefiting from the movement between classes. What remains to be explained therefore is not the contrast between the continuing immobility and the belief in mobility, but why this frustrating tension between the two terms functioned better than the old ideal of partitioned worlds.

General Conclusion

The Republican model of new strata and new elites succeeded at first by achieving a compromise which defused the pressure from the most turbulent urban and rural working classes by the invention of an enemy common to both the '*capacités*' and the people: the Church and the old notables, in decline in the new urban society. Similarly Bonapartism played on fear of the reds in order to win the support of notables and peasants. The new system of domination handled the conflicts gently through decentralisation and a preventative policy of defusing them, setting up intermediary institutions (pressure groups, group representation, locally elected members and a variety of client groups). In this way the infernal logic of the early nineteenth century of violent confrontations through general crises was gradually removed until 1930–1950.

This evolution was not solely the result of conscious social and political strategies on the part of the elites or leaders of the dominated classes. The general conditions of social life were also involved. Increasing geographical mobility and improvement in the standard of education destroyed the classical foundations of the earlier domination by the notables which was based on spatial distance (the notable as the intermediary between the centre and the periphery) and on the gulf between educational standards and citizenship (and thus on keeping the rural working classes outside of political life). Consequently the 1848 democratic ideal, appropriated by the *capacités*, could now be extended not only to the new sections of the bourgeoisie and middle classes but also to the elite elements of the working classes. Admission to public office, the boom in teaching posts, education beyond primary level, and access to the acquired skills for modern economic life were just as responsible as the official ideology for the spread of the belief in general social mobility, making confrontation harmful to these groups which had formerly been breeding-grounds for leaders of the people. The abolition of the political division between the electorate and the real country was assimilated into the ending of all privilege. This was the best screen for the preservation of sectorial privileges, more impalpable to expose and slower, harder and more protracted to challenge. The main ideological obstacle to effective social criticism was socialist theory itself, which projected a schema borrowed from the mid-nineteenth century social situation onto an increasingly complex society.

The other petty bourgeois model of social mobility, through personal accumulation of wealth and diffused private property, was only able to survive as a lasting social ideal because it was based on a cultural mutation specific to France in these early days; the Malthusianism of the rural and middle classes. The decline in the birth rate halted the enlargement of the self-reproducing and self-enlarging proletariat which the new industrialisation required. This indirectly strengthened the workers' ability to resist the employers and maintained the possibility of a channel of promotion capable of replacing both the educational model and proletarianisation through the continued existence of a category of 'little men'. These latter, in their turn, were the breeding-ground for new petty notables located in the centre of society and political life in several medium-sized regions. They provided ready-made support for reverence to the ideal of the French Revolution and therefore, for the entrenchment of the Republic.

The other side of this invisible cultural revolution was the closing of frontiers to commodities but their opening to men in order to balance the shortage of indigenous manpower. This introduced a new element of division and weakness into the worker movement, which was not able to take root within this potential clientele. In the longer term, therefore, this dual movement created renewed social fears and what can be summed up as a beleaguered fortress mentality. These fears crystallised at the end of the nineteenth century and came to a head in the confrontations of the mid-twentieth century. Conversely, impatience born of a voluntarily limited social mobility drove one faction of intellectuals to suggest a new social utopia in which the social hierarchy would be based purely on selection by a unified educational system, a programme which would be the rock of Sisyphus for the twentieth century school. In contrast, another group of intellectuals formulated strategies to defend the educational privileges thus threatened. To a large extent, therefore, the seeds of the conflicts which marked twentieth century social history were contained in these pre-First World War debates and anxieties.

Bibliography

Abbreviations
AESC: *Annales (Économies, Sociétés, Civilisations)*
ARSS: *Actes de la recherche en sciences sociales*
HES: *Histoire, Économie, Société*
MS: *Le Mouvement social*
RH: *Revue historique*
RHMC: *Revue d'histoire moderne et contemporaine*

General Works

The size of this book does not leave room for a complete list of the very large number of sources or surveys which are useful for social history. The reader is referred to the sources and bibliographies in the principal theses cited below as well as the *Bibliographie annuelle de l'histoire de France*, edited by Colette Albert-Samuel, Paris, Éditions du CNRS, since 1953, which contains several items relating to social history. Also useful as general guides to research or as thematic aids to beginning research:

Barbier, Frédéric, *Bibliographie de l'histoire de France*, Paris, Masson, 1987
Dreyfus, Michel, *Les Sources de l'histoire ouvrière, sociale et industrielle en France*, Paris, Éd. ouvrières, 1983
Charle, Christophe, Jean Nagle, Michel Richard, and Denis Woronoff, *Prosopographie des élites françaises (XVIe–XXe siècles), guide de recherche*, Paris, IHMC, 1980
Fourcaut, Annie (ed.), *Un siècle de banlieue parisienne (1859–1964), guide de recherche*, Paris, L'Harmattan, 1988

Numbers 22, 24, 30, 31, 32 and 37 of the present bibliography also contain valuable bibliographies and guides to research, although they are old. Any use of nineteenth century statistical documents must always employ the methods of the contributions to the colloquium *Pour une histoire de la statistique*, Paris, Economica-INSEE, new ed., 1984.

Documents and Evidence

We have deliberately limited ourselves to evidence on the popular or middle classes, the evidence on the ruling classes being superabundant and well known.

1. Bédé, Jacques-Étienne, *Un ouvrier en 1820*, unpublished mss., introduction and notes by R. Gossez, Paris, PUF, 1984
2. Bouvier, Jeanne, *Mes Mémoires ou 59 Années d'activité industrielle, sociale et intellectuelle d'une ouvrière (1876–1935)*, ed. D. Armogathe and M. Albistur, Paris, Maspero, 1983
3. Chabot, Michel, *L'Escarbille: histoire d'Eugène Saulnier, ouvrier verrier*, Paris, Presses de la Renaissance, 1978
4. Chabot, Paul, *Jean et Yvonne domestiques en 1900*, Paris, Tema, 1977
5. Dumay, Jean-Baptiste, *Mémoires d'un militant ouvrier du Creusot, 1841–1905*, introduction and notes by Pierre Ponsot, Grenoble, Presses universitaires de Grenoble, 1976
6. Grenadou, Éphraim and Alain Prévost, *Grenadou, paysan français*, Paris, Éditions du Seuil, 1966, new edn, coll. 'Points', 1978
7. Guillaumin, Émile, *La Vie d'un simple* (1904), new edn, Paris, Livre de poche, 1972
8. Halévy, Daniel, *Visites aux paysans du Centre* (1934), new edn, Paris, Livre de poche, 1978 (The countryside of the Bourbonnais at the beginning of the century seen by an intellectual and peasant elite.)
9. Hélias, Pierre Jakez, *Le Cheval d'orgueil, mémoires d'un Breton du pays Bigouden*, Paris, Plon, 1975
10. Lejeune, Philippe, 'Les instituteurs du XIXe siècle racontent leur vie', *Histoire de l'éducation*, 25, Jan. 1985, pp. 53–104, with an index and a summary of the main autobiographies.
11. Lejeune, Xavier-Édouard, *Calicot*, an inquiry by Michel and Philippe Lejeune, Paris, Montalba, 1984
12. Le Play, Frédéric, *Les Ouvriers européens*, Paris, Mame et fils, 1877–9, 6 vols
13. ——, *Les Ouvriers des deux mondes*, Paris, Mame et fils, 1856–1913; partial new edn with a postscript by B. Kalaora and A. Savoye, Paris, A l'Enseigne de l'arbre verdoyant, 1983
14. Nadaud, Martin, *Léonard maçon de la Creuse*, Paris, Hachette or Maspero, 1976
15. Perdiguier, Agricol, *Mémoires d'un compagnon*, new edn, Paris, Maspero, 1982
16. Poulot, Denis, *Le Sublime ou le Travailleur comme il est en 1870 et ce qu'il peut être* (1872), new edn with a preliminary study by Alain Cottereau, Paris, Maspero, 1980

17. Sandre, Bertrand, Baptiste, Joseph, Marie, *La classe ininterrompue, Cahiers de la famille Sandre enseignants, 1780–1960*, introduced by Mona Ozouf, Paris, Hachette, 1979
18. Silvère, Antoine, *Toinou, le cri d'un enfant auvergnat*, Paris, Plon, 1980
19. Truquin, Norbert, *Mémoires et Aventures d'un prolétaire à travers les révolutions*, Paris, Maspero, 1977
20. Villermé, Louis-René, *Tableau de l'état physique et moral des ouvriers employés dans les manufactures de coton, de laine et de soie*, Paris, 1840, new edn by J.-P. Chaline, and F. Demier, Paris, EDI, 1990

Society as a Whole

21. Ariès, Philippe, *Histoire des populations françaises et de leurs attitudes devant la vie*, Paris, Éditions du Seuil, 1971
22. Ariès, Philippe, and Georges Duby (eds), *Histoire de la vie privée*, vol. 4, ed. Perrot, Michelle, Paris, Éditions du Seuil, 1987
23. Armengaud, André, *La Population française au XIXe siècle*, Paris, PUF, 1976
24. Braudel, Fernand and Ernest Labrousse (eds), *Histoire économique et sociale de la France*, Paris, PUF, vol. 3/1–2, 1976, and vol. 4/1, 1979
25. Centre d'histoire contemporaine du Languedoc méditerranéen et du Roussillon, *Économie et Société en Languedoc-Roussillon de 1789 à nos jours*, Montpellier, 1978
26. Chevalier, Louis, *La Formation de la population parisienne au XIXe siècle*, Paris, PUF, 1950
27. *Conjoncture économique, Structures sociales, hommage à Ernest Labrousse*, Paris, Mouton, 1974
28. Crossick, Geoffrey, and Heinz-Gerhard Haupt (eds), *Shopkeepers and Master Artisans in Nineteenth Century Europe*, London, Methuen, 1984
29. Daumard, Adeline et al., *Les Fortunes françaises au XIXe siècle*, Paris, Mouton, 1973
30. Duby, Georges (ed.), *Histoire de la France urbaine*: vol. 4, *La Ville de l'âge industriel*, by M. Agulhon, F. Choay, M. Crubellier, Y. Lequin and M. Roncayolo, Paris, Éditions du Seuil, 1983
31. Duby, Georges and Armand Wallon (eds), *Histoire de la France rurale*: vol. 3, by M. Agulhon, G. Désert and R. Specklin, Paris, Éditions du Seuil, 1976
32. Dupâquier, Jacques (ed.), *Histoire de la population française*, vol. 3, 1789–1914, PUF, Paris, 1988 (An excellent synthesis which makes it unnecessary to read earlier works.)

33. Dupeux, Georges, *La Société française (1789–1960)*, Paris, Colin, 1972

34. Gildea, Robert, *Education in Provincial France, 1800–1914*, Oxford, Clarendon Press, 1983

35. Haupt, Heinz-Gerhard, *Sozialgeschichte Frankreichs seit 1789*, Frankfurt-a-Main, Suhrkampf, 1989

36. Howorth, Jolyon and Philip G. Cerny (eds), *Elites in France*, London, Frances Pinter, 1981

37. Lequin, Yves (ed.), *Histoire des Français (XIXe et XXe siècles)*, vol. 2, *La Société*, Paris, Colin, 1983

38. ——, *La mosaïque France*, Paris, Larousse, 1988

39. Lévy-Leboyer, Maurice and François Bourguignon, *L'Économie française au XIXe siècle, analyse macroéconomique*, Paris, Economica, 1985

40. Price, Roger, *A Social History of 19th Century France*, London, Hutchinson, 1987

41. Prost, Antoine, *L'Enseignement en France, 1800–1967*, Paris, Colin, 1968

42. Valette, Jacques and Alfred Wahl, *Les Français et la France (1859–1899)*, Paris, SEDES-CDU, 1986 (A textbook for the *agrégation*, educational but full of facts.)

43. Verley, Patrick, *Nouvelle Histoire économique de la France contemporaine, 2. L'industrialisation 1830–1914*, Paris, La Découverte, 1989 (A short but elegant synthesis.)

44. Zeldin, Theodore, *France 1848–1945*, Oxford, Clarendon Press, 1973–1977, 2 vols (A mine of scholarly information but its impressionism is sometimes misleading.)

Social Groups Studied over a Long Period

45. Anglade, Jean, *La Vie quotidienne dans le Massif central au XIXe siècle*, Paris, Hachette, 1971

46. Aron, Jean-Paul (ed.), *Misérable et glorieuse, la femme au XIXe siècle*, Paris, Fayard, 1980

47. Aubert, Jacques, et al., *Les Préfets en France (1800–1940)*, Geneva, Droz, 1978

48. de Baecque, Francis, et al., *Les Directeurs de ministère en France aux XIXe et XXe siècles*, Geneva, Droz, 1976. (Variable studies.)

49. Baillou, Jean, (ed.), *Les Affaires étrangères et le Corps diplomatique*, Paris, Éditions du CNRS, 1984, vol. 2

50. Bergeron, Louis, *Les Capitalistes en France (1780–1914)*, Paris, Gallimard-Julliard, coll. 'Archives', 1978 (A very good collection of portraits of the various employers.)

51. Bois, Paul, *Paysans de l'Ouest*, 1st. edn, 1960, new abridged edn, Paris, Flammarion, 1971 (A classic of the new rural history.)

52. Brekilien, Yann, *La Vie quotidienne des paysans en Bretagne au XIXe siècle*, Paris, Hachette, 1966

53. Brunot, André and René Coquand, *Le Corps des ponts et chaussées*, Paris, Éditions du CNRS, 1982 (A great corps as seen by one of its own, but useful nonetheless.)

54. Caron, François (ed.), *Entreprises et Entrepreneurs, XIXe–XXe siècles*, Paris, Presses de l'Université de Paris-Sorbonne, 1983

55. Carter, Edward C., Robert Forster and John N. Moody (eds), *Enterprises and Entrepreneurs in Nineteenth and Twentieth-Century France*, Baltimore, John Hopkins University Press, 1976

56. Chaline, Jean-Pierre, *Les Bourgeois de Rouen: une élite urbaine au XIXe siècle*, Paris, Presses de la FNSP, 1982 (The most substantial study of a provincial bourgeoisie.)

57. Charle, Christophe, *Les Hauts Fonctionnaires en France au XIXe siècle*, Paris, Gallimard-Julliard, coll. 'Archives', 1980

58. Châtelain, Abel, *Les Migrants temporaires en France (1800–1914)*, Lille-III, 1977, 2 vol (A reference book on a long-neglected section of social history.)

59. Codaccioni, Félix-Paul, *De l'inégalité sociale dans une grande ville industrielle. Le drame de Lille de 1850 à 1914*, Lille, Université de Lille-III - Éditions universitaires, 1976 (When the quantitative manages to recreate the depth of the social conflicts.)

60. Corbin, Alain, *Les Filles de noce, misère sexuelle et prostitution aux XIXe et XXe siècles*, Paris, Aubier, 1978, new edn, Flammarion, coll. 'Champs', 1982

61. Crebouw, Yvonne, *Salaires et Salariés agricoles en France des débuts de la Révolution aux approches du XXe siècle*, State thesis, Université de Paris-I, 1986

62. Day, Charles R., *Education for the Industrial World: the École d'Arts et Métiers and the Rise of French Industrial Engineering, (1800 to the Present)*, Cambridge (Mass.), MIT Press, 1987 (The limits of promotion through technical skill.)

63. Désert, Gabriel, *Une société rurale au XIXe siècle. Les paysans du Calvados (1815–1895)*, Lille, Atelier de reproduction des thèses de Lille-III, 1975, 3 vols

64. Dewerpe, Alain, *Le Monde du travail en France, 1800–1950*, Paris, Colin, coll. 'Cursus', 1989 (Very original on the technical aspect of work.)

65. Farcy, Jean-Claude, *Les Paysans beaucerons au XIXe siècle*, Chartres, Société archéologique d'Eure-et-Loir, 1990, 2 vols

66. ——, *Agriculture et Société rurale en Beauce pendant la première*

moitié du XIXe siècle, typed thesis, Université Paris-X-Nanterre, n.d.

67. Farge, Arlette and Christiane Klapisch-Zuber (eds), *Madame ou Mademoiselle? Itinéraires de la solitude féminine XVIIIe–XXe siècles*, Paris, Montalba, 1984 (Some chapters on women's history.)

68. Faÿ-Sallois, Fanny, *Les Nourrices à Paris au XIXe siècle*, Paris, Payot, 1980

69. Gaillard, Jeanne, 'La petite entreprise en France aux XIXe et XXe siècles', *Rapport français à la Commission internationale d'histoire des mouvements sociaux et des structures sociales, consacré à la petite entreprise et à la croissance industrielle dans le monde*, Paris, Éditions du CNRS, 1981

70. Garrier, Gilbert, *Paysans du Beaujolais et du Lyonnais (1800–1970)*, Grenoble, Presses universitaires de Grenoble, 1973, 2 vols

71. ——, *Vignerons du Beaujolais au siècle dernier*, Roanne, Horvath, 1984

72. ——, *Le Phylloxéra. Une guerre de trente ans (1870–1900)*, Paris, Albin Michel, 1989

73. Gavignaud, Geneviève, *Propriétaires-viticulteurs en Roussillon, Structures, Conjoncture, Société (XVIIIe–XXe siècles)*, Paris, Publications de la Sorbonne, 1983

74. Geison, Gerald L., *Professions and the French State, 1700–1900*, Philadelphia, University of Pennsylvania Press, 1984 (An Anglo-Saxon view of the liberal professions.)

75. Gerbod, Paul, *La Condition universitaire en France au XIXe siècle*, Paris, PUF, 1965 (The liberation of the teachers corps.)

76. Goldstein, Jan, *Console and Classify: the French Psychiatric Profession in the 19th Century*, Cambridge, Cambridge University Press, 1987

77. Guillaume, Pierre, *La Population de Bordeaux au XIXe siècle*, Paris, Colin, 1972

78. Guiral, Pierre and Guy Thuillier, *La Vie quotidienne des domestiques en France au XIXe siècle*, Paris, Hachette, 1978

79. Haupt, Heinz-Gerhard and Philippe Vigier (eds), 'L'atelier et la boutique', *MS*, no. 108, July–Sept. 1979

80. ——, 'Petite entreprise et politique', *MS*, no. 114, Jan.–Mar. 1981

81. Heywood, Colin, *Childhood in 19th Century France: Work, Health and Education among the 'classes populaires'*, Cambridge, Cambridge University Press, 1988

82. Higgs, David, *Nobles in 19th Century France: The Practice of Inegalitarianism*, Baltimore and London, John Hopkins University Press, 1987 (A slightly premature synthesis.)

83. Houssel Jean-Pierre (ed.), *Histoire des paysans français du XVIIIe siècle a nos jours*, Roanne, Horvath, 1976, re-pub., 1987

84. Hubscher, Ronald, *L'Agriculture et la Société rurale dans le Pas-de-Calais du milieu du XIXe siècle à 1914*, Arras, Mémoire de la commission départementale des monuments historiques du Pas-de-Calais, 1980, 2 vols (A classic but also innovative thesis.)

85. Katznelson, Ira and Aristide R. Zolberg, *Working-Class Formation: Nineteenth-Century Patterns in Western Europe and the United States*, Princeton, Princeton University Press, 1986

86. Köpeczi, Bela and Eva H. Balazs (eds), *Noblesse française, Noblesse hongroise*, Rennes colloquium (1975), Budapest, Akademiai Kiado, Paris, Éditions du CNRS, 1981

87. Lachiver, Marcel, *Vins, Vignes et Vignerons, histoire du vignoble français*, Paris, Fayard, 1988 (The most complete and up-to-date synthesis on a category of peasants typical of nineteenth-century France.)

88. Lambert-Dansette, Jean, *Quelques Familles du patronat textile de Lille-Armentières*, Lille, Imprimerie Raoust, 1954 (A milieu seen by one of its own.)

89. Lamy, Yvon, *Hommes de fer en Périgord au XIXe siècle*, Lyons, La Manufacture, 1987 (The decadence of a rural industry.)

90. Langlois, Claude, *Le Catholicisme au féminin. Les congrégations françaises à supérieure générale au XIXe siècle*, Paris, Éditions du Cerf, 1984 (Portrait of an unknown but enormous group of women.)

91. Launay, Marcel, *Le Bon Prêtre. Le clergé rural au XIXe siècle*, Paris, Aubier, 1986

92. Laurent, Robert, *Les Vignerons de la Côte d'Or au XIXe siècle*, Paris, Les Belles Lettres, 1958, 2 vols

93. Léon, Pierre, *Géographie de la fortune et Structure sociale à Lyon au XIXe siècle*, Lyons, Presses universitaires de Lyon, 1974

94. Léonard, Jacques, *Les Médecins de l'Ouest au XIXe siècle*, Atelier de reproduction des thèses de Lille-III, 1978, 3 vols (A thesis which revives a formerly neglected sector of society. More accessible to non-specialists are the three following works:)

95. ——, *La France médicale au XIXe siècle*, Paris, Gallimard-Julliard, coll. 'Archives', 1979

96. ——, *La Médecine entre les savoirs et les pouvoirs*, Paris, Aubier, 1981

97. ——, *La Vie quotidienne du médecin de province au XIXe siècle*, Paris, Hachette, 1977

98. Lequin, Yves, *Les Ouvriers de la région lyonnaise (1848–1914)*, Lyons, Presses universitaires de Lyon, 1977, 2 vols (A classic of the new working class history.)

99. Merriman, John M. (ed.), *French Cities in the 19th Century*, London, Hutchinson, 1982

100. ——, *The Red City. Limoges and the French Nineteenth Century*, London, 1985

101. Moulin, Annie, *Les Paysans dans la société française, de la Révolution à nos jours*, Paris, Éditions du Seuil, coll. 'Points', 1988 (A valuable summary of present research.)

102. *Les Noblesses européennes au XIXe siècle*, proceedings of the colloquium organised by the French School of Rome, Milan-Rome, Università di Milano-École française de Rome, 1988 (The most recent summary with an international perspective.)

103. Noiriel, Gérard, *Les Ouvriers dans la société française, XIXe–XXe siècles*, Paris, Éditions du Seuil, coll. 'Points', 1986 (An original synthesis.)

104. Pinaud, Pierre-François, *Les Receveurs généraux des finances, 1790–1865*, Geneva, Droz, 1990 (A historic study, with an index of names and places.)

105. Pierrard, Pierre, *La Vie quotidienne du prêtre français au XIXe siècle (1801–1905)*, Paris, Hachette, 1986

106. Pinchemel, Philippe, *Structures sociales et Dépopulation dans les campagnes picardes de 1836 à 1936*, Paris, Colin, 1957 (When geography becomes social history.)

107. Plessy, Bernard and Louis Challet, *La Vie quotidienne des canuts, passementières et moulinières au XIXe siècle*, Paris, Hachette, 1987

108. Pourcher, Yves, *Les Maîtres de granit. Les notables de Lozère du XVIIIe siècle à nos jours*, Paris, Orban, 1987 (Describes the persistence of an old system of domination.)

109. Raison-Jourde, Françoise, *La Colonie auvergnate de Paris au XIXe siècle*, 1976 (A fine analysis of a group typical of nineteenth-century France.)

110. Schnapper, Bernard, *Le Remplacement militaire en France. Quelques aspects politiques, économiques et sociaux du recrutement au XIXe siècle*, Paris, SEVPEN, 1968 (The army and social classes before conscription.)

111. Segalen, Martine, *Mari et Femme dans la société paysanne*, Paris, Flammarion, 1980 (Reacts against too patriarchal an image of the peasant family.)

112. Sellier, François, *Les Salariés en France depuis cent ans*, Paris, PUF, coll. 'Que sais-je', 1979

113. Shinn, Terry, *Savoir scientifique et pouvoir social, l'École polytechnique, 1794–1914*, Paris, Presses de la FNSP, 1980 (The transition over the century of an elite; at times over-simplified.)

114. Shorter, Edward and Charles Tilly, *Strikes in France, 1830–1968*, Cambridge, Cambridge University Press, 1974 (The power and the limitations of quantification in social history.)

115. Smith, Bonnie, *Ladies of the Leisure Class: Bourgeoises of Northern France in the 19th Century*, London, 1981 (An original psychological and ethnographic approach.)

116. Thuillier, Guy, *Bureaucratie et Bureaucrates en France au XIXe siècle*, Geneva, Droz, 1980 (A lot of small minor facts and a mine of erudition.)

117. ——, *La Vie quotidienne dans les ministères au XIXe siècle*, Paris, Hachette, 1976 (Surpasses Courteline on a world that we believed we knew.)

118. Tilly, Charles, Louise Tilly and Richard Tilly, *The Rebellious Century, 1830–1930*, Cambridge (Mass.), Harvard University Press, 1975 (A project analysing the rejection of authority in France, debatable but stimulating.)

119. Vigier, Philippe (ed.), *Maintien de l'ordre et Police au XIXe siècle*, Paris, Creaphis, 1987 (A new sector of social history in the process of emerging.)

120. Weiss, John H., *The Making of Technological Man: The Social Origins of French Engineering Education*, Cambridge (Mass.), MIT Press, 1982 (A history of the 'Centraliens' and civil engineers.)

1 French Society Circa 1815

121. Agulhon, Maurice, *La Vie rurale en Provence intérieure au lendemain de la Révolution*, Paris, Société d'études robespierristes, 1970 (A fine analysis of a still traditional society.)

122. ——, *Le Cercle dans la France bourgeoise, 1815–1848, étude d'une mutation de sociabilité*, Paris, Colin, 1977

123. d'Angeville, Comte Adolphe, *Essai sur la statistique de la population française considérée sous quelques-uns de ses rapports physiques et moraux*, Paris, Mouton, 1969, introduction by Emmanuel Le Roy Ladurie (The two Frances seen by a notable.)

124. Armengaud, André, *Les Populations de l'Est aquitain au début de l'époque contemporaine, 1845–1871*, Paris, Mouton, 1961 (The origins of the under-development of the Toulouse Midi.)

125. Aron, Jean-Paul, Paul Dumont and Emmanuel Le Roy Ladurie, *Anthropologie du conscrit français*, Paris, Mouton, 1972 (The two Frances seen through the military archives.)

126. Beck, Thomas D., *French Legislators, 1800–1834: A Study in quantitative history*, Berkeley, UCLA Press, 1974 (Corrects and discusses Pinkney (200).)

127. Bénichou, Paul, *Le Sacre de l'écrivain*, Paris, Corti, 1973

128. ——, *Les Mages romantiques*, Paris, Gallimard, 1988 (The premises of a new intellectual power.)

129. Bergeron, Louis, *Banquiers, Négociants et Manufacturiers parisiens du Directoire à l'Empire*, Paris, EHESS-Mouton, 1978 (Business circles during a troubled period.)

130. Bergeron, Louis and Guy Chaussinand-Nogaret, *Les Masses de granit, cent mille notables du Premier Empire*, Paris, EHESS-Jean Touzot, 1979 (Breaks and continuity after the Revolution at the summit of society.)

131. Bourdelais, Patrice and Jean-Yves Raulot, *Une peur bleue, histoire du choléra en France au XIXe siècle*, Paris, Payot, 1987 (The epidemic as a social revealer.)

132. Bourguet, Marie-Noëlle, *Déchiffrer la France. La statistique départementale à l'époque napoléonienne*, Paris, Éditions des Archives contemporaines, 1988 (Post-revolutionary France seen through the administrative elites.)

133. Caty, Roland and Eliane Richard, 'Contribution à l'étude du monde du négoce marseillais de 1815 à 1870', *RH*, Oct.–Dec. 1980, pp. 337–64

134. Chassagne, Serge, *Le coton et ses patrons: France 1760–1840*, Paris, Éditions de l'EHESS, 1991

135. Chaussinand-Nogaret, Guy, *Une histoire des élites (1700–1848)*, Paris, Mouton, 1975 (A very useful choice of texts from different periods and historians.)

136. Chevalier, Louis, *Laboring Classes and Dangerous Classes*, New York, Fertig, 1973 (An increasingly questioned classic.)

137. Church, Clive H., *Revolution and Red Tape, the French Ministerial Bureaucracy (1770–1850)*, Oxford, Clarendon Press, 1978 (The only comprehensive book on the administration in the first half of the nineteenth century.)

138. Compère, Marie-Madeleine, *Du collège au lycée (1500–1850)*, Paris, Gallimard-Julliard, coll. 'Archives', 1985 (The persistence of the classical educational mould despite the revolutions.)

139. Couailhac, Marie-José, *Les Magistrats dauphinois, 1815–1870*, Grenoble, Université des sciences sociales de Grenoble, 1987 (Primarily valuable for its analysis of the relationships between a rural population and the justice of the notables.)

140. Dhombres, Nicole and Jean Dhombres, *Naissance d'un nouveau pouvoir, sciences et savants en France, 1793–1824*, Paris, Payot, 1989 (The reconstruction of the scholarly society in the world of the notables.)

141. Figeac, Michel, 'La noblesse bordelaise sous la Restauration', *HES*, 5, 1986, pp.381–405 (A study of a social group affected by the Revolution.)

142. 'La France sous le Premier Empire', special issue of the *RHMC*,

July–Sept. 1970

143. Furet, François and Jacques Ozouf, *Lire et Écrire, l'alphabétisation des Français de Calvin à Jules Ferry*, Paris, Éditions de Minuit, 1977, 2 vols (An essential book for an understanding of the cultural dynamic of the nineteenth century.)

144. Gayot, Gérard and Jean-Pierre Hirsch (eds), *La Révolution française et le Développement du capitalisme*, special issue of the *Revue du Nord*, 5, 1989

145. Goubert, Jean-Pierre (ed.), *La Médicalisation de la société française (1770–1830)*, Waterloo (Ontario), Historical Reflections, 1982

146. Higgs, David, *Ultraroyalism in Toulouse*, Baltimore, John Hopkins University Press, 1973 (Describes the social foundations of Legitimism.)

147. Jessenne, Jean-Pierre, *Pouvoir au village et Révolution, Artois 1760–1848*, Lille, Presses universitaires de Lille, 1987 (The birth of the power of the cocks of the walk in the village.)

148. Knibielher, Yvonne, 'Les médecins et la "nature" féminine au temps du Code civil', *AESC*, no. 4, July–Aug. 1976, pp. 824–45 (On anti-feminism in the nineteenth century.)

149. Lebrun, François and Roger Dupuy (eds), *Les Résistances à la Révolution*, proceedings of the Rennes colloquium (1985), Paris, Imago, 1987

150. Lepetit, Bernard, *Les Villes dans la France moderne (1740–1840)*, Paris, Albin Michel, 1988

151. Mayaud, Jean-Luc, *Les Paysans du Doubs au temps de Courbet*, Paris, Les Belles Lettres, 1979

152. Mazoyer, Louis, 'Catégories d'âge et groupes sociaux, les jeunes générations françaises de 1830', *Annales d'histoire économique et sociale*, no.53, Sept.1938, pp.385–423 (An old article but with interesting information on an area of tension in the society of the notables.)

153. Merley, Jean, *La Haute-Loire de la fin de l'Ancien Régime aux débuts de la Troisième République (1776–1886)*, Le Puy, Cahiers de la Haute-Loire, 1974, 2 vols

154. Petitfrère, Claude, *L'Oeil du maître. Maîtres et serviteurs de l'époque classique au romantisme*, Brussels, Complexe, 1986 (The rise of the bourgeois spirit in relationships with domestic servants.)

155. *La Révolution française et le Monde rural*, proceedings of the Rennes colloquium, Paris, Comité des travaux historiques et scientifiques, 1989

156. Soulet, Jean-François, *Les Pyrénées au XIXe siècle*, Toulouse, Éché, 1987, 2 vols (The France of the notables seen from the dissident fringe.)

157. Vidalenc, Jean, *La Société française de 1815 à 1848*, vol. 1, *Le Peuple des campagnes*, Paris, Marcel Rivière, 1970; vol.2, *Le peuple des villes et des bourgs*, ibid., 1973 (Scholarly but often heavy.)

158. ——, *Les Demi-Soldes*, Paris, Marcel Rivière, 1955 (Against Balzac-type simplifications.)

2 Notables, Educated Classes, *Capacités*, Peasants and Proletarians

159. Aguet, Jean-Pierre, *Les Grèves sous la monarchie de Juillet*, Geneva, Droz, 1954 (A mine of information.)

160. Agulhon, Maurice, *The Republic in the Village: The People of the Var from the French Revolution to the Second Republic*, Cambridge University Press, New York, 1982 (A classic.)

161. ——, *Une ville ouvrière au temps du socialisme utopique: Toulon de 1800 à 1852*, Paris, Mouton, 1970 (Complements (160).)

162. ——, *1848 ou l'Apprentissage de la République*, Paris, Éditions du Seuil, 1973; new edn, 1987

163. ——, *Les Quarante-huitards*, Paris, Gallimard-Julliard, coll. 'Archives', 1975 (Aims to rehabilitate the unloved republicans.)

164. Amann, Peter, *Revolution and Mass Democracy: The Paris Club Movement in 1848*, Princeton, Princeton University Press, 1975

165. Barral, Pierre, *Les Périer dans l'Isère au XIXe siècle*, Paris, PUF, 1964 (The permanence of a family of great notables.)

166. Best, Heinrich, *Die Männer von Bildung und Besitz, Struktur und Handeln parlamentarischer Führungsgruppen in Deutschland und Frankreich 1848–1849*, Düsseldorf, Droste Verlag, 1989 (A comparative sociological study of the political elites in France and Germany in the revolutionary period.)

167. Bouillon, Jacques, 'Les démocrates-socialistes aux élections de 1849', *Revue française de science politique*, VI, no. 1, 1956, pp.70–95 (A classic article.)

168. Caron, Jean-Claude, *La Jeunesse des écoles à Paris, 1815–1848, étude statistique, sociale et politique*, new system thesis, University of Paris-I, 4 vols, 1989; abridged edn, *Générations romantiques 1814–1851, les étudiants de Paris et le Quartier latin*, Paris, Colin, 1991 (On the students as a social and political force.)

169. Caspard, Pierre, 'Aspects de la lutte des classes en 1848: le recrutement de la garde nationale mobile', *RH*, no. 511, 1974, pp.81–106 (A fine sociological analysis of the two contending proletariats.)

170. Corbin, Alain, *Archaïsme et Modernité en Limousin au XIXe siècle*,

1845–1880, Paris, Marcel Rivière, 1975, 2 vols (Economic tardiness and political advance.)

171. Daumard, Adeline, *La Bourgeoisie parisienne de 1815 à 1848*, Paris, SEVPEN, 1963; abridged edn, Paris, Flammarion, 1970

172. Delsalle, Paul, *La Brouette et la Navette. Tisserands, paysans et fabricants dans la région de Roubaix-Tourcoing, 1800–1848*, Dunkirk, Éditions des Beffrois, 1985 (The predominance of peasant individualism within a proletariat in process of formation.)

173. Denis, Michel, *Les Royalistes de la Mayenne et le Monde moderne, XIXe–XXe siècles*, Paris, Klincksieck, 1977 (The slow decadence of a type of domination in the 'white' West.)

174. Faure, Alain, 'Mouvements populaires et mouvement ouvrier à Paris (1830–1834)', *MS*, no. 88, 1974, pp. 51–92.

175. ———, 'Petit atelier et modernisme économique: la production en miettes au XIXe siècle', *HES*, 5, 1986, pp. 531–57

176. Frey, Michel, 'Du mariage et du concubinage dans les classes populaires à Paris (1845–1847)', *AESC*, no. 4, 1978, pp.803–29 (The complexity of matrimonial behaviour in the working-class milieu.)

177. Girard, Louis, William Serman, Rémi Gossez and Émile Cadet, *La Chambre des députés en 1837–1839*, Paris, Publications de la Sorbonne, 1976

178. Gossez, Rémi, *Les Ouvriers de Paris*, book I, *L'Organisation*, La Roche-sur-Yon, Bibliothèque de la révolution de 1848, Imprimerie centrale de l'Ouest, 1967 (The corporative eruption of the Parisian workers between February and June 1848.)

179. Guillemin, Alain, *Le Pouvoir de l'innovation. Les notables de la Manche et le développement de l'agriculture (1830–1875)*, Paris, typed thesis, EHESS, 1980 (The rivalry between old and new notables in the West.)

180. ———, 'Patrimoine foncier et pouvoir nobiliaire: la noblesse de la Manche sous la monarchie de Juillet', *Études rurales*, 1976, pp. 117–40

181. ———, 'Aristocrates, propriétaires et diplômés, la lutte pour le pouvoir local dans le département de la Manche, 1830–1875', *ARSS*, 42, 1982, pp. 33–60

182. ———, 'Rente, famille, innovation. Contribution à la sociologie du grand domaine noble', *AESC*, no. 1, 1985, pp. 54–70

183. Hilaire, Yves-Marie, *Une chrétienté au XIXe siècle? La vie religieuse des populations du diocèse d'Arras (1840–1914)*, Lille, Presses universitaires de Lille, 1977, 2 vols

184. Huard, Raymond, *La Préhistoire des partis, le mouvement républicain en Bas-Languedoc (1848–1881)*, Paris, Presses de la

FNSP, 1982 (The slow entrenchment of the Republic in the France of the 'little man'.)

185. Ibarrola, Jésus, *Structure sociale et Fortune mobilière et immobilière à Grenoble en 1847*, Paris, Mouton, 1965

186. Jardin, André and André-Jean Tudesq, *La France des notables (1815–1848)*, Paris, Éditions du Seuil, 1973, 2 vols

187. Labrousse, Ernest (ed.), *Aspects de la crise et de la dépression de l'économie française au milieu du XIXe siècle, 1846–1851*, La Roche-sur-Yon, Imprimerie centrale de l'Ouest, 1956 (Contributions which continue to be indispensable to throw light on the social climate of the Second Republic.)

188. Lévêque, Pierre, *Une société provinciale, la Bourgogne sous la Monarchie de Juillet*, Paris, Éditions de l'EHESS, Jean Touzot, 1983

189. ——, *Une société en crise: la Bourgogne au milieu du XIXe siècle (1846–1852)*, Paris, Éditions de l'EHESS, Jean Touzot, 1983 (With (188) two works giving an exhaustive view of provincial society between 1830 and 1851.)

190. Le Yaouanq, Jean, 'La mobilité sociale dans le milieu boutiquier parisien au XIXe siècle', *MS*, no. 108, 1979, pp. 89–112

191. Marcilhacy, Christiane, *Le Diocèse d'Orléans au milieu du XIXe siècle: les hommes et leurs mentalités*, Paris, Plon, 1962

192. Margadant, Ted W., *French Peasants in Revolt: the Insurrection of 1851*, Princeton, Princeton University Press, 1979 (A remarkable analysis of the process of mobilisation against the coup d'État.)

193. Martin-Fugier, Anne, *La Vie élégante ou la Formation du Tout-Paris, 1815–1848*, Paris, Fayard, 1990 (High society through its own eyes.)

194. Mayaud, Jean-Luc, *Les Secondes Républiques du Doubs*, Paris, Les Belles Lettres, 1986 (On the birth of a conservative peasantry.)

195. Ménager, Bernard, *Les Napoléon du peuple*, Paris, Aubier, 1988 (The social foundations of popular Bonapartism.)

196. Moss, Bernard H., *The Origins of the French Labor Movement. The Socialism of Skilled Workers*, London, 1976

197. Perrot, Michelle (ed.), *L'Impossible Prison, recherches sur le système pénitentiaire au XIXe siècle* (debate with Michel Foucault), Paris, Éditions du Seuil, 1980

198. Petit, Jacques-Guy, *Des peines obscures, histoire de la prison au XIXe siècle*, Paris, Fayard, 1989 (An outline of the prison system from the Ancien Regime to the beginnings of the Third Republic.)

199. Pinkney, David H., *Decisive Years in France, 1840–1847*, Princeton, Princeton University Press, 1986 (Describes far-reaching innovations under Guizot's 'reign'.)

200. ——, *The French Revolution of 1830*, Princeton, Princeton

University Press, 1972 (An alternative and disputed view of the 'bourgeois' revolution.)

201. Price, Roger, *The French Second Republic: A Social History*, London, Batsford, 1972

202. Rancière, Jacques, *La Nuit des prolétaires, archives du rêve ouvrier*, Paris, Fayard, 1981 (The voice of the elite workers.)

203. Richardson, Nicholas, *The French Prefectoral Corps (1814–1830)*, Cambridge, Cambridge University Press, 1966

204. Rousselet, Marcel, *La Magistrature sous la monarchie de Juillet*, Paris, Sirey, 1937

205. Rude, Fernand, *Le Mouvement ouvrier à Lyon de 1827 à 1832*, new edn, Paris, Anthropos, 1969

206. ——, *Les Révoltes des canuts 1831–1834*, Paris, Maspero, 1982

207. Scott, Joan W., '"L'ouvrière, mot impie, sordide", le discours de l'économie politique française sur les ouvrières (1840–1860)', *ARSS*, 83, June 1990, pp. 2–15

208. Sewell, William H., *Structure and Mobility. The Men and Women of Marseille, 1820–1870*, Cambridge, Cambridge University Press, 1985 (The social mixture and its limitations in a large provincial town.)

209. ——, *Work and Revolution in France: The Language of Labour from the Old Regime to 1848*, Cambridge, Cambridge University Press, 1981 (Corporatist spirit and class consciousness.)

210. ——, 'La classe ouvrière de Marseille sous la Seconde République: structure sociale et comportement politique', *MS*, no. 76, 1971, pp. 27–65

211. ——, 'La confraternité des prolétaires: conscience de classe sous la monarchie de Juillet', *AESC*, no. 4, 1981, pp. 650–71

212. Singer-Kerel, Jeanne, *Le Coût de la vie à Paris de 1840 à 1954*, Paris, Colin, 1961

213. Stearns, Peter N., *Paths to Authority, The Middle Class and the Industrial Labor Force in France, 1820–1848*, Chicago, University of Illinois Press, 1978

214. Spitzer, Alan B., *The French Generation of 1820*, Princeton, Princeton University Press, 1987 (The misunderstanding between intellectual youth and the gerontocracy of the Restoration.)

215. Tilly, Charles and Lynn Lees, 'Le peuple de juin 1848', *AESC*, no. 5, 1974, pp. 1061–91

216. Traugott, Mark, *Armies of the Poor*, Princeton, Princeton University Press, 1985 (A new attempt at a synthesis of social analysis of June 1848.)

217. Tudesq, André-Jean, *Les Grands Notables en France (1840–1849), étude historique d'une psychologie sociale*, Paris, PUF, 1964, 2 vols

(A fundamental thesis.)

218. ——, *Les Conseillers généraux au temps de Guizot*, Paris, Colin, 1967

219. Vigier, Philippe, *La Seconde République dans la région alpine*, Paris, PUF, 1963, 2 vols. (Another classic thesis.)

220. ——, *Essai sur la répartition de la propriété foncière dans la région alpine*, Paris, SEVPEN, 1963

221. Vigreux, Marcel, *Paysans et Notables du Morvan au XIXe siècle jusqu'en 1914*, Château-Chinon, Académie du Morvan, 1987

3 Imperial Stabilisation and Society in Motion

222. Anderson, Robert, 'Secondary Education in Mid-Nineteenth-Century France: Some Social Aspects', *Past and Present*, 50–53, 1971, pp. 121–46

223. Auzias, Claire and Annick Houël, *La Grève des ovalistes, Lyon, juin-juillet 1869*, Paris, Payot, 1982

224. Barbier, Frédéric, *Le Patronat du Nord sous le Second Empire: une approche prosopographique*, Geneva, Droz, 1989

225. ——, *La Maison Fould: finances et politique en France à l'époque contemporaine*, Paris, Colin, 1991

226. Barjot, Dominique (ed.), 'Les entrepreneurs de Normandie, du Maine et de l'Anjou à l'époque du Second Empire', *Annales de Normandie*, 2/3, May–July 1988

227. Bertho, Catherine, *Télégraphes et Téléphones, de Valmy au microprocesseur*, Paris, Livre de poche, 1981 (How to reconcile Bonapartism and modernity in a technical administration.)

228. Bourienne, Véronique, 'Boucicaut, Chauchard et les autres, fondateurs et fondation des premiers grands magasins parisiens', *Paris et Ile-de-France, mémoires publiés par la Fédération des sociétés historiques et archéologiques de Paris et de l'Ile-de France*, 1989, vol.40, pp. 257–335

229. Boutry, Philippe, *Prêtres et Paroisses au pays du curé d'Ars*, Paris, Éditions du Cerf, 1986

230. Bouvier, Jean, *Les Rothschild*, Paris, Fayard, 1967

231. ——, *Histoire économique et Histoire sociale*, Geneva, Droz, 1971 (Essential monographs on the business milieus.)

232. Cayez, Pierre, *Crises et Croissance de l'industrie lyonnaise, 1850–1900*, Paris, Éditions du CNRS, 1980

233. Chaline, Nadine-Josette, 'Le recrutement du clergé du diocèse de Rouen au XIXe siècle', *RHES*, 1971, pp. 385–405

234. Chamboredon, Jean-Claude, 'Peinture des rapports sociaux et invention de l'éternel paysan: les deux manières de Jean-François

Millet', *ARSS*, 17–18, Nov. 1977, pp. 6–28 (Painting as a means of constructing an idyllic image of the peasantry.)

235. Cholvy, Gérard, *Géographie religieuse de l'Hérault contemporain*, Paris, PUF, 1968

236. Corbin, Alain, *Le village des cannibales*, Paris, Aubier, 1990 (A dive into the depths of the peasant's soul at the end of the Second Empire in the lands of Jacquou le Croquant.)

237. Dalotel, Alain, Alain Faure and Jean-Claude Freiermuth, *Aux origines de la Commune. Le mouvement des réunions publiques à Paris, 1868–1870*, Paris, Maspero, 1980 (On how the masses found their voice again.)

238. Darmon, Jean-Jacques, *Le Colportage de librairie en France sous le Second Empire*, Paris, Plon, 1972 (Describes a fundamental change in popular culture.)

239. Delefortrie, Nicole and Jane Morice, *Les Revenus départementaux en 1864 et en 1954*, Paris, A. Colin, 1959 (A mine of figures.)

240. Dubois, Jacques, *Le Vocabulaire politique et social en France de 1869 à 1872*, Paris, Larousse, 1962 (On language as a clue to the confrontation between social views.)

241. Dupeux, Georges, *Aspects de l'histoire sociale et politique du Loir-et-Cher (1848–1914)*, Paris, Colin, 1962 (A classical 'Labroussian' thesis.)

242. Duveau, Georges, *La Vie ouvrière sous le Second Empire*, Paris, Gallimard, 1946 (A heavily researched picture.)

243. Fohlen, Claude, *L'Industrie textile sous le Second Empire*, Paris, Plon, 1956

244. Foucault, Pierre, 'L'origine socio-professionnelle du clergé sarthois durant la période concordataire (1801–1905)', *Cahiers des Annales de Normandie*, No. 8, Caen, 1976, pp. 149–70

245. Gaillard, Jeanne, *Paris, la ville (1852–1870)*, Lille, Atelier des thèses de Lille-III, Paris, Champion, 1976 (A thesis central to the study of the Second Empire.

246. ——, 'Les usines Cail et les ouvriers métallurgistes de Grenelle', *MS*, nos. 33–4, 1960, pp.35–53

247. Gerbod, Paul et al., *Les Épurations administratives (XIXe et XXe siècles)*, Geneva, Droz, 1977

248. Girard, Louis, Antoine Prost and Rémi Gossez, *Les Conseillers généraux en 1870*, Paris, PUF, 1967 (Study of the notables before their decline.)

249. Harrigan, Patrick and Victor Neglia, *Lycéens et Collégiens sous le Second Empire, étude statistique des fonctions sociales de l'enseignement secondaire public d'après l'enquête de Victor Duruy (1864–1865)*, Paris-Lille, Université de Lille-III, Éditions de la

MSH, 1979 (Austere but useful.)

250. ——, *Mobility, Elites and Education in French Society of the Second Empire*, Waterloo (Ontario), Wilfred Laurier University Press, 1980 (Commentary on the previous book but less original.)

251. Jacquemet, Gérard, *Belleville au XIXe siècle*, Paris, Éditions de l'EHESS, 1984 (A look into working-class Paris.)

252. Jobert, Philippe (ed.), *Les Patrons de la Bourgogne sous le Second Empire*, Paris-Le Mans, Éditions Cenomane, Picard, 1991 (On the co-existence of two employer societes at a turning-point in time.)

253. Launay, Marcel, *Le Diocèse de Nantes sous le Second Empire*, Nantes, CID, 1982, 2 vols (Religion and society in the West at the apogee of clericalism.)

254. Le Clère, Bernard and Vincent Wright, *Les Préfets du Second Empire*, Paris, Colin, 1973 (Qualifies an over-authoritarian image of prefectoral power under the Empire.)

255. Lelièvre, Claude, 'Bourses, méritocratie et politique(s) scolaire(s) dans la Somme', *RFS*, XXVI, 3, 1985, pp. 409–29 (Aims to destroy the myth of the scholarship boy.)

256. Léonard, Jacques, 'Femmes, religion et médecine. Les religieuses qui soignent en France au XIXe siècle', *AESC*, no.5, 1977, pp. 887–907

257. ——, 'Les guérisseurs en France au XIXe siècle', *RHMC*, July–Sept. 1980, pp. 501–16

258. Le Roy Ladurie, Emmanuel and Nicole Bernageau, 'Étude sur un contingent militaire (1868): mobilité géographique, délinquance et stature mises en rapport avec d'autres aspects de la situation des conscrits', *Annales de démographie historique*, 1971, pp. 311–37

259. Locke, Robert R., 'A Method for Identifying French Corporate Businessmen (The Second Empire)', *French Historical Studies*, X, no. 1, 1977, pp. 261–92 (The birth of financial groups.)

260. L'Huillier, Fernand, *La Lutte ouvrière à la fin du Second Empire*, Paris, Colin, 1957

261. Marnata, Françoise, *Les Loyers des bourgeois de Paris, 1860–1958*, Paris, Colin, 1961

262. Miller, Michael B., *The Bon Marché: Bourgeois Culture and the Department Store, 1869–1920*, Princeton, Princeton University Press, 1982 (Essential for an understanding of the bourgeois and urban civilisation of the end of the century.)

263. Murard, Lion, and Patrick Zylberman (eds), *L'Haleine des faubourgs. Ville, habitat et santé au 19e siècle*, Fontenay-sous-Bois, Éditions Recherches, 1978 (Articles which are still useful despite a dated Leftist bias.)

264. Pierrard, Pierre, *La Vie ouvrière à Lille sous le Second Empire*, Paris,

Bloud et Gay, 1965

265. Plessis, Alain, *De la fête impériale au mur des fédérés (1852–1871)*, Paris, Éditions du Seuil, 1973

266. ——, *Régents et Gouverneurs de la Banque de France (1852–1870)*, Geneva, Droz, 1985 (On the elite of wealth.)

267. ——, *La Banque de France et ses deux cents actionnaires (1852–70)*, Geneva, Droz, 1982 (Capitalism and traditional elites.)

268. Richter, Noë, *Les Bibliothèques populaires*, Paris, Cercle de la librairie, 1978 (On the appetite for culture in the mid-nineteenth century.)

269. Roudié, Philippe, *Vignobles et Vignerons du Bordelais, 1850–1980*, Paris, Éditions du CNRS, 1988 (A fine monograph on an famous rural region.)

270. Rougerie, Jacques, *Procès des communards*, Paris, Julliard, coll. 'Archives', 1964

271. ——, *Paris libre 1871*, Paris, Éditions du Seuil, 1971 (Two reference books.)

272. ——, 'Remarques sur l'histoire des salaires à Paris au XIXe siècle', *MS*, no.63, 1968, pp. 71–108 (A classic article.)

273. Roy, Joseph-Antoine, *Histoire de la famille Schneider et du Creusot*, Paris, Marcel Rivière, 1962

274. Royer, Jean-Pierre, Renée Martinage and Pierre Lecocq, *Juges et Notables au XIXe siècle*, Paris, PUF, 1982 (Sociology of a system of class justice.)

275. Scott, Joan Wallach, *The Glassworkers of Carmaux*, London, 1974 (On the resistance of a worker elite to loss of status.)

276. Serman, Serge William, *Le Corps des officiers sous la Deuxième République et le Second Empire*, Lille-III, Atelier de reproduction des thèses, 1979, 3 vols (A thesis which has overturned many accepted ideas.)

277. Thabault, Roger, *1848–1914. L'ascension d'un peuple. Mon village, ses hommes, ses routes, son école*, Paris, Delagrave, 1944; new edn, Presses de la FNSP, 1982 (A classic on emancipation through education.)

278. Toutain, Jean-Claude, 'La consommation alimentaire en France de 1789 à 1964', *Économies et Sociétés*, V, no. 11, 1971, pp. 1909–2049

279. Trempé, Rolande, *Les Mineurs de Carmaux (1848–1914)*, Paris, Éditions ouvrières, 1971, 2 vols (A classic thesis.)

280. Verley, Patrick, 'Exportations et croissance économique dans la France des années 1860', *AESC*, no. 1, Jan.–Feb. 1988, pp. 73–110

281. Voilliard, Odette, *Nancy au XIXe siècle (1815–1871), une bourgeoisie urbaine*, Nancy, 1968 (An interesting monograph

despite its conceptual limitations.)
282. Wright, Vincent, *Le Conseil d'État sous le Second Empire*, Paris, Colin, 1962 (A remarkable sociology of one of the centres of imperial power.)
283. ——, 'Les préfets du gouvernement de Défense nationale', *Bulletin de la Société d'histoire moderne*, 1965, nos. 11–2, pp. 11–24
284. Zeldin, Théodore, *The Political System of Napoleon III*, London, Macmillan, 1958

4 A New Class: The Peasants

285. Augustins, Georges. 'Mobilité résidentielle et alliance matrimoniale dans une commune du Morbihan au XIXe siècle', *Éthnologie française*, 1981, no. 4, pp. 319–28
286. Barral, Pierre, *Les Agrariens français de Méline à Pisani*, Paris, Colin, 1968 (An innovative and essential book.)
287. ——, (ed.), 'Aspects régionaux de l'agrarisme français avant 1930', *MS*, no. 67, 1969. (Complements the preceding book.)
288. Bernard, Philippe, *Économie et Sociologie de la Seine-et-Marne, 1850–1950*, Paris, Colin, 1953
289. Bourdieu, Pierre, 'Une classe objet', *ARSS*, 17–8, 1977, pp. 2–5
290. Brunet, Pierre, *Structure agraire et Économie rurale des plateaux tertiaires entre la Seine et l'Oise*, Caen, Caron et Cie, 1960
291. Brunet, Roger, *Les Campagnes toulousaines, étude géographique*, Toulouse, Imprimerie Boisseau, 1965
292. Cholvy, Gérard, 'Sur l'histoire occitane', *AESC*, no. 4, 1978, pp. 863–79
293. Claverie, Élisabeth and Pierre Lamaison, *L'Impossible Mariage. Violence et parenté en Gévaudan (XVIIe–XVIIIe–XIXe siècles)*, Paris, Hachette, 1982 (Family dramas in a traditional society.)
294. Farcy, Jean-Claude, 'L'artisanat rural dans la Beauce au XIXe siècle', *HES*, 5, 1986, pp. 573–90
295. Fillaut, Thierry, *L'Alcoolisme dans l'Ouest de la France pendant la seconde moitié du XIXe siècle*, Paris, La Documentation française, 1983
296. ——, 'Manières de boire et alcoolisme dans l'Ouest de la France au XIXe siècle', *Ethnologie française*, no. 4, 1984, pp. 377–86
297. Garrier, Gilbert, 'L'Union du Sud-Est des syndicats agricoles avant 1914', *MS*, no. 67, 1969, pp. 17–38
298. Goujon, Pierre, 'Les débuts du syndicalisme agricole en Saône-et-Loire', *Bulletin du Centre d'histoire économique et sociale de la région lyonnaise*, nos. 1–2, 1981, pp. 15–25
299. Gratton, Philippe, *Les Luttes de classes dans les campagnes*, Paris,

Anthropos, 1971

300. ——, *Les Paysans français contre l'agrarisme*, Paris, Maspero, 1972

301. Hubscher, Ronald, 'La petite exploitation en France: reproduction et compétitivité (fin XIXe–début XXe siècles)', *AESC*, no. 1, 1985, pp. 3–34

302. Jones, Peter M., *Politics and Rural Society, the Southern Massif Central, c. 1750–1880*, Cambridge, Cambridge University Press, 1985

303. Le Roy-Ladurie, Emmanuel and André Zysberg, 'Anthropologie des conscrits français (1868–1887)', *Ethnologie française*, no. 1, 1979, pp. 47–68

304. Leveau, Rémy, 'Le syndicat de Chartres', *MS*, no. 67, 1969, pp. 61–78

305. Luc, Jean-Noël 'La scolarisation en France au XIXe siècle: l'illusion statistique', *AESC*, no. 4, 1986, pp. 887–911 (Makes particularly good use of educational statistics.)

306. Maurin, Jean, *Armée-guerre-société, soldats languedociens (1889–1919)*, Paris, Publications de la Sorbonne, 1982

307. Mesliand, Claude, 'La fortune paysanne dans le Vaucluse (1900–1938)', *AESC*, no. 1, 1967, pp. 88–137

308. ——, *Paysans du Vaucluse (1860–1939)*, Aix, Publications de l'Université de Provence, Aix-Marseille-I, 1989, 2 vols

309. Pech, Rémi, *Entreprise viticole et Capitalisme en Languedoc-Roussillon. Du phylloxéra aux crises de mévente*, Toulouse, Presses universitaires du Mirail, 1975

310. Pennetier, Claude, *Le Socialisme dans le Cher, 1851–1921*, La Charité-Paris, Éditions Delayance-Éditions de la MSH, 1982

311. Pingaud, Marie-Claude, 'Chronologie et formes du pouvoir à Minot (Côte-d'Or)', *Études rurales*, 63–4, 1976, pp. 191–206

312. Ponton, Rémy, 'Les images de la paysannerie dans le roman rural à la fin du dix-neuvième siècle', *ARSS*, 17–18, 1977, pp. 62–72

313. Postel-Vinay, Gilles, 'Pour une apologie du rentier: ou que font les propriétaires fonciers?', *MS*, no. 115, 1981, pp. 27–50

314. Price, Roger, *The Modernization of Rural France: Communication Networks and the Agricultural Market Structures in 19th Century France*, London, Hutchinson, 1983

315. Raymond, Justinien, *La Haute-Savoie sous la Troisième République, histoire économique, sociale et politique, 1875–1940*, Seyssel, Éditions du Champ Vallon, 1983, 2 vols

316. Rinaudo, Yves, *Les Paysans du Var (fin du XIXe–début du XXe siècle)*, Lyons, Presses universitaires de Lyon, 1982

317. ——, 'Le syndicalisme agricole varois au début du XXe siècle',

Bulletin du Centre d'histoire économique et sociale de la région lyonnaise, nos. 1–2, 1981, pp. 9–13

318. ——, 'Un travail en plus: les paysans d'un métier à l'autre (vers 1830–vers 1950)', *AESC*, no. 2, 1987, pp. 283–302

319. Segalen, Martine, *Quinze Générations de Bas-Bretons*, Paris, PUF, 1985 (Using ethnography as social history.)

320. Weber, Eugen, *Peasants into Frenchmen, the Modernization of Rural France, 1870–1914*, London, Chatto and Windus, 1977 (Impressive scholarship but with the limitation of impressionism.)

5 The Rise of the Middle Classes

321. Bachrach, Susan, *Dames employées, The Feminization of Postal Work in Nineteenth-Century France*, New York, Haworth Press, 1984

322. Beaud, Olivier, *Aux origines du syndicalisme des 'cadres' de la fonction publique, le cas des fonctionnaires des ministères (1870–1914)*, thesis of the third cycle, typescript, University of Caen, 1984

323. Bertinotti, Dominique, 'Carrières féminines et carrières masculines dans l'administration des postes et télégraphes à la fin du XIXe siècle', *AESC*, no. 3, 1985, pp. 625–40

324. Bourdelais, Patrice, 'Employés de la grande industrie: les dessinateurs du Creusot. Formations et carrières (1850–1914)', *HES*, 3, 1989, pp. 437–46

325. Charle, Christophe, 'Pour une histoire sociale des professions juridiques. Note pour une recherche', *ARSS*, 76–77, 1989, pp. 117–9

326. Faure, Alain. 'L'épicerie parisienne au XIXe siècle ou la corporation éclatée', in H.-G. Haupt, and P. Vigier, (eds), 'L'atelier et la boutique', *MS*, no. 108, July–Sept. 1979, pp. 113–30

327. Fontvielle, Louis, 'Évolution et croissance de l'État français', *Cahiers de l'ISMEA*, serie AF no. 13, 1976, pp. 1657–2149

328. Frischmann, Georges, *Histoire de la fédération CGT des PTT*, Paris, Éditions sociales, 1967

329. Haupt, Heinz-Gerhard, 'Kleine und grosse Bürger in Deutschland und Frankreich am Ende des 19. Jahrhunderts', in J.Kocka (ed.), *Bürgertum im 19. Jahrhundert*, Munich, DTV, 1988

330. Karady, Victor, 'Les professeurs de la République. Le marché scolaire, les réformes universitaires et les transformations de la fonction professorale à la fin du XIXe siècle', *ARSS*, 47–8, 1983, pp. 90–112

331. ——, 'Normaliens et autres enseignants à la Belle Époque. Note sur l'origine sociale et la réussite dans une profession intellectuelle',

RFS, XIII, 1, 1972, pp. 35–58

332. ——, 'Recherches sur la morphologie du corps universitaire littéraire sous la Troisième République', *MS*, no. 96, 1976, pp. 47–79

333. Launay, Michel, *La CFTC*, Paris, Publications de la Sorbonne, 1986

334. Luc, Jean-Noël and Alain Barbé, *Des normaliens, histoire de l'École normale supérieure de Saint-Cloud*, Paris, Presses de la FNSP, 1981 (A remarkable combination of the history and sociology of education on a group embodying republican meritocracy.)

335. Martin, Jean-Clément, 'Hiérarchie et structure de la société commerçante: les listes d'électeurs du tribunal de commerce de Niort', *MS*, no. 112, 1980, pp. 57–77

336. Mayeur, Françoise, *L'Enseignement secondaire de jeunes filles sous la Troisième République*, Paris, Presses de la FNSP, 1977

337. Muel-Dreyfus, Francine, *Le Métier d'éducateur*, Paris, Éditions de Minuit, 1983 (A subtle analysis of the investigation by J. Ozouf based on the evidence of teachers in the Belle Époque.)

338. Nord, Philip, *Paris Shopkeepers and the Politics of Resentment*, Princeton, Princeton University Press, 1985. (A remarkable monograph on a little-known milieu.)

339. Ozouf, Jacques, *Nous les maîtres d'école: autobiographies d'instituteurs de la Belle Époque*, Paris, Gallimard-Julliard, coll. 'Archives', 1967

340. Pezerat, Pierrette and Poublan, Danielle, 'Femmes sans maris, les employées des postes', in Arlette Farge and Christiane Klapisch-Zuber (eds), *Madame ou Mademoiselle? Itinéraires de la solitude féminine XVIIIe–XXe siècles*, Paris, Montalba, 1984, pp. 117–62

341. Serman, Serge William, *Les Officiers français dans la nation (1848–1914)*, Paris, Aubier, 1980 (On the adaptation of the officers to the Republic.)

342. Siwek-Pouydesseau, Jeanne, *Le Syndicalisme des fonctionnaires*, Lille, Presses universitaires de Lille, 1990

343. Sorlin, Pierre, *Waldeck-Rousseau*, Paris, Colin, 1967 (The example of a social success through the bar.)

344. Suleiman, Ezra N., *Centralization and Democracy in France: the 'Notaires' and the State*, Princeton, Princeton University Press, 1987 (The persistence of a corporation.)

345. Thuillier, Guy, *Les Femmes dans l'administration depuis 1900*, Paris, PUF, 1988. (A possibly premature synthesis.)

346. Turquan, Victor, *Essai de recensement des employés et fonctionnaires de l'État*, Paris, the secretariat of the Société d'économie sociale, 1899 (A mine of statistics on public office.)

347. Verger, Jacques (ed.), *Histoire des universités en France*, Paris,

Payot, 1986, especially the contribution by Victor Karady, pp. 261–366

348. Vincenot, Henri, *La Vie quotidienne dans les chemins de fer au XIXe siècle*, Paris, Hachette, 1975

349. Vincent, Gérard, 'Les professeurs du second degré au début du XXe siècle: essai sur la mobilité sociale et la mobilité géographique', *MS*, no. 55, 1966, pp. 47–73

350. ——, 'Les professeurs de l'enseignement secondaire dans la société de la Belle Époque', *RHMC*, Jan. 1966, pp. 49–86

351. Weisz, George, *The Emergence of Modern Universities in France, 1863–1914*, Princeton, Princeton University Press, 1983

6 Old and New Elites

352. Agulhon, Maurice, Jean-Louis Robert et al., *Les Maires en France de 1800 à nos jours*, Paris, Presses de la Sorbonne, 1986

353. Barjot, Dominique, *La Grande Entreprise française de travaux publics (1883–1974), contraintes et stratégies*, State thesis, University of Paris-IV, 1989, 7 vols, typescript

354. Bécarud, Jean, 'Noblesse et représentation parlementaire, les députés nobles de 1871 à 1958', *Revue française de science politique*, 23, 5, Oct. 1973, pp. 972–93

355. Boime, Albert, 'Les hommes d'affaires et les arts en France au XIXe siècle', *ARSS*, 28, Jun. 1979. pp. 57–76 (An English version can be found in (55).)

356. Buttoud, Georges, *Les Conservateurs des eaux et forêts sous la Troisième République, 1870–1940*, Nancy, Laboratoire d'économie forestière de l'ENGREF, 1981

357. Carré de Malberg, Nathalie, 'Le recrutement des inspecteurs des finances de 1892 à 1946', *Vingtième Siècle revue d'histoire*, Oct.–Dec. 1985, pp. 67–91

358. Chadeau, Emmanuel, *Les Inspecteurs des finances au XIXe siècle (1850–1914)*, Paris, Economica, 1987

359. Charle, Christophe, *Les Élites de la République (1880–1900)*, Paris, Fayard, 1987

360. ——, *Naissance des 'intellectuels' (1880–1900)*, Paris, Éditions de Minuit, 1990

361. ——, (ed.), with R. Ferré, *Le Personnel de l'enseignement supérieur en France aux XIXe et XXe siècles*, Paris, Éditions du CNRS, 1985

362. ——, 'Le recrutement des hauts fonctionnaires en 1901', *AESC*, 2, 1980, pp. 380–409

363. ——, 'Naissance d'un grand corps, l'inspection des finances à la fin du XIX siècle', *ARSS*, 43, 1982, pp. 3–26

364. ——, 'Le pantouflage en France (vers 1880–vers 1980)', *AESC*, no. 5, 1987, pp. 1115–37

365. ——, 'Noblesse et élites en France au début du XXe siècle', in *Les Noblesses européennes au XIXe siècle*, Milan-Rome, Università di Milano-École Française de Rome, 1988, pp. 407–33

366. Cohen, William B., *Rulers of Empire: The French Colonial Service in Africa*, Hoover Institution Press, Stanford University, 1971.

367. Conze, Werner and Jürgen Kocka (eds), *Bildungsbürgertum im 19. Jahrhundert*, pt. I, Stuttgart, Klett-Cotta, 1985

368. Daviet, Jean-Pierre, *Un destin international. La Compagnie de Saint-Gobain de 1830 à 1939*, Paris, Éditions des archives contemporaines, 1988

369. Dogan, Mattei, 'La stabilité du personnel politique sous la Troisième République', *Revue française de science politique*, Apr.– June 1953, pp. 319–48

370. ——, 'Les filières de la carrière politique', *RFS*, VIII, 4, 1967, pp. 441–67

371. Elwitt, Sanford, *The Making of the Third Republic: Class and Politics in France, 1868–1884*, Baton Rouge, Louisiana State University Press, 1975 (A stimulating Marxist approach.)

372. ——, *The Third Republic defended: Bourgeois Reform in France, 1880–1914*, Baton Rouge, Louisiana State University Press, 1986 (The continuation of the previous volume, but less original.)

373. Estèbe, Jean, *Les Ministres de la République (1871–1914)*, Paris, Presses de la FNSP, 1982 (Revives the political world view.) To be complemented by the more complete type-written version, Université de Toulouse-Le Mirail, 1978, 3 vols

374. Fox, Robert, and George Weisz, *The Organization of Science and Technology in France (1808–1914)*, Paris, Éditions de la MSH, Cambridge, Cambridge University Press, 1980

375. Gadille, Jacques, *La Pensée et l'Action politique des évêques français au début de la Troisième République, 1870–1883*, Paris, Hachette, 1967, 2 vols

376. Gaudemet, Yves-Henri, *Les Juristes et la Vie politique de la Troisième République*, Paris, PUF, 1970 (The Republic of lawyers.)

377. Genet-Delacroix, Marie-Claude, 'Le statut social de l'artiste professionnel aux XIXe et XXe siècles', in *La Condition sociale de l'artiste*, Saint-Étienne, Presses universitaires-CIEREC, 1987, pp. 87–104 (The measure of a financial success through art.)

378. ——, *Art et État sous la Troisième République*, typewritten State thesis, University of Paris-I, 1989 (The artist between the State and the market.) First part published by 'Publications de la Sorbonne', 1992.

379. Gillet, Marcel, *Les Charbonnages du Nord au XIXe siècle*, Paris, Mouton, 1973

380. Girault, René, 'Pour un portrait nouveau de l'homme d'affaires à la Belle Époque', *RHMC*, July–Sept. 1969, pp. 329–49

381. Guiral, Pierre and Guy Thuillier, *La Vie quotidienne des députés en France de 1871 à 1914*, Paris, Hachette, 1980

382. Halévy, Daniel, *La Fin des notables*, Paris, Grasset, 1930, a new edn, Livre de poche, 1972

383. ——, *La République des ducs*, Paris, Grasset, 1937, new edn, Livre de poche, 1972 (Two works which remain classics.)

384. Hau, Michel, 'La longévité des dynasties industrielles alsaciennes', *MS*, no. 132, 1985, pp. 9–26

385. ——, *L'Industrialisation de l'Alsace (1803–1939)*, Strasbourg, Association des publications près les universités de Strasbourg, 1987

386. Kessler, Marie-Christine, *Les Grands Corps de l'État*, Paris, Presses de la FNSP, 1987

387. Lalumière, Pierre, *L'Inspection des finances*, Paris, PUF, 1959

388. Levillain, Philippe, *Albert de Mun, catholicisme français et catholicisme romain du Syllabus au Ralliement*, Rome, École française de Rome, 1983

389. Lévy-Leboyer, Maurice (ed.), *Le Patronat de la seconde industrialisation*, Paris, Éditions ouvrières, 1979 (Very new, with a comparative dimension.)

390. ——, 'Le patronat français a-t-il été malthusien?', *MS*, no. 88, 1974, pp. 3–49

391. ——, 'Le patronat français a-t-il échappé à la loi des trois générations?', *MS*, no. 132, 1985, pp. 3–8

392. Locke, Robert R., *French Legitimists and the Politics of Moral Order in the Early Third Republic*, Princeton, Princeton University Press, 1974 (A successful marriage of social and political history.)

393. Mercier, Lucien, *Les Universités populaires: 1899–1914, Éducation populaire et mouvement ouvrier au début du siècle*, Paris, Éditions ouvrières, 1986 (The difficult encounter between the intellectuals and the people.)

394. Martin, Marc, 'Journalistes parisiens et notoriété (vers 1830–1870)', *RH*, July–Sept. 1981, pp. 31–74 (On the confirmation of a new bourgeois profession.)

395. Mayer, Arno J., *The Persistence of the Old Regime*, London, Croom Helm, 1981 (Debatable but interesting from a comparative point of view.)

396. Moine, Jean-Marie, *Les Barons du fer, les maîtres de forge en Lorraine du milieu du XIXe siècle aux années 30, histoire sociale d'un patronat sidérurgique*, Nancy, Éditions Serpenoise-Presses

universitaires de Nancy, 1989 (On the emergence of new bourgeois dynasties under the Republic.)

397. Nye, Mary-Jo, *Science in the Provinces: scientific communities and provincial leadership in France, 1860–1930*, Berkeley, University of California Press, 1986 (On scientific elites and industrial applications.)

398. Ory, Pascal and Jean-François Sirinelli, *Les Intellectuels en France de l'affaire Dreyfus à nos jours*, Paris, Colin, 1986

399. Palmer, Michael B., *Des petits journaux aux grandes agences, naissance du journalisme moderne*, Paris, Aubier, 1983 (On the emergence of a new profession.)

400. Paul, Harry W., *From Knowledge to Power, the Rise of the Science Empire in France (1860–1939)*, Cambridge, Cambridge University Press, 1987 (On the process of legitimisation of a new social figure, the scientist.)

401. Peiter, Henry D., 'The Consolidation of the Business Community in Bourgeois France (1880–1914)', *Journal of Social History*, vol. 9, no. 4, summer 1976, pp. 510–25

402. Perrot, Marguerite, *Le Mode de vie des familles bourgeoises (1873–1953)*, Paris, Colin, 1961. (A study of the bourgeoisie through its accounts.)

403. Pinaud, Pierre-François, *Les Trésoriers-payeurs généraux au XIXe siècle, 1865–1914*, Paris, Éditions de l'Erudit, 1983 (A prosopographic catalogue of a disputed but coveted profession.)

404. Ponton, Rémy, *Le Champ littéraire de 1865 à 1905*, typewritten thesis, EHESS, 1977 (On the birth of the profession of author and the tensions of an intellectual milieu.)

405. Rust, Michael Jared, *Business and Politics in the Third Republic: the Comité des forges and the French Steel Industry*, Ph.D. thesis, Princeton, 1973, typescript (Describes the political strategy of a pressure group.)

406. Saint-Martin, Monique de, 'Une grande famille', *ARSS*, 31, 1980, pp. 4–22 (The adaptation of a great noble family, the Cossé-Brissacs.)

407. Siegfried, André, *Tableau politique de la France de l'Ouest sous la Troisième République*, Paris, Colin, 1913 (The persistence of the France of the notables; debatable but always stimulating theses.)

408. Siwek-Pouydesseau, Jeanne, *Le Corps préfectoral sous la Troisième et la Quatrième République*, Paris, Colin, 1969 (This book is still useful although it is based on superceded sources.)

409. Smith, Robert J., *The École normale supérieure in the Third Republic*, Albany, SUNY Press, 1982 (On the cradle of the teachers' Republic.)

410. Thépot, André (ed.), *L'Ingénieur dans la société française, Cahier du mouvement social*, Paris, Éditions ouvrières, 1985 (A colloquium with some very interesting discussions.)

411. Wright, Vincent, 'L'épuration du Conseil d'État en juillet 1879', *RHMC*, Oct.–Dec. 1972, pp. 619–53 (On the social limitations of a political revolution.)

7 The Working Classes: Dissent or Integration?

412. Bastié, Jean, *La Croissance de la banlieue parisienne*, Paris, PUF, 1964

413. Berlanstein, Lenard R., *The Working People of Paris, 1871–1914*, Baltimore, John Hopkins University Press, 1984 (An excellent general view of Paris after the Commune.)

414. Brunet, Jean-Paul, *Saint-Denis la ville rouge?*, Paris, Hachette, 1980 (Describes the birth of a workers' suburb.)

415. Caron, François, 'La grève des cheminots de 1910, une tentative d'approche', in *Conjoncture économique, Structures sociales, hommage à Ernest Labrousse*, Paris, Mouton, 1974, pp. 201–19

416. Cazals, Rémy, *Avec les ouvriers de Mazamet*, Paris, Maspero, 1978

417. ——, *Les Révolutions industrielles à Mazamet, 1750–1900*, Paris-Toulouse, La Découverte Maspero-Privat, 1983

418. Cottereau, Alain, 'Usure au travail, destins masculins et destins féminins dans les cultures ouvrières en France au XIXe siècle', *MS*, no. 124, 1983, pp. 71–112

419. ——, 'The Distinctiveness of Working Class Cultures in France 1848–1900', in I. Katznelson and A.R. Zolberg, *Working-Class Formation: Nineteenth-Century Patterns in Western Europe and the United States*, Princeton, Princeton University Press, 1986, pp. 111–54

420. Dauphin, Cécile and Pierrette Pézerat, 'Les consommations populaires dans la deuxième moitié de XIXe siècle à travers les monographies de l'école de Le Play', *AESC*, nos. 2–3, 1975, pp. 537–72

421. Debouzy, Marianne (ed.), 'Paternalisme d'hier et d'aujourd'hui', special number of *MS*, no. 144, 1988

422. Devèze, Michel, *Cayenne, déportés et bagnards*, Paris, Julliard, coll. 'Archives', 1965 (On the hell-hole of the Third Republic.)

423. Dubief, Henri, *Le Syndicalisme révolutionnaire*, Paris, Colin, 1969

424. Ewald, François, *L'État providence*, Paris, Grasset, 1986 (The issues at stake at the beginning of social legislation under the Republic.)

425. Fridenson, Patrick, *Histoire des usines Renault*, vol. 1, *Naissance de la grande entreprise*, Paris, Éditions du Seuil, 1972 (A model

monograph.)

426. ——, 'Die Arbeiterpolitik grosser Unternehmer in Frankreich und ihre Auswirkungen auf die Arbeitschaft', in J. Kocka (ed.), *Arbeiter und Bürger im 19. Jahrhundert*, Munich, Oldenbourg, 1986

427. ——, 'Un tournant taylorien de la société française (1904–1918)', *AESC*, no. 5, 1987, pp. 1031–60

428. Geslin, Claude, *Le syndicalisme ouvrier en Bretagne avant 1914*, Nîmes, Sedilan, 1984

429. Green, Nancy, *Les Travailleurs immigrés juifs à la Belle Époque, le 'Pletz' de Paris*, Paris, Fayard, 1984 (A look at an unknown working class.)

430. Guerrand, Roger-Henri, *Les Origines du logement social en France*, Paris, Éditions ouvrières, 1967

431. Guilbert, Madeleine, *Les Femmes et l'Organisation syndicale avant 1914*, Paris, Mouton, 1966 (A book in the avant-guard of its day.)

432. Guin, Yannick, *Le Mouvement ouvrier nantais, essai sur le syndicalisme d'action directe à Nantes et à Saint-Nazaire*, Paris, Maspero, 1976 (Militant but informed.)

433. Hardy-Hémery, Odette, *De la croissance à la désindustrialisation: un siècle dans le Valenciennois*, Paris, Presses de la FNSP, 1984

434. Hanagan, Michael P., *The Logic of Solidarity. Artisans and Industrial Workers in three French Towns, 1871–1914*, Chicago, Urbana University Press, 1980

435. Julliard, Jacques, *Autonomie ouvrière*, Paris, Éditions du Seuil-Gallimard, 1988 (A collection of articles on direct action trade-unionism by one of the best experts in the subjet.)

436. ——, *Fernand Pelloutier et les Origines du syndicalisme d'action directe*, Paris, Éditions du Seuil, 1971

437. Knibiehler, Yvonne, *Cornettes et Blouses blanches. Les infirmières dans la société française, 1880–1980*, Paris, Hachette, 1984

438. Legendre, Bernard, *Les Chaussonniers de Fougères, essai sur le développement d'un syndicalisme*, third cycle thesis, typescript, University of Paris-VIII, 1974, 2 vols

439. ——, 'La vie d'un prolétariat: les ouvriers de Fougères au début du XXe siècle', *MS*, no. 98, 1977, pp. 3–41 (Summary of the preceding thesis.)

440. Maîtron, Jean, 'La personnalité du militant ouvrier français dans la seconde moitié du XIXe siècle', *MS*, nos. 33–4, 1960–1961, pp. 66–86

441. Magri, Susanna and Christian Topalov (eds), *Villes ouvrières, 1890–1950*, Paris, L'Harmattan, 1990 (The latest trends in worker history.)

442. Marec, Yannick, *Le 'Clou' rouennais, des origines à nos jours, du Mont de Piété au Crédit municipal*, Rouen, Éditions du Petit

Normand, 1983 (A social history of poverty.)

443. Martin-Fugier, Anne, *La Place des bonnes: la domesticité féminine à Paris en 1900*, Paris, Grasset, 1979 (Below stairs with the bourgeoisie.)

444. Melucci, Alberto 'Action patronale, pouvoir, organisation. Règlement d'usine et contrôle de la main-d'oeuvre au XIXe siècle', *MS*, no. 97, 1976, pp. 139–59

445. Néré, Jacques, *La Crise industrielle de 1882 et le Mouvement boulangiste*, State thesis, typescript, Paris, Paris faculty of letters, 1959, 2 vols (Economic situation and political crisis under the Republic.)

446. Noiriel, Gérard, *Longwy, immigrés et prolétaires 1880–1980*, Paris, PUF, 1984 (The formation of a new proletariat.)

447. ——, *Le Creuset français, histoire de l'immigration en France XIXe–XXe siècles*, Paris, Éditions du Seuil, 1988 (A new field of research.)

448. Offerlé, Michel, 'Illégitimité et légitimation du personnel politique ouvrier en France avant 1914', *AESC*, no. 4, 1984, pp. 681–716 (The obstacles to the democratisation of the political personnel.)

449. Papayanis, Nicholas, 'La prolétarisation des cochers de fiacre à Paris (1878–1889)', *MS*, no. 132, 1985, p. 59–82 (The ambiguities of the social situation of the workers in the service sector.)

450. Perrot, Michelle, *Workers on Strike, France, 1871–1890*, Berg, Leamington Spa-Hamburg-New York, 1984, French edn, 1971 (Fundamental.)

451. ——, 'Comment les ouvriers parisiens voyaient la crise d'après l'enquête de 1884', in *Conjoncture économique, Structures sociales, hommage à Ernest Labrousse*, Paris, Mouton, 1974, pp. 187–200

452. ——, 'Délinquance et système pénitentiaire en France au XIXe siècle', *AESC*, no. 1, 1975, pp. 67–91

453. ——, 'La fin des vagabonds', *L'Histoire*, no. 3, July–Aug. 1978, pp. 23–33

454. ——, (texts collected and introduced by), 'Travaux de femmes au XIXe siècle', special number of *MS*, no. 105, 1978

455. ——, 'Le regard de l'autre: les patrons français vus par les ouvriers (1880–1914)', in M. Lévy-Leboyer (ed.), *Le Patronat de la seconde industrialisation*, Paris, Éditions ouvrières, 1979, pp. 293–306

456. Pigenet, Michel, 'L'usine et le village: Rosières (1869–1914)', *MS*, no. 119, 1982, pp. 33–61. See also his thesis *Les Ouvriers du Cher (fin XVIIIe–1914)*, Montreuil, Institut CGT d'histoire sociale, 1990

457. Rebérioux, Madeleine (ed.), *Jaurès et la Classe ouvrière*, Paris, Éditions ouvrières, 1981

458. Regourd, Florence, *La Vendée ouvrière*, Les Sables d'Olonne, Le

Cercle d'or, 1981

459. Ribeill, Georges, *Les Cheminots*, Paris, La Découverte, 1984

460. Rondeau, Daniel and François Boudin, *Chagrin lorrain, la vie ouvrière en Lorraine, 1870–1914*, Paris, Éditions du Seuil, 1979

461. Sagnes, Jean, *Le Mouvement ouvrier en Languedoc, syndicalistes socialistes dans l'Hérault de la fondation des bourses du travail à la naissance du Parti communiste*, Toulouse, Privat, 1980

462. Salais, Robert, Nicolas Baverez et Bénédicte Raynaud, *L'Invention du chômage*, Paris, PUF, 1986

463. Scott, Joan W. and Louise Tilly, *Women, Work and Family*, New York/London, Routledge, 1978

464. Shapiro, Anne-Louise, *Housing the Poor of Paris, 1850–1902*, Madison, University of Wisconsin Press, 1985

465. Stearns, Peter N., *Revolutionary Syndicalism and French Labor: A Cause without Rebels*, New Brunswick (NJ), Rutgers University Press, 1971

466. Sternhell, Zeev, *La Droite révolutionnaire (1885–1914)*, Paris, Éditions du Seuil, 1978

467. Thiesse, Anne-Marie, *Le Roman du quotidien, lecteurs et lectures populaires à la Belle Époque*, Paris, Le Chemin vert, 1984 (The ethnology and sociology of popular literature.)

468. Trempé, Rolande, 'Le réformisme des mineurs français à la fin du XIXe siècle', *MS*, no. 65, 1968, pp. 93–107

469. ——, 'Pour une meilleure connaissance de la classe ouvrière. L'utilisation des archives d'entreprise: le fichier du personnel', *Mélanges offerts à Jean Maîtron*, Paris, Éditions ouvrières, 1976, pp. 249–63

470. ——, 'Travail à la mine et vieillissement des mineurs', *MS*, no. 124, 1983, pp. 131–52

471. Willard, Claude, *Le Mouvement ouvrier en France, les guesdistes (1893–1905)*, Paris, Éditions sociales, 1965

472. Wilson, Stephen, *Ideology and Experience: Antisemitism in France at the time of the Dreyfus Affair*, Rutherford, Fairleigh Dickinson University Press, 1982

8 The Ideal of a Democratic Society?

473. Daumard, Adeline, *Les Bourgeois et la Bourgeoisie en France*, Paris, Aubier, 1987

474. 'L'enseignement technique et professionnel. Repères dans l'histoire (1830–1960)', special number of *Formation emploi*, nos. 27–28, July–Dec. 1989

475. Levasseur, Émile, *Questions ouvrières et industrielles en France*

sous la Troisième République, Paris, A. Rousseau, 1907 (A mine of statistics and commentaries typical of the mentality of a republican liberal.)

476. Martin, Benjamin F., *Crime and Criminal Justice under the Third Republic*, Baton Rouge, Louisiana State University Press, 1989

477. Mayeur, Jean-Marie, *Les Débuts de la Troisième République, 1871–1898*, Paris, Éditions du Seuil, 1973

478. Pigenet, Michel, 'L'École nationale professionnelle de Vierzon et le problème de la formation professionnelle dans une ville ouvrière (années 1880–1914)', *RH*, no. 572, 1989, pp. 367–90 (The limitations of technical training for worker promotion.)

479. Prost, Antoine, 'Mariage, jeunesse et société à Orléans en 1911', *AESC*, no. 4, 1981, pp. 672–701 (A provincial society seen across the civil State.)

480. ——, 'La population d'Orléans en 1911: une enquête d'histoire sociale informatisée', *Histoire et Mesure*, II, 1/2, pp. 121–46 (Complements the preceding article.)

481. Rebérioux, Madeleine, *La République radicale? 1898–1914*, Paris, Éditions du Seuil, 1975 (The best general synthesis on the period.)

482. Sohn, Anne-Marie, 'Les rôles féminins dans la vie privée, approche méthodologique et bilan de recherche', *RHMC*, Oct.–Dec.1981, pp. 567–623 (The slow evolution of customs under the Republic.)

483. Dupâquier et al., *La société française au XIXème siècle*, Paris, Fayard, 1992

484. Duby, Georges and Michelle Perrot (eds), *Histoire des femmes en Occident*, Paris, Plon, 1991, vol. 4

485. Magraw, Robert, *A History of the French Working Class*, Oxford, Blackwell, 1992, 2 vols

486. Moriceau, Jean-Marc and Gilles Postel-Vinay, *Ferme, entreprise, famille. Grande entreprise et changements agricoles, XVIIe–XIXe siècles*, Paris, Éditions de l'EHESS, 1992

Index

academics 213, 214
Académie des Sciences Morales et
    Politiques 31
Académie française 187
agrarianism 125–7, 184
agriculture *see also* peasantry; rural
    society:
    Belle Époque prosperity 132–3;
    capitalist landowners 19–22; class
    struggle 128–30; creation of
    government Minister 109; cycle of
    unrest 20; day labourers 21; farm sizes
    112; golden age for peasants 64–8;
    great depression at end of 19th century
    122–5; ground rents 120; mid-century
    crisis 43–6; Ministry 153, 204; mixed
    farming adopted 124; mortgage debt
    123; new feudalism 29; new rural
    communication 117–18; notables 181–
    2, 184; proletarianisation 138–9;
    protectionism 120; return to hierarchy
    20–2; revolution in technology 67;
    sharecroppers 21, 124; small land
    owners 65–6, 67, 111; tenant farmers
    19–21, 65–6, 113; unanimism 130–1;
    unionism and agrarianism 125–8;
    vicious circle of underdevelopment 12–
    13
Albert, Marcellin 131
Ancien Regime: decline in urbanisation
    12;
    education 15; effect of old economy 7;
    food riots 20; long-lasting 216; women,
    young and prisoners 24–6
Andler, Charles 214
anti-semitism 222–3, 246
d'Arenberg, Prince Auguste 186
Arlès-Dufour, François Barthélemy
    (businessman) 78
army *see* military
L'Artisan (newspaper) 38
arts: liberal professions 170
Arts et Métiers 192, 197, 199
Association générale des agents des PTT
    162
L'Atelier (newspaper) 38
Aubin 101
Aynard family 78, 192

de Balzac, Honoré: *Les Employés* 146, 152
Bank of France 79, 191–2

banks 191; employees 147; increase in
    savings accounts 87
Barbier, Frédéric 77
Barrès, Maurice 212
Baudelaire, Charles: *Les Fleurs du Mal* 64
Bazar de l'Hôtel de Ville 150
Beauce 111, 113
Beaujolais 123, 124
Béhic, Armand 54–5
Bel Ami (de Maupassant) 171
Belgium: immigrant workers 111–12, 222,
    223
Benoist d'Azy (banker) 79
Bergasse, Henry 194
Bergeron, Louis 193
Berliet, Marius 197
Bernard, Claude 212
Berthelot, Marcellin 212
Bertillon, Alphonse 259
Bigo, Louis 194
Bigo-Daniel, Émile 194
Blanc, Louis 42; *L'Organisation du travail*
    31
Bois, Paul 183
Bon Marché 150, 189; employees 147,
    148–9
Bonaparte, Louis Napoleon *see* Napoleon
    III
Bonaparte, Napoleon *see* Napoleon
    Bonaparte
Bonnardel family 192
bookshops 98
boot and shoe industry 225, 232, 250
Bordeaux 23; health of working class 233;
    wealth of liberal professions 171
Bordelais 123
Boucicaut family 148–9, 189
Boulanger, General Georges 145, 155, 180
'Boule de Suif' (de Maupassant) 259
Bourdieu, Pierre 139
bourgeoisie 188–90, 216–17 *see also*
    petty bourgeoisie; acquires property 16;
    administrative elite 57; businessmen
    and Louis Napoleon 54–6; *capacités*
    32–5; categories of status 178; defined
    188; domestic servants 253; dynamic of
    careers 207–9; establishing dynasties
    189, 190–5; financial aristocracy 191–
    3; higher administration of government
    206; illusion of egalitarianism 266;
    intellectuals 211–16; June revolt of

Index

1848 47; lifestyles 80–1, 195–7; lobbies 199–201; marriage and social mobility 164, 187, 208, 267; Members of Parliament 202–3; ministers 204–5; Napoleon suppresses 31; new industrialists 76–8; new strata 99–100, 217; nostalgia for revolution 26; Paris restructuring 95; provincial employers 193–5; self-made men 197–9; socialist writings 42; towns 22; wealth and incomes 188–9, 265
Bourget, Paul 212
Bourguignon, François 68, 70
Bouvier, Jeanne 253
Breton language 115
Brittany 111, 135–6, 183
de Broglie, duc Albert 186
Burgundy 123
business: Bonapartist state 54–6; bourgeois employers 189–90, 196–7; bureaucracy and paternalism 148–50; discipline and authority 246–7; distinctive lifestyle of businessmen 80–1; the employee 146–51, 235; family networks 77; lobbies 199–201; reformed paternalism 242–6; self-made men 76–8; small retail trader 141–6; speculators and the two hundred families 78–80; unscrupulous 205; urban employers 75–81; worker action 236–42

Cail, Jean-François 76, 84
Calvados 122
Cambefort family 192
capacités 32–5, 271; and craftsmen 39; unrest of 1848 47
capitalism 189–90; bourgeois dynasties 190–5; populist socialism 226; self-made men 197; social barriers 269
Carmaux basin 224
de Castellane, Boni 187
Catholic Church: absorbs unemployed bachelors 137; acceptance of Republic 213; agrarianism 126; anti-clericalism in education 159; and birth control 12; business paternalism 243, 244; clergy's relationship with Napoleon III 61–4; education 15, 96–7, 168, 211; former protector of social order 7; hierarchy 222; loss of property 16; and notables 182; notables enlist against peasants 50; and officers 164; restoration 62; and social reality 42; women 25
Cavallier, Camille 199

censorship 64
Chabot, Jean 252
Chabot, Yvonne 252
Chagot, Léonce 243
Chaline, Jean-Pierre 193
Chambre syndicale des constructeurs de navires 200
Charentes 123, 124
Charles-Roux, Jules 194
chemical industry 193, 197, 220–1
Chevalier, Louis 24
Cheysson, Émile 244
children: abandonment 13; factories 41; gangs of youths 260; labour 25, 81–2, 229; labour law (1841) 82; rural exodus 114; working-class life cycle 228–9
cholera 13
Clemenceau, Georges 240
clergy: class origins 61, 63; liberal professions 169; official status 152
clerks: legal 175
clothing: employees dress-requirements 150; sewing machines 134
Comité des forges 200
Comité des houillères 200
The Commune 103–4, 239, 249
communications 59
Comte, Auguste 212
Concordat: and clergy 62, 63
conscription: control of deviants 259; effect of revolution and wars 8; family life of conscripts 87; geographical origins 9, 11; health improves 135; men's heights 72; officers' view 163; resented by peasantry 119; rural burden 22; substitution 8–9, 72–3
Conseil d'État 156
Constituent Assembly 48
Côte (banker) 78
Council of State 205, 208–9
Cour de Cassation 210
Cour des Comptes 156, 206, 208–9
craftsmen: arrests by trade 102; blurring of worker numbers 82; mid-century crisis 43; new social identity 35–6, 38–9; petty bourgeoisie 141–6; rural exodus 110–11; rural life 19, 20, 22; skilled industrial work 84–5; small farm and artisans 114; social mobility 269; social model inappropriate 32; standard of living 86; towns 23–4; worker origin 226; workshop v factory 220
Crédit Lyonnaise 192
Crédit Mobilier 79
Le Creusot 93; strikes 101

Index

crime: concentration on working classes 256–7; the imprisoned 259–60
culture: Second Empire 96–8
Cumay, Charles 210

Danel, Léonard 194
Daumard, Adeline 185
Declaration of the Rights of Man 30
Delesalle, Paul 249
Democratic Socialists: capacités 35
demography: about 1815 7–27; education and literacy 13–15; rural Second Empire 64–5
dentists 171
diplomatic service 206
doctors 172–4; dubious practices 34; liberal professions 169–2; Parliament 202–3; rural 71–2; workers prefer amateurs 234
domestic servants 251–6
Dorizon, Louis 192
Doumer, Paul 205
Draveil, M. 240
Dreyfus (Alfred) affair 145, 156; effect on military 163–4; intellectuals criticize government 211; power of intellectuals 214, 216; return to secularism 159
Ducos, Théodore 54
duelling 165
Dumay, Jean-Baptiste 85, 203
Dupeux, Georges 113
Durkheim, Emile 213
Duruy, Victor 55, 96, 98
Duveau, George 86–7

Eaux et Forêts 206
L'Écho de la fabrique (newspaper) 38
École centrale 192; science and technology 197, 198
École de droit 58
École de mines 197
École de physique et de chimie de la Ville de Paris 198
École supérieur d'électricité 198
École des mines 192
École Génie Maritime 197
École normale 157–8
École normale de Saint-Cloud 269
École normale supérieure 57, 166, 214
École Polytechnique 58, 192; Roads and Bridges inspectors 206; self-made men 197–8
École polytechnique 148
École Ports et Chaussée 197
École supérieure de guerre 164

Écoles primaires supérieures 267
education: academics 213; administrative elite 206–7; adminstrative elite 57–8; adults 97–8; advance of science and technology 197–8; agrégation 165–6, 174; agriculture 128; anti-clericalism 159; capacités 34–5; and Church 96–7, 168; content and standards 167–8; contributes to militant movement 100–1; democratic ideals 272; doctors 174; employee statistics 152; Guizot's faith in 31–2; Guizot's law (1833) 14, 96; high level bourgeoisie 191–2; intermediate schools and colleges 154; literacy 72; and literacy 13–15; militarization of lycées 14; new strata 98–100, 99; notables' patronage 187; partial meritocracy 217; peasants in Third Empire 114–16; reading rooms 97–8; reforms 55; religious 61–2; republic of professors 168; rural society 137; scholarship students 268–9; schools for non-commissioned officers 163–4; Second Empire 96–8; secondary and higher 211; secondary school-teachers 165–8; social mobility 116, 267–8; teachers 152, 157–60; universities 14–15; women 97
egalitarianism 265–6
electricity industry 197, 220
emigration 22 see also urbanisation; to other countries 128
engineers 197–9; State engineers 206
England: agriculture 110, 122; rural style 73
Étienne, Eugène 205

Fabre family 192
fairs 70
Falloux law 50, 61, 97
families and marriage see also women: bourgeoisie 190–5, 195–6; business 77, 147; chaining up of marriages 136; children 87; domestic servants 252–3; employed wives 162; employees 150; government adminstration 206; life cycle of working class 228–9; Paris aristocracy and high bourgeoisie 187; peasant girls and dowries 195; proof of dowry military regulation 164; seasonal workers 114; small businesses 143; social mobility 267; systems of bequeathing property 135–9; tension caused by education 116; working-class trades 223–4

Index

families and marriages: bourgeoisie 208
Fédération des mineurs 248
Fédération générale des travailleurs agricoles 129
finance: mortgage credit for small farmers 67–8; speculators and the two hundred families 78–80
Finance Inspectorate 206, 207
financial agents 171
Flaubert, Gustave: *Madame Bovary* 64
Les Fleurs du Mal (Baudelaire) 64
Fontvielle, Louis 151–2
food 133; home gardens 229; riots 26, 43, 45
Fortoul, Hippolyte (teacher) 55
Fould, Achille 54
Fridenson, Patrick 225
Furet, François 2

Gaillard, Jeanne 75–6, 94
Galeries Lafayette 150
Gambetta, Léon Michel: agricultural union 126; creates ministry of Agriculture 153; new strata 98, 100, 179, 206; son of a grocer 176
Gaxie, Daniel 203
geography: natural barriers 117; peasantry 9, 12; working-class mobility 89–90, 221–6
Gerbod, Paul 166
Germain, Henri 55, 78
Germain family 192
Germany: agriculture 110, 122; intellectuals 213; universities 211–12
glassworks 232
government: administration v. political power 210–11; civil servants 60–1; dynamic of administrative careers 207–9; higher administration 205–11; Ministers 203–5, 210
grandes Écoles 168, 192
Granet, Félix, Minister for Post Office 156
Grenadou, Ephraim 125, 138, 139
Grenoble 198
Griffuelhes, Victor 249
grocers 143
Guesdism 250
Guillain, Florent 205
Guimet, Émile 78, 192
Guimet, Jean-Baptiste 78
Guizot, François: education 14, 31–2, 96; get rich by hard work and saving 17, 33; open to Legitimists 28

Halbwachs, Maurice 146, 227

Halévy, Daniel 118, 216–17
Harmel, Léon 243
Haupt, Heinz-Gerhard 144
Haussman, Baron Georges Eugène 58; rise in workers' rents 95; workers feel victim of 104
Haute-Garonne 124
Haute-Savoie 125
health: alcoholism 133; clergy provides medical care 62; crime and Moral Order 257; doctors 172–4; epidemics 13, 93; food 133; improvements in rural life 134–5; men's height 8, 10; *officiers de santé* 172–3; Paris 96; rural 71–2; scholarship 212; urbanisation 24; working classes 229, 233–5
Hérault 111
Herr, Lucien 214
historiography 1–3
Hottinguers (bankers) 79
housing: Belle Époch 134; bourgeois lifestyles 195, 196; growth of towns 93–4; Paris 94–5; rural 70–1; working class 227, 234
Hubscher, Ronald 66, 138

industry 75; bourgeois capitalism 189–90; conditions of work 88–9; decline in worker numbers 81–2; discipline and authority 246–7; employees 146–8; fuel 83; growth of towns 92–3; hierarchy of skills 232; mechanisation 246; nascent 17; notables 29, 181–2, 184–5; old and new sectors 220–1; provincial bourgeoisie 193–5; reformed paternalism 242–6; rival worker tactics 247–50; self-made men 197–9; small traders against 145; Taylorism 225; unwholesome conditions 233–4; workers 41, 82–5, 236–42; workers become small employers 226; workshop v factory 220, 224–5, 247
insurance companies 191
intellectuals 211–16; academics 213; German 211–12, 213; journalists and authors 170, 211–12, 213; painters 213–14; power 214–16; social origins 213–14; socialism 214
iron and steel industry 82–3; mechanisation 225
Isère 221
Italy: foreign workers 222, 223, 258

Jaluzot, Jules 189, 203
Jews 222–3, 266

- 308 -

journalists 170, 211–12, 213, 214
Julliard, Jacques 249

Karady, Victor 166

labour: agrarian proletariat 138–9;
agrarianism 125–8, 184; arrests and
trade 102; blurring of categories 81–2;
children 25, 81–2, 229; collective
wages 90; the Commune 103–4;
conciliation boards 92; discipline and
authority 246–7; employees 146–51;
factory proletariat 40–1; Guesdism 250;
hierarchy in industry 224–5; hours of
work and conditions 88–9, 229–32;
industrialisation 82–5; job conditions
for state employees 61; joint
management and profit-sharing 248;
massacres of striking workers 101;
militant movement 100–3, 104;
Ministry 109, 153–4; mobility 22–4,
89–90; Paris, 1848 47–8; paternalism
185, 242–6; piecework 88, 230;
reformist tactics 247–9; registration
book 89; relations with employers 236–
8; revolutionary trade unionism 249–
50; rise in workers' rents 95; rural work
64–5; school-teachers 159–60; social
Bonapartism 91–6; strikes 36–8, 39–40,
90; sub-contracting 230; urban
employers 75–81; women 24–5, 83–4,
220; workers against engineers 198;
workers' position deteriorates 27
Labrousse, Ernest 2; agricultural crises 20;
portrait of father 145–6
languages: Breton 115; dialects and
literacy 14; local dialects and languages
115
Languedoc 124, 129–31
Lavisse, Ernest 212
Le Play, Frédéric 68, 137; influence on
industrialists 200, 244; influence on old
notables 184; role of engineers 198; on
seasonal workers 114; *Unions pour la
paix sociale* 245; workers' lives 86
legal professions 174–8; higher
administration 206; liberal professions
169–2; Parliament 202–3
legislation: social 42
Legitimism: conscription 9; map 183;
nobility open to 28; Paris aristocracy
186
Léonard, Jacques 171
Lépine, Louis: *Souvenirs* 177
Lequin, Yves 231

Le Roy Ladurie, Emmanuel 72
Les Employés (Balzac) 146, 152
de Lesseps, Ferdinand 186
Lévy-Leboyer, Maurice 68, 70, 122, 190
Leygues, George 264
Liard, Louis 210
liberal professions: doctors 172–4;
incomes 265; intellectuals 211–16; new
strata 99; wealth 171
liberalism 205; *capacités* 33–5; contract
between employer and worker 243
*Ligue syndicale du travail, de l'industrie
et du commerce* 145
Lille 23; business bourgeoisie 80;
education 198; growth 92, 93;
literacy: adult education 97–8; domestic
servants 254; transition of peasants to
citizens 114–15
literature: bourgeoisie lifestyles 196;
censorship 64; intellectuals 211;
political alignment 214; prostitutes
258–9; worker-poets 42–3
local authority 119–20; republican
timidity 201–2
Locke, Robert 183
Loir-et-Cher 124; agricultural depression
122; craftsmen 111; rural exodus 113
Loire: industry 221; miners 101
Lorraine 222, 258
Louis Napoleon Bonaparte *see* Napoleon
III
Louis-Philippe 56, 183, 186
Lumière brothers, Auguste and Louis 197
Luxemborg commission 42
Lyautey, Hubert 198
lycées 157, 165–6; scholarship students
268–9; and social mobility 267–8
Lyons 23; business bourgeoisie 80;
education 198; growth 92, 93;
immigrants 223; industry 221; patriciate
192; silk weavers revolt 38, 39–40, 101;
silk workers' strike 239; wages 231;
wealth of liberal professions 171

Madame Bovary (Flaubert) 64
magistrates 209–10
Mallets (bankers) 79
Malthusianism: bourgeoisie 155, 193;
foreign labour 266; rural 12, 111–12,
255; social effect 272
Marseilles 23, 78; bourgeoisie 80, 194;
industry 221; prostitutes 257; Second
Empire 92; urbanisation 23, 24
Marx, Karl: on Louis Bonaparte 52;
perception of elite 179

Marxism: agriculture 127; historical interpretation 2; workers and strikes 40, 250
Massif Central: notables 183; property 136–7
de Maupassant, Guy 155; *Bel Ami* 171; 'Boule de Suif' 259
Mayenne 181, 183
Mayer, Arno 216
mayors 120–1
men: height 72; tavern and smithy 71
metallurgy industry 191, 197, 221; wage differentials 232
migration *see* mobility
militant movement 100–3
military: anti-militarism 165; changes the life of rural conscripts 119; conscription 8–9; duelling 165; exemption for doctors and lawyers 170; officers 163–5; proof of dowry regulation 164; Second Empire expands officer class 59–60
mining: coal miners' death rate 233–4; conditions 88; family life 229; reformist tactics 247–9; sons prefer other jobs 224; strikes 101; wage differentials 232; workers 82, 84, 221; workers' conditions 90
Mirès, Jules (banker) 79
mobility: foreign workers 222–3
mobility (geographic): labour 89–90, 221–6; natural barriers 117; peasants 9, 12
mobility (social) 266–7 *see also* education; barriers 269–70; changing status 267–8; democratic ideals 271–2; petty bourgeoisie 272
Monatte, Pierre 249–50
Monod, Gabriel 212
Monod, Henri 210
Moral Order 155; and crime 257, 259
Moral Order government 205
Morbihan 115
mortgages: small farmers 123
Morvan 183
motor industry 220, 221; division of skills 225
Motte, Eugène 203
Moulin, Annie 1
Mulhouse 32, 92
de Mun, Albert 187
Murger, Henry 171

Nadaud, Martin 203
Nana (Zola) 259
Nancy 92; education 198

Nantes 23
Napoleon Bonaparte: suppresses Académie 31; workers' registration book 89
Napoleon III: army service 9; authoritarian administrative system 153; book on Julius Caesar 55; peasant support 48, 50; satisfied demands 52; social programme 91–2; support from peasantry 271; tries to reconcile ruling class 56
National Guard: excludes workers 36
National Workshops 42
nepotism 57
newspapers 98, 118–19
Noiriel, Gérard 1
Normandy 194; labour reservoir 111; pasturage 125
notables *see also* ruling class: agriculture 181–2, 184; decline in power 180–2; illusion of egalitarianism 266; industry 181–2, 184–5; Napoleonic compromise 51; Paris aristocracy 185–7; provincial 183–5; return to countryside power 73–4; reunite against the masses 48; shareholder in Bank of France 79–80; social mobility 269–70; state service 187; struggle against the peasants 48–50; wall of money 46; wealth and incomes 263–5; world-view 182; yearn for order and protection 53
notaries 175–6

L'Oeuvre (Zola) 171
L'Organisation du travail (Blanc) 31
Orleanists: against other classes in politics 28; Paris aristocracy 186; prevent reform 31
Orléans: immigrants 223

painters 213–14
Pareto, Vilfredo 179
Paris: aristocracy of Belle Époque 185–7; brothels 257; business bourgeoisie 80; disparity in wealth 18; domestic servants 253; health of working class 233; immigration 223; industry 221; most militant workers 104; retail traders 143, 144; Second Empire changes 94–6; teachers 167; urbanisation 23–4; wages 231; wealth of liberal professions 171; white collar workers 147
Paris Basin: bequeathing land 137–9
Parliament: elite 202–3
Pas-de-Calais: bequeathing land 137–9;

notables 183; small farms 112
Pasteur, Louis 172, 212
peasantry: acquires property 16; character in Third Republic 109–10; daily life in Second Empire 68–73; education 114–16; emerge as political force in 1848 48–52; escape from patronage 182; fear return of feudalism 26; golden age in Second Empire 64–8; mid-century crisis 43–6; mobility 9, 12; part-time or migrant 81; resist military 8–9; return to hierarchy 20–2; rural exodus 110–11; status 114; yearn for order and protection 53
peddling 70; reading material 97–8
Péguy, Charles 214
Pelloutier, Fernand 249
Penal Code (1810) 26
pensions 233
Pereire family 55, 78–80, 194
Perrot, Michelle 225, 240, 242
Le Petit Journal 98
petroleum industry 197, 220
petty bourgeoisie 178, 217 *see also* bourgeoisie; education 267–8; employee 146–51; legal professions 174–8; liberal professions 168–72; military officers 163–5; new strata 140; politics 144–6; post office employees 160–3; retail tradesmen 141–6; school-teachers 157–60; secondary school-teachers 165; social mobility 272; state officials 151–6; wealth and incomes 265
pharmacists 171, 174
philanthropy 32
phylloxera 123–4
Pinot, Robert 200
police 60
Polish workers 223
politics: administrative elite 56–9, 201–11; business lobbies 199–201; conservatives shocked by provincial bourgeoisie 205; corruption 54; democratic ideals 271–2; doctors in Chamber of Deputies 173; Members of Parliament 202–3; new strata 179–80; notables 29–31, 184; petty bourgeoisie 144–6; right and left divisions 214–16, 262–3; unequal finances of candidates 54
pollution: growth of towns 93
population: birth control 12, 34, 63, 87, 111–12, 272; counter-tactics 136; rural exodus 110–11; urbanisation 22–4

Post Office 118; conflicts of PTT employees 160–3; creation of ministry 153; officials 152
Poulot, Denis 89
poverty: clergy provides for 62; created by situations 87–8; disappearance of beggars 132; Haussman policies in Paris 95–6; mid-century crisis 43–4; Paris 24; prisons 26; rural 82; social barrier 269–70
printing trade 84
prisons 26, 259–60
profit-sharing 245, 248
property: effect of revolution and empire 15–19; inequality 26; and political power 17–19; small land ownership 65–6; systems of bequeathing 135–9; wealth and incomes 263–5
prostitutes 257–9
protectionism 200
Protestants 266
Proudhon, Pierre-Joseph: *Qu'est-ce que la propriété?* 31
Proust, Marcel 255
Provence 126–7
public houses 142
public utilities 191
Pyrénées 112

Qu'est-ce que la propriété? (Proudhon) 31

railways 59; decentralising Parisian stations 94; employees 147, 148; ends rural isolation 66, 70, 116–17; family owned or joint stock 191; reading pedlars 98; rural labour 65; rural society 137; service workers 235–6
regionalism: democratic-socialists 51; provincial craftsmen 36
religion 188, 266 *see also* Catholic Church
Renan, Ernest 212
Renault 225
Restoration 16
Revolution 130; change in aristocracy 186; doctors 172; effect on population 7–13; effect on property 15–19; petrified nobility 28–9
Revolution of 1848: economic unrest turns to politics 46–8; fear in ruling class 31; leading up to 32–3
La Ricamarie 101
Richet, Denis 2
Ringer, Fritz 170
Rive-de-Gier 92
roads 116–17

Index

Roads and Bridges inspectors 206, 207
Rogé, Xavier 199
Rolland, Georges 193
Rothschild family 79, 263
Roubaix 92, 93, 257
Rouen 23; bourgeoisie 80, 194; domestic servants 253; growth 92, 93
Rougerie, Jacques 103
de Rousiers, Paul 200
de Roussy de Sales, Marquis 138
Rouvier, Maurice, Minister for Post Office 156
rubber industry 197, 220
ruling class *see also* notables: acquisition of property 16; challenge from new strata 179–80; education 14–15; fear return of Terror 26–7; inability to cope with masses 44–6; monopoly on political power 29–31; petrified by Revolution and Terror 28–9; political power 17; reconciled by Napoleon III 56; rural change 22; sons and gerontocracy 25–6; transition from agriculture to industry 32. *see* socialism as attack on property 40
rural society *see also* agriculture: blurring of worker categories 81–2; craftsmen 19, 20, 22; disparity in wealth 16–19; doctors 172; education 158–9; effects of crisis 124–5, 131–2, 139; farm servants 254; golden age for peasants 64–8; increased prosperity 132–5; migration 85; newspapers 118–19; notables 73–4, 183–5; overpopulation 12; postal communication 118; roads and railways end isolation 116–18; systems of bequeathing land 135–9; urban way of eating 133

Saint-Étienne: growth 92, 93; wages 231
Saint-Olive (banker) 78
Saint-Simon, Claude Henri Comte de 42
Sandre, Joseph 158–9
Sandre, Marie 160
sanitation 134
Sarthe 183
Schneider, Eugène 44, 55, 93, 200; miners strike 101
Schneider, Henri 187
Schneider family 79, 193, 243–4
school-teachers 14, 157–60; class origins 158, 166–7; incomes 265; secondary education 165–8; women 166
Second Empire 53 *see also* Napoleon III; adminstrative elite 56–9; civil public

office 60–1; and clergy 61–4; daily life of peasants 68–73; education and culture 96–8; expands officer class 59–60; golden age for peasants 64–8; labour policy 88, 89–91; political establishment 54–6; progressive changes 105; social Bonapartism fails 91–2
Seine-et-Marne 130
Serman, Serge William 163
Sewell, William 38
sharecroppers 21, 124, 126
Shorter, Edward 38
Siegfried, André 183
Siegfried, Jules 203
silk weavers revolt 38, 39–40
silk workers revolt 101
social reforms 31–2, 205
socialism: agriculture 127; the Commune 103–4; democratic-socialists 51; intellectuals 214; new paternalism 245–6; new perspectives by utopian thinkers 41–3; notables create social repression 40–1; populist anti-capitalism 226; unanimism 130–1
Société des agriculteurs de France 126
Société des ingénieurs civils 198
Société des participations aux benéfices 245
Société fraternelle des ouvriers mineurs 101
Société Marseillaise de Crédit 194
Société nationale d'encouragment à l'agriculture 126
de Solages, Marquis 203
Somme 111
Souvenirs (Lépine) 177
status: illusion of egalitarianism 265–6; social mobility 266–70
Strasbourg 23
strikes 237–42; agriculture 129; employee unrest 149–51; general strike 239, 249; service workers 236
Suez Canal Company 186
Syndicat de Chartres 127
Syndicat des agriculteurs de France 184
Syndicat des constructeurs et fabricants de chemins de fer 200

Taine, Hippolyte 212
Talabot family 79
taxes 71, 141
Taylorism 225
telegraph 59, 60, 161
telephones 161

Index

La Terre (Zola) 70

Terror: petrified nobility 28–9

textile industry: bourgeoise dynasties 192; convent factories 90; family networks 77; forty percent of industrial population 220–1; geography 221; mechanisation 83, 225; peasant clothing market 68, 70; workers 87

Thabault, Roger 70, 116

Third Republic: aristocracy in state service 187; budgets 151–2, 156; crisis in authoritarian administrative system 152–7; elite administration 201–11; politics of petty bourgeoisie 144–5; state officials 151–6

Tilly, Charles 38

timber 21, 129

Toulouse 23, 124, 171, 198

trade unions *see also* strikes: business lobbies against 200–1; domestic servants 256; Guesdism 250; and new paternalism 245–6; revolutionary 249–50; rival worker tactics 247–50

tradeguilds 36

transport industry 191, 197; service workers 235–6

Tristan, Flora 42

Tudesq, André-Jean 30

Ultras: abandon social protection out of revenge 22; attack on education 15; conscription 9; domination of politics 30; wanted restoration of property 16

unanimism 130–1

Union centrale des syndicats agricoles de France 126

Union de Sud-Est des syndicats agricoles 126

Union des industries métallurgiques et minières 200

Unions pour la paix sociale 245

university 14–15

urban society: blurring of worker categories 81–2; disparity in wealth 18–19; employers 75–81; influence on rural 133–4; lifestyle of businessmen 80–1; mid-century crisis 44; officials 152; Paris in Second Empire 94–6; professionals and towns 34; simple model of development 74–5; towns in Second Empire 92–4; workers' standard of living in Second Empire 85–8

urbanisation: decline 12; education introduces towns to young 116; peasants transformed into petty

bourgeoisie 140–1; towns 22–4

vagabonds 260

Vaisse, Prefect of the Rhône 58

Valenciennois 223, 224

Var 257

Vendée: red of 1851 51; white of 1793 51

Le Ventre de Paris (Zola) 233

Vilar, Pierre 218

Villermé, Louis-René 42

Vincent, Gérard 166

viticulture *see* wine and vineyards

voting: county councils unchanged 74; old notables support in 1871 180; peasants 109–10; property qualifications 17–18; struggle for universal suffrage 35; universal suffrage 48, 54; workers excluded 36; youth 26

Vougy, Vicomte de 60

Vuitry, Adolphe 55

Waldeck-Rousseau, René 176; agricultural unionism 125; law against criminals 257; post office 161

wealth and incomes 263–5

Weber, Eugen 115

Weber, Max: perception of elite 179

Weiss, Jean-Jacques 57

de Wendel family 193

Werlé, Mademoiselle 187

wine and vineyards 66; class struggle 129–30; consumption of wine 133; farm sizes 112; new rural communication 117–18; phylloxera 123–4; sharecropping 126; workers' 1907 movement 130–1

women *see also* families and marriage: bourgeois lifestyles 195–6; Catholic education 61–2; convent factories 90; domestic servants 251, 252–6; dowries and small business 143; education 97; employees 150; factory proletariat 41; introduction into workforce 220; labour 24–5, 75, 81–2, 83–4; legal professions 177; liberal professions 178; post office employees 160–2; proof of dowry military regulation 164; prostitution 257–9; salons 25; schoolmistresses 158, 160; secondary school-teachers 166; social roles 25; state typists 154; strikes 238–9; wages compared to men 231; water and washing 71

working classes 218–19; blames for social problems 31–2; changing status 225–6; dissidence 261; divisions and demography 219–21; domestic servants 251–6; education and social mobility 268; equated with danger 31; factory proletariat 40–1; family budgets 227–8; family trades 223–4; geography and mobility 221–6; health 233–5; hours of work and wages 229–32; identified as dangerous 256–7; illusion of egalitarianism 266; incarceration 259–60; leisure 227–8; life cycle 228–9; marriage and social mobility 267; Parliament 203; political power 179–80; prostitutes 257–9; relations with employers 236–8; school-teachers 159–60; service sector 235–6; standard of living in Second Empire 85–8; violence of 1848 47–8; wealth and incomes 263–5

xenophobia 222, 246

Yvetot, Georges 249

Zola, Emile: *Nana* 259; naturalism 212; *L'Oeuvre* 171; portrays social changes 74; *La Terre* 70; *Le Ventre de Paris* 233